SPYMASTERS

SPYMASTERS
TEN CIA OFFICERS
IN THEIR OWN WORDS
Edited by RALPH E. WEBER

A Scholarly Resources, Inc. Imprint
Wilmington, Delaware

© 1999 by Scholarly Resources Inc.
All rights reserved
First published 1999
Printed and bound in the United States of America

Scholarly Resources Inc.
104 Greenhill Avenue
Wilmington, DE 19805-1897

Library of Congress Cataloging-in-Publication Data

Spymasters : ten CIA officers in their own words / edited by Ralph E.
  Weber.
       p.   cm.
    Includes index.
    ISBN 0-8420-2714-9 (cloth : alk. paper). — ISBN 0-8420-2715-7
(paper : alk. paper)
       1. Intelligence officers—United States—Interviews. 2. United
States. Central Intelligence Agency—History. I. Weber, Ralph Edward.
JK468.I6S69   1999
327.1273'092'2—dc21   98-21588
                                                               CIP

♾ The paper used in this publication meets the minimum requirements
of the American National Standard for permanence of paper for printed
library materials, Z39.48, 1984.

For Rosemarie

About the Editor

RALPH E. WEBER is professor of history at Marquette University and a former scholar in residence at the Central Intelligence Agency as well as the National Security Agency. He served in the U.S. Navy during World War II. Professor Weber's earlier research on codes and ciphers resulted in *United States Diplomatic Codes and Ciphers, 1775–1938* (1979), which won the Scholarly Book Award of the National Intelligence Study Center in Washington, DC. He edited *The Final Memoranda: Major General Ralph H. Van Deman, USA Ret., 1865–1952, Father of U.S. Military Intelligence* (1988). Some of his other works include *Masked Dispatches: Cryptograms and Cryptology in American History, 1775–1900* (1993), *From the Foreign Press: Two Centuries of American History* (1980), and *Voices of Revolution: Rebels and Rhetoric* (1972). The father of nine children, Professor Weber resides with his wife in Milwaukee, Wisconsin.

Contents

Acknowledgments

Many friends assisted with the preparation of this book: Thomas E. Hachey, dean of the College of Arts and Sciences at Marquette University; Steven Avella, chair of the History Department at Marquette; colleagues and students of the foreign intelligence profession who over the decades have guided me through the maze of intelligence and counterintelligence histories and sources, in particular Samuel Halpern, who reviewed the introduction and biographical profiles, Paul Arnold, Elizabeth Bancroft, Helene Boatner, the late Russell J. Bowen, Charles A. Briggs, Ann Caracristi, the late Ray Cline and Paul H. Corscadden, Harold P. Ford, David W. Gaddy, Donald P. Harvey, David Hatch, John Hedley, Wayne Kiyosaki, Brian Latell, Woodrow Kuhns, William J. McCaffrey, Newton S. Miler, Carole Minor, the late Nate Nielsen, Hayden B. Peake, Walter L. Pforzheimer, Edward Proctor, Henry Schorreck, the late Louis Tordella, Thomas F. Troy, David D. Whipple; Robert H. Ferrell, who, though retired from the teaching ranks at Indiana University, still instructs us with insightful counsel and new books on American history; David Kahn, editor at the Long Island daily, *Newsday*; L. A. Anderson; and University Press of Kansas editor-in-chief Michael Briggs.

Sabbatical and financial support from Marquette University and the Bradley Institute for Democracy and Public Values of Marquette University enabled me to initiate this research and travel to six presidential libraries, from Harry S. Truman's through Gerald R. Ford's. Research grants from the Eisenhower World Affairs Institute, Gerald R. Ford Foundation, John F. Kennedy Library Foundation, and Harry S. Truman Library Institute made it possible to gather extensive research notes in Abilene, Kansas, Ann Arbor, Michigan, Boston, Massachusetts, and Independence, Misssouri, on the personal and official relationships between these Presidents, their staffs, and their Directors of Central Intelligence.

Thanks go to James W. Leyerzapf and David J. Haight at the Eisenhower Library; Karen B. Holzhausen and her husband, Richard (who prepared the Ford Library on a Saturday morning for a production crew filming my interview on codes and ciphers for a televised program on "What Is, Isn't: Coded Communication" for the Library of Congress),

Sandra Deline, Geir Gundersen, David Horrocks, William McNitt, Jenny Sternaman, and Leesa Tobin at the Gerald R. Ford Library; Yolanda Boozer (who kindly arranged a personal visit with Lady Bird Johnson at the Johnson ranch in Texas), John Barr, Regina Greenwell, Linda Hanson, Alan Fisher, John Powers, and Philip Scott at the Lyndon Baines Johnson Library; librarian Elizabeth Safly and staff members Dennis Bilger, Ray Geselbracht, Sam Rushay, and Randy Sowell at the Harry S. Truman Library; William Johnson, who gave excellent counsel, and his associates Megan Desnoyers, James Hill, June Payne, and Maura Porter at the John F. Kennedy Library; and Milton Gustafson, Clarence Lyons, and the legendary John Taylor at the National Archives II. These staff members at the presidential libraries and National Archives II provided expert counsel and offered numerous suggestions for locating other foreign intelligence documents.

My appreciation also goes to Sir David Frost of London, England, who gave permission for the publication of his interview with Richard Helms; to Jane Gray, who carefully typed significant portions of the manuscript for this book; and to Douglas Charles for his research skills. My special thanks are owed to Richard M. Hopper, vice president of Scholarly Resources, who shared my enthusiasm for this project and guided it to completion. And once again, a thank-you goes to my gracious wife, Rosemarie, whose careful assistance shortened the sabbatical research trips, whose patience survived the lines at the copy machines at the National Archives and the presidential libraries, and whose good humor softened daily life at modest motels and restaurants.

Especially talented persons at the presidential libraries conducted insightful and probing oral history interviews: Ted Gittinger, Joe B. Frantz, and Paige E. Mulhollan at the Johnson Library; Thomas F. Soapes at the Eisenhower Library; Thomas W. Braden and Joseph E. O'Connor at the Kennedy Library; and William Hillman and David M. Noyes at the Truman Library. Their penetrating questions and comments enrich the history of American foreign intelligence. Moreover, these historians and presidential assistants fashioned invaluable perspectives and primary sources for understanding presidential foreign policy resources and leadership. In addition, the interrogations by Rockefeller Commission members and staff proved to be insightful.

For ease of reading and out of respect for the integrity of the interviews, spelling and typographical errors have been emended in this edition. Most of the original transcripts have been shortened by omitting redundancies as well as topics not directly relevant to the Central Intelligence Agency and American foreign relations.

Due to the legal requirements of the secrecy agreement that I signed as a Scholar in Residence at the Central Intelligence Agency, and also as a Scholar at the National Security Agency, I submitted the manuscript for this book to both agencies' publications review boards. Because my research was based on open documents and literature, and some declassified and therefore now publicly available sources, the security reviews were a formality. The boards' approvals do not constitute an endorsement of the contents' accuracy; rather, they simply mean that no classified information on foreign intelligence sources and methods is included. I am responsible for any omissions and errors.

Abbreviations and Acronyms

AEC   Atomic Energy Commission

AID   Agency for International Development

AMLASH   Code name for Maj. Rolando Cubela Secades, Cuban agent recruited by CIA to eliminate Castro

ARVN   Army of the Republic of Viet Nam

CAS   Civil Action Support cadres organized in early years of Diem regime in South Vietnam

CHAOS   CIA-FBI operation begun in 1967 to determine if anti-Vietnam War movement had foreign support

CI   Counterintelligence

CIA   Central Intelligence Agency

CIG   Central Intelligence Group

COI   Coordinator of Information

COMINT   Communications Intelligence

CORDS   Civil Operations and Rural Development Support

COSVN   Central Office of South Vietnam

CRP   Committee to Re-elect the President

CS   Clandestine Service

DCI   Director of Central Intelligence

DD   Deputy Director

DDI   Deputy Director for Intelligence; Directorate of Intelligence

DDO   Directorate of Operations

DDP   Deputy Director for Plans; Directorate of Plans

DIA   Defense Intelligence Agency

DOD   Department of Defense

ECA   Economic Cooperation Act

FAA   Federal Aviation Administration

FBI   Federal Bureau of Investigation

5412   committee organized during Eisenhower Administration to review covert action and clandestine activities

FOIA	Freedom of Information Act
G-1	U.S. Army Assistant Chief of Staff for Personnel
G-2	U.S. Army Assistant Chief of Staff for Intelligence
G-4	U.S. Army Assistant Chief of Staff for Logistics
GAO	General Accounting Office
GS	Government Service
GVN	Government of Viet Nam
HTLINGUAL	CIA selective mail-opening project based in United States and begun in 1950s
IG	Inspector General
INR	State Department's Bureau of Intelligence and Research
ISA	International Security Affairs
JCS	Joint Chiefs of Staff
MAAG	Military Assistance Advisory Group
MACV	Military Assistance Command, Vietnam
MK-ULTRA	CIA code name for drug and counter-drug research projects
MONGOOSE	operation to overthrow Castro regime in Cuba in early 1960s
MUDHEN	operation of surveillance of columnist Jack Anderson in 1971 and 1972
NASA	National Aeronautics and Space Administration
NATO	North Atlantic Treaty Organization
NIE	National Intelligence Estimate
NSA	National Student Association
NSAM	National Security Action Memorandum
NSC	National Security Council
OAS	(Algerian) Secret Army Organization
OB	order-of-battle information
OCI	Office of Current Intelligence
OEOB	Old Executive Office Building, Washington
ONE	Office of National Estimates
ONI	Office of Naval Intelligence
OP 34A	Covert action plan against North Vietnam approved by President Johnson in early 1964
OPC	Office of Policy Coordination
OPEC	Organization of Petroleum Exporting Countries
OSO	Office of Special Operations
OSS	Office of Strategic Services
PBSUCCESS	operation to overthrow Arbenz regime in Guatemala
PFIAB	President's Foreign Intelligence Advisory Board
POW	prisoner of war
PRU	Provincial Reconnaissance Units

R & D	research and development
RDF	rural development force
ROTC	Reserve Officers' Training Corps
SAM	surface-to-air missiles
SHAEF	Supreme Headquarters, Allied Expeditionary Forces
SI	Secret Intelligence (OSS)
SIGINT	Signals Intelligence
SNIE	Special National Intelligence Estimate
SPA	Special Political Action
SRPOINTER	CIA Office of Security project at John F. Kennedy Airport begun in 1953 for opening incoming and outgoing Russian mail
SSU	Strategic Services Unit
TCP	Technological Capabilities Panel
TDY	temporary duty
1290-D	joint CIA and AID project for training internal police forces in 1950s
10/2	presidential committee for reviewing covert action and clandestine activities
U-1	State Department intelligence unit created by Secretary of State Robert Lansing
U-2	reconnaissance aircraft ordered by CIA and designed by Lockheed Corporation
UAR	United Arab Republic
UN	United Nations
USIA	U.S. Information Agency
VC	Viet Cong
WH	Western Hemisphere Division

Preface

Thoughtful Central Intelligence Agency officers and the persons who interviewed them, most often on special assignment from the presidential libraries administered by the National Archives and Records Administration, provide engrossing descriptions of American foreign intelligence issues. Combining expert research, careful questioning, and insightful answers, these experienced professionals sketched portraits that reveal fascinating information and perspectives about U.S. foreign intelligence collection together with clandestine and covert activities during the anxious decades of Cold War threats and espionage. Beginning with President Harry S. Truman, officers from a civilian central intelligence agency supplied their Presidents with intelligence collection in both human and technical areas, extensive research, and analyses for the conduct of foreign affairs. They also became involved with covert activities ranging from foreign political movements to paramilitary action during the first generation after World War II.

Established by Truman in the early tense months of Cold War threats, the Central Intelligence Agency (CIA) would quickly begin attracting confident and intelligent men to its leadership posts. Most of these leaders, initiated as citizen soldiers in World War II, were trained and hardened by their experiences against German or Japanese forces in the brutal warfare that began for Americans with a major intelligence failure, the surprise attack on Pearl Harbor. The majority of the intelligence officers featured in *Spymasters* knew, respected, and admired Gen. William J. Donovan, who brought the idea and office of centralized intelligence to America in 1941, first as Coordinator of Information and later as head of the Office of Strategic Intelligence.

Donovan, already trained in law, first experienced war's violence and ugliness as an officer during World War I on the western front, where he won the Medal of Honor. During the 1930s, as a reserve officer, he witnessed firsthand the armaments race in Germany and Italy's conquests in Ethiopia. With the support of Navy Secretary Frank Knox and strong encouragement from British intelligence officers, Donovan convinced President Franklin D. Roosevelt that America must unmask enemy intentions.

Brave, moral, honorable, and clever, Donovan and his staff set high standards in their selection and training of Office of Strategic Services recruits. Instruction in special operations, radio propaganda, guerrilla and commando raids along with intelligence collection and analysis attracted talented people, scholars as well as warriors. As with their leader, patriotism and deep faith in American freedoms served as foundations for these young people during World War II and the Cold War decades.

These oral history accounts reveal fascinating, sometimes discouraging, aspects of the CIA as the President's agency. As Truman's first Director of Central Intelligence and head of the Central Intelligence Group in 1946, Adm. Sidney Souers served only a few months (as he wished) with several military bosses and neither money nor people of his own. As Thomas Troy writes in *Donovan and the CIA: A History of the Establishment of the Central Intelligence Agency* (1981), Souers "trod lightly." Souers's own account of this beginning reflects the power struggles involving the military services and other administrative agencies. After the establishment of the CIA in 1947, many of his successors enjoyed far greater support from other Cabinet officers and the Congress, although still mixed and grudging endorsement from the military services.

As Director of Central Intelligence in President Dwight D. Eisenhower's administration, Allen Dulles inherited a CIA that his immediate predecessor and former Ambassador to Moscow, Gen. Walter Bedell Smith, had redesigned and strengthened in the first year of the Korean War. Dulles, as Smith's Deputy, had directed with enthusiasm numerous covert operations during that conflict. With strong support from President Eisenhower and also from his brother, Secretary of State John Foster Dulles, Director Allen, with the flair of General Donovan, sent Agency officers into covert operations to change the governments in Iran and Guatemala.

First begun in the Eisenhower Administration, a covert design for overthrowing Fidel Castro in Cuba fascinated newly elected and energetic President John F. Kennedy. The debacle at the Bay of Pigs in 1961 forced Kennedy, Dulles, and presidential advisors to search for insights and answers to this stunning failure. The covert design's architect, Richard Bissell, who earlier had achieved magnificent victories for the CIA in building the U-2 and SR-71 spy planes, agonized while reflecting on the anatomy of this defeat. Once again, the Agency had feet of clay.

In their oral history accounts, Samuel Halpern, Lyman Kirkpatrick, Robert Amory, Jr., and Ray Cline add further insights into the Bay of Pigs operation, as well as Operation MONGOOSE. Moreover, two of them describe fascinating details about CIA operations in the Far East during the 1950s as well as candid evaluations of Directors of Central Intelligence Allen Dulles, John McCone, and Richard Helms. And finally, the critical observations about intelligence and covert action from Richard Helms, William Colby, and John McCone frequently reflect the daring and courage of General Donovan, who sought to "unmask the intentions of the enemy" and lessen foreign threats to the United States. In his autobiography, William Colby called CIA officers "honorable men"; these oral history narratives add substantial evidence for this evaluation.

Introduction

Capt. Dean Rusk, a future Secretary of State, was recalled to the U.S. Army's military intelligence unit, G-2, in Washington, DC, two months before the attack on Pearl Harbor and directed to organize a new geographical section covering the region from Afghanistan through the Indian subcontinent, Burma, Ceylon, Malaya, Australia, New Zealand, and the British Pacific islands. Searching for research materials in the army office, he found a single file drawer containing: one volume of *Murray's Handbook* for travelers to India and Ceylon, marked "Confidential" because it was the only copy in Washington; clippings from the *New York Times* dating back to World War I; and one 1925 military attaché's report from London on the British Army in India!

On his second day in office, Captain Rusk received a phone call from a colonel in the War Plans Division of the General Staff who asked whether Indochina was in South China or North China. The colonel was pleased when Rusk explained its exact location. Gaps in the G-2 files were gradually filled by reports from businessmen and missionaries familiar with those areas and by additional British information. Maps, however, even on a scale of 1:1,000,000, were lacking. Moreover, Rusk continued,

> we tried to organize a Burmese language program in our army and we looked around the United States for a native Burman. We asked the Census Bureau for a list of the people living here who had been born in Burma and they came up with about twelve names, but most of them were McDougall or McLanahan, the children of British soldiers who were born in Burma. We finally found one and we looked him up and he was in an insane asylum.[1]

Rusk had him released and made him a Burmese language instructor.

Japan's surprise attack on Pearl Harbor on December 7, 1941, shocked the War Department, the Navy Department, and the American nation. It was the worst intelligence failure in U.S. history. Army and Navy intelligence data, especially intercepted Japanese diplomatic messages, lacked centralized analysis. The intelligence process in Washington and Hawaii had failed, and this defeat reflected American prewar intelligence weaknesses as well as too much confidence in the supposed protection offered by the Atlantic and Pacific oceans. The Pearl Harbor baptism of fire outraged American political and military leaders. The so-called Day of Infamy ended both the peacetime age of intelligence innocence for the United States and any historic ambivalence about espionage in peacetime.

In the early years of the new nation, George Washington had postulated the first commandment for American foreign intelligence:

> The necessity of procuring good Intelligence is apparent and need not be further urged. All that remains for me to add is, that you keep the whole matter as secret as possible. For upon secrecy, success depends in most Enterprises of the kind, and for want of it, they are generally defeated, however well planned and promising a favourable issue.[2]

Espionage, secret codes and ciphers, and clandestine tactics blossomed during the Revolution. Wartime in America brought European peace and war espionage practices into vogue. Spies on Long Island sent encoded messages to General Washington, informing him about British troop placements and movements.[3] Especially in foreign affairs, dispatches to and from American diplomats were masked in special ciphers, codes, and codesheets.[4] Charles William Frederic Dumas in the Netherlands, for example, sent a special code to Benjamin Franklin in 1775 for use in their correspondence.

In the last days of the war, an ordinance for regulating the U.S. postal system passed the Congress of the Confederation. It ensured security and a privileged status to almost all mail, with one crucial exception: the President of Congress, or in wartime the Commander in Chief of the Armies or commander of a separate army, or the chief executive officer of a state could, with a warrant, open, delay, or destroy letters. In September 1785, John Jay, the Secretary for Foreign Affairs, wrote to Congress describing reports about the encouragement given by Canadian officials to "our People" to settle around British trading posts that had not been surrendered as called for in the 1783 Treaty of Peace. Very anxious about losing U.S. citizens and territory to Great Britain, Jay urged Congress to keep a cloak of secrecy around his request that "there may be Occasions where it would be for the Public Interest to subject the Post Office to the Orders of your principal executive Officers."[5] He wanted to stop the growing number of persons seduced by the British offer.

Congress promptly considered Jay's request and passed a secret resolution, valid for twelve months, that the Secretary, if he believed the safety or the interest of the United States required it, could inspect any letter in the post offices except those franked by or addressed to members of Congress.[6] One year later, Congress secretly passed an identical resolution but with no time limit. An anxious new republic feared foreign threats to its survival, and for the next several years secret inspections of correspondence continued.

Soon after the Constitution was ratified and Washington was elected the first President of the United States, it became clear that in the conduct of foreign relations the Chief Executive nominated and, with the advice and consent of the Senate, then appointed ambassadors and other ministers. President Washington also appointed executive diplomatic agents without Senate consent. Their powers, duties, and compensation were based simply on the executive power in the Constitution. The only channel of communication between the United States and foreign nations, wrote Secretary of State Thomas Jefferson, was the President.[7] Supremacy of the President in foreign affairs also is illustrated in the contingent or secret fund. Although the Senate approved treaties and the House controlled the purse, there was a secret fund on which the President could draw, or he could have the Secretary of State certify an expenditure without specifying the reason. (In the rigid accounting program in the U.S. government, this fund is the only exception.) Most of the executive agents have been paid from this source.[8] Secret visits to Lisbon and Madrid in the 1790s and in the early 1800s to Brazil, Cuba, and Constantinople (where George B. English in 1823 wore Oriental clothes to appear as an American Muslim visiting the heart of Islam—he quietly obtained a secret copy of the Turkish treaty with the French) were just the first few confidential missions by the President's executive agents.[9]

Secret communications, using codes and ciphers, continued in the decades between the Revolution and the War of 1812. Indeed, President Thomas Jefferson, who had served as Minister to France in the 1780s, feared foreign espionage. An astute code-maker, he had even prepared a special cipher for the Lewis and Clark expedition that explored the newly purchased Louisiana Territory.[10] Following the outbreak of war with England in 1812, America's espionage and clandestine activities commenced again. Badly prepared for war, its military forces were ignorant of the order of battle for English troops as well as details of terrain and geography. Due to these intelligence gaps, as well as incompetent American military officers and panic-stricken troops, British forces were able to set fire to the city of Washington. The Treaty of Ghent, consented to by the Senate in 1815, halted the warfare and most American espionage.

Encoded diplomatic correspondence from the State Department to its ministers in Europe also declined. On this continent, however, in the 1820s, tensions with the newly independent Mexican nation resulted in many secret dispatches as Ministers Joel Poinsett and Anthony Butler attempted the purchase or cession of Mexican territory to the United States. When war broke out between the two countries in 1846, U.S. military leaders again lacked geographical and terrain data, this time for Mexico. Centralized military and diplomatic intelligence improved slowly and modestly during this conflict. With war's end in 1848, the War and State Departments still had not instituted peacetime intelligence, nor did this situation improve in the 1850s.

The Civil War opened a new chapter in secret intelligence as Northern and Southern armies probed the other side for its military strengths and weaknesses. The Pinkerton detective agency provided order-of-battle data to Gen. George B. McClellan's Northern troops during the first eighteen months of the war. The Navy Department sent two agents to England with $10 million in bonds in an effort to prevent the Confederates from purchasing iron-clad rams and cruisers.[11] Despite this mission, Southern agents managed to buy several British-built commerce raiders. For the first time on the American continent, observation balloons were used, by Northern troops to gather intelligence on troop maneuvers.[12] The Civil War also witnessed the introduction of innovative battlefield communications by telegraph and flag wigwag systems. Both armies protected their dispatches through enciphering; however, counterintelligence units devised interception and deciphering techniques with considerable skill and fed disinformation to their opponents.

The Confederate government established the Signal and Secret Service Bureau in Richmond, Virginia, which sent numerous secret agents to the Northern states, Canada, and Europe. Agents in the North supplied Confederate government officials with newspapers from New York, Philadelphia, Washington, and Baltimore, since news columns often printed maps as well as valuable information about troop strengths, casualties, and Army operations. Gen. William T. Sherman, angered by these often uncensored accounts, had little sympathy for war correspondents. The Southern correspondents, fewer in number, were under tighter censorship regulations.

Overseas, Union agents in British seaports reported on ships and cargoes destined for the Confederacy. They, as well as Confederate agents, bribed British ships' officers and crewmen for information. Soon after the outbreak of the war, intelligence networks spread to France, Belgium, and Spain, where Confederate agents were especially skillful in courting European sympathizers and also carefully subsidizing journalists and editors in the propaganda campaigns.[13]

With war's end in 1865, the Union Army reduced its numbers from one million men to twenty-five thousand. And once again, only a few American leaders appreciated the fact that European peacetime espionage practices, especially the interception of diplomatic dispatches, continued. In 1866, John Bigelow, the American Minister to France and a former editor of the *New York Evening Post*, warned Secretary of State William Seward about French practices: all cables to the U.S. Legation in Paris were first read by the Ministry of the Interior. Moreover, Bigelow cautioned, the standard State Department code, designed and first used by James Monroe in France in 1803, had probably been given to principal European governments by "traitors to the Government under Mr. [James] Buchanan's administration [1857–1861]."[14]

Seward's naive reply to Bigelow's warning dismissed the likelihood that traitors had turned over the code because the code sheets were always in the secure hands of the State Department's loyal chief clerk. And he added that if a dishonest person wished to make a copy, he would need two long working days if he had the proper blank forms, or one week without them. With confidence he wrote that the code was the "most inscrutable ever invented," and therefore the Department rejected five or six new cipher designs each year.[15] Obviously, Seward had never encoded or decoded a dispatch. In another message, Bigelow again sought to advise Seward of French espionage practices; however, the stubborn Secretary of State rejected the counsel, and thus French officials probably read confidential American diplomatic dispatches before they reached the Minister.[16]

The Keefer incident is an even more significant reflection of Seward's belief that American espionage should be practiced only in wartime. Charles A. Keefer, a cipher clerk for Gen. Philip Sheridan in New Orleans in 1866, was almost certainly the first operator to use American telegraph communications intelligence during peacetime. In mid-December, Keefer wrote to Gen. Ulysses S. Grant that he had happened to be in the New Orleans telegraph office one week earlier when a message from Emperor Napoleon III of France to Gen. François Castelnau in Mexico was being transmitted via the French Consulate in New Orleans. Keefer copied the message, translated it, and gave it to General Sheridan, who in turn sent it to Grant.

Keefer also copied an encrypted cable message from Castelnau and Marshal Achille François Bazaine to Napoleon III, dated December 3, but he could not decipher it. With luck, Keefer explained to Grant, the 373-word cable might be published in plaintext in a French newspaper. If that happened, Keefer asked that a copy be sent to him so that he could work out the key and decipher any future correspondence between Napoleon III and Maximilian, the French-backed Emperor of Mexico. Keefer also asked that his name be kept secret because the telegraph lines were controlled by Southern men, and if they learned of this secret dispatch it would harm his prospects of becoming a telegraph operator for the Southern lines.[17]

Writing directly to Secretary Seward in early January 1867, Keefer informed him that the New Orleans newspapers were printing a telegraphic synopsis of the Castelnau-Bazaine dispatch, and he asked him to send a plaintext copy so that he could work out the key. In addition, he reported that he had intercepted a dispatch from a *New York Herald* reporter, sent from New Orleans to the editor, James Bennett. This dispatch, containing information about an Austrian corvette at Vera Cruz, was datelined Paris; however, Keefer wrote that the dispatch originated in New Orleans and the reporter told Bennett to publish the story as European news from Paris.

Keefer's January 11 letter to Seward included a forty-nine-word message transmitted via the French Consul in New Orleans in plaintext from Napoleon III to Castelnau, which urged no delay in the return of French troops from Mexico—a clue to the Emperor's policy for Mexico.[18] One week later, Keefer's final letter to Seward, who was apparently troubled by these intercept practices (and wrote as much to Keefer), was an apology. The embarrassed cipher clerk explained that his only motive was to be of service to his government: "I did not exactly consider myself as playing the part of a spy but on the contrary I considered it my duty as a cipher operator . . . to send you copies of the dispatches concerning Maximilian."[19]

Continuing with his apologia, Keefer wrote that he knew that the Secretary of War had removed all restrictions on telegraphic correspondence the previous April; however, Keefer judged that current affairs in Mexico "would warrant" his telling Seward about Napoleon III's policy toward Mexico. He concluded his letter by asking Seward to keep the episode confidential so as not to harm his prospects as an operator on the Southern lines. This melancholy supplication concluded a major peacetime communications intelligence effort. Keefer was taught by Secretary of State Seward what another secretary of state, Henry L. Stimson, allegedly told intercept operator Herbert Yardley in 1929: "Gentlemen do not read each other's mail." Nevertheless, General Sheridan rewarded Keefer's intercept practices with a cash prize of $1,600.[20]

While American military forces were reduced in the late 1860s and the 1870s, European land forces were supplied with new guns, rifled artillery, and other advanced matériel such as shrapnel. Naval forces perfected long-range rifled guns, torpedoes, steel warships, and steam engines. The need for better intelligence about the latest European naval weapons and shipbuilding resulted in the establishment of the Office of Naval Intelligence (ONI) in 1882. The annexation of Midway Island, increased international trade, and the purchase of Alaska from Russia in 1867 had brought new defensive responsibilities to the U.S. Navy. Naval attachés soon served in American legations in European capitals and sent back naval technology data. Several years later, the Army created the Military Information Division, which gathered domestic data on militia strength, transportation routes, and foreign armed forces. In 1889, Congress passed legislation that permitted the Army to send officers overseas. These attachés collected publications, observed ordnance trials, and sought other open information.

The Naval War College, established near Newport, Rhode Island, in 1884, transformed the Navy into an intelligence organization. College faculty members such as William Little, William Livermore, and Henry C. Taylor introduced war games where students dealt with hypothetical naval threats. On huge map tables a paper force of five battleships, fifteen cruisers, and several smaller vessels was challenged by a British invasion force of sixteen battleships, thirty cruisers, and several troopships trying to take over New York City. Students and faculty concluded that they could defeat the superior force by combat in coastal waters rather than the open sea. In 1895, during the crisis in Venezuela between Great Britain and the United States, these college students devised a contingency war plan and sent it to the ONI and the Secretary of the Navy.[21] A short time later, Lt. Comdr. Richard Wainwright, the new Chief of Naval Intelligence, drew up intelligence requirements with the College, and thus the ONI became a genuine intelligence organization.

In 1896 the War College devised a naval strategy for a possible war with Spain, a real threat at the time. After a thorough analysis, the class recommended the capture of Manila, Spain's colonial jewel in the Philippines, as a bargaining device for helping the Cuban people. Included in the students' tactics were the blockades of Puerto Rico and Cuba together with landing troops for the capture of Havana. Assistant Secretary of the Navy Theodore Roosevelt, fascinated by the research and recommendations, carefully reviewed these creative ideas. Most of them would be followed in 1898.

Three months before war was declared against Spain, John Haswell, a former State Department clerk, warned the elderly Secretary of State, John Sherman, that European espionage practices included the copying and attempted code-breaking of all telegraphic cipher messages. In France, he reported, the Ministry of Foreign Affairs, with fifteen to twenty code clerks, classified all encoded messages and attempted to decipher them. Since the U.S. diplomatic code, designed by Haswell, was twenty-five years old, he urged that a new one be prepared.[22] Also on the eve of the Spanish-American War, Gen. Horace Porter, the American Minister in France, sent an alarming dispatch to Sherman. According to General Porter, a former secretary in the American Legation in Madrid now living in Paris was told by a secret informer that he had seen the State Department codebook in a Spanish government official's Madrid office.[23] "Am sure Madrid knows State Department cipher," he cabled. Porter also alerted Gen. Stewart Woodford, the American Minister in Madrid.[24] Nevertheless, Woodford, having no substitute, continued to employ the codebook. As war fevers climbed, Sherman gave Haswell $3,000 to prepare a new one.[25] One year later the Department finally had a new codebook.

Early in 1898, Roosevelt ordered Commo. George Dewey, commander of the Asiatic Squadron, to Hong Kong to prepare for an attack on the Spanish squadron in Manila Bay if war with Spain should occur. In Hong Kong, Commodore Dewey gathered specific information on Spanish ships and personnel; however, he still lacked maps and charts on the Philippines. Despite this gap in information, his squadron destroyed the Spanish ships in Manila Bay one week after war was declared.

In western Europe, young American naval officers organized a network of intelligence agents in Paris, London, and Madrid. Army intelligence sent Lt. Andrew S. Rowan, who had earlier collected data along the Canadian Pacific Railroad lines for the War Department, to southeast Cuba two days after the war began. He brought back maps and several insurgent officers to Washington. Lt. H. Whitney carried out a similar covert reconnaissance of Puerto Rico. The Secret Service chief, John E. Wilkie, investigated Spanish clandestine activities in the United States and Canada. By eavesdropping on Spain's diplomats in Montreal and intercepting their agents' mail, Wilkie and his men foiled espionage plans.

The American occupation of Manila, Cuba, and Puerto Rico, together with the virtual destruction of the Spanish ships, brought an end to hostilities by mid-August, and feverish intelligence operations against Spain subsided. During the first years of the twentieth century, Capt. Charles D. Sigsbee, Chief of the Office of Naval Intelligence, focused on possible German naval threats. His successors and the General Board of the U.S. Navy war-gamed a possible crisis involving Germany in the Far East and then, shortly before World War I, a counteroffensive operation against Germany in the West Indies, code-named War Plan Black. Likewise, in 1904–05 careful war planners sent observers to watch the Japanese naval forces in their maneuvers against the Russian squadron in the Russo-Japanese War. Young naval officers were assigned to Japan for language study.

Following the Boxer Rebellion in China, several nations, including the United States, established garrisons in Beijing (Peking) and Tianjin (Tientsin) with detachments along the railroad between Tianjin and Shenyang (Mukden) to protect foreign nationals from another xenophobic uprising. In order to prepare a topographical map of the area, the future Father of American Military Intelligence, Capt. Ralph H. Van Deman, was sent from the Military Information Division of the Philippines to this region. Working under cover out of Tianjin in civilian clothes, Van Deman was surprised when the postmaster from the Japanese post office in Tianjin brought him a letter where he was staying in the British Concession and then addressed Van Deman as "Captain." "How did you know where I live?" Van Deman asked. With a smile the postmaster replied, "You have Japanese cook."[26] Van Deman deduced quickly that agents of the Japanese government living in other countries kept up with the activities of foreigners. Several years later, another group of American Army officers tried clandestinely to map this same region; however, Japanese informers told Chinese government officials, who questioned the U.S. Government and then forced their removal.

Shortly before World War I began in 1914, War Plan Green was designed for American intervention in Mexico, which then was plagued by revolution. War Plan Orange, a contingency plan in case of war with Japan, soon followed. Only modest progress was being made by American civilian leaders and military officers in the collection and dissemination of intelligence. Chaotic conditions in Mexico after 1912 found President Woodrow Wilson ill served by weak Army and Navy intelligence units. Moreover, the outbreak of war in Europe in August 1914 surprised most leaders in Washington, although Wilson's advisor, Col. Edward House, had warned of intense European rivalries and hatred several months earlier.

Gradually, American intelligence collection began along the Mexican border. In 1916, Pancho Villa's brutal raid on Columbus, New Mexico, forced Wilson to send soldiers into Mexico in pursuit under Gen. John Pershing. Young William Donovan of future Office of Strategic Services fame commanded New York troops on this long, unsuccessful search mission. With the presidential election coming in the same year, Wilson feared that contingency war planning might be seen by his opponents as pushing the United States into war. Quietly, the ONI again displayed intelligence leadership by employing agents throughout Latin America to report on German and Japanese activities. However, the central issue remained— no centralized intelligence collection and analysis organization existed in the United States.

Even before U.S. entry into World War I, German propaganda experts had sought to decrease American sympathies for Belgium, England, and France. Soon after the dastardly attack on the passenger ship *Lusitania* by a German submarine in May 1915, Wilson ordered that German and Austro-Hungarian embassies be placed under surveillance by the Secret Service. Moreover, from wiretap transcripts, Service agents read daily reports on German plans and activities.

Wilson's angry reaction to German submarine attacks on the *Lusitania* and merchant ships resulted in the resignation of William Jennings Bryan as Secretary of State and the nomination of his successor, international lawyer Robert Lansing. As the belligerents practiced espionage in America, the State Department, under counselor Frank L. Polk, now involved itself in intelligence issues. The Yale-educated Polk, who had been caught up in New York municipal reform and violence (seated next to Mayor John P. Mitchel, he was wounded in the jaw when an assassin fired at the mayor), had supported Wilson for the presidency and was rewarded with a position in the State Department's central intelligence office, U-1. In this post, Polk supervised counterespionage agencies, monitored units that gathered overseas data, and also served as liaison with British and French agencies. His coordination system may have "allowed the sinister hand of the spy to be regulated by the dexterous hand of the diplomat."[27] In 1919, Polk would serve as Acting Secretary of State and support the surprising establishment of the American Black Chamber, or code-breaking office, and another new State Department codebook.[28] (The U-1 office was abolished by Secretary of State Frank B. Kellogg in 1927.)

The quiet arrival of thirty-year-old William Wiseman as a representative of the British War Office in New York City in early 1916 and his establishment of an intelligence station added vigor, experience, and basic intelligence to American counterintelligence. Earlier, as an investment banker, he had worked in Canada and Mexico; then, with the declaration of war against Germany, he served in the British Army and was gassed at Ypres. Several months after his arrival, Wiseman visited with Colonel House at the latter's New York City apartment, and a genial friendship began between the two anti-German counselors.

Lt. Col. Claude Dansey, on Wiseman's team, began advising Maj. Ralph Van Deman, a physician who had joined the army in 1893 and, as noted earlier, had served in the Philippines and briefly in China. By 1908, when the Military Information Division merged with the War College Division, intelligence efforts declined rapidly, and Van Deman became very frustrated. Convinced of the value of centralized intelligence in the War Department but unable to win over Maj. Gen. Hugh L. Scott, he, through Dansey and Wiseman, gained House's support. The Army began a small Military Intelligence Section in 1916 under Van Deman, two other officers, and two clerks. To date, foreign intelligence collection had focused primarily on foreign threats in the Americas, but Van Deman widened the perspective. And he leaned heavily on British intelligence organizational models in building his staff to several thousand before war's end.[29]

Early on, Major Van Deman's team lacked talented code-breaking officers; however, two months after the United States declared war on Germany in April 1917, Herbert O. Yardley, a former railroad telegrapher and then State Department code clerk, convinced Van Deman of his cryptographic skills. Many years earlier, so-called Black Chambers had been established for intercepting and reading foreign coded communications in Vienna, Paris, London, and Madrid. Yardley now began America's first Black Chamber, and foreign messages in ciphers, codes, secret ink, and shorthand became prey for his several hundred officers and clerks.[30]

Communications support by the British Naval Intelligence's Room 40 together with Van Deman's expanding intelligence section kept German secret agents from attempting acts of sabotage in America's munitions factories. Moreover, joint British-French-American counterintelligence strategies decreased German covert operations in Mexico. Gradually, the United States, with British assistance, became educated to the vast undercurrent of espionage and sabotage that threatened this naive democracy, which had considered the Atlantic Ocean a sort of medieval moat of protection. During the war years, American leaders such as Wilson, House, Lansing, Polk, and Van Deman realized that this ocean also transmitted European conflicts to American shores.

Eager for a postwar settlement based upon knowledge and justice, Wilson and House in September 1917 formed a secret commission made up of over one hundred academics and known as "the Inquiry." Wilson demanded secrecy lest the American people, hearing of the group, would think that war's end was imminent. Individuals such as James T. Shotwell, Frederick Jackson Turner, Samuel Eliot Morison, Charles Seymour, William E. Dodd and the young journalist Walter Lippmann prepared two thousand reports with maps, charts, and other data on problems in Europe, Asia, Africa, and the Middle East that might be discussed at the upcoming peace conference. Financed from the President's contingency fund and incorporating data from the State Department, Military Intelligence Section, and other federal government units together with U.S. corporations such as Standard Oil, the Inquiry's recommendations were woven into Wilson's famous Fourteen Points address to Congress in January 1918.

At the Peace Conference in Paris, the academics were dismayed by the ease with which the diplomats disregarded their recommendations. Nonetheless, the Inquiry proved to be a milestone in the history of American intelligence: "It was the first American government agency charged with the production of national—as opposed to departmental—intelligence. Departmental intelligence is that used by a government department—for example, the army or the navy—in carrying out its mission; national intelligence is that regarded by the president and his advisers in order to formulate national policy."[31] To President Wilson's credit, planning for a peace based upon researching the past and estimating the future finally, though briefly, became elemental in the conduct of American foreign relations.

Wilson remained convinced that gathering intelligence in peacetime was done only by military nations in search of commercial and industrial superiority. In a speech at the St. Louis Colosseum on September 5, 1919, he sought popular support for his League of Nations when he emphasized that the United States must not stand alone from the other world powers. If this nation chose to stand apart, he warned, a great standing army with costly arms and munitions, an increase in taxes, and an undemocratic government would result. And the President of the United States would serve not as "chief counselor," elected for a time, "but as the man meant constantly and every day to be the commander in chief of the army and navy of the United States, ready to order it to any part of the world where the threat of war is a menace to his own people."[32] In such a military nation no free debate or public counsel is permitted:

> Plans must be kept secret. Knowledge must be accumulated by a system which we have condemned, because we have called it a spying system. The more polite call it a system of intelligence. (Laughter.) And you can't watch other nations with your unassisted eye. You have got to watch them by secret agencies planted everywhere. Let me testify to this, my fellow citizens. I not only did not know it until we got into this war, but I did not believe it when I was told that it was true, that Germany was not the only country that maintained a secret service. Every country in Europe maintained it, because they had to be ready for Germany's spring upon them, and the only difference between the German secret service and the other secret services was that the German secret service found out more than the others did. (Applause and laughter.) And therefore Germany sprang upon the other nations unawares, and they were not ready for it.[33]

For Wilson, if the American nation rejected a peaceful partnership with the rest of the world, then it would stand alone in armed isolation with a spying system called intelligence. Nevertheless, ambivalence by American leaders regarding peacetime foreign intelligence continued after the end of the war.

In the war's aftermath, fears of Communist and terrorist attacks on government officials, federal judges, and financiers led Attorney General A. Mitchell Palmer to appoint twenty-five-year-old J. Edgar Hoover to the newly created Radical Division in the Justice Department. Beginning in early 1920 over four thousand suspected radicals, seized without search warrants in homes, poolhalls, and lecture halls, were jailed during Palmer's Red Scare raids. The Military Intelligence Division monitored domestic subversive activities before being prohibited from collecting domestic intelligence in late 1922. At the State Department, Robert F. Kelley and Robert D. Murphy in the Division of East European Affairs monitored and evaluated threats from the Soviet Union in the 1920s and 1930s. Together with George F. Kennan and Charles E. Bohlen, these Foreign Service officers urged firmness in facing Soviet threats.

Soon after their return from Europe in the spring of 1919, Brig. Gen. Marlborough Churchill of military intelligence and Herbert Yardley, now a captain, initiated a peacetime code-breaking Black Chamber in the War Department with the State Department paying $40,000 (or 40 percent) of the budget.[34] After moving to New York City with his unit, Yardley also established a front company, Code Compiling Inc., which sold codes at a profit. He also managed to obtain copies of cables transmitted by the Western Union Telegraph Company and the Postal Telegraph Company to and from correspondents in numerous foreign countries, including Japan. When Great Britain, the United States, and Japan, then having the first, second, and third largest navies, respectively, met in November 1921 to establish limits on capital warship tonnage, Yardley decoded and read the instructions transmitted from Tokyo's Foreign Office to its diplomats at the Washington Naval Conference and supplied Secretary of State Charles Evans Hughes with this information.

In the years after 1921, Yardley's team received fewer cables, and they turned to intercepted Japanese radio messages. Later in the decade, the Chamber's budget was lowered to $25,000. According to Yardley, between 1917 and 1929 his staff read forty-five thousand cryptographic messages to nineteen nations. In May 1929 the new Secretary of State, Henry L. Stimson, learned of the Black Chamber and immediately withdrew State Department funds from the six-person staff. Much later, Stimson allegedly told his biographer, "Gentlemen do not read each other's mail."[35] With bitterness, Yardley closed it down.

William F. Friedman, a Cornell University graduate in agricultural genetics and later a young scholar at the Riverbank Laboratories outside Chicago, in the two years prior to World War I found the study of codes and ciphers a fascinating project. Shortly after the entry of the United States into the war, Van Deman's office sent him encoded messages for solution, and soon he was training Army officers in cryptology at Riverbank. Commissioned in May 1918, he went to France to study German code systems. At the war's end he returned to Riverbank, but one year later he moved with his brilliant wife, Elizabeth, to Washington and became a cryptanalyst in the Signal Corps's Code and Cipher Compilation Section of the War Department. With the termination of Yardley's Black Chamber, Friedman took charge of a new group, the Signal Intelligence Service, with responsibilities for code-breaking and code-making.

Joined by recent university graduates Frank B. Rowlett, Abraham Sinkov, and Solomon Kullback, who had mathematics and foreign language skills, Friedman, with $17,000, established a section that included an intelligence school for Signal Corps officers.[36] Intercept traffic came from radio receivers in Virginia, Texas, the Philippine Islands, Hawaii, and Panama. Apparently to protect the Service from prosecution under the Communications Act of 1934, Secretary of War Harry H. Woodring gave approval in 1938 to the intercept and cryptanalytic operations as "necessary for training purposes."[37] Beginning in August 1940 staff members began reading top-secret Japanese diplomatic messages masked by a cipher system named Purple by Friedman.

The Navy's cryptographic section under Lt. Laurence F. Safford and Lt. Ellis Zacharias during the 1920s had focused on Japanese radio naval dispatches.[38] From stations in Washington State, Hawaii, Maryland, Maine, the Philippines, Guam, California, Long Island, and Florida, intercepted traffic flowed to Washington. At sea, U.S. Navy units monitored Japanese fleet maneuvers and communications during the 1920s and 1930s.

Early in 1929, John A. Gade, naval attaché in Copenhagen during World War I, at the time employed in a banking firm in New York City, offered a plan for a "National Intelligence Service," in effect a central intelligence agency that would report directly to President Herbert Hoover. He discussed his seven-page proposal with two low-ranking military intelligence officers stationed at Governors Island. Accurately describing U.S. intelligence collection and analysis systems as amateurish, confusing, and lacking coordination, Gade praised British and French intelligence services. He told of the "wheel of British intelligence" with spokes radiating out to private citizens and government agencies. Crucial to the process, he added, was the fact that the wheel revolved in wartime and peacetime. The United States should have such an intelligence wheel in the State Department that would involve the various federal government departments and agencies. Copies of his proposal were forwarded to the ONI and the Military Intelligence Division, where Navy captains and Army colonels gave it negative reviews. The blueprint was filed.[39]

Five months before the Pearl Harbor attack, Gade's proposal became a partial reality when President Franklin D. Roosevelt, by executive fiat, established the office of Coordinator of Information (COI), headed by William Donovan. Roosevelt endorsed Donovan's intelligence office design, which incorporated a close relationship between strategy and information. Donovan stressed the critical need for domestic as well as foreign-based federal offices to collect data not only on the resources but also on the intentions of the enemy. Analyses should be made by the military officers as in the past; however, civilian scholars should also subject the informational data to rigorous analysis.

As in World War I, a British intelligence officer, this time William S. Stephenson, played a major role in assisting Donovan as friend and collaborator with his organization.[40] Donovan, then fifty-eight, had been born Irish, Catholic, and Republican in Buffalo, New York. He had attended local schools before enrolling at Niagara University and then transferring to Columbia University, where he received his bachelor's degree and then a degree in law in 1907. Returning to Buffalo, he joined a law firm in that city. In 1914 he married Ruth Ramsey, the daughter of a wealthy and prominent Buffalo couple. Before U.S. entry into World War I, Donovan served on the American War Relief Commission in Europe for several months before joining his National Guard unit with General Pershing in pursuit of Pancho Villa in Mexico.

During twenty-two months of service in World War I, Colonel Donovan was wounded several times and received a number of awards, including the Medal of Honor. During the 1920s he served as U.S. Attorney for the Western District of New York and Assistant Attorney General in the Department of Justice. When President Hoover failed to nominate him as U.S. Attorney General, Donovan moved to New York City and established a law firm that specialized in defending clients involved in antitrust suits. In the 1930s he became concerned with foreign affairs issues, ranging from Italy's overseas adventures to military developments in Germany,

Spain, the Balkans, the Low Countries, and France. As violence flared in Europe, Donovan lectured on the lack of preparedness in the United States.

Donovan's close friend, Chicago newspaper publisher Frank Knox, became Secretary of the Navy in June 1940, when an anxious President Roosevelt added notable Republicans (Knox was Alf Landon's running mate in 1936) to his Cabinet. Worried about the stunning successes of the Nazi armies, Knox asked Donovan to visit England and investigate its defenses against an invasion and also learn about the threats then posed by a Fifth Column (a clandestine organization in a country that gave assistance to invading armies). Enthusiastic about this assignment, Donovan toured defense installations, met the King and Queen, and consulted with major British intelligence officials. Soon after his return to Washington, Donovan impressed upon Roosevelt, Secretary of War Henry L. Stimson (also a recent Republican addition to the Cabinet), and Congressional leaders the high morale and basic courage of the British people. He also emphasized their desperate need for aircraft, pilots, destroyers, and Enfield rifles. In collaboration with forty-three-year-old William Stephenson, who had established a British security coordination office in New York City, Donovan supported Roosevelt's decision to send fifty destroyers to England. In the following months, Stephenson and Donovan went to London for further consultation and Stephenson urged Donovan to help in creating a secret government agency patterned after the British system and collaborating with it. Also, such an organization could give needed support to Stephenson's intelligence operations in Latin America.

Thus, in midsummer 1941, and supported by the President's secret fund, Coordinator Donovan began a complex organization that gathered information, analyzed data, developed propaganda, and studied sabotage and guerrilla actions. "The program was, at one and the same time, commonplace and unusual, academic and operational, overt and covert, peaceful and forceful, legal and illegal."[41] Collection and analysis became the COI's greatest strength as language specialists and other scholars researched information on potential threats from foreign enemies. The Foreign Information Service monitored Axis radio broadcasts and supplied U.S. bureaus with propaganda; films also were distributed. Recent immigrants from Fascist countries supplied valuable information. All foreign countries were open to COI authority with the exception of those in South America, where J. Edgar Hoover's Federal Bureau of Investigation (FBI) ran operations. The military services gave Donovan control of their undercover activities but retained their tactical and strategic units. Very little support came to the COI from the State Department.

Following the Japanese attack on Pearl Harbor in December 1941, the President, Congress, and the military acknowledged that central intelligence unpreparedness and military rivalries together with serious gaps in secret intelligence and counterintelligence were responsible for the disaster. After the United States entered the war, Donovan, realizing that the military now offered greater power and influence, sought to ally the COI with the military and place it under the control of the Joint Chiefs of Staff. Donovan won the support of the Joint Chiefs; and, despite Hoover's and the State Department's objections, Roosevelt in June 1942 turned the COI into the Office of Strategic Services (OSS) with Donovan as Director, under the Joint Chiefs. Donovan proudly wrote that for the first time in U.S. military history a civilian unit had become a member of the military. Moreover, "there had been great neglect of the new elements in modern warfare and we have succeeded in getting them set up and all under one tent, including special intelligence, special operations, and psychological warfare."[42]

Although also charged by the Joint Chiefs with responsibilities for espionage, covert action, counterespionage, sabotage, moral subversion of the enemy, and creating Fifth Column activities, the OSS became especially valuable for its work in research and analysis, with much of the data coming from open sources. By war's end, the OSS had twenty-five thousand employees. It often remained a junior partner to the more experienced British Secret Intelligence Service and the Special Operations Executive in Europe. In the Far East, the OSS never received Gen. Douglas MacArthur's approval; nevertheless, it established bases in Burma, India, Ceylon, Thailand, China, and north Indochina.

Nine months before Germany's defeat in May 1945, Donovan was convinced that the United States would remain an engaged world power, but he now feared the Soviet Union's hunger for world supremacy. In a notable report he called for a permanent postwar central intelligence agency with a status equal to the Army, Navy, and Army Air Force, and subject only to the President. He also wrote that an advisory board of State, War, and Navy Secretaries plus any other presidential appointees would work with the Director. Opposition quickly formed as Brig. Gen. George V. Strong together with Maj. Gen. Clayton Bissell, the Army's G-2 director, strongly rejected the plan; they stated that the OSS should dissolve at war's end. Before this issue was decided, Roosevelt died, a tragedy for the nation and a personal one for Donovan. Vice President Harry S. Truman became President in April 1945.

Intense personal and bureaucratic opposition to Donovan's report by the State, War, and Justice Departments and the Navy continued in the early days of Truman's administration. It soon became apparent that the President, like William Seward, Woodrow Wilson, and Henry Stimson, had an instinctive distrust of espionage in peacetime. Moreover, Donovan had little rapport with Truman. A series of negative, tabloid-style newspaper articles attacking Donovan and the OSS (Oh So Social, Oh So Secret) appeared in the late winter and spring of 1945. In addition, British subversive influences were charged. Harold D. Smith, director of the

Bureau of the Budget, always anxious to reduce federal government expenditures, counseled Truman against Donovan's blueprint. Germany's defeat in May and Japan's surrender in August provoked talk in Congress of rapid demobilization and greatly reduced military budgets. On September 20, Truman signed an Executive Order terminating the OSS as of October 1. The Research and Analysis Branch was transferred to the State Department, and the Operations Branch went to the War Department, where it became the Strategic Services Unit under Gen. John Magruder. Truman signed a second order that day, which authorized Secretary of State James Byrnes to head an interdepartmental group for planning coverage of the foreign intelligence field. He also approved the continuation, in collaboration with the British, of signals intelligence, which led to "an unprecedented peacetime Anglo-American intelligence alliance that still remains."[43]

In the autumn, discussions by supporters such as Magruder and Secretary of the Navy James Forrestal for a peacetime centralized intelligence service continued. And as the Soviet Union's ambitions for global expansion became more evident, Truman hastened the research and reappraisal of U.S. national security goals and methods. In January 1946 he created the Central Intelligence Group (CIG), staffed and funded by the War, State, and Navy Departments. He also established the National Intelligence Authority, composed of War, Navy, and State Secretaries and his presidential representative, Fleet Adm. William Leahy. The director, Adm. Sidney W. Souers, was responsible to the Authority. Representatives from military and civilian intelligence operations served on the Intelligence Advisory Board.

At a White House luncheon on January 24, 1946, with only staff members present, Truman read an amusing proclamation to his "Brethren and Fellow Dog House Denizens." Acting upon his authority as Top Dog, the President stated, "I require and charge that Front Admiral William D. Leahy and Rear Admiral Sidney W. Souers, receive and accept the vestments and appurtenances of their respective positions, namely as Personal Snooper and as Director of Centralized Snooping."[44] Exhorting them to improve foreign relations through more "intensive snooping," the President presented them with black cloaks, black hats, and wooden daggers. Truman's sense of humor masked the often tense debate surrounding the creation of the CIG.

Truman wanted important intelligence summaries from the Group; and Souers, who had several bosses, gradually organized his staff and cooperated with the Authority and the Board. In effect, the CIG was not an agency of analysis but a "cooperative interdepartmental activity," managed by the Director but dependent upon other departments for funds, staff, and facilities.[45] Certain military offices continued to feud with staff members because they viewed the CIG as a temporary intelligence service in time of neither war nor peace. Congress also proved reluctant to support a peacetime intelligence service.

Souers served only five months as Director, and in June his successor, Gen. Hoyt S. Vandenberg, the nephew of Senator Arthur Vandenberg, sought to strengthen his authority over the analysis and control of all intelligence collection. He wanted legislation to establish the Group's independence and authority over the conduct of espionage and counterespionage abroad. Then forty-seven, this ambitious West Point graduate had served earlier as the Ninth Air Force's commanding general. As he consolidated intelligence activities, he took over the Foreign Broadcast Information Service, the Strategic Services Unit (SSU), and, from the FBI, Latin American intelligence jurisdiction.

During the months following Vandenberg's appointment, increasing anxiety about Soviet threats together with memories of the Pearl Harbor disaster fueled action by Truman, Congress, and the public to reorganize the U.S. military establishment by adding a Secretary of Defense and a separate Department of the Air Force and by coordinating military responsibilities with other agencies involved with national security. Legislation also provided for a National Security Council and a Central Intelligence Agency headed by the President's intelligence officer, who reported to the President through the Council.

General Vandenberg's testimony before the Senate Committee on the Armed Services in April 1947 on the proposed National Security Act gave powerful reasons for establishing postwar intelligence and espionage despite the prewar abhorrence of such operations:

> In my opinion, a strong intelligence system is equally if not more essential in peace than in war. Upon us has fallen leadership in World affairs. The oceans have shrunk until today both Europe and Asia border the United States almost as do Canada and Mexico. The interests, intentions and capabilities of the various nations on these land masses must be fully known to our national policy makers. We must have this intelligence if we are to be forewarned against possible acts of aggression, and if we are to be armed against disaster in an era of atomic warfare.[46]

And Vandenberg quoted Gen. George C. Marshall's observation, made the previous year, that prior to 1941 the United States "had little more than what a military attaché could learn at a dinner, more or less over the coffee cups."

For Vandenberg, the earlier national ambivalence about espionage and foreign intelligence no longer existed. He stated that Pearl Harbor and the ensuing global war had taught the nation that all intelligence is not sinister, nor is it an "invidious type of work." Failure by the United States to tap open sources of information, which provided 80 percent of intelligence, together with failure by the intelligence services to coordinate their results had hindered the nation before Pearl Harbor. And never again, he urged, should this nation have to go "hat in hand," begging any foreign government as we did Great Britain for "the eyes—the foreign intelligence—with which to see." Vandenberg emphasized that this nation must be self-sufficient, and the intelligence agency must prepare national intelligence estimates for the President based on data provided also by other departments such as State, Navy, and War. Moreover, this agency would also disseminate information to other government officials. Finally, he added, the kind of men who are able to execute successful intelligence missions would be attracted to such an agency.[47] Vandenberg's testimony to the Committee was well received, especially because he was not building his own empire. That same month he moved to become Chief of Staff of the new U.S. Air Force.

On May 1, 1947, Rear Adm. Roscoe H. Hillenkoetter became the CIG's director. The National Security Act of 1947, signed on July 26, provided for a strengthened director of central intelligence who took charge of the agency directly. Although the director was the head of the Intelligence Community, he did not have the budget or the practical administrative authority to direct this total community. In this legislation, Congress, determined to empower civil authority, also included a provision wherein the Council could give the agency other intelligence functions and duties affecting national security. This provision would later answer the question as to whether this agency could engage in covert action.

The Central Intelligence Agency (CIA), formally founded on September 18, 1947, thus became the first U.S. independent civilian intelligence service that collected and analyzed foreign information and offered counsel to the President and the National Security Council. Although established primarily for intelligence collection and analysis, the Agency had a small Office of Special Operations (the former SSU) for secret collection.[48] The decades after 1947 would witness an America sensitive to foreign threats in peacetime as well as in wartime. The Agency often provided a vital layer of security against foreign threats. CIA officers—some brilliant, some clever, some astute—were dedicated to the United States and the profession of intelligence. They organized, guided, and defended the finest intelligence organization in the world. There would be no more single file drawers on Asia, no more frantic searches for language instructors, no more fragmented communications intercepts. And, one hopes, no more Pearl Harbors.

NOTES

1. Files of the President's Commission on CIA Activities within the United States (Rockefeller Commission), Box 32, Testimony of Dean Rusk, April 21, 1975, Gerald R. Ford Library, Ann Arbor, Michigan.

2. George Washington to Col. Elias Dayton, July 7, 1777, *The Writings of George Washington*, ed. John C. Fitzpatrick, 39 vols. (Washington, DC, 1931–1944), 8:478–79.

3. Morton Pennypacker, *General Washington's Spies on Long Island and in New York*, 2 vols. (Garden City, NY, 1948).

4. Ralph E. Weber, *United States Diplomatic Codes and Ciphers, 1775–1938* (Chicago, 1979).

5. John Jay to President of Congress, September 2, 1785, *Journals of the Continental Congress*, ed. W. C. Ford and Gaillard Hunt, 34 vols. (Washington, DC, 1904–1937), 29:679.

6. Ibid., 29:685.

7. As quoted in Henry Merritt Wriston, *Executive Agents in American Foreign Relations* (Baltimore, 1929; reprinted by Peter Smith, 1967), 122–23, 128.

8. Ibid., 122–23, 695.

9. Ibid., 695ff.

10. Weber, *United States Diplomatic Codes*, 178.

11. Wriston, *Executive Agents*, 124.

12. See Edwin Fishel, *The Secret War for the Union* (Boston, 1996), for the most recent and fascinating appraisal of Civil War military intelligence.

13. G. J. A. O'Toole, *Honorable Treachery* (New York, 1991). Chapter 12 highlights the propaganda war waged in Europe.

14. John Bigelow to William Seward, August 3, 1366, Department of State, Record Group 59, Dispatches from U.S. Ministers to France, Microcopy 34, Roll 62, National Archives, Washington, DC (hereafter cited as RG59, M, R, and NA).

15. Seward to Bigelow, August 21, 1866, Department of State, RG 59, Diplomatic Instructions of the Department of State, M77, R58, NA.

16. Bigelow to Seward, October 12, 1866, RG59, M34, R62, NA.

17. Charles A. Keefer to Ulysses S. Grant, December 17, 1866, William Seward Papers, Library of Congress, Washington, DC microcopy roll 98 (hereafter cited as Seward Papers).

18. Keefer to Seward, January 11, 1867, Seward Papers, Roll 99.

19. Ibid., January 17, 1867. Strangely, copies of Seward's letter(s) to Keefer are not in the Seward Papers or in the files of the State Department at the National Archives.

20. Sheridan's memorandum and reports on Keefer's operations were filed in the Chicago headquarters of the Military Division of Missouri but were destroyed in the Great Fire of 1871. Sheridan had clerks reconstruct his papers from files in the War Department, and these copies are in the Philip Sheridan Papers, Library of Congress, Washington, DC, microcopy roll 2.

21. O'Toole, *Honorable Treachery*, 181–85.

22. John Haswell to John Sherman, January 26, 1898. Copy in author's possession.

23. Horace Porter to Sherman, March 31, 1898, Department of State, RG59, Diplomatic Dispatches from U.S. Ministers to France, 1789–1906, M34, R118, NA.

24. Porter to Stewart Woodford, March 30, 1898, ibid.

25. Sherman to Haswell, March 24, 1898. Copy in author's possession.

26. Ralph Van Deman, *The Final Memoranda: Major General Ralph H. Van Deman, 1865–1952, Father of U.S. Military Intelligence*, ed. Ralph E. Weber (Wilmington, DE, 1988), 11–12.

27. Thomas Troy argues that Polk's office served as a clearinghouse—as a liaison service rather than primarily a coordinating office. See Thomas Troy, *Wild*

Bill and Intrepid: Donovan, Stephenson, and the Origin of CIA (New Haven, 1996), 206–7.

28. Weber, *United States Diplomatic Codes*, 249.

29. Van Deman, *Final Memoranda*, 103–14. Van Deman's memorandum on March 2, 1916, to the War College division chief outlined major weaknesses in the current intelligence collection efforts, especially regarding individual and encyclopedic monographs on foreign powers. He warned that complete military data were available for only three—Guatemala, Mexico, and El Salvador—out of forty-nine nations!

30. Herbert O. Yardley, *The American Black Chamber* (Indianapolis, 1931), revealed publicly for the first time the support by the War and State Departments for these activities.

31. O'Toole, *Honorable Treachery*, 310.

32. Woodrow Wilson, *The Papers of Woodrow Wilson*, ed. Arthur S. Link, 69 vols. (Princeton, NJ, 1966–1994), 63:46.

33. Ibid., 69:46–47.

34. Yardley, *American Black Chamber*, 240. Yardley believed that no protest would be made by the Great Powers if the Chamber was discovered because all of them maintained cipher bureaus: "Just as in warfare armies do not attempt to bomb each other's headquarters, so also in diplomacy statesmen do not protest against the solution of each other's messages. However, if foreign governments learned that we were *successful* they would immediately change their codes, and we would be obliged after years of struggle to begin all over again." Ibid., 322–23.

35. Ibid., 332.

36. David Kahn, *The Codebreakers* (New York, 1963), 386.

37. James Bamford, *The Puzzle Palace: A Report on America's Most Secret Agency* (Boston, 1982), 33.

38. According to Yardley, Navy code-breakers were asked to decode Mexican telegrams published in the Hearst newspapers about Secretary of the Interior Albert B. Fall in the Teapot Dome scandal. When they asked the War Department for assistance, they were told that no cipher bureau existed despite the fact that Yardley's Chamber had already analyzed these telegrams. Yardley, *American Black Chamber*, 324–25.

39. Thomas Troy, *Donovan and the CIA: A History of the Establishment of the Central Intelligence Agency* (Washington, DC, 1981), 3–5.

40. Troy, *Wild Bill and Intrepid*, provides a careful analysis of Stephenson's influence on Donovan.

41. Troy, *Donovan*, 74.

42. William Donovan to Gen. Sir Archibald Wavell, July 6, 1942, in ibid., 153.

43. Christopher Andrew, *For the President's Eyes Only: Secret Intelligence and the American Presidency from Washington to Bush* (New York, 1995), 3.

44. January 24, 1946, Diary of William D. Leahy, Library of Congress, Microcopy, Reel 4.

45. Troy, *Donovan*, 353.

46. U.S. Congress, Senate Committee on the Armed Services, *Unification of the Armed Services*, 79th Congress, 2d Session, 1947, 491.

47. In this he echoed Allen Dulles's memorandum to the Committee. Dulles believed that the Agency should be predominantly civilian and that the Director, like the FBI head, should make it his life's work. Moreover, his appointment should be somewhat comparable to an appointment to high judicial office and be

free from interference due to political changes. "Memorandum Respecting Section 202," ibid., 525–26.

48. In June 1948, George Kennan, with backing from George Marshall and Dean Acheson, won approval from the National Security Council for creating a major covert operations organization, the Office of Policy Coordination (OPC). Staffed and financed by the CIA, its manager was chosen by the Secretary of State and reported to him and the Defense Secretary. In 1950, Gen. Walter Bedell Smith took control of the OPC, and in 1952 the Office of Special Operations and the OPC merged into a Plans Directorate in the CIA.

1

Sidney W. Souers

ORN IN DAYTON, OHIO, on March 30, 1892, to Edgar Daniel and Catherine Rieker Souers, Sidney later attended schools in that city and then Boys' High School in New Orleans. During his high-school years he worked part-time in the local newspaper's press room. After graduation, he left New Orleans on a freighter for New York City, where he took a steamer for Europe. Upon his return to New York he found a job on a Hudson River night passenger boat. When he had saved $1,000 for college tuition, he enrolled at Purdue University in 1911. After two years, with his funds depleted, he transferred to Miami University in Ohio, where a special work-study program enabled him to complete his bachelor of arts degree in 1914.

Returning to New Orleans, he spent two more years at the Item Publishing Company as an advertising salesman. Hired at the Mortgage and Securities Company, he would become president in 1925.

A succession of executive positions in banking and life insurance took him from New Orleans to Memphis, back to New Orleans, to Nashville, and then in 1930 to St. Louis, where he became an officer in the General American Life Insurance Company for the next ten years.

Commissioned Lieutenant Commander in the United States Naval Reserve in April 1929, Souers served as an intelligence officer. During his years in St. Louis, his Navy responsibilities included public relations, officer procurement, and organizing intelligence units. Volunteering for active duty in July 1940, Souers recalled that he gave up his $30,000 salary as executive vice president in the private sector for government pay of $3,000. His intelligence assignments took him to Great Lakes, Illinois; Charleston, South Carolina; and San Juan, Puerto Rico. During this last tour, he married Sylvia Nettell, formerly of Stanton, Missouri. In July 1944, Souers and his wife moved to Washington, where he became assistant director in the Office of Naval Intelligence. Sixteen months later, he became Deputy Chief of Naval Intelligence with the rank of Rear Admiral.

With support from Secretary of the Navy James Forrestal and Adm. Thomas Ingles, Souers supported the plan of the Joint Chiefs of Staff for a peacetime intelligence organization during the fall months of 1946. Because of Souers's energetic advocacy, President Harry S. Truman sometimes referred to the Chiefs' plan as the Souers Plan or the Navy Plan. Truman's Executive Order establishing the Central Intelligence Group in January 1946 pleased Souers, who was appointed Director. Recognizing that the new organization had modest funds and few personnel, Souers believed that the Group was a temporary milestone on the road to a fully funded and staffed intelligence organization. Daily summaries of information and operational matters began in February; and, in the next few months, Souers attracted a staff numbering one hundred. In his final report before he left the post as Director on June 10, Souers called for an independent budget and more authority. (His successor, Gen. Hoyt Vandenberg, secured both.)

After going back to private life for a few months, Souers accepted a special assignment on intelligence for the Atomic Energy Commission. In September 1947 he became the first executive secretary of the National Security Council and held that crucial post until January 1950. During the remainder of Truman's term as President, Souers served as his consultant. Apparently he served his boss well. Truman noted on the Souers oral history interview transcript in the Truman Library, "You can depend on this guy. He was one of my greatest assets." Returning to St. Louis, and to the General American Life Insurance Company, Souers soon rose to the posts of president and chairman of the board. He later became chairman of the board of the National Linen Service Corporation in Atlanta, Georgia. Souers died in St. Louis in January 1973.

WILLIAM HILLMAN AND DAVID NOYES: *You briefed the President every morning on all that had come in. Can you give us a running account?*

SIDNEY SOUERS: During World War II, I served the entire time in the intelligence end of the Navy and rose to Rear Admiral and Deputy Chief of Naval Intelligence. I spent the last year and a quarter, from about October 1944 to the end of January 1946, endeavoring to work out a central intelligence agency that would serve the President of the United States, as well as the Cabinet members, who are primarily responsible for the national security, so that all would get the same intelligence—in contrast to the system that had prevailed, where the OSS would give one bit of intelligence to the President and not any to the secretaries of the military departments and the State Department, who had some responsibility to advise the President. This languished, this effort, until President Truman succeeded to the Presidency in April of 1945. At that point I had known Mr. Truman only casually. But he directed the Secretary of State, Mr. [James] Byrnes, to come up with a plan for a central intelligence agency. The Joint Chiefs of Staff had been working on a plan which had been referred to them by Admiral [William] Leahy and which had been submitted to the White House by General [William] Donovan. This plan proposed that the organization be immediately under the President and responsible solely to the President. The Navy plan, which was later adopted by the Joint Chiefs of Staff, had taken the position that a central intelligence agency should serve as the overall intelligence organization but that each of the departments responsible for national security should have a stake in it. It was coordination at a national intelligence level. Every department needed its own intelligence, but there needed to be a central intelligence organization to gather together everything that had to do with the overall national policy. Each agency would contribute to the pool. The estimates would be made at top level to guide those who were making top policy in the foreign, political, and military fields.

Secretary Byrnes took the position that the organization should be responsible solely to the Secretary of State, and he advised the President that he thought he should be in control of all intelligence. I personally fought this, and the Navy backed me in it. And we had Mr. [Robert] Lovett, who was on the special committee of the Army. I represented Secretary [James] Forrestal. We took the position that our plan of having a coordinating agency reporting directly to the President through a national intelligence authority, consisting of the Secretaries of State, War, and Navy, was the one that should be submitted to the President. Byrnes had appointed Al McCormack to prepare the plan for State, and he stood pat on

Conducted by William Hillman and David M. Noyes on December 15, 1954, in Kansas City, Missouri. Student Research File, CIA, Box 23 B File, Harry S. Truman Library, Independence, Missouri.

Byrnes's idea—I don't remember exactly the language that Byrnes expressed in it, or his reasoning, but it was that the agency should be under his jurisdiction. In the meantime, in January 1946, Secretary Forrestal and—I'm not sure whether it was Secretary [Robert] Patterson and Secretary [Kenneth C.] Royall, or whether Royall did it as Acting Secretary of War or as Secretary. Anyway, he and Forrestal went to Byrnes's apartment in the Shoreham Hotel [in Washington] on Sunday afternoon and stated that they were prepared to go to the President with a plan they had both signed. It was substantially as it was later approved by President Truman. Secretary Byrnes was invited to join them, but if not, they could each go up with separate plans, but the military felt very definitely that this plan was the best for the country. Byrnes, after making one or two minor word changes, did sign it, and that was then submitted to President Truman on Monday.

The President then called a meeting in his office of Harold Smith, the Director of the Budget; Admiral Leahy; Mr. [Samuel] Rosenman and, I think, J. K. Vardaman; and me. He opened the meeting by saying he thought this plan submitted by the three secretaries, namely, Byrnes, Forrestal, and the Secretary of the Army, was a good one. Harold Smith took the position it was not, and Secretary Byrnes was opposed to it. I recall stating that it was hard for me to believe that the Secretary of State would sign a recommendation to the President in which he didn't believe, and I thought therefore that the President would have to accept his written resignation because he was a wishy-washy compromiser. Harold Smith then stated that he would like to have his people go over the plan. And Mr. Rosenman said, "Do you mean from a budgetary standpoint?" and he said, "No, the intelligence aspects," because he had expert intelligence men in his organization, and he wanted to go over it from an intelligence standpoint. President Truman spoke up in his characteristic manner and said, "I like this plan. If they want to make it slightly better, that's all right, but this is what I have been wanting to do for a long time. You appoint your men, and I'll ask Leahy, Souers, and representatives of the Justice Department to meet in Admiral Leahy's office." We met there and listened to the arguments of the Budget people who were, in effect, co-authors of the State Department plan. And we told them that the President had said he wanted our plan, and if they could make any suggestions for a workable improvement on it, we were willing. The Justice Department was representing Mr. [J. Edgar] Hoover and reflecting his viewpoints. Mr. Hoover wanted to insert a paragraph which would state that the FBI was responsible for all investigations within the continental limits of the United States and the Territory of Hawaii and Puerto Rico. I volunteered the suggestion that we simply state that the Central Intelligence Agency had no responsibility for internal security within the United States and its territories. We all agreed to it, and the President issued an Executive Order on or about the 20th of January 1946. The institution was immediately put into operation . . . by the contributions of the officers and personnel of the State Department and the War and Navy Departments.

What was its name?

It was the Central Intelligence Group serving under the direction of the National Intelligence Authority. The National Intelligence Authority consisted of the three Secretaries, above named, a representative to be designated by the President who happened to be Admiral Leahy, and a Director of Central Intelligence who would serve on the Authority without a vote. I was designated that Director.

You were the first Director?

It was understood that I would serve until the three Departments and the President could agree upon a permanent one. There had been such a feud over the issue that they could not agree on someone who would be satisfactory to all. So I fell heir to it until they could agree on a permanent Director. In about six months I recommended, and all parties agreed to, General Hoyt Vandenberg, who was then G-2 of the Army, to be the Director. My reason for recommending his appointment was twofold. First, the President didn't want it in politics, and Vandenberg seemed to symbolize the nonpolitical angle, but it was nice that he was a nephew to the Senator [Arthur Vandenberg], because we had to keep in mind that we needed legislation to finally set up the agency as an independent agency under the President.

Could we go back to the origin of the thing? It's not too clear yet. Who originally conceived the idea and wanted it on a White House level? Why did the President need a central intelligence agency?

There were two angles. First, I have explained why I was for it. I had seen the Army and the Navy and the State Department just duplicating efforts, and nothing came up correctly as was intended. One result of this was Pearl Harbor. It was easy to see intelligence in the government, but it never did reach the top level that should have had it in proper form. If it was communication intelligence, it would be whispered maybe to Admiral [Harold] Stark or Secretary [Frank] Knox. They would say, "Uh-huh" and then forget it. My feeling was that messages like that should be evaluated and placed on the desks of all concerned. If intelligence had been available in that form before Pearl Harbor, it might have eliminated the disaster that occurred. I had been plugging at it from the beginning. I served on [Ferdinand] Eberstadt's committee, which wrote the chapter on intelligence which gave arguments for a central intelligence agency substantially the same as was finally worked out. But who started the

President on it I wouldn't know. It may have been Jack Vardaman—he was in on it, I had talked to him. He was dissatisfied with the intelligence handled by the OSS, and he felt that Donovan wasn't doing much of anything except writing books and making speeches and propagandizing his own great achievements. And he was determined to stop that and said he would order it dissolved, and he did, as you remember. He ordered part of it into the State Department; he ordered a part into the War Department.

At that stage I had not been in contact with President Truman. We were trying to beat that order. We knew it was coming. We tried to have him hold up on that order until we could determine what we could use out of the organization and what we could not. A communication went over from the Joint Chiefs to the President to take no action, but the President got the order an hour before from Harold Smith. There was no doubt what the President wanted, but anyway ours was held back, and the President signed theirs. That order was published immediately transferring the two parts as I stated. The President must have had it in mind that he wanted a central intelligence outfit. He wanted to know what his own Secretaries were doing because shortly after, or immediately after, the Central Intelligence Agency was formed, we had quite a row. He wanted to digest every day a summary of the dispatches flowing from the various Departments, either from State to our ambassadors or from the Navy and War Departments to their forces abroad, wherever such messages might have some influence on our foreign policy. For instance, the Navy might send a cruiser to the River Plata to try to influence Argentina. The President thought he ought to know that. And he had a feeling that Secretary Byrnes didn't keep him properly informed. I'm sure he didn't. He wanted this daily summary to keep him fully informed on exactly what was going on. And we had a fight with Byrnes. He objected strenuously to that on the grounds that that wasn't intelligence, and under a strict interpretation of intelligence, it wasn't. Intelligence is information properly evaluated about foreign countries, and this was operational. It was a report of what they were doing within the United States. Byrnes said it was up to him to report that to the President, that it was solely within his jurisdiction to report to the President. Therefore, he was opposed to it. Admiral Leahy spoke up and said, "The President wants it this way." And Byrnes said, "I ask that no action be taken until I see the President." He saw the President, and the President was adamant that it should be handled his way. But that was what the daily summary was. He needed that intelligence to find out what his own people were doing. That was right after January 20 (?), 1946, near the time of Byrnes's Moscow episode.

Mr. Hoover was always very jealous of his prerogatives, and he didn't want any investigatory forces existing within the United States, particularly in the security field. Incidentally, he opposed the organization of the Central Intelligence Agency because he was already in the foreign field of South America and I think, in some capitals of Europe. So he was bitterly opposed and so expressed himself. But when the die was cast, he recognized the necessity for it and that it was going to go forward. He wanted no conflict in the United States, and he continued for awhile in South America. The President expressed himself as opposed to his being down there. That was passed on to the Appropriations Committee, and they withdrew two or three million dollars that had been voted for that purpose. My own feeling was that it was wrong to stop him from doing it there because he was already operating, and we couldn't hope to get all the rest of the things done that we needed to do to replace it. It wasn't our idea to diminish our sources of intelligence. My feeling was that South America was primarily a Commie sort of thing and should be left with him, and that we should confine ourselves to finding out what the Russians were doing in Europe, and I knew that we were going to be overtaxed to get that done. The President agreed, and Hoover got his money back within a year. His budget was restored to him by that amount. [Hoyt] Vandenberg, however, was eager to build up a big machine, and he had a good chance to do it in a quick stroke. A month after he was in, he caused it to be cancelled. Hoover kept the budget money, but Vandenberg took over the responsibility. He spent his time working out South America, and the rest of the world was left alone and uncovered.

Hoover? I got along fairly well with him. The President was anxious to have our intelligence all in one overall Group. He didn't want to have one man responsible for the world, one man for the United States and another for the rest of the world. Central Intelligence is counterintelligence also, and it does do security work. It has to protect our men. It is a coalition of preventive intelligence, but it should not have any responsibility on the inside. If the CIA learns that agents are coming over, they should tie in with the man in charge of domestic intelligence and security so that he takes over at the shore. Or if the Navy would intercept messages to the effect that agents were being planted here, they would go to the FBI. Hoover dealt through Justice officially. He always maintained the proper decorum. He gave his ideas to Justice, and Justice tried to carry them out.

What was your role after Vandenberg became head?

I went back into active duty. I had been ordered over there by the Navy Department as director. It was like an assignment, and I think the President did appoint me too, but I was ordered there to serve President Truman.

2

Allen W. Dulles

"**D**ECEPTION AS A WAY OF LIFE was strange to a young man reared in the manse of a Presbyterian minister. But over a long life in the Chancelleries and war rooms of powerful nations, the reality grew upon him that the means for shaping the world's destiny might be manifest—or they might be covert."* This man, Allen Dulles, was born in Watertown in upstate New York on April 7, 1893, to the Rev. Allen Macy Dulles, pastor of the town's Presbyterian church, and his wife, Edith Foster, daughter of Secretary of State John Watson Foster and sister-in-law to another Secretary of State, Robert Lansing. Tutored by governesses, the brilliant Dulles children, soon numbering five, thrived as their parents made education their top

*Peter Grose, *Gentleman Spy: The Life of Allen Dulles* (Boston, 1994), 565.

priority. Shortly before his eighth birthday, Allen wrote a twenty-six-page booklet, *The Boer War*, and his proud grandfather, General Foster, had seven hundred copies printed and sold; proceeds went to the fund for Boer War widows and orphans.

Following his graduation in 1914 from Princeton University, where he was elected to Phi Beta Kappa, Dulles, uncertain about his future, toured India, China, and Japan for several months before returning to Princeton for a year's postgraduate study. He then joined the Foreign Service in the State Department. Posted as an Embassy secretary to Vienna and later to Bern during World War I, Dulles was surrounded by the fog of wartime diplomacy. His European tour ended with service at the Versailles Peace Conference. Back in the United States, he married Clover Todd in 1920. Evening classes at George Washington University led Allen to a law degree. He resigned from the State Department in 1926 and joined his brother, John Foster, in New York at Sullivan and Cromwell, a prominent and powerful Wall Street law firm.

Increasingly apprehensive because of Adolf Hitler's threats and Nazi Germany's power, Dulles, well known to American reporters and foreign leaders, urged the United States to adopt a posture of benevolent neutrality rather than follow the strict neutrality legislation of the mid-1930s. By May 1941 his public speeches claimed that "isolationist folly" had led America to throw off the responsibility of world leadership. Shortly after Pearl Harbor, Dulles joined William Donovan's fledgling intelligence organization, and he leased office space in Rockefeller Center next to the British intelligence office of William Stephenson. In late autumn 1942, now a member of the newly established Office of Strategic Services, Dulles returned to Switzerland to Bern where, fascinated by clandestine activities, he established a network of German and other foreign agents in opposition to Nazi Germany. His informants infiltrated the Abwehr, the Nazi military espionage agency. Within nine months his network penetrated Hitler's high command. The sophisticated spymaster, code-named "110," gathered crucial enemy intelligence data and surrender proposals. Operation SUNRISE, a secret negotiation promising the unconditional surrender of a million German and Italian forces in Italy, was masterfully processed by Dulles.

With war's end he returned to Sullivan and Cromwell. Although he played no direct role in establishing the Central Intelligence Group in 1946, during the following year he became a very public spokesman, urging a national civilian intelligence service. Such an organization, he believed, would collect data and analyze intelligence reports from the military services and the State Department. He insisted that this new service be managed by men who would make it their life's profession. Dulles assisted in drafting the 1947 National Security Act that created the Central Intelligence Agency, and one year later he headed a commission that designed a blueprint for reorganizing the CIA.

As CIA Director, Walter Bedell Smith, brilliant at his job, remodeled the CIA soon after his appointment in October 1950. He turned to Dulles to combine the two clandestine units, the Office of Policy Coordination and the Office of Special Operations, into the Directorate of Plans, which became responsible for all covert activities. In August 1951, Dulles became Deputy Director of the CIA. Following the election to the Presidency of GOP candidate Dwight D. Eisenhower in 1952, Dulles, dedicated to the Republican party, gratefully accepted the appointment as the first civilian Director (four military officers had preceded him) and the first professional intelligence officer to head the Agency, a post he had coveted five years earlier.

Dulles's clandestine experiences in two world wars, his boundless enthusiasm, and his wide range of contacts in Western Europe and the United States all combined to bring vigor, prestige, and excitement to the Agency reconstructed by Smith. In particular, covert action capabilities would be enhanced. During the 1950s, Dulles's secret operations for replacing the governments in Iran and Guatemala together with securing the U-2, a highly sophisticated photoreconnaissance aircraft, enhanced the Agency's reputation with the White House and with government leaders cleared for top-secret information.

Hostile criticism about America's failure to aid Hungarian freedom fighters, inept covert action in Indonesia, and the shoot-down of Francis Gary Powers in a U-2 plane over the Soviet Union produced only modest public reaction. However, the failed Bay of Pigs paramilitary invasion of Cuba in April 1961, designed by U-2's manager, Richard Bissell, and ordered by an inexperienced President John F. Kennedy, brought Dulles's resignation from the CIA in November, and John McCone was named Director. At Lyndon Johnson's request, Dulles then served on the Commission to Report upon the Assassination of President John F. Kennedy, or Warren Commission, and also took part in a civil rights investigation in Mississippi. In the years prior to his death in 1969, Dulles continued to defend the CIA in speeches, interviews, and articles. He believed in shaping world power through either open or covert means.

THOMAS BRADEN: *I would like to begin this by asking you, Allen, just to sort of get going, when did you first meet John F. Kennedy?*

ALLEN DULLES: Tom, when I knew I was going to be talking with you about President Kennedy, I tried to think back and I can't be absolutely certain when I first met Jack Kennedy. I believe it was when he was Senator and I believe it was in Palm Beach. He used to go down there a good

Conducted by Thomas Braden in Washington, DC, on December 5–6, 1964. Oral History Interviews, John F. Kennedy Library, Boston, Massachusetts.

deal, you know, and I think I met him through his father, Joe [Joseph P. Kennedy]. I knew Joe quite well; I knew Joe from the days of being a lawyer and in the securities business to some extent myself. I knew him from the days when he was head of the Securities and Exchange Commission, wasn't he, in 1933 or thereabout? I used to go down to Palm Beach from time to time. I was quite a friend of Charlie [Charles B.] Wrightsman—you know, the Wrightsmans who are close neighbors of the Kennedys—and Charlie was an old client of mine in the law. I used to go down occasionally with Charlie and Jayne Wrightsman, and I recall a series of visits I made—I'm not awfully good on dates without a lot of paper before me, and I haven't got any paper here. Maybe you can help me out on this, but I remember at the time that Jack Kennedy was working on his *Profiles in Courage*.

That would have been while he was ill.

It was while he was ill. He was quite ill. He was suffering a good deal of pain, and he was lying on the sofa there in the study in Joe Kennedy's house there at Palm Beach, and as I recall that was the first time I saw him. I might have seen him before that, but that's the first I recollect having seen him.

Did you have any impression about him at that time—just a young fellow that was writing a book, a fellow that had a particularly tough time? What was your impression, or did you have any?

Well, I had more of an impression than that. I had the impression that here was a fellow that had been grievously wounded in the war, and that he was just bound that he was going to make a comeback, that he was going to conquer the physical ills that he had. Now, I don't know what his ambitions were at that time, but I don't think he was looking at that moment at the Presidency. His job then, as he saw it, was to get well, but it was a hard struggle. I could see many times—he would get up, you know, in the room and walk a few paces; he was wincing with pain. Then he overcame it. But that was the impression that I got of those early days, and we used to have quite long times together. I mean, I'd go and stay a couple of hours. I would rely on Joe a good bit because I knew Joe would let me know when Jack had had about all he ought to take.

Do you remember what you talked about?

Mostly foreign affairs, various stages of foreign affairs.

He was very obviously interested.

Oh, fascinated, fascinated!

Was he informed, intelligent?

Oh, yes. But he obviously wanted to learn. I was trying to think whether I wasn't Director of Central Intelligence at that time. I came in in 1953; in 1951 I was Deputy Director, you see, and I think it was during that period—'51, '52, '53, along then. Am I correct on that, do you think?

Yes. So you would have been either Director of Central Intelligence or Deputy Director.

At that time my brother [John Foster Dulles] was Secretary of State, and we used to have dinners over at Charlie Wrightsman's. As I recall, about this time we had a very interesting dinner there with my brother, Charlie Wrightsman, and several others and spent the long evening together discussing foreign policy problems. Jack Kennedy was quite a modest man in those days. In those meetings particularly—I remember my brother was there—I don't say he was overawed, but he [Kennedy] was very respectful. I mean, he didn't throw any weight around, and he was trying to find out what the facts were. The Middle East was worrying us particularly at that time, and a good many other things.

This was the time of [Iran's Mohammed] Mossadegh, perhaps?

Yes, I think it was just after. . . . Charlie Wrightsman was an oil man, and he was interested and we were all deeply interested in the developments of the Middle East at that time. That was one of the main subjects of that particular dinner conversation, as I recall it.

Now, when he recovered and came back to Washington, and during the time he was a Senator and recovered from his back injury, did he have any particular interest in intelligence affairs? I don't remember any of this, but did he come over to the Agency a good deal and ask questions? Or did he take particular interest in it in the Senate?

I can't speak about the Senate. He took great interest in it. As I say, he was always trying to get information. I don't mean secrets or things of that kind particularly, but to get himself informed. He wanted to get my views, and when my brother was there his views on what we thought about things, and we had many, many talks together. As I say, very often Joe was there at the same time.

Allen, to go on a little bit there—do you remember any period of succeeding relationship with him between that time and the time he became President? Just social in Washington, or occasional interviews, or was there no contact at all?

Oh, no, the contact was fairly continuous because my trips to Palm Beach were quite frequent. He was very often there, and whenever he was there we always got together. I respected his views. I thought he had a very keen appreciation of foreign problems; and, being in the intelligence business, I pumped him as much as I could to get his views on things and his reaction to things, and that continued on during those days until the days when I served under him for a short time as Director.

I remember that, Allen. I remember the announcement in the newspapers, and it seems to me I saw you within a few days after that by an odd chance in your office. Were you surprised when he called you and asked you to become Director or did you think this . . .

No, I was surprised.

You were? Why?

Well, I'll tell you I wasn't surprised that he considered my continuance on in the job. Our relations were such and our friendship such that I thought that might happen. I didn't think it would happen as soon as this. It was one of the first things he did after the election. . . . I was in my office in Washington, and I remember my secretary coming to me and she said the President-elect wanted to speak to me, and he went right to the point.

What did he say?

He said, "Allen, I'd like to have you stay on as Director of Central Intelligence when I take over next January 20th," and I admit I was surprised, and I was flattered and I was pleased. As you know as well as anyone, Tom, intelligence has been my lifeblood. and I have tremendous interest in building up the Agency, and developing it. I thought that the one thing that could be most damaging to the Agency at the time of presidential change is that if you establish the precedent that when a new President. new Director of Central Intelligence, new party is in, change the Director and get somebody that is the same party as the President. I've always felt that intelligence ought to be kept out of politics, and I therefore was gratified and thrilled that I was given the chance to help establish the precedent that here we have a Democrat coming in [and] taking over from a Republican. . . .

And you, after all, with your brother as Republican Secretary of State had a certain—oh, let's say, a certain independent type of Republican . . .

Oh, yes, I generally voted Republican, and. I said—I think I called him a Senator then—"Senator, I'm beyond retiring age, you know, normal retiring age." Let's see, I was 58 or 59 at that time—how long ago was that? Well, it was November of 1960; I guess I was 67 or thereabouts—born in '93, is that mathematics right? I said, "Look here, I ought to retire fairly soon. I don't think a man should stay on in this job indefinitely. There are a lot of young men in this shop that are coming along, and a lot of able people, and I would like to see a change come about in an orderly way and be around when it was made. But if you want me to stay on, I'll certainly stay on for a period, a year or so, whatever you want, and then I think I probably ought to retire." That was about the way it went.

What did he say?

Well, he said, "We can talk about the other later. I'm also communicating with J. Edgar Hoover, and I would like to announce that both you and J. Edgar Hoover will continue on in your present functions, respective functions, after I take over as President. I want to announce that right away." That was the way he was.

On that particular question, did you ever hear later of the ways in which he came to this decision? As far as you knew, did he just decide that this was what he wanted, or do you think there were advisors who suggested this? Do you know of any particular facet of this decision other than what you just said?

It came so soon that, as far as I know, people weren't talking or thinking about it. If it had come a couple of months later, there would have been time. I don't think there was time for anybody to bring a lot of pressure on him even if anybody wanted to do it. So I have every reason to believe that this was his own idea because, as I say, this was a matter of forty-eight hours after the results of the election were known.

I believe you said at the time, I've forgotten now, but it seems to me that it was either the sixth President or the seventh that you had served since [Woodrow] Wilson . . .

I think I've served nine now. Let me see . . . Well, I don't need to stop and count up now, but, starting with Woodrow Wilson, I've served every President since Woodrow Wilson, including Mr. Kennedy and now Mr. [Lyndon B.] Johnson.

He took office then on January 20. Do you remember your first official business with him? Or was it before January?

We had a good deal of official business before January. Let's discuss—I think it's an interesting subject and I'd like to get a little down on it—this question of briefings of Kennedy.

Oh, that's right. I'd forgotten about that. This involved the Quemoy-Matsu business, didn't it?

It involved that, and it involved Cuba, and it involved the problem with [Richard M.] Nixon, you know. Well, what happened was this. Back in—I was trying to think what campaign it was—back in the [Thomas E.] Dewey campaign . . .

Forty-four.

No, let me see—'44, yes. Back in '44, I had been working with Tom Dewey as a candidate in New York—weren't you there at the time? Don't you remember being in a hotel room—yes, that's another story. I had an office set up at Dewey's request in the Hotel Roosevelt, and interestingly enough I had Chris [Christian A.] Herter and Mac [McGeorge] Bundy—do you remember both of them were working with me? We were gathering together—this was particularly in '48 but seriously started in '44—information that would be necessary after the Republican victory of '48. We were thinking of '48 particularly because we thought we knew the results in '48 a little more surely than we did in '44. Forty-four for the Republicans was a pretty uphill campaign, as you know, against FDR, but in '48 it looked as though the Republicans would come in. We set up that office, and my brother was there and we were advising him as to what was going on and this was with the full consent of the State Department. It was all set up. What we got was official information, and I passed that on to Tom Dewey—Chris Herter did, Mac Bundy, all of us working there together.

Was this your idea—that the presidential candidate ought to have at least the official records so that he could speak wisely, is that the idea?

No, I don't think so. That went back a bit earlier. [Arthur H.] Vandenberg—of course, you recall the role he had played and was playing in these days, and I think Vandenberg had something to do with it. And my brother had been called in to consult with regard to the Dumbarton Oaks Conference when they were working on the new United Nations and so forth and so on. So it was the idea of a bipartisan foreign policy, or nonpartisan foreign policy insofar as one could possibly get it, that that ought to be carried over into the electoral period; that the candidate, once he was nominated, should have access and should have briefings from the Administration in power or from the State Department so that the two rival candidates would each know the essential facts so as to keep as far as possible the campaign somewhat on the track. It didn't always work out that way. I'm not absolutely sure the system is a sound system; I've had some qualms about it since, in some ways growing out of this misunderstanding that took place in the time of the Kennedy campaign. Should I just go into that for a minute?

I think you should, yes.

Let me get this straight. During the campaign, of course, and this is the Nixon-Kennedy campaign, Cuba was a major issue; [Fidel] Castro was behaving like a Communist and the American people were disturbed. The question was what to do, what could you do? And at one stage of the campaign—not going into the details 'cause it's all a matter of record— Nixon was under pretty heavy attack from Kennedy on the grounds that we weren't doing enough. What were we doing? Here were these Cuban refugees who wanted to get into the battle, and who was doing anything for them?

Ninety miles away and all of that.

Ninety miles away, and were we doing anything? And Nixon was pretty vigorously attacked by Kennedy on that point. The suggestion was made, as I recall, that we ought to be training these Cubans, we ought to be sending them back and so on. Well, then candidate Kennedy jumped in—I don't know if Adlai [E. Stevenson] was back of this or not or whatever caused it—anyway, he jumped in and he attacked Nixon and said, this was improper, you ought not to propose this. We have all these treaties, noninterference, and you are recommending that the President of the United States should violate the neutrality laws of the United States by arming people to go landing in Cuba.

You mean, Nixon came back with this, or do you mean Kennedy came back?

Yes, Kennedy came back—did I say Kennedy?

Yeah, you did.

Kennedy went on the attack. I think he made a mistake in that but anyway—no, let me see—I think Nixon made a mistake. Then the issue arose as to whether or not Kennedy, when he had said this, knew that there were certain covert operations going on because he was being briefed. Nixon was quite annoyed, and he thought Kennedy might be making use of the fact that there was secret information of this kind, but it couldn't be used, and that he was violating a confidence. Well, that wasn't the case.

Well, how much secret information were you giving Kennedy?

Well, that is the question. Just to carry along with the story, Nixon, after this incident, got hold of one of [Dwight D.] Eisenhower's close advisors—I've forgotten which one it was at the moment—and he called up Jerry [Wilton B.] Persons in the White House; and he said, will you find out for me whether Allen Dulles, in connection with his briefings of the candidates, has briefed Mr. Kennedy on Cuba, and left it vague—it was on Cuba, you see. They didn't make it clear. What they meant was whether he'd briefed Kennedy on the secret operations that Nixon knew about as a member of the National Security Council, but that was not in the public domain. The word came back—and it was a perfectly honest mistake, I'm quite sure—that Kennedy had been briefed by me on Cuba, but just that, that was all there was to it: "on Cuba." They didn't get in touch with me; I think maybe I could have straightened the thing out early if they had. I had briefed the candidate, Kennedy, on Cuba, and I told him about what was going on there, and about Castro, and about the whole situation on Cuba. But I did *not* tell Mr. Kennedy that there was on the back of the stove a project to arm some of these Cuban refugees, to help the underground in Cuba. At that stage there was no plan of an invasion or of a military operation directed from the outside against Cuba.

We weren't then training people?

We were training people, but we had not decided at that time whether they would be infiltrated individually as guerrillas, or whether they were going to be dropped in to add to the underground there—one or two at a time, or a few at a time. There had been no planning as to how they were to be used; that is, we had them in training in various places in Latin America, Panama, and other places, in relatively small numbers. The number at this time I would imagine—by this time I'm talking about September, October—we might have had a couple hundred being trained, but mostly for guerrilla operations, sabotage, and things of that kind. I'm afraid this is getting a little bit long, and I would like to get back now to the point of it.

So I told Jerry Persons—if it was Jerry who was called at the White House, and I think it was Jerry—yes, I'd briefed Mr. Kennedy on Cuba. When that word got back—you see, that was passed back to Nixon—Nixon thought that I had briefed Kennedy on these secret operations which Nixon knew about because of being a member of the Security Council, and I knew about, but Jerry Persons I don't think did. So you see how the misunderstanding arose. So then. . .

Was Nixon furious?

Nixon was quite furious—it comes out in that book he wrote, *Six Crises*—because he thought Kennedy, being in the know, had made use of this, but knowing that there couldn't be any comeback on it, really, because this was confidential information. Well, now, I had not deliberately withheld this from Kennedy, but the ground rules under which I was operating, in the briefing of the President, did not cover covert operations unless they were going to blow before the elections. Now if you had a long-range covert plan that was being developed, but which wasn't going to be put into effect until after the elections, you did not bother the candidate with it because it wasn't going to affect anything politically. At least that was the ground rule under which I was operating; because no matter how discreet one is in the heat of a campaign, if you fill his mind full of all kinds of information, this is going to come out. No matter how good he is. No matter how careful he is. And so the general rules under which I was operating—I don't know whether I made them up myself or whether they were given to me—but I did not brief candidates on secret operations which were destined to come out only in the future, and with respect to which the candidate, if elected, would have all the opportunity in the world to pass his own judgment on as to whether he wanted to go ahead. The candidate, if he became President, would then have complete control of the situation; and if he said, I don't like this operation, you'd better stop it. . . . In the Cuban matter we weren't even going to get anything committed except a little money and except a little time on training. That was about all.

Did you have to brief Kennedy on any secret operations that were going to take place? I don't recall any.

I don't remember any on which we did brief him prior to the election. Now, I was trying to think of the date when I went down to Palm Beach to brief him, whether that was after the elections. I did go down but before he took office; I went down to Palm Beach later and told the candidate-elect what was going on, but I did not ask at that time any judgment on it. I took this up with Eisenhower because at that time there was a good deal of pressure on [George A.] Smathers and others. The Senators from Florida, they were getting worried about the situation in Cuba; they wanted something to be done, and there was quite a demand and pressure to get going, do something. Well, now, we were at that time—this was after the election but before the President took over—we wanted the President-elect to know for his own guidance in dealing especially with pressure from the Congressmen, Senators, and so forth, that this was not being neglected, something was being done. And at that time we did not say to Mr. Kennedy: we want your views on this; we want you to know this is going on; when you've taken over, you can turn it off or you can turn it on; we will not in the meantime—in connection with this—we will not be taking any action which commits you as to the future.

Let's go back for just a second now. A little while ago you said you doubted—at least you had some grave doubts about—whether this system worked, of briefing candidates. I'd like to just ask you, what are your doubts?

Well, my doubts are these. This system is subject to abuse in that in the particularly delicate foreign affairs situation, you might give a full briefing to a candidate and he might be afraid that then you would say, well, now, look here, this is all very confidential, you can't use this. You could restrict the freedom of action of a candidate in a very important situation or make it very uncomfortable for him; and yet you are going to brief on delicate situations. You are going to brief on situations where, even between the period of the election and change of Administration, if there is a change, you may even have to reach some decision in this field.

But don't you risk on the other hand, by not briefing, the possibility that he might make a completely irresponsible statement because he didn't know the facts? Do you think that's a better risk? Maybe it is.

I think that you have to sort of weigh the pros and the cons. I have found candidates on the whole not anxious to get briefings in depth.

What was Kennedy like during this period? How many times did you brief him—five or six, or was it often?

Three times, I think, and as I recall General [Charles Pearré] Cabell, who was my Deputy, briefed him once. The first briefing was a very general briefing and covered the waterfront. I think briefings of that kind probably at that stage are a good thing, but I have found that candidates don't generally want to be told too much. That is, say they want to attack Policy B that the Administration is following. Now, if you have a lot of briefers that are going to him and filling him full of all the virtues of Policy B and so forth and telling him all about it and giving him secret information about it, what's he going to do then? Is he free then to go up and attack Policy B, and is he going to use this information in doing it, or what is he going to do? There is a grave danger that the freedom of debate of foreign policy issues might be hampered unless this briefing is done very carefully, unless the ground rules are perfectly clear, and unless the candidate is able to keep complete freedom of action.

Yes, I see. Well, in any event, the first briefing you gave him was very general, and after that do you remember any particular incident? Was he particularly interested in the briefing?

Oh, yes, we went over country by country.

Did he ask a lot of questions, or was it a hurried thing?

No, it wasn't hurried at all. We went up there—let's see, he was up on the Cape—and we spent most of the day at it, and went over the situation, and then we had a couple of other briefings. I've got—somewhere tucked away—a list of the various subject matters. One was related, I remember, to the question of developments in the atomic field in which he was extremely interested, and he asked half a dozen questions, I would say, during the period; and we had two or three or four briefings altogether, and we went over these various questions that he had.

Did you remember that he ever asked you specifically about the Cuban thing?

Well, you see, I covered that right after the election.

No, but before, I mean, during the campaign briefings. Did he ever ask you, well now, is there anything going on there? I just say he might have because . . .

No, I was trying to think as to whether he did. I don't recall that he did. When this issue came up with Nixon, Mr. Nixon indicated he thought he'd been double-crossed. I said, this is all a misunderstanding because as far as I know, President Kennedy did not know about the training— from me, anyway. Now, if he knew about it—there had been some press comments on it, he might have believed the press comments. He didn't know anything about it from me, until after the election took place.

All right, then, do you think we've covered this question of briefings? Or did you want to say anything more about that?

No, I think probably we've pretty well covered it. I wouldn't go so far as to say that I would absolutely change the present system as it has developed, but I do think I would try to get the ground rules, particularly the ground rules with regard to covert operations, a little clearer so that there wouldn't be this misunderstanding that took place this last time.

Now, let's go ahead, then. Do you remember, after he took office, the first official time you met him? Did you show up the first day for your normal briefing of the President? Didn't you do that—let's see, how often?

Well, that's a fairly complicated question, and the answer is going to be fairly complicated too. Every President has his own system. Under Eisenhower the briefing system was quite largely developed around the meetings of the National Security Council. The National Security Council met every Thursday unless there was some reason for postponing it or some reason for having an extra meeting. The Director of Central

Intelligence was afforded an opportunity, at the opening of every meeting, to give a briefing and generally took it. It was my practice in the days when I was Director of Central Intelligence; this covers about the eight years of Eisenhower and some of the period prior to that under President Truman. [Dulles was Deputy Director under Truman.]

Yes, I was going to ask you about that in a minute because I remember that you used to go over and brief Truman—it seems to me in the morning . . .

That's right. That's different.

. . . and I remember you commenting to me that he was extremely interested.

Yes, he was. He followed it very closely. I would always be in touch before the meeting of the National Security Council with the director, Bobby [Robert] Cutler or Mac Bundy or whoever it might be who was the director of the National Security Council staff. I generally would go over with him the subject matters which I felt were important. I would ask him—it was Gordon Gray for awhile, it changes you know—was there anything he wanted to have me cover. And if there was anything, then I'd say, all right, we'll add that in, and then I would cut my time down on the others. That was sort of the routine that had been established during the Eisenhower Administration and followed fairly closely what had been done in the Truman Administration, although a good deal more briefing was done of President Truman in his office alone, generally before a National Security Council meeting. He would get some briefing papers, and some of them he would read, some of them he would keep and give back to you later, and that was the way it was done under Truman.

Then I've described a bit how it was done under Eisenhower, and under Kennedy the National Security Council procedures were somewhat changed, partly due to the different temperament of the men. I only, of course, was in on this for about a year. You see, I resigned at the end of November—well, he became President—I mean, he was "acting" President before that, so that it was almost a year. President Kennedy liked to get snappy, short, but at the same time reasonably comprehensive—as to subject matter—notes, and we'd get to him every morning several sheets of paper. It might be four or five pages, and on these pages we'd say, here are the important things that have happened in the last twenty-four hours, if anything important had happened. Then we would often find that there would be quite a barrage of questions. You'd often get telephone calls and so forth.

Was this daily?

Yes, this was daily. Now, how long that lasted I can't say because I wasn't there the whole time. . . . Then there were certain other papers that were prepared and presented on a daily basis that were a little bit longer.

You said you'd often get telephone calls. You mean you'd get them personally?

Sometimes you'd get them personally; sometimes you'd get them from the particular aide who was working with him on the particular matter for the National Security Council. It might sometimes be his military aide or whoever was working very closely with him on current developments in the foreign field.

Was this set up right away as soon as he took office? Did he decide this or did you?

Oh, it took a little time to work it out. We carried on for a time the system that we had developed before he came in, and then there were certain changes he wanted made—this is too long; I want this worked out a little differently; I want one or two sheets of paper and I want to get the main points of crisis, points of difficulty, in the foreign field, and I want to get that quickly, and then you can supplement that and add to it as you want, but give me that every morning.

Do you remember any particular things that he asked questions about, or were they just too frequent to recall?

No, I wouldn't. Well, we had the Dominican [Republic] business— do you remember [Rafael] Trujillo and all that business—and that blew up. We had constantly the Cuban situation. We had the developing problems in NATO [North Atlantic Treaty Organization], and I worked out a system at the time—whether it's carried on or not, I don't really know— of trying to pinpoint in one or more documents that we would hand to the President, not always every morning, developing crisis situations. He, more than almost anyone I ever knew, said: I don't want to get caught short on this thing, I want to know; you can't give me all the details but if you see a crisis situation, point it out to me quickly so that I can do my own homework and get a background on it. He didn't want something to happen in, say, Nicaragua and find himself not knowing anything about the current situation in Nicaragua. Nicaragua, say, might have been quiet for six months and then all of a sudden you see a crisis coming up; he wanted to have that crisis pinpointed to him so he could get the background. He was always very accessible on the telephone; I would telephone him from time to time. If anything happened in the world, you never made a mistake if you called up Mr. Kennedy and said here's what's happened. He might differ from you as to whether it was urgent or not, but he wanted you to do it and he accepted your judgment if you saw it was urgent to tell him about it.

Let's go back for a minute, if it's all right with you, to when you first told him about the Bay of Pigs—not about the Bay of Pigs, but when you first briefed him on the covert operation in Cuba. That was down in Palm Beach, after he had been elected but before he took over the Presidency. When did you first go to him to say, well, now, here's what the plan is and here's a prospective timetable—or did you do that?

By the way, I might just add at that time, when I went down to brief the President, I took up with him—and I don't think it's necessary to put on the record what I took up with him—two or three other covert operations that were going on, that were significant, so that he would have an opportunity to study and decide promptly whether he wanted these things to continue or not.

Did he?

I think in most cases he did, as I remember. We then had some rather delicate problems about the U-2 [reconnaissance plane] and made quite a thorough review of that situation. He wasn't timid and he wasn't rash, but we wanted to lay before him everything that was being done that might have implications. This particular briefing, as I recall, was after the election but before he took over, so that he did not technically have responsibility; but still he was in a situation where he was going to inherit the responsibility for anything you did in the meantime, and we didn't want to be doing anything in that delicate field of covert operations.

I gather—maybe I'm reading this into it—he wasn't a man who was simply fascinated with the covert operations arm as some people are. He was not?

No, but I didn't feel he was frightened by it.

He didn't seem to think that it was reprehensible or immoral or anything?

No, oh, no, I think he took that quite in his stride because I recall he didn't cut off anything that was being done, and we gave him that opportunity. He was the boss. But we did not say, we are bringing this to you now for a final decision on your part. We said this is going on—let's say, a U-2 flight. You will have the problem when you take over as President; you will have the problem of whether you want this to continue or not. Meanwhile, we will bring to your attention the pros and cons and the benefits and the possible difficulties.

Right. And not then or even later did he tell you—do you remember, anyway, that he told you—to cut out any particular covert operations?

I wouldn't want to say yes or no on that; I don't recall any at this moment. There were some that were sort of being developed on which no very formal decision had been reached which later were stood down, but it might well have been that they would have been stood down anyway. When the time came to reach a decision, those that were working on them, including myself, might have said to the President: we've worked on this, but on reviewing the whole situation we don't recommend it, or we recommend it be changed, something of that sort.

To go back for just a minute, somebody told me once that you had made the President interested in the James Bond thrillers, which everyone knows he read. Is that the way you remember it?

Well, really, I think that the shoe's on the other foot. I recall, in those days I was down in Florida a good deal, that on one occasion Jackie [Jacqueline Bouvier] Kennedy gave me the first James Bond that I ever had. I think it was *From Russia, With Love,* which is, I think, one of his best books, and then after that I got so much interested in them that I bought up the next two or three that he got out. I know I sent them to Senator Kennedy and President Kennedy and we often talked about James Bond, and we both of us kept up our interest in it until his sad death recently. I'm speaking there of James Bond.

Of James Bond's death, or [author Ian] Fleming?

Rather, Fleming, yes.

Let's go back now to the operations of the Agency and of your relationship with the President during the time that you served as DCI under him. We were talking about the covert plan for Cuba. When, do you recall—it doesn't matter when, I think, because that will be a matter of record perhaps—but do you recall what the circumstances were and what it was like when you first went to him in his official capacity, after he had become President in the White House, and said, here's the plan? Did you say, here's the plan; what are we going to do? Or what did you say?

As I recall, this took place at the time of that meeting after the elections. I think we fixed that for late November, didn't we, or around that time in Palm Beach? Maybe this is repetition, but the circumstances of that were that after the elections, I went to President Eisenhower and I said to him, knowing the pressures he was under from his friends in the Senate and Congress, to get going on Cuba in some way or another. I said to President Eisenhower that I had never briefed Mr. Kennedy, the President-elect, on what was being done with regard to training exiles and others for possible operations in Cuba, and I recommended that he be brought up to date on that as soon as possible so as to avoid any misunderstanding or embarrassing situation between the President-elect and respected members of the Senate who were importuning him to do something. President Eisenhower agreed; and Dick [Richard] Bissell, who had been my particular deputy for the Cuban matter and who was the Deputy Director for Operations in the CIA, went down with me. We spent the better part of a day with President-elect Kennedy and told him of what had been done, who had been trained, where they had been trained—talking now about Cuban patriot refugees who wanted to do something—and I told him something of the timetable. As I recall, and I'm speaking now without any records before me, when we went down there to do the briefing there had been no plans formulated for anything like an invasion of [Fidel] Castro's Cuba. The training which had been given had been very largely training that one would give to guerrillas, and there were bands of guerrillas in Cuba. And the original idea had been that these bands would be strengthened and built up with accretions from the outside, and it was sometime later that the plans changed from a purely guerrilla-type operation to a more directly military-type operation.

Did you go to him then when the plan changed and say, here's our plan? How did that work out?

Immediately after the new Administration came in following the election, and you had a certain number of new faces, there was quite a briefing operation to do. Many of the same people were in the State Department and many in Defense, but there were many new faces also, and then a more definite plan was formulated and was discussed at a great many meetings of the National Security Council and its Cuban and Latin American subcommittees. As I said earlier, there were certain changes in operation of the National Security Council. President-elect Kennedy had indicated that he wanted to change a little bit the method of procedure and to develop ad hoc task forces, sometimes called subcommittees of the National Security Council, on which there should be people who were expert in the ad hoc question that was up—whether it was Cuba, or whatever it might be. The plans then began to take shape in meetings of the task force committee within the general structure of the National Security Council, and with the Joint Chiefs of Staff and the military establishment being fully brought in on the plans, which took on more and more of a military character.

Did the President from the beginning, do you remember, review these plans which you showed him first down at Palm Beach? Did he like them, did he think they were interesting, or did he just oppose them right away or anything like that?

No, now I'm drawing on memory, but my recollection is that his initial attitude was, well, what is your timetable on this? And we gave that to him in that we said we won't be ready until the late spring probably to do anything, and we were given a go-ahead to continue to plan but without any commitment.

When you told him about this, was he alone present with you and Bissell, or were there others?

As I recall, at that time we were alone. I don't remember anybody else being there.

In any event he did ask you what your timetable was and then apparently looked upon it with some equanimity.

If I'm right that I was doing this sometime in November—let me get my year now—November '60, and I was talking of the spring—that would be '61: February, March, April, along there.

All right, then, do you recall, Allen, as you look back on when you began to present these plans, as they firmed up in a more military fashion, did he still look upon it with equanimity? Was he doubtful, distrustful, worried, harried?

He was inquiring. He had a certain amount of skepticism. He studied them pretty carefully, very carefully. There was that one period along there where there was a rather dramatic change in the planning. I'll go back just a bit here to pick up the thread. I've already described the situation our country faced: communism taking over in Cuba; more and more tie-ins with the Kremlin; a great many Cubans, refugees, exiles, some of them, in this country—they wanted to do something to save their country. There was a certain amount of pressure—political pressure, Congressional pressure—on the President to do something more definite, more dramatic than had been done in the past. What were we going to do with these high-minded, young, able, patriotic Cubans? Our military people looked into it and measures were taken so that they could get, under certain conditions, military training under the procedures that had been set up by the Defense Department. And then there had been the very specific training that the CIA had done, starting, as I reported before, with relatively small groups of men who had been trained, many of them, in the jungles of Central America and the tough terrain that you had there—trained to be ready, trained in guerrilla tactics.

And by this time—I'm speaking shortly after the Kennedy election—we had several hundred of these trainees, and not only did we have these, but we had many more that were pressing, that were ready to be trained, that were in touch with the various recruiting organizations that had been set up to maintain contact with them. So we were in a position where we could recruit several hundred in addition to the few hundred that we had at this time, and at the time of the change that I mentioned—the change really was from sending in scattered guerrilla fighters to join the existing underground. The plan was to consider the formation of a brigade, a military formation; the number of that we hadn't finally fixed at that time. It was going to be somewhere between five hundred and a thousand with the possibility of later increasing that so that you would have a small *force de frappe* [strike force], a small military formation, a brigade fully equipped, armed, and ready to make a descent upon Cuba at the time and under the circumstances that the military, our military people, would think the wisest.

Now, then, you had various plans that were presented as to if you were going to make a landing in Cuba, where would you make it? The decisions on that point were very largely dictated by the military, our military advisors in the Defense Department. You had to consider certain things; you had to consider the availability of some airstrip so that you could develop quickly some air coverage for the operation, particularly so that you would have possession of a runway from which aircraft could take off to protect the ships which were bringing in the men and the military matériel—the equipment, including later even tanks, mechanized units, armored units, and the like.

Plans were formulated, military plans on paper; various sites for a possible landing were considered. You had to consider the many factors: how you get your men ashore and their equipment; how once ashore, then would they have access either to roads of ingress or lines of communications so they could get where they wanted to. One had in mind, too, that while we had moved at that time from the purely guerrilla concept to the concept of a strike force, we still had in mind that if the strike force failed, we wanted to be able for it to join, if possible, other military Maquis-type underground forces that were already in the mountains of Cuba and had some organization there and some protection from being overrun by the Castro forces and by the Cuban militia.

I take it that the military phase of this, as you described it, the change in plans which made it more of a military type of operation than merely an infiltration of some guerrillas, individual guerrillas or bands, came after the Inauguration of January 1961 then, didn't it?

The preliminary decision to prepare a plan on the basis of a strike force was reached on a very tentative basis before the change of Administration, as I recall. I have in mind the date of November with the change of Administration taking place the next January. But you must realize that this was very tentative because it hadn't yet been processed in the Defense Department; it hadn't been looked at by the Joint Chiefs of Staff; you hadn't as yet finally decided on, let's say, the place to attack, or even whether to attack.

It was almost a paper idea?

It was on paper without having been approved. Of course, there was no go-ahead signal having been given at all.

Of course not. As you described it, it wasn't completely staffed out as yet.

It wasn't completely staffed out; it was for planning purposes, and it was a plan to be staffed out.

Now, when was that? What was the new President's reaction when this particular plan, as distinguished from the guerrilla operation idea, was first revealed to him? Do you remember what his reaction was, or was that the same plan that was shown him, as you described earlier, when you went down to Palm Beach with Dick [Bissell]?

No, I don't think that when I went down to Palm Beach—and I might be wrong on this—I don't think even for planning purposes we had finally decided on that.

Do you recall . . .

I might be wrong on that because it was about that time—I have a date in mind of the 7th or 8th of November, let's see, what year am I talking about, November 1960—that this plan was discussed with me in a very tentative way inside the CIA.

Inside the organization. So it must have been just about the date of the election?

Yeah.

I think the election that year was the 8th of November, so therefore do you recall then when this particular plan was first shown to the President or discussed with him?

I can't say definitely when it was. It was a good bit later before it got to the point of being a plan that had been considered by the Joint Chiefs of Staff and that you had before you a military paper.

Just for the sake of history—not that it perhaps is very important in terms of the long-range interests of the United States—but was the plan that you are now talking about, the military plan, ever discussed with President Eisenhower?

Funny, I don't remember clearly. It was not discussed with President Eisenhower as a formulated plan on paper stating we have X number of well-trained, highly trained, equipped Cuban refugees; they are now in a task force in a brigade; we have the equipment for this number and certain additional ones that will be added to it; and we have a brigade, eight hundred men or whatever it may be, all equipped and ready to go. I don't know whether that was discussed with President Eisenhower in that form or not. I would doubt whether it was.

I think you're indicating to me, or at least you seem to be indicating, that general ideas of this sort of thing might have been discussed in a casual way, perhaps, not in a formal way.

Yes, that would be fair enough.

Then let's get down to the time when you first showed a conceived plan to the new President, Kennedy. Do you recall anything about that?

Oh, yes, I recall a good deal about it, but I'm rather chary about giving dates because I am speaking here without any papers before me at all.

Yes, that's right, let's not bother with the dates.

We had a period now to deal with which goes from the time of the election, which was the first week early in November, and the date when the final decision to proceed was taken, which was next April. I think that's correct, I think it was in the first ten or fifteen days of April. That was dictated by various other considerations, the rainy season, questions of weather, and so forth. I mean, you had certain periods when it was better to do this than others, and that whole period following the election. . . . And of course, there was some little time between the election [and the Inauguration]; there were some new faces coming in; there were certain personnel changes being made at that time so that it wasn't immediately after the election. The numerous meetings that we held with the task force of the National Security Council that was assigned to this took place over a relatively long period of seven or eight weeks, I should say.

Do you suppose that you were the first man to tell the President about the plans, or do you suppose that he got it from the papers of the National Security Council or the task force report?

I would have thought that—my best memory serves me now—this would have been done in a task force meeting and a paper which would probably have been prepared by Dick Bissell, gone over by me, reviewed by the military, and then presented merely as a talking paper in this meeting of the task force of the National Security Council.

Then we have the question of what you recall of his reaction to this?

At this stage it was purely study. You didn't present this to him at that time saying, it's important that you reach a decision at this meeting, or that we have to reach a decision before next week or the next two or three weeks. It wasn't even as close as that, and you may recall from written history of this period that there was some difference in views with regard to how one should use the brigade, where it should go, the nature of its equipment. I think you probably remember what's called the Trinidad Plan. That was very carefully considered; that involved certain somewhat different considerations because you were going into a more highly populated area there. It was a kind of an operation where if you won, you won big, but if you lost, you lost awful quick because you were going into an area where there were certain known hostile forces. That plan was, after a good deal of consideration, finally set aside, partly because of opposition at the White House level and partly because the military thought that another plan, another place where we finally went—the Bay of Pigs—was better.

Eventually, however, over a series of weeks, I suppose, as you've described it, the President must have at some time or another become involved in this . . .

Oh, yes, he did, very deeply.

Was he interested? Do you remember anything about that? What we're trying to find here, of course, is not dates [but] his reaction and what he thought.

Yes, I understand that. I remember during the discussion it was realized by him from the beginning that this was tricky business, it was difficult business. No one could hold out the assurance of success, and he was therefore anxious to see what alternative possibilities there were. Say, we were met in force as we went ashore, what do you do then? Say, that we succeeded in a penetration in some depth, what would happen then? Were you planning your landing so that if there were these guerrilla forces that we knew were on the island, if they could help, were we landing in the best place to aid them; or were we landing in the best place so that your force, if it was knocked about to begin with as an organized military force, could still become a guerrilla force and join the guerrillas that were on the island? I remember discussions of things of that kind. He was very much interested to know what the chances were. What was the worst that could happen? What was the best that could happen? What was the situation on the island? How effective were these other guerrillas? How much could we count on them for some help, and how much could we count on being able to help them through this force?

It's been said, and you've no doubt read, that you or Dick Bissell, or I guess you and Dick Bissell, sold the President. Do you feel as though you sold him on this, or do you think it was a kind of joint decision that was reached?

Naturally, one ought never to sell anybody a bill of goods. I mean, of course, that wasn't one's job.

Well, did you feel the role of a salesman?

You've put a hard question to me there, and I'd like to be very honest about it. I didn't feel that, although maybe instinctively I was drawn into that situation a little bit. Obviously, you present a plan and it isn't your job to say, well, that's a rotten plan I've presented. You can only say, here are the merits of the plan, and in presenting the merits of the plan the tendency is always—because you're meeting a position, you're meeting this criticism and that criticism—to be drawn into more of a salesmanship job than you should. I know the President was terribly disturbed about this and very thoughtful about it. I think we'd been meeting in the Cabinet Room, and then we went aside into the room next to the Cabinet Room there—I think they call it the Fish Room—in the White House. Several of us were there; I think the Chairman of the Joint Chiefs of Staff was there, and I think the Vice President was there that day. He was in on a good many of these meetings.

You're talking about President Johnson.

President Johnson, yes. I remember the President came up to me—I was just alone—and he said, "Allen, what do you think of this? Would you do it or would you not do it?" And at that time—and this was, oh, a month before the final decision—I said, "Mr. President, I think we ought to study this further before reaching a final decision. I know what a tough one this is." And we did study it some more; we weren't ready then for a decision. I remember that incident very clearly.

Do you recall, Allen, whether opposition to the plan came largely from the White House staff, or the military, or people within the Agency, perhaps, who thought it wasn't such a good idea?

Well, there was no really organized center of opposition to it. Later, you may recall, there was that meeting where the President went around the group and asked everybody to stand up and be counted on it; and you remember what was attributed to [Senator J. William] Fulbright—the accounts given of that are more or less accurate. It was a general feeling that it is very important to do something here. We had been working now—the time I'm speaking of when we get on to April—a good many months with these trainees. Some of them had reached a point in their training where they pretty nearly had a stomach full of it. I mean, you can train just so long and then you go too fine. Now that was only the case with a few of them.

You may recall that at that time, just shortly before the decision was made, I wanted to get a further appraisal of the situation, so we sent down to the head military people who were in charge of the training, and there was one Marine colonel, a brilliant fellow, who had been doing a good deal of supervision of the training, and I wanted to get a report from him, and we got a report from him. It was a very optimistic report; I guess it was too optimistic, as it turned out. That report had a great deal of influence on the President.

It was written, was it?

Oh, yes.

It was a written report, not made in person?

No, it was a written report. Later the man came up and did report in person, I believe, to the President; he certainly reported to the task force.

Just to get the record straight . . .

It came up by cable, and that cable was presented and was read in these meetings.

Just as a guess, and I suppose there wouldn't be any record of this so maybe a guess will have to stand—how many times do you think you discussed this whole idea with the President?

You mean in an organized manner with a plan?

Yes, either through a National Security Council staff meeting or personally. Would you say you talked about it with him five or six times?

Oh, more than that, if you take in all of these meetings with the particular task force that was working on this.

He, of course, wasn't present at those task force meetings?

Oh, yes, he was. I don't say he was present during all of the meetings, but at some stage of the meeting and during a good deal of it he would be present himself.

And by the time these meetings were shaping up to the point where decisions had to be made, do you feel that he, President Kennedy, was in support of it or still dubious certainly . . .

I think he wanted to do it. Yes, I think he wanted to do it, but he wasn't quite persuaded it was going to work out. That was the impression I got.

Now, let's go to the time then when the decision had to be made and he must have been persuaded. I presume he was persuaded—maybe I shouldn't do that. Let's go to the last meeting when the thing was decided. Did you tell him, for example, now look, we must decide this now, or we have to either do it now, or we have to wait so many months, or just how was it put to him?

There were certain factors which made it necessary to reach a decision not later than a certain date—I can't remember what date it was in April—around the time the decision was reached. As I recall, you were approaching the rainy season, which was a problem. You had certain technical questions in connection with the landing operations where the time made a good deal of difference, the weather made a good deal of difference. You had certain problems that I've already referred to with regard to the state of the training. We had to reorganize our training because we had brought certain of the trainees up to a point where they almost had to go or else be put into a different kind of a training for a different period. The people that were in charge of the training felt, as we got into April, that we were approaching the time limit when these particular men were at the peak of their efficiency for the particular job to which they were assigned.

I have made it a practice in my relations with the National Security Council not to keep personal notes of National Security Council meetings. There is a note made of decisions reached and so forth, but the conversations have to be so confidential that I always thought it would be improper for any single individual to prepare notes. The temptation to use those notes some day is very great, and there have been cases where I think notes of Cabinet meetings and National Security Council meetings had been abused. You have no way of checking off these personal notes that are made, you know.

You're talking now of what people said and their reactions?

What people said and their reactions, and the decisions were registered. Notes were taken by the National Security Council staff. Generally, those notes, as I recall, were not formally typed up; certainly they were not circulated. There was a note generally circulated that [at a] meeting of the National Security Council on a certain date, it was decided that this or that agency should prepare this or that, or this individual in this agency should study a certain point and bring it back to the National Security Council, or the Joint Chiefs of Staff should give a further summary on certain questions presented, but I never kept any notes. I always made just a notation of what the CIA was supposed to do before the next meeting. I would always get that confirmed, though, by a written note that went to the CIA or to what other agency was involved.

Let me philosophize just a moment here. We formulated a plan, a plan was drawn up jointly by the military and the CIA. Bissell was very active in the CIA in the preparation of those drafts and various people, [Lyman L.] Lemnitzer, [Arleigh A.] Burke—[Earle G.] Wheeler came on a little later, I think. He was there but I don't think he was—of course, he was appointed Chairman of the Joint Chiefs later. Lemnitzer was Chairman, but he was away a good deal of this period on NATO business, and Arleigh Burke was acting in his place a good deal during this particular period, but many of the papers were prepared by Burke and Lemnitzer on the basis, of course, of consideration by the Joint Chiefs as a body. I'm not trying to impose responsibility on any particular place. It was done as an operation which had military connotations of grave importance, to see that the military aspects of it were considered by the military authorities of the United States Government. That was done, and in those days preceding the final decision in April we met very frequently, prepared quite a large number of papers. and eventually reached decisions.

There was one other thing I wanted to add to that. When the attempt was made and there was the failure, the President, without any hesitation, assumed personally full responsibility for the action that had been taken. And without issuing orders he made it clear that, having done this, he did not expect his subordinates, others that had been working on this matter, to go out and do some after-game quarterbacking on the thing and do a lot of talking about it. I have always felt that the President, having taken what I believed was the honorable and right and courageous stand that he did, there was a very strong duty on the rest of us to respect the almost unspoken injunction that he gave to us not to go around talking about it or shove responsibility here, there, or the other place. He said, I was President, this was done under my Presidency, I was responsible, I assume the responsibility, and that closes the chapter as far as that is concerned. I think the country owed him a great deal for that very courageous decision.

In all cases of this kind where the Central Intelligence Agency is involved, I have always felt the Director should naturally assume full responsibility for anything his Agency had done, and wherever he could shield or protect the President in any way, he should do it. Some people say, well, you ought to always deny all these things, and they said that after the U-2 and they said it again after the Bay of Pigs. You ought not to let the President get so deeply involved that this situation arises. Well, no Director of the Central Intelligence Agency can really control that. He stands there ready at any time to take any responsibility that the President wants him to take, to resign if the situation calls for it, but at any rate to take any responsibility that he can. But there are certain situations, and I've said this often—I wrote it in my book, *The Craft of Intelligence*, in discussing the U-2 issue—there is a greater issue than the responsibility of a particular individual. There's a whole question of what kind of government we run. Do we run a responsible government or an irresponsible government? And no President can admit that we run an irresponsible government. No President can properly admit that people are going around doing irresponsible things when he, the President, is responsible, and he has that choice. He boldly took the responsibility here. I admired him for that stand. As I say, I think it was the only stand that he could take, because he either had to say, look here, a lot of strange things are going on in my Administration right under my nose and I don't know what's going on. But I don't say that was his motive; that wasn't necessarily the reason why he did it. That is why I personally feel that there wasn't any great choice, but he took it because that's the kind of man he was. He had to study the matter, he had reached his decision, and he stood by the decision he had reached, and he wasn't going to blame anybody.

I talked to him a great deal about it afterwards, and while I did have a feeling that maybe he thought I had let him down, there never was one harsh or unkind word said to me by him at anytime thereafter. He never blamed. He never said, you ought to have warned me more about this. You ought to have made it more clear to me—and I think there maybe we did make a mistake—that this air cover was absolutely a sine qua non, that this was absolutely essential. We kind of thought we had made that clear, but I guess we hadn't. You can't land naked vessels with ammunition and supplies on board in the face of any kind of hostile aviation that controls the air. I mean, whether they are bombers or whether they are C-47s, they can drop a bomb and blow an unarmed merchant vessel to pieces, and that's what happened. But I just want to say that he never at any time addressed a word of criticism afterwards. We had many talks about it. I'm sure it had some effect on his views about my judgment; maybe he felt that I had persuaded him too much. I tried not to. I don't think if you had the record here, I would be accused of being a salesman on this thing, but I may have appeared in that light to him. It was a very difficult decision because if you didn't do it, you had the problem of trying to reverse a line of policy in connection with the training of these men which had set in motion a great many hopes, expectations. Policies were affected, and you [couldn't] easily turn off the spigot and go off and forget it. You left behind quite a trail that would have affected our relations with Cuba and affected, if we ever wanted to do anything like it, our ability to do that again.

Just to mention what you are talking about now. when the thing had ended in failure, did you go see the President, or call him, or did he call you, or what?

Oh, we were together a good deal those days . . .

It seemed to me that you, following a precedent which I think you established on some other occasion, had gone off from Washington at that time. Am I wrong?

No, you're not wholly wrong. I had planned to be in Puerto Rico for other business a good many months before the date of this operation was fixed.

But if I can ask you this, isn't this a ruse, in effect, that you've followed before?

Yes, I have followed that before; during certain phases of the Iranian matter I was deliberately away. I wasn't deliberately away here. I was in a situation where I had one very important speaking engagement. The only reason I mention that is that I would have had to cancel out at a time when everybody would say, why has he cancelled out? It wasn't just a thing that you give up and say you had a bad cold or something of that kind. It would have had significance because it just happened to be on the eve of the landing, and so I knew I could get back with the speed of aircraft; it was only a question of six or eight hours. So I was in Puerto Rico the night of the landing, and then I came right back, and I saw the President during that following period several times.

While things were still uncertain?

Well, while things were going badly.

And, as you say, besides not delivering any blame and behaving in the fashion you described, was he particularly crestfallen, nervous, upset, did he appear . . .

Oh, this was a shock to him, there's no doubt about it. He never allowed it, as far as I could see, to affect his judgment or he wasn't short, he wasn't . . .

Did he swear?

No, I don't remember. It moved fairly fast so the time wasn't awfully long, but there were forty-eight hours there—twenty-four or forty-eight hours of when the thing was hanging like this.

Were you spending most of your time in the White House at that time or on the phone?

I was a great deal at our own operations in the CIA, but I was in touch with the White House.

Was he devoting full time . . .

He was in the White House. Oh, yes, he was devoting full time to this.

And who did you have over there with him—Dick?

Dick was over there, General Cabell was over there, the military, of course, were there, Burke and others, and I think Lemnitzer was back by this time.

I would just like to raise one point because I think it has some bearing upon President Kennedy and the kind of man he was. What about the calling off of the second air strike, which has been said by historians we've had so far to be the crucial decision which may or may not have determined the enterprise? The inference is that it did. Did it, and how was that made? What lessons can we draw from it?

Well, the lesson I would draw from it is that one ought never to leave the Chief of State, the man who has to reach the final decisions, in any state of uncertainty, as I think the President must have been, as to the points of a plan which are absolutely essential. I don't think he appreciated fully the vital importance, the absolutely essential character of these particular air strikes. Now, when you say the air strikes might have failed, and the whole plan ought not to have been based on something which might fail, but that's inherent in almost all planning.

The first air strike did fail, did it not, or almost failed?

It wasn't a complete success, it was a partial success; it wasn't a complete failure, it was a partial failure.

So, we have decision number one here to go in, and decision number two to call off a part of the plan which was essential to it, is that right?

Well, when you say an essential part of the plan in a sense that if all air strikes and all air coverage were removed, your plan was a faulty plan. I don't think the essentiality of that point was clearly enough and absolutely decisively enough brought to the President's attention in connection with the planning work. And if I blame myself for many points, I might engage in self-criticism, but that's rather useless here at this stage. But there's one thing that I do feel badly about, because I think I had a responsibility there that I didn't fully carry out. That is before we went into this, I should have said, Mr. President, if you're not willing to permit us to take the steps necessary to immobilize for X period, or substantially immobilize, the Cuban air force, which was a very small and crotchety and defective air force at that time, the plan to get this brigade ashore with its equipment and supplies is a faulty one. As I say, if I was looking back on it, if I engaged in self-criticism, which is always a useful thing to do, I think, that's the point that I would stress, that I don't think I made that absolutely crystal clear to the President.

Let me interject a couple of questions here to finish up this part about the Bay of Pigs. To start with, what did the military think about the plan? What was their view?

That, of course, you will find in the military records, and they ought to speak for themselves. It was my understanding that they felt that the plan was a plan which held out some hope of success. I don't recall we ever asked them to put a percentage figure on it. They felt that the brigade was well equipped, they felt that the place selected for landing was appropriate for the various purposes that we had in mind for the brigade. They never guaranteed success of the plan. They never underwrote it from that angle, and, as I say, their general position was that this plan has a possibility, if the brigade is well trained.

There's one other aspect of this. When the President called off the second air strike and you discussed this to some extent, he did it for reasons which were said to have been presented to him by other officials of the government—the exposure of the plan in the United Nations [UN], for example, and for the rising public and press criticism and anxiety. And I suppose that those factors which caused him to call off the second air strike are factors that you, in a sense, can't comment on. After all, you were charged with trying to make the plan a success. You were not charged with the other facets of the decision.

No, I think that you're right on that, and further I don't have all the information available on which to pass judgment. I have never discussed this with Adlai Stevenson or anyone else at the UN. I don't know what he said to the President or whether he said anything to the President on this particular subject. I assume that he did, but I never have gone into that. It certainly was his business to present that viewpoint. Of course, there are two features, and I haven't gone into this air coverage question in any great detail. There was the question of an air strike, and there was a question of some air coverage.

The air coverage was to follow, though, wasn't it? The following morning the air strike had already been called off; is that correct?

That is correct. There had been certain discussions, though, during the planning period and a good deal of discussion about certain air coverage that might be furnished in the event of attack, or threatened attack, on the merchant vessels which were taking the supplies and the equipment and the brigade itself into the place of landing. This involved possibly operations over international waters, and it might have involved some beyond that. I don't think I should say any more about that at this stage.

Well, can I just ask, is it true that the President also decided, so it's been reported, on the following morning not to furnish this air cover? He made that decision, didn't he?

There was air coverage to be furnished for a limited period of time.

I see.

And there was some mix-up with regard to that. In a great event some small things often make a lot of difference. The time element—Greenwich time, local time—got a little fuzzed up, and so one bit of air coverage that had been planned didn't, due to a misunderstanding of the time, get quite at the place at the right time. I think probably I had better leave it at that. As you say, it's not up to me to judge of the pressures, which I know were very great, on the President on many phases of this matter, the consequences resulting from it, and a great many other factors. That's for history to judge and for those that had that phase of American foreign policy particularly within their scope of judgment and decision.

Did you, when this was all over, continue to see the President a good deal on other matters? Did you feel from that point on that you had to some extent lost his confidence, or were your relations good?

I think I've said before that I did see the President. Let me see, I continued on as Director of Central Intelligence until roughly the end of November of—let's see, where are we now—'61.

You served another six months.

About six months—let's see, from April to November, after the Bay of Pigs—and I saw the President a good deal. I think I've said that there was never any recrimination on the President's part. I might well have lost to some extent in the measure of confidence he placed on me. That's inevitable in things of this kind, I think, but I may say in his personal attitude toward me, in the many meetings we had, he never let that appear, and I retired at about the time I had planned to retire when he first asked me, as I've explained earlier, to stay on after he took over the duties as President.

You have, I know, in the course of a long lifetime, met a lot of people. And in the particular job you have, something I've always noticed about you is that you have a variety of friends from many different fields and walks of life. You are friendly with people who were spies, you are friendly with people who are musicians, you are friendly with people who are lawyers—the whole spectrum really, and you have rated a lot of men. How did you rate personally, in your own mind, President Kennedy as a man?

Oh, I rated him high. Maybe that's trite to put it that way, but I rated him high. I shall never forget when I first heard the news of the Dallas tragedy [Kennedy's assassination]. I felt that here is a man who hadn't had a chance really to show his full capabilities, that he was just reaching a point where his grasp of all the intricacies of the Presidency was such that now he could move forward. He'd gone through the very difficult days, problems with [Soviet Premier Nikita S.] Khrushchev, the confrontation after the Cuban business, and all that, that he had put behind him, the [nuclear] testing crisis, and he was at a point to move forward and show us the full possibilities of a very extraordinary man. That tragedy was brought out again and again when I was asked to serve on the Warren Commission and go into all the tragic details of that event, November '62 ['63].

As we were doing that work, I felt here was an extraordinary happening in history. Here was a man, [Lee Harvey] Oswald, who had been a failure at everything he had done. He was almost a misfit in the world, and yet he carried through successfully the intricate details of this mad act, and as I studied all that record I could see literally hundreds of instances where if things had just been a little different, if one fact had been known that wasn't known but which might have been known just as the fact of his earlier attack on General [Edwin A.] Walker. I'm not criticizing anyone of that because it just wasn't known, but there were so many factors—if the employees of the Book Depository had eaten their lunch in a little different place, if somebody had been at one place where he might easily have been instead of another at one particular time, the "ifs" just stand out all over it. And if any one of these "ifs" had been changed, it [the assassination] might have been prevented. I don't know how we got off on that, but I mean it was just your question about the man. That was a hard task, you know, because of that; it was so tantalizing to go over that record, as we did, trying to find out every fact connected with the assassination, and then to say if any one of the chess pieces that were entered into the game had been moved differently, at any one time, the whole thing might have been different.

3

Richard M. Bissell

RICHARD BISSELL, ONE OF THREE CHILDREN, was born in Hartford, Connecticut, on September 18, 1909, to Marie Truesdale Bissell and wealthy insurance executive Richard Bissell, Sr. The Bissells resided in the old Mark Twain house, designed by Samuel Clemens. Each year the family, accompanied by a cook, two maids, and more than twenty steamer trunks, summered at Dark Harbor, Maine. They also traveled frequently to Europe: in 1919 they toured the battle-fields of northern France and witnessed the ruins of war. These scenes horrified young Richard and would influence his isolationist stance in the 1930s. Boarding-school years at Groton were followed by enrollment in 1928 at Yale University; four years later, as a history major, he graduated with an A.B. degree.

Bissell's postgraduate studies at the London School of Economics for a year inspired more courses in economics at Yale, which led to a Ph.D. in 1939 and then to full-time faculty status at Yale. He married Ann Cornelia Bushnell in 1940 (they later would have five children). Moving to Washington, DC, in 1941, Bissell first took a post in the Department of Commerce and, after Pearl Harbor, a job at the War Shipping Administration, where he predicted dry-cargo requirements. In 1945, as a member of the American delegation at the Yalta and Potsdam summit conferences, Bissell grew skeptical about Joseph Stalin's postwar promises.

Peacetime brought new challenges. After a brief stint as an economics professor at the Massachusetts Institute of Technology, Bissell returned to Washington and began working with Averell Harriman on the brilliant European Recovery Program, or Marshall Plan. Paul Hoffman, the astute administrator for the Economic Cooperation Act of 1948, recruited Bissell and appointed him as ECA deputy administrator and also spokesman at Congressional hearings for the next four years. In this post, Bissell first learned about postwar covert action when the Office of Policy Coordination's director, Frank Wisner, requested ECA counterpart funds for OPC operations such as aid to European anti-Communist newspapers, labor unions, and political parties.

At the urging of Hoffman, who headed the Ford Foundation in 1952, Bissell joined the staff; however, he continued to take independent consulting assignments, such as designing the National Security Council's NSC-141, the Truman Administration's final international security document, which advised that Western nations must resist expansion by the powerful Communist bloc. He also joined the Central Intelligence Agency's group of consultants who met every few months at Princeton University.

He became a member of the CIA family in 1953 when Allen Dulles offered him a position at the Agency. Dulles, his mentor, assigned him to Wisner's covert operation, PBSUCCESS, against the Arbenz government in Guatemala. In this hectic classroom of operations, Bissell learned an important lesson: the successful disinformation propaganda beamed by radio into Guatemala should be in the blueprint for future covert actions. After the Bay of Pigs failure, Bissell regretted that the CIA's operational successes in Iran and Guatemala had led policymakers to overestimate the Agency's covert action abilities.

Recognizing Bissell's management talents, Dulles placed him in charge of the U-2 reconnaissance aircraft project: this amazing plane made its first overflight of the Soviet Union in July 1956. Several years later, another of his managerial products, the SR-71, joined the secret squadron. And in 1960 a new generation of technological marvels, photoreconnaissance satellites, continued the revolution in collecting intelligence data. Bissell quickly proved, as Lyman Kirkpatrick would write years later, that he was one of the most brilliant individuals ever to serve in intelligence. As Deputy Director for Plans, Bissell also became involved in removing Patrice

Lumumba from the Congo's government (now Zaire), promoting a pro-Western solution in Laos, and devising a strategy for overthrowing Fidel Castro in Cuba.

American policymakers became convinced that a Communist government only ninety miles from the U.S. mainland was intolerable, and in January 1960 the Eisenhower Administration decided that Castro's regime must be ousted. Socn, radio propaganda messages were beamed into Cuba. Twenty Cuban exiles, trained for sabotage, were recruited; they would teach 100 to 150 more exiles, and this force would be infiltrated into Cuba. In addition, early planning called for a small paramilitary force of a few hundred exiles who would invade the island in a coordinated attack.

The architects of this operation, recalling European guerrilla successes in World War II, gave high priority to building first an underground network in Cuba with safe houses, code names, and compartmentation. This attempt failed, however, as Castro jailed local resistance leaders. This failure and other problems forced major changes in the covert operation between John F. Kennedy's election and his inauguration. A new plan in January 1961 called for a force of 1,500 men; and before the invasion was launched in April, still more modifications were made. The failed Bay of Pigs invasion led to the resignation of both Dulles and Bissell several months later. Bissell would head the Institute for Defense Analyses for several years and then join United Aircraft Corporation until 1974. For two decades before his death in 1994 he served as an independent management consultant.

In the final months of his life, Bissell acknowledged the hostile criticisms aimed at the CIA, especially at the covert activities of the 1950s and 1960s: "Having rethought this policy many times since then, I am convinced that the Agency acted in the government's best interest in attempting to preserve the highly desired principle of democracy." And deeply aware of current perspectives, he added: "Many episodes might be considered distasteful, but during the Eisenhower and Kennedy years the Soviet danger seemed real and all actions were aimed at thwarting it" (*Reflections of a Cold Warrior* [New Haven, 1996], 142).

JOSEPH O'CONNOR: *I wanted to begin this by asking you if you had any contacts with John Kennedy before he became President.*

RICHARD BISSELL: Yes, I had rather occasional and fleeting contacts. I think the first time I actually met him, under circumstances where I sat down and talked to him, was when I went up to see him in his office in the

Conducted by Joseph E. O'Connor in Providence, Rhode Island, on April 25, and July 5, 1967. Oral History Interviews, John F. Kennedy Library, Boston, Massachusetts.

Capitol. This was at a fairly early stage in his campaign, and he invited me to contribute, in writing, any ideas that I might have that could be fed into the campaign that would be valuable to him. I was eager to do so, but the press of business kept me fairly busy, and I think, as it turned out, I never did make such contributions. I may have seen him once or twice more during the campaign, but really very little until after the election.

Did he have any things particularly in mind when he asked you for help?

I had the impression that he didn't have, at that point, anything much in mind having to do with the CIA, where I was, of course, then working and had been for about six years. I'm inclined to think he was more interested in economic policy, but we didn't really bring it to the point of sharply defining a field. I think there's one more reason that may have influenced him to make the suggestion, which is that I was one individual known to him and known quite well to a number of his close associates as being a Democrat, a professed Democrat, and also being interested in his candidacy. I was one such person who was active in the Executive Branch of the government and at a fairly senior Civil Service level. I don't mean for one moment that there was any intimation that he wanted to use me to find out what was going on in the inner councils of the administration; that was not the thrust at all. It is simply that I was an individual who had had, and was still having, current experience inside the Executive Branch. I think he was well aware that many problems of government inevitably looked different from inside than from outside, even where that difference doesn't have anything to do with privileged information or classified information.

Okay, then I would presume your next contact with him would have come just during the campaign. Were you involved at all in the briefing that he received?

I really wasn't very much involved in that, and I was a little reticent to be. I don't remember any specific suggestion to that effect being made, but I would have been a bit reticent simply because of my position in the government.

But I thought specifically of the briefing that he received regarding— well, various matters, undoubtedly, but regarding the Bay of Pigs. There was, as you're well aware, a controversy over whether or not he had known anything about the invasion, about the plans for infiltration or invasion of Cuba before the election was actually held.

My impression is that he didn't know anything about those plans before the election. The next time that I remember seeing him at any length was an occasion that has been widely reported when Allen Dulles and I went down just after Thanksgiving, after the election, and gave him a pretty extensive briefing on the Bay of Pigs, and on many other things as well. I think he probably had intelligence briefings during the campaign; that is to say, briefings in which he was apprised of the latest intelligence on the state of the world. But I took no part in those—that wouldn't have been a part of my job in the CIA anyway—and I would be fairly surprised if those had covered the Bay of Pigs at all.

When the briefing with you and Allen Dulles took place at Thanks-giving time, had the decision been made at that time to advance the Bay of Pigs or the Cuban operation from infiltration, perhaps, to a modified invasion? Had this decision taken place yet?

I would say that the decision had taken place because the plan, as we outlined it to him, did contemplate some form of landing of a significant force to act as a catalyst in inducing, ultimately, a revolutionary situation in Cuba. It's difficult to answer the question, however, because that decision as to the character of the operation was rather gradually modified during the late autumn, and it's very difficult, even for someone who was close to those developments, to put a finger on the exact moment when a clear decision was made or the circumstances or, really, the people who made it. It was a decision rather forced by circumstances.

Well, much has been made of the pressure on the President-elect and President from the fact that a body of men was training for this opera-tion. Was this pressure very great before the Inauguration? Are you aware of this . . .

I don't believe it was, because I don't think that before the Inaugura-tion he tried to concern himself in any detail with this activity. My im-pression was that this was a period when his efforts were overwhelmingly directed to the selection and choice of people for various positions and in which he really didn't have very much time to spend on the Bay of Pigs.

When does this become a major factor? Or did it ever, the pressure of . . .

Oh, it did become so. Yes, it did become so later; I think the pressure began to be felt, as such, perhaps as much as a month after the Inaugura-tion. I say that as much time as that elapsed simply because my recollec-tion is that it was possible and logical to allow the preparatory phase to go forward for at least that period of time before the ultimate decisions began to seem imminent and had to be faced very seriously. Of course, the pressure in the first month of a new Administration of the decisions that have to be made is so intense—I think in some ways more so than in any subsequent period except the most extreme crises—that anything that doesn't absolutely demand attention is bound to be pushed off.

Much has been made of this pressure, and the defenders of John F. Kennedy have said, in effect, that he was presented almost with a fait accompli, *that it was very, very difficult to reverse this measure once it had begun rolling. Now, do you agree with that or not? How strong do you feel the pressure was, or what chance, what opportunity, do you feel the President had to reverse the decision? I know he, legally, always had the chance up until the move was actually taken.*

Yes. Well, I think I would agree that the pressure—which I'll for the moment call the pressure of circumstances, but also a pressure applied through people, including myself—was very strong. By the time this began to be a serious issue requiring major decisions, there was a significant military force; it was in training under circumstances that could not be maintained for very long. There were a variety of circumstances—the impending arrival of the rainy season, the inadequacy of the facilities of the training camp in Guatemala, the increasingly precarious political position of this venture vis-à-vis [Miguel] Ydígoras [Fuentes], the President of Guatemala, the impossibility of maintaining the Cubans as a force and maintaining their morale and discipline if they weren't committed to action fairly soon.

There were many circumstances, of which I have perhaps enumerated the principal ones, which made some action to change radically the location, status, and role of that military force absolutely essential and urgent. So the alternative was not, as I'm sure has been said many times, that of continuing to train and prepare a military force or else to commit it to action. The alternative to committing it to action would have been to move it back to the U.S. or to break it up and disperse it, or both. This would have been a very difficult and messy operation. It not only would have been difficult and messy at the level of the Cubans themselves and the Cuban force, but, as we all know, it had domestic political overtones that were pretty serious. Because of what would have had to have been done, the action would have been widely publicized, and there would have been a great many Cubans expressing their view that here they were, ready to recapture their homeland by their own efforts, and the U.S. Government was actively preventing it.

The President, therefore, within a couple of months of coming into office, would have been open to the accusation that he was dismantling the government's major effort to unseat [Fidel] Castro. Castro was extremely unpopular then. The whole issue of relations with him was much more exacerbated at that point than it is now. I think, therefore, that the pressures—ultimately built up by the circumstances in being, but expressed as potential political pressures and a very real concern about the wisdom of breaking up the only effective anti-Castro force—became very power-ful indeed.

Because of these pressures, this force of circumstance, to an outsider there seems to be a sort of inevitability about the Bay of Pigs Operation. I don't know whether you'd agree with that or not, but I would like to ask you if, or when, consideration was given to alternatives. What would be done with the men training if it was decided to call off the operation?

Consideration was given to that off and on all through those early months—really, from the beginning in February until the operation was actually mounted—because we had to face this possibility a number of times. The plan, as I remember it, that was ultimately adopted as a fallback plan was that they would be embarked on the vessels that had been char-tered for the invasion, but those vessels would have been taken into convoy by American Naval vessels and brought to a U.S. port or to Guantánamo or to the Marine station on Vieques [off Puerto Rico] or some place of this kind. As far as it went, that was feasible. I don't think anyone had tried to think through all the details of then disarming and demobilizing these people and actually returning them to the U.S., al-though that part would not have been too difficult.

Frankly, I thought that would be the most difficult part. I think that's what everyone was worried about, the problem of disarming the force and returning it to . . .

What I really mean is that if they'd been under U.S. Naval escort, they would really have had no choice. If they'd been taken first to some port other than in the continental U.S., let us say some military base in the Caribbean, and they had there been disembarked and disarmed, per-haps that's when the political and similar difficulties would have started, but the military problem, I think, would have been under control by that time.

Okay. There is a controversy over what the role of the Joint Chiefs of Staff was, or the military in the United States.

Could I go back and add a little to your preceding question because one is bound to speculate about might-have-beens of all kinds. As I look back, I think one of our failures, collectively, in the course of the decision-making process—one of the respects in which that process was, with hindsight, unsatisfactory—is that some other alternatives were not considered, perhaps because some of the basic underlying assumptions of the operation were not brought out and reviewed.

Let me expand on this point and make a little clearer what I'm driv-ing at. A decision that was at no point questioned during the period we're talking about, the early months of the new Administration, was that if this operation were to be carried forward at all, it would be so as, ostensibly, an activity of the Cubans—one which was certain to be suspected of receiving some support from the U.S. Government but nevertheless basically undertaken and carried forward on Cuban initiative with the possibility of a plausible disclaimer of support by the U.S. Government. This was the concept of this as an operation, and, of course, this is the reason that the CIA rather than the Pentagon was in charge of it.

I think one simple failure of observation on the part of really all of us who were involved, including the President and [Secretary of State Dean] Rusk and very definitely all of us in the CIA, was that despite reading the daily papers and listening to the radio, we didn't really grasp the extent to which it was believed by everyone else that whatever operation was in preparation was very much on the initiative of the U.S. Government and under the direction of the U.S. Government, rather than on Cuban initiative and under effective Cuban control. In the public discussion it was more and more taken for granted that this was, in effect, an activity of the U.S. Government, which, to be sure, was using Cubans, but really only using them.

Therefore, I believe that, just as a matter of fact, the concept of this as an operation, responsibility for which could be plausibly disclaimed by the U.S. Government, had lost its validity many weeks before the invasion itself took place. It was this fact, as I now believe it to have been, that really, it seems to me, was never faced by those of us in the CIA who were advocating the operation and deeply committed to it emotionally, or by someone like Rusk, who was on the whole opposed to it, or by the President or others in the circle of advisors. The one thing that seemed to be taken sort of for granted throughout was that if anything was going to be done, it would be done within this original concept.

My feeling is that if the breakdown of that concept had been faced, some other possible courses of action would have been considered. One was to decide that the Administration would go forward with the operation but would do so in ways that took full advantage of the fact that it was going to be attributed to the U.S. Government no matter what denials and what official positions were taken. And there are quite a few things that could have been done to enhance the chances of success of this operation, if it was once admitted that U.S. Government responsibility was going to be established in the public mind beyond any possibility of doubt. For instance, using U.S. volunteers as pilots would have made a significant difference. If this decision had been made some weeks in advance, the whole scale of the operation could have been different. Probably more sophisticated weaponry could have been used. Even without committing any U.S. citizens or any but a handful of volunteers to action on the ground, it still would have been possible to make it a more militarily effective operation.

Alternatively, if the complete breakdown of that concept had been faced, I am inclined to think Dean Rusk would have argued even harder than he did, and he might very well have won the day in favor of complete cancellation of the operation. But as I look back on it, almost everybody continued, really without much debating of this point, to believe that the fig leaf was still in place. And that belief, the deep reluctance of Rusk to drop the fig leaf if the operation was going to be done at all, the President's own reluctance to drop the fig leaf—these, I think, in the final weeks did contribute to the ultimate failure of the operation.

Do you think sufficient attention also was paid to the domestic political consequences early enough in the operation, early enough in the planning?

You mean the U.S. domestic political consequences? I think probably not, because certainly the people who were concerned, like myself, with the conduct of the operation simply weren't spending any time on the domestic political implications. We were very concerned with the political platform, as it were, of the [Cuban Revolutionary] Council, which was the political arm of the invasion. A lot of nonsense has been written about the degree to which this was a conservative group and the degree to which the U.S. Government's influence was in the direction of conservative doctrines. This is just plain false; it was quite the other way. But I don't think much attention was paid to the political implications or possible repercussions in the U.S.

I started to ask you a little bit ago about the role that the Joint Chiefs of Staff played in this. There's been much question about this; much has been written about this. Can you tell me at what point the Joint Chiefs of Staff or the Pentagon became involved? In other words, was it ever strictly a CIA operation?

Let me answer in these phases: For the first eight months or so of the whole activity, which took it up almost to the change of Administration, the military had been involved, as they are or have been in a number of CIA operations. There were military personnel assigned to the CIA to work as part of the CIA staff. This was the source of the men who did most of the military training, of course. The principal military officer in charge of the planning and finally the military conduct of the operation was a very fine Marine colonel [Jack Hawkins], an outstanding officer. Then we had made some use of various military facilities. We got our B-26s, as I remember it, a release from the National Guard; we got some

National Guard pilots or air crews to volunteer primarily for training purposes; we used the ex-military base at Miami as a logistics base; we undoubtedly—and I don't know the details of this—used other military installations on occasion for loading ships and doing things of this sort. All of this involvement, however, was at a relatively low level, and it comes under the heading of support by the Department of Defense to CIA activities.

I would say that the most decisive change in the role of the Joint Chiefs came early in the Administration. I don't remember just how soon, but I do know that the very first time this was discussed in a policy meeting in the White House, the President said, "Have the Joint Chiefs made a careful evaluation of this operation?" The answer was negative. And he said, "I want that done as the very first step."

One reason that the subject was then fairly quiescent at the policy level in Washington, at least through February, was that the Joint Chiefs formed a committee, a senior officer from each of the three services chaired by an Army brigadier general, to carry out an evaluation. This committee, first of all, came and reviewed the provisional operational plans. They then went down to Central America and elsewhere, wherever we had operational activities, and looked them over. My recollection is they got back to Washington and finished their appraisal in the latter part of February, then made a report in the first instance to the Joint Chiefs. The Joint Chiefs accepted their conclusions. Their report was then, in effect, presented either by General [David W.] Gray, who was the chairman of that group, or else by the Chairman of the Joint Chiefs to the President in one of those policy meetings.

From that point on, the involvement of the Joint Chiefs was very much more intimate because that review committee remained in existence to review variations in and new versions of the military plan, also to keep an eye on the implementation of these plans. That committee of three military officers worked very, very closely with us, and they spent, I think, as much time in the office where this project was quartered in Washington as they did over in the Pentagon. Theoretically, they were a committee to oversee and report to the Joint Chiefs. They had no authority, and in the CIA no one had any authority over them. In practice, however, they worked very closely with the senior military commander, the Marine colonel I spoke of, who was on assignment to the CIA and in the line of command reported to me.

When the Joint Chiefs of Staff first became involved, or this committee selected by the Joint Chiefs of Staff, was it understood by them that they could reject this operation, or was it simply the feeling that they were to implement . . .

No, very definitely, in that first month the question was whether the operation should go forward. What they were invited to do at that point had nothing to do with implementation. They were acting at that point very clearly and explicitly in their role as the President's advisors and not in the role of an implementing or directing body.

It seems to me, from what little I know about the operation, that the plan tended to have a series of weak points, or at least from an overall military standpoint it was a rather fragile plan. It depended on the perfect execution of various things. Did you ever feel that the Joint Chiefs of Staff [JCS] or that the committee, the military committee, did not emphasize sufficiently to you or to the President the fragility of the plan?

The answer to that is affirmative. I did have that feeling on several specific occasions. I suppose the reason I felt it, however, was that it affected the President's attitude toward the form and implementation of the plan. I had great confidence in the Marine officer who was directing the military side of this operation. He was trained and experienced in amphibious warfare. From the moment when it began to appear that this would involve the landing of a significant body of troops—how we were first talking of four or five hundred as against three times that number that eventually went in—he emphasized that if the group were large enough so they couldn't make what would amount to a completely clandestine entry into Cuba, then air cover of the operation was absolutely essential, and if the air cover was not fully effective, the operation wouldn't succeed. He said flatly, "This is accepted doctrine. And every military officer who knows anything about amphibious operations knows that unless you can count on solid air cover, the chances of success are small."

This he was saying to you?

To me and to Allen Dulles, and to [C. Pearré] Cabell, Allen's Deputy, my boss. And we, all of us, accepted this position. The feeling I had then, and I have never changed this in any degree, is that as a piece of military doctrine it was surprising and later horrifying to me that the Joint Chiefs did not emphasize this point nearly as strongly as the colonel who was in charge of the operation himself did.

There was one interesting and alarming occasion at one of the sequence of policy meetings in the White House. Before the meeting started, those of us who were to participate in it were talking outside the Cabinet Room, which was still occupied by a preceding meeting I was told, I think it was by General Gray (the chairman of this Joint Chiefs review committee), who shared, I may say, our view on the essentiality of air cover, something of a discussion that had taken place the preceding day in the meeting of the Joint Chiefs. In that discussion two of the three Chiefs present had said that they weren't at all sure the operation really had to have air cover, that it had a good chance of success without air cover.

I relayed this view to the military director of the operation, who was also there in the group; he had heard something of the same thing and was, again, absolutely horrified. He said that if the Commandant of the Marine Corps had been at that particular meeting of the Joint Chiefs, he felt sure there would have been a rather different tone taken.

Let me make clear, in none of those meetings did [Lyman L.] Lemnitzer or Arleigh Burke, who was Acting Chief whenever Lemnitzer was away, nor did the chairman of the JCS review group, General Gray, say to the President, "We don't believe that air cover is absolutely vital for this operation." As to General Gray, I don't think he believed any such thing, and of course the Joint Chiefs, I'm sure, would all have agreed that effective air cover enhanced the chances of success. Nevertheless, I don't exclude the possibility that the President became aware, one way or another, that the Chiefs placed less emphasis on pre-invasion air strikes to knock out the Castro air force than did those in charge of planning the operation. And I may say that, as a civilian with no military experience, I was put in a very odd position to know that at the level of the Chiefs themselves there was a real question about the doctrine that the colonel reporting to me regarded as so essential.

I think it has to be said that if there's anything hindsight tends to prove, it is that the colonel was right. With hindsight, I think one is not justified in saying that, given adequate air cover, the operation would surely have been a success. I've never thought that one could be at all certain of that. I do think you could pretty well say, however, that without air cover it didn't have a chance.

This apparently wasn't brought out very strongly in the meetings with the President in discussion.

No, particularly the representatives of the Chiefs there didn't take this position strongly. You see, a great many of the policy questions that kept arising in those planning meetings with the President had to do with whether "you really have to have these air strikes?" I'm sure that in advance of the event, both he and Secretary Rusk were more worried about the effect on world opinion of the air operations than they were about the landing itself. They were eager to see the landing done as unobtrusively as possible—indeed, we all were—and hence their desire, which was, of course, what was done, to trim back the preparatory air operations.

Well, the thing that Arthur Schlesinger brought out in his book [A Thousand Days: John F. Kennedy in the White House (1965)] was that the military men who were involved in this, the Joint Chiefs commit-

tee or the Joint Chiefs themselves—now this is what he says, I believe— never really had an opportunity to make their views known effectively because there was no agenda to meetings, things kept changing, and by the time they realized the change had taken place, the planning was already past that. Do you agree or disagree with that?

By and large, I disagree with that, although I think you can shade this one way or the other. It is perfectly true that there were no agendas for the policy meetings with the President. It is not true that as the military plan changed in certain respects, major respects, the Chiefs did not have an opportunity themselves to consider and then to make known their views on such a revision of the plan as, for instance, the much discussed shift from a plan for a landing at Trinidad [on Cuba] to a landing at the Bay of Pigs.

The Chiefs always knew in what respects the plan was being revised or reconsidered because their review committee under General Gray, as I have said, was in daily intimate touch with the planners and in a sense was helping with the planning of the operation. Furthermore, the chairman of that committee reported to the Chiefs, I believe, at every meeting of the Joint Chiefs during all of this period. So the Joint Chiefs were up to date on what was happening in the planning.

Now, in the case of that major change of locale from Trinidad to the Bay of Pigs, the Chiefs—as again I'm sure has been said in the books— not only knew of it but they had a chance to consider it, and they did have a written comment on that. In the last rather hectic days, that was not true. After all, the famous decision to cancel an air strike scheduled for Monday morning wasn't made until six o'clock Sunday evening. It was made, to the best of my knowledge and belief, without consultation with the Chiefs. The Chiefs were not consulted on a decision that the air strike that was made on Saturday morning would be cut to about half strength or less. And indeed, the way that decision was made was rather odd because I was simply instructed by the President to reduce the scale of the strike and make it "minimal." No figure was set, and that was a decision that I made myself. The Chiefs weren't consulted on that. So there is some truth in Arthur's contention in these cases, but I rather doubt if this is what he had mainly in mind.

In any case, without trying to guess what he did have in mind, I would say this: that although the Chiefs did receive orderly reports from their Joint Staff committee, although they did discuss the operation (and, by the way, with nobody from CIA or from the project office present), and although they did express views, only on two occasions that I'm aware of were these views reduced to writing. Moreover, so far as I'm aware, it was not the practice, either in the meetings which I attended or in other private meetings, for the Chairman of the Joint Chiefs to give the

President an orderly account of the Joint Chiefs' most recent deliberations on this matter. If the Joint Chiefs met on a Tuesday and spent half an hour on this and then passed on to other business, I very much doubt whether anyone that afternoon or the next day saw the President and said, this was discussed in the Joint Chiefs. There was no action item before the Joint Chiefs. So I think I would agree with Arthur that the way the system worked, the President was not exposed to a kind of orderly reporting of the Joint Chiefs' deliberations. . . .

In hindsight we can see many aspects of the plan, I think, that could very well have been strengthened by the Joint Chiefs of Staff, and I wonder if there were any specific instances that you could recall . . .

Remember that the curtailment of strategic air strikes, pre-invasion air strikes designed to knock out the Castro air force, were something that they really didn't ever have much opportunity to express an opinion on. I am confident that they would have opposed that, but I'm not at all sure they would have opposed it in terribly strong terms to the President for the reason that I've indicated to you. As to other deficiencies, well, I think with hindsight there are some that the Chiefs and, indeed, the military officers who were working for me should have foreseen and exposed. As a matter of fact, I came to feel immediately after the event that in straight military terms, aside from curtailing the air strikes, the worst mistake by all odds was that the air force we'd assembled wasn't big enough to begin with. I feel very guilty on this point because I think I could have foreseen the deficiency, but I think that our military people had, if I may say so, a greater responsibility for this. We had something like seventeen aircraft and air crews. A single sortie required about ten hours in the air for about an hour and a half to two hours over Cuba.

If you'll just do the arithmetic on the back of an envelope, it's clear that you can't turn one aircraft around more than twice a day, and you probably can't turn an air crew around more than one and a half times a day. That means that the most you can get is three hours a day over the target area per aircraft and maybe two hours a day per air crew. Well, this means that if you did all your scheduling perfectly and if you had no attrition, you could have about one and a half aircraft over the target area all the time.

Now this, as I feel with hindsight, was very definitely insufficient. We were counting on our aircraft not only for the strategic role before the invasion to knock out Castro's aircraft on the ground, but we were also counting on it very heavily as, in effect, the artillery of the ground forces. No one ever thought that the [Cuban] Brigade could hold Castro's armies off unless you had favorable terrain, which we did, and unless you could call in very strong air support. It's been clear to me ever since that this was a serious miscalculation. And I think that I should have foreseen this, and I think others should have foreseen it. It is for this reason, among others, that I have always been unwilling to say that if the President hadn't called off that air strike, the operation would surely have been a success. I'm about 90 percent certain that the Joint Chiefs never commented on this inadequacy. Indeed, I don't remember the Joint Chiefs ever making this simple analysis.

I had come in here, frankly, with the impression that there must have been perhaps an institutional lack of communication between the Joint Chiefs of Staff and the CIA. I don't get that impression now from talking with you.

No, I think that is incorrect. I think the communication in the last two months before the operation and during it was excellent, was very good. I think the Chiefs had the mechanism as a result of Kennedy's action. I may say, this had not been the case previously. But with that review committee under General Gray, they had the means of keeping themselves continuously informed, and yet, just as a comment on government procedures, they were able to do so without any improper interference with the activity of the people who had the line responsibility. I also feel that they had every opportunity to state specific objections because they could either make any objections or comments directly to us through General Gray or, if they'd wished to do so, face to face; or the Chairman could have made any objections that he thought it important to make directly to the President and the whole circle of the President's advisors.

One of the reasons I had this impression was because President Kennedy has been criticized for disrupting older channels of communication and, during the first six months, not instituting new channels to replace them. And again, because of the appointing of Chester Cooper as a sort of liaison man between McGeorge Bundy's group in the White House and intelligence groups in various other places, I thought—well, evidently there was a lack of communication during the time of the Bay of Pigs. But apparently, this lack, if it did exist, wasn't relevant to the Bay of Pigs operation.

I don't believe it was relevant to the Bay of Pigs, no, because that received so much attention that the communications were really very good on that. I would like to make a comment on the general point, though. I think one thing that happened during these first few months of the President's term, as others have remarked, is that he largely lost confidence in his senior professional military advisors. That was certainly due in part to the Bay of Pigs, and I've always assumed, rather than actually learned from the President himself, that he felt the Joint Chiefs, in their capacity as his advisors, should have been more vigilant in pointing out shortcomings or causing shortcomings to be corrected, one of the two.

However, I think it's a mistake to assign the major role to the Cuban experience in explaining his at least temporarily reduced confidence in the Joint Chiefs because I also saw very intimately during these months what was going on in Laos and the decisions that were being made there. One reason that the Bay of Pigs operation didn't have much attention for the first few weeks after the Inauguration was that the Laotian war was in a state of acute crisis as he assumed office. The first meeting I attended with members of the new Administration—Paul Nitze for one, [Robert S.] McNamara for part of the time, Dean Rusk for part of the time—was one of a series of meetings in the State Department on Laos. I was present at most of these informal policy meetings that were the successor to the formal NSC [National Security Council] that dealt with Laos. Now there was a case where I think the communication certainly didn't work, although it wasn't, I think, because of institutional changes that he made or procedural changes.

What would happen at successive meetings was that the President would be briefed either by the Chairman of the Joint Chiefs personally or, as is more apt to be the habit, a more junior officer would actually do the briefing of the whole group in the presence of the Chairman of the Joint Chiefs and with the Chairman's comments from time to time. I still remember very clearly the occasion when the long-planned major offensive by the Royal Laotian Army against the Nationalists under Kong Le and Communists in the Plaine des Jarres was outlined.

Well, it was a nice piece of planning to have been carried out in a military college as an exercise in how you would dispose troops, given the terrain and the dispositions of the enemy. It predicted that the Plaine des Jarres would be seized on the tenth day of the operation, or something of this kind, by parachute troops. All of this, you understand, was to be done by the Royal Laotian forces. I left this briefing with a sense of complete unreality. I had been close for a year and a half, I guess, to the goings-on in Laos, and it just never occurred to me that the Royal Laotian [Army] could, or would, carry out any such elegant military operation of this sort, and of course they didn't.

It really didn't occur to me until after that whole event that the President had taken this plan seriously. And why shouldn't he? He assumed, correctly, I believe, that when he was given a briefing by the Joint Chiefs on the plans of the Laotian Army, plans formulated with U.S. military advisors at every level, that the Joint Chiefs endorsed the plan and thought it would work. I'm sure that if he'd asked the Chairman, the Chairman would have said, "Yes, we think there's a pretty good chance this will work."

On that occasion there were a lot of others of us civilians in the room who would have expressed extreme surprise at the notion that this was going to work out the way it was planned because a number of us had had much more intimate experience than the members of the Joint Chiefs, individually, of observing the imperfections of military execution in a tiny, backward, backwoods Asian country. It is no particular criticism of the Joint Chiefs, perhaps, that they had no feel for that, but it is a grave criticism of the way the system worked. Either because the Joint Chiefs were permitted to be quite unrealistic about what the Laotians could accomplish or because they assumed the President would do his own discounting, he was given, I believe, a completely false picture about what was going to happen in that little war. And I think this was disillusioning to him.

Then that was followed by the Bay of Pigs, and I'm sure he felt that here again the Chiefs had given a kind of formal comment on a plan, a superficial comment that did not reflect the results of probing deeply, and that this was another example of the same thing. Nevertheless, I am suggesting that in the Cuban case they certainly were better informed, or at least as well informed, and they certainly had every opportunity to probe deeply and had certainly made an effort through a Joint Staff group to do so. . . .

You mentioned that the Marine Corps colonel who served as an advisor, in effect, and a trainer of men had had experience in amphibious operations, and I know for a fact that he did have experience in Iwo Jima.

Yes.

But I've, at the same time, heard the criticism made of the operation that not enough people with experience in amphibious operations were involved, and that particularly within the CIA organization itself, among civilians in the CIA, there were men—and I'm thinking offhand of Robert Amory—who had had experience in amphibious operations whose experience was not drawn upon.

Well, there's no doubt that the last is true. There were civilians whose experience wasn't drawn upon, and this is because of their place in the Agency. Perhaps, with hindsight, that was a mistake. I don't feel this in itself was a serious source of inadequacy in the plan or in its execution. The Marine colonel had also, as you probably know, been a year and a half behind the lines in the Philippines, so he'd had extensive guerrilla experience as well as amphibious. I think some of the usual mistakes that seem to be made in any amphibious landing were made in this case, but not really by want of foresight. I'm thinking of the fact that we did find a reef where we didn't expect one. And this is despite the fact that we had really looked very hard for that with reconnaissance photography. . . .

There is also an important question about the plan or the possibility that these invaders or infiltrators might be able to escape into the Escambray Mountains and become guerrillas. Was Kennedy actually told this very, very strongly? Was this very definitely a part of the final plan?

No. I think it is certainly true that it was in the minds of everyone concerned with the final plan that, given the Bay of Pigs location, there was little likelihood they could make an escape to the Escambray. We did feel there was some chance that guerrilla activity could be continued in the marshes around and especially to the north and west of the Bay of Pigs. Classically and historically that's been an area that's supported guerrilla operations. I do feel the impression we attempted to give the President was just that—that the chances of a retreat to the Escambray from the Bay of Pigs, by contrast with a landing around Trinidad, which is right next to the Escambray, were very poor, but that there would be some chance of organizing effective guerrilla activities right around the Bay of Pigs. I feel myself that this is a respect in which all of us were derelict. The President was given, or was allowed to form, a much too optimistic impression of this as a possibility, as a fallback in the Bay of Pigs case. . . .

There was a very famous April 4 meeting, among many meetings, in which it is said the President asked various people to stand up and give their opinions. Apparently he never got around to the whole group, but at least he did ask various members. And at this meeting, it is said, or has been said, that Senator [J. William] Fulbright voiced an objection to the plan. And yet I've heard from other people that he did not. Now, what was your recollection of that? Do you recall Senator Fulbright's opinions as outstanding at all?

Yes, my impression is that he did voice some objection.

Well, we're dealing with impressions here all around because . . .

Yes. That is my impression. By the way, the President did get around to almost everybody in that meeting.

I wasn't aware of that. I was under the impression that . . .

If that's the meeting I have in mind. There was one where he went around, and he asked everyone for their votes. One reason I remember this quite clearly, he came to Adolf Berle. Adolf gave a rather long reply, which was, well, the alternatives aren't very good, and it has dangers, but if it succeeded, it would be effective, and so on. Finally, when he was through, the President said, "Well, Adolf, you haven't voted." And Berle said, "I'd say, let her rip."

I've heard that "Let her rip" a number of times, but I didn't know who it came from, actually.

That's it. Several of the people gave, ultimately, inconclusive comments, sort of no-objection comments. I remember particularly, however, that pro votes were given specifically by Nitze, who was there, McNamara, Berle in the terms I've spoken of, Tom [Thomas C.] Mann, I think, when finally pinned down in somewhat the same way. Well, these are the people whom I remember, and I don't know who was there for the Joint Chiefs. I don't know whether it was Lemnitzer or Burke, but I suspect that whoever it was gave an affirmative reaction. And I know that also the Marine colonel was there in that room. No, I guess he wasn't in that room because he was at that point down at the embarkation. He had been at an earlier session. He may have been there; I'm not sure of that. I think General Gray was there for the Joint Chiefs committee and so on. But it was a pretty complete canvass.

Another controversy involves what was expected of the dissident elements in Cuba. Would you comment on that? What exactly did you expect from the dissident elements, and when?

I thought we'd get nothing. Oh, possibly a few sporadic incidents, but nothing of significance until a beachhead was consolidated and had been held for three or four days. By that time, if we had had aircraft operating out of the beachhead and had, in effect, demonstrated that the Castro forces could not successfully attack and destroy the beachhead, if we'd had aircraft able to attack communications and the railroad and targets of this kind, then I thought there was a very real possibility that you'd begin to get significant action.

One of the criticisms that is made in connection with the dissident elements is that they were not told satisfactorily or in time that their cooperation was to be expected eventually, and that this led to their being defenseless when Castro moved effectively against them.

Yes, right.

How did that come about? Can you explain that at all?

Yes. I think that the second half of that criticism especially has some validity. It came about as the final climax of one of the developments in the whole course of the operation that had a lot to do with its ultimate failure. This was the complete failure of the effort to organize a disciplined underground in Cuba. As you remember, of course, when the operation was started a year before the Bay of Pigs, it was intended in the first instance as an operation involving the training of guerrilla leaders and organizers, radio operators, and a few technicians, the infiltration of these men and their subsequent resupply by air. It wasn't until months after the operation had been initiated that the concept was evolved of a small landing force to detonate, as it were, an internal revolt that would have been already organized. It wasn't until the latter part of the preceding autumn with the complete failure of the effort to organize a disciplined underground that the whole emphasis shifted to the landing force, to the invasion.

These facts, I think, are pretty well known, but they need a little more explanation. The key to what I mean by a disciplined underground is perhaps not quite accurately described by this term because its essential feature is a secure command and control and communications net. What I mean by a command and control and communications net is not a large body of men. Perhaps in the whole of a country the size of Cuba it could be one or two hundred people, but people who were highly disciplined, would obey orders, who were compartmented so they knew one another, for instance, only by code name and pseudonyms, who had means of communicating with one another in such a fashion that if one man was apprehended, he would not be able to give away the identity of many others in the net. And to be effective, the individuals who constitute a communications net of this kind must have radios. Quite possibly, these would serve as a major means of internal communication, and certainly they have to be in a position to receive communications from outside and to send them by radio.

Given a command and control net that is secure, it then becomes possible to have guerrilla groups which by their very nature are more numerous, less well trained, therefore less susceptible to tight discipline, and much less able to be secure than those who comprise the "net." If there's a guerrilla band of twenty men, it's just inevitable that if one of them is picked up, he knows the identities of the other twenty. But if your basic communications and command and control net is disciplined and competent and secure, then it becomes the means of establishing communication with actual groups of dissidents and also with all kinds of groups of would-be dissidents inside the country. Furthermore, there's no need for one group of dissidents to know the identity of another group. There can be some university students in a cell, and there can be some guys in the Escambray, and there can be some industrial workers who are still at their jobs, and they don't need to know one another.

It's in this way that something that can be called a controllable and reasonably disciplined resistance movement can be, and has to be, built up. A resistance that is held together by this kind of net, then, becomes a collection of forces from which operational intelligence can be quickly obtained and to which information and instructions can be given. For instance, if you have an organization of this kind, a group that wants and needs an air drop of supplies, and is in a place in the country where it can receive it, can communicate (a) its needs, and (b) where it is and when it will be there and what the recognition signal will be, and you can organize these things.

In the course of the autumn I don't know how many air drops were made, and I think one was reasonably successful, but only one of the entire series. For the most part, after an air drop had been carried out in response to a request that had been forwarded in a cumbersome chain through Havana and the U.S. Embassy, we never knew whether the recipients had been anywhere near the drop zone, and they never knew whether the aircraft had been anywhere near what they thought was the drop zone. I certainly felt that I received a liberal education in the fact that what I've called a communications and command and control net of some sort, an underground, is doomed to ineffectiveness.

Well, for a whole lot of reasons—and some of them, I'm sure, reasons that I have never understood—the efforts during the late summer and autumn to build an underground of this sort, specifically to establish contact with guerrilla groups, to send in a radio operator and technician to each so that they'd communicate to the outside, to identify and recruit agents in fishing villages who were reliable people with whom communications would be possible, for infiltration by small boats—all of these efforts failed abysmally. In late autumn we had a number of very successful small-boat infiltrations of supplies and people, but, as a general rule, the people were picked up within forty-eight hours and the supplies immediately thereafter. Why? Because when you land guys on a beach at night, even if it's completely secure and they're completely safe and, after all, are of the nationality of the country and all the rest of it, there has to be a house in a village nearby where they can go and sleep and get a meal. Then there has to be another place to pass them along to. This simply was not accomplished. That being the case, the dissidents inside Cuba at the time of the Castro uprising were a very diverse group, or set of groups of people. Mainly, the dissidents were people who were emotionally in opposition to Castro, but not in any kind of organizational framework. And short of a broadcast on the radio, there wasn't any way to communicate with these people. There were still a few with whom we could communicate, but very, very few. The whole effort, of course, was to make this invasion a tactical surprise, which it was. To that end, it, of course, was quite out of the question to warn Castro semi-publicly, by broadcasting to the dissidents that something was going to happen on such and such a day.

One of the myths of the discussions of that operation—a myth that's uttered by many Cubans, too—is to the effect that there was an organized underground with which communication was possible, which could have been warned to get out of the way on a certain date so as to avoid arrest without giving the date away to Castro. That is a myth. There probably weren't more than a dozen people, if that many, inside of Cuba to whom it was possible with any security whatever to communicate, let alone give, an order and expect to have it carried out.

One of the lessons that can be drawn from this is that the whole thing should have been aborted, not just after Kennedy came into office but way back in November when it was pretty clear that the effort to build an underground wasn't working. Here again this is where one, both at the time and looking back on it, has a feeling of inevitability. A great effort had been mounted, let us say, by November, and there seemed to be really no pressing reason then for giving it up. What I think we did not foresee as early even as December is that there plainly wasn't going to be time to start all over again at the building of an underground and have that job done before the rainy season. Because it seemed that there wasn't time to do that job and because we were quite aware that it had not been a success, everyone concerned began to pay more and more attention gradually to the other alternative.

I [am] curious to know whether or not the intelligence side of the CIA was involved in attempts to set up, prior to the Bay of Pigs invasion, a communications net or a communications organization of dissident elements within Cuba.

It was not involved. I've used the terms "the intelligence side" of the Agency to refer to that part of it which, in those days, was under the Deputy Director, Intelligence. All of these components of the Agency were concerned in one way or another with intelligence analysis and intelligence interpretation. They did not at any time have operational responsibilities. On the operational side, the responsibility for clandestine intelligence collection was with the same organization that was responsible for all other operational matters. Hence, it was natural and in accord with normal procedure that the intelligence side of the Agency didn't have anything to do with the operation.

I was going to ask you if it would have been better if they had, but apparently it just doesn't enter into the question.

It didn't, really. That question never arose. . . .

In view of your feeling on Sunday night that the President probably would not accede to a request for a second air strike or for additional air cover, do you feel that you or anyone else in the CIA failed in any way in presenting the importance of this air cover or air power to the President?

Yes, I do. I think not only should we have insisted on speaking to the President that evening—although I still believe that that wouldn't have made any difference—but I have the feeling that in the previous discussions this point of military doctrine, the absolute essentiality of command of the air for the success of this sort of operation, had somehow not been given. We hadn't succeeded in giving it the emphasis that it deserved.

And you would include then, also, that the Joint Chiefs of Staff or their representatives as well had not given it the emphasis . . .

I believe that to be true, yes.

The CIA has taken a great deal of the responsibility for this. A great deal of the criticism, at any rate, is focused on the CIA, and I wonder if you would care to comment on where you think additional responsibility lies with regard to the failure of the operation. Now this is, again, ground that we have dealt with and covered before, but I'm particularly interested in who you consider at fault in areas aside from the CIA.

I think the only way that I can answer that question, and I am being completely honest in giving this answer, is that this decision was participated in, as is a matter of record, by a lot of people and a lot of parts of the government. I suspect that some of the individuals who were involved in the many meetings with the President and who were finally asked by the President to give their recommendations in the meeting where an affirmative decision was reached, feel, or would argue, that they were led astray by the CIA; that we were the operating organization, and that they pretty much had to accept our estimates of the likelihood of success. I think to a degree, and in the case of some individuals and organizations, that's a valid argument. I think it's fair to say that neither the President nor most of his political advisors—especially I'm thinking of the State Department people—could have been expected to form an independent judgment of the likelihood of a military success. That kind of judgment is always, of course, a complex one; and, as I think I said to you when we were talking about this before, the only judgment you can make is a probability judgment. The one that was made—and was supported, de facto, by the Chiefs of Staff—was that there was a considerably better than even chance of success in the first phase, that is, in establishing a beachhead.

So if we absolve the people who participated in the decision but who couldn't be expected on their own authority or knowledge to review that judgment, you then have to say that insofar as that judgment, in turn, was proven to have been false, the blame lies with the people to whom the President did look for such an assessment. And that was the CIA and the Joint Chiefs and the Joint Staff.

I think one point that has to be made here is that if you make a probability judgment that outcome "A" is twice as likely as outcome "B" and then "B" is what turns up, that doesn't necessarily prove the original

judgment was wrong, because that's the character of probability judgments. It's a two-to-one chance of "A"; it's still a one-in-three chance of
"B"; and if you do it only once, "B" can be the one that turns up, and it
still doesn't prove that the original assessment of probability was wrong.

But to come back to your question and pursue it a bit further, I think
that the responsibility for the military assessment, it has to be said, did
rest between the CIA and the Joint Chiefs. The Joint Chiefs had certain
advantages in making such an assessment. First, they commanded military expertise, which the CIA possessed only in the persons of officers
assigned to it. And secondly, this wasn't a military operation under the
command or cognizance of the Joint Chiefs, and therefore one presumes
that they could be objective about it. However, you have to set against
that the fact that, ultimately, the responsibility is much heavier on the
people who are in the line of command.

So I think I would summarize what I've been saying here as follows:
if the military assessment was at fault, and as a probability statement I'm
not sure to this day that it was—I know that long after the event, General
Gray, I believe, would have defended the original probability judgment
as probably having been correct—but if that was at fault, I think some of
the blame falls on the Joint Chiefs and the Joint Staff.

There were other nonmilitary judgments involved. I think I said to
you last time that to my mind one of the most serious errors was a failure
to realize how thoroughly the disclaimability by the U.S. Government of
this operation had been compromised. This failure to realize that the whole
world accepted what was going on as a U.S. Government operation, on
the one hand, induced the political authorities in Washington, who didn't
much like it, nevertheless to go along with it. But on the other hand, this
unclear view of how the whole operation looked to the public prevented
the Administration from philosophically accepting a degree of responsibility and then authorizing some of the actions that could have greatly
enhanced the chances of success that I mentioned to you, I'm quite sure,
the possibility of making considerably more use of American volunteers
and especially American volunteer air crews, and perhaps using some
more sophisticated aircraft. Now, if I'm correct in diagnosing this as one
of the mistakes of judgment, and I'm very sure that I am, I believe the
blame for this error in judgment is much more widespread.

Do you think particularly in the State Department?

I feel quite strongly that the State Department, especially, should have
been more—I was going to say more aware, and yet that isn't quite the
phrase that I want to use because, of course, they were well aware of
what was coming out in the press; we all were. But I think the State Department, as well as the CIA and even to a degree the Pentagon, should

have been clearer on the significance of the climate of public discussion that had grown up. I think they should have realized that however much we might legalistically say the operation was disclaimable by the U.S. Government because nobody could actually prove that a U.S. Government-authorized representative had dealt with the Cubans, this sort of rather legalistic defense was almost irrelevant.

The fact of the matter was that this had about it, to all other Americans and to everybody else, clearly the earmarks of a U.S. operation. I feel that the State Department was at least as much to blame as we are. And I think I may say that in this respect the President and his own advisors have to share a significant part of the blame because this judgment that I'm talking about—the assessment of how this looked from outside of Washington and then, given how it looked, how should you handle it— these are judgments that are not highly technical; there is no reason to expect the military to be particularly good at them. Unfortunately, there's no reason to expect the CIA to be any better at these than the other parts of the civilian administration. So I'm not trying to get out of a fair share of the blame for this mistake, but I do think the blame was widely shared. . . .

Were there any people within the CIA who were, let's say, opposed to this operation, or who were criticizing it perhaps as it went along, that you were aware of?

No. As you probably know, [Lyman] Kirkpatrick, the Inspector General, ultimately issued an unfavorable report. That was entirely an after-the-fact report, and I am unaware of any time when the operation was in progress when he expressed any considerable concern about it. My own hunch is that very possibly Dick Helms, who was then my Deputy and now the Director, and some others in the operational side of the CIA, in the Clandestine Service, were gravely concerned about an operation that had become so big and so public. But they did not, in fact, raise any of these doubts with me or, to the best of my knowledge and belief, with Dulles or Cabell while the operation was in progress.

In connection with the two inspections or two investigations that went on after the fact, the President's committee of inspectors . . .

You mean the one that was headed by General [Maxwell D.] Taylor?

Right. Do you have any comments on the one that was headed by General Taylor, on the satisfactoriness of this investigation? Do you have any criticisms or comments of that investigation?

No, I thought that was a very thorough and, on the whole, a very fair-minded inquiry.

Was it as thorough as the CIA's own investigation?

I would say it was as thorough in the sense that it probed as deeply into the whole progress of the operation, its successive phases. It did not inquire into what I will call organizational matters and personnel assignments and things of this kind within the CIA as deeply as Kirkpatrick did, for the obvious reason that it was really done by senior people, Burke, Dulles, and the Attorney General, and they simply didn't know people within the Agency as well or the organization in as much detail.

Well, I take it that the CIA's investigation, its own investigation, was more directly concerned with the CIA rather than the broader aspects.

That's correct, yes.

Do you have any comments or criticisms of that investigation or of the report? Did you read the report?

Oh, yes, I read the report, and I wrote, in fact, a rejoinder to the report. Yes, I would have some pretty strong comments on that. I think some of the points made in the report were well made, but I thought this was a typical report that uses hindsight illegitimately for criticism. I would have to go back and get my hands on and read parts of the I.G.'s [Inspector General] report, and parts of our own comment thereon to go into it in any detail, which I would be rather reluctant to do anyway, I think. But I felt that it had internal inconsistencies in it, and that generally the broad criticism to be made of it, which I would not make of the Taylor report, was that it did take advantage of hindsight and, in effect, criticized the participants for judgments that allegedly turned out to be incorrect after the fact, rather than trying to assess them on the basis of the evidence available to those who made them when they made them.

The Director of the CIA, I think, has referred to that report as a hatchet job. You would go along with that?

I would agree with that, yes.

Well, that's a rather strange situation. I wonder if there were any personality conflicts which might have led to this sort of thing. Was the Inspector General attempting to . . . Do you think his motives were base in any way?

Yes, but I think maybe this is as much as I will say. I think it probably doesn't serve any good purpose to go beyond [that] because one then begins to get into a matter of voicing views on motivations.

I will simply say that the then Inspector General was known to be, to I think everyone that knew him, extremely ambitious. He was an individual who, as I felt well before this incident, was not above using his reports and his analysis of situations to exert an influence in the direction that he chose; and these directions were, not always but sometimes, tied up with his own personal ambitions. I think in this case he had a number of purposes he was trying to serve, more or less of that character. But I don't really think it does any good to go any deeper into that.

All right. Much has been made of John Kennedy's accepting respon-sibility for this operation publicly; and, in particular, people have complimented him very, very sincerely for directing that there should be no personal recriminations or anything of this sort I wondered if your own personal experience after the Bay of Pigs would lead you to believe that this was sincerely the way he felt.

I think it was sincerely the way he felt, yes.

I wondered if he had ever expressed to you, or to others which came back to you, an irritation with the CIA or with anyone in particular?

I talked to him, oh, probably a couple of times beyond the immediate aftermath about it. He was always extremely generous as far as I person-ally was concerned. I never heard him express directly any criticism. I get the impression mainly, I suppose, from comments repeated by others that he had a mixture of attitudes. First of all, I think he very sincerely meant no recriminations. I think he wished strongly to discourage people in the State Department or on his own staff who might have been critical of the CIA from voicing this criticism either within the Administration or outside. I think he wished genuinely to discourage in the aftermath of a disaster the kind of mutual recrimination that would reduce the effective-ness of cooperation between the agencies. . . .

Do you feel the Bay of Pigs seriously undermined John Kennedy's confidence in the CIA? His confidence apparently was very high when he first came into office.

I thought he had genuinely not only a desire to avoid recriminations among members of the Administration, but that he himself had no strongly adverse feelings toward any of the people involved. I think he felt that the responsibility for the decisions had indeed been rather widely dif-fused in the Administration and that even in his own mind he was not prepared to pick out a few people and mentally place the blame on them. I do not think it shook his confidence, therefore, in the basic competence or loyalty of people in the Agency. I know that he felt there had to be a change at the top of the Agency because he told me that perfectly straight-forwardly. And his comment was that if this had been a Cabinet govern-ment, he would have resigned; but being the kind of government it is, somebody else had to; and inevitably, he thought, this had to be Allen Dulles and Pearré Cabell.

I suppose it did, in part, undermine his confidence in the Agency. Perhaps, however, it would be more accurate to say that it definitely undermined his confidence in the decision-making process with respect to major Agency activities. I think what he felt most strongly, perhaps, was not that the CIA as such had revealed grave deficiencies, but that as decisions had been made in the Administration concerning CIA activities, the process of making such decisions and of assessing the opportunities and the risks was deficient and had to be quite radically changed.

Now, of course, in the event there were no radical changes or sudden changes made in either the Agency or the decision-making process, the changes in personalities were made. Gradually over a period of years there have been important changes, in my view, in the role of the CIA. I've had a chance to observe these, and in no significant degree, really, were they set in motion by actions taken under Kennedy. For the most part, they have not been the result of initiatives taken from the White House and resulting in instructions to the Director of CIA. They've been changes of another sort that have grown more from within the Agency and from the evolution of its relationship with the Pentagon than they have from any White House-instituted moves, at least to the best of my information.

It has been said that greater outside supervision of the CIA would have, perhaps, avoided the situation of the Bay of Pigs. I understand that John Kennedy took steps to . . .

It is true that he reactivated the Foreign Intelligence Advisory Board to take that one first. I think he may have increased its effectiveness and its vigor. My recollection is that he did this even before the Bay of Pigs, but it may have been afterward.

It was May 1961, so it was immediately afterward.

It was immediately afterward. But my answer to your question is that I don't really think that a committee of that kind—meeting less often than once a month, meeting for a day at a time, necessarily reviewing matters of structure and doctrine and operating philosophy—could have, in fact, offered any safeguard against the sorts of errors of judgment that were made in the Bay of Pigs operation.

I don't know to what extent it can be said that Kennedy further activated the 5412 Committee [an NSC group to review covert actions]. That had existed, of course, for years. It had been much more active in the last year or year and a half of the Eisenhower Administration than previously. My recollection is that its functioning did not change greatly under Kennedy. It is true that beginning a few months after the Bay of Pigs the activities of the 5412 Committee were somewhat formalized, and another committee on, as I remember it, insurgency and counterinsurgency was established with about the same membership. For a time, General Taylor was chairman of both of these.

I think it is fair to say that in the aftermath of the Bay of Pigs especially, the 5412 Committee was much more conscious of its responsibility and reviewed proposed operations both more rigorously and more formally than it had before. I suspect that change has persisted. It is my own view, again, however, that nothing of that sort would have made any significant difference in this case because, after all, the one point never to be forgotten about the Bay of Pigs was that the plans for that activity and its progress were meticulously reviewed for weeks before it came off by the President and the whole circle of his advisors, and in even more detail daily by a committee of the Joint Staff for the Pentagon and by a group in the Western Hemisphere Bureau of the State Department who were working actively on the political aspects of it. All that the 5412 Committee does is to bring these operations before the scrutiny of top people in State, Defense, and the White House. This operation and any others of this magnitude have always been under the scrutiny of these same individuals when the operations were imminent or in progress. And having a more formalized committee wouldn't have made its members any wiser. So I think the answer has to be that if there's anything clear on the record of the Bay of Pigs, it is that lack of supervision and coordination was not the reason for failure.

DAVID BELIN: *During the time that you were with the Agency, did you ever have any discussions with anyone in the White House concerning the planning of what was called an Executive Action Capability, which was defined in substance as a capability of the Agency carrying out assassinations, if required?*

RICHARD BISSELL: My recollection of this is far from clear. But I am satisfied that very early in the Kennedy Administration I did participate in such conversations.

DB: *And do you have any recollection of with whom you might have participated?*

I am almost certain it was either Walt Rostow or McGeorge Bundy, or probably the former, and possibly both.

Conducted by the President's Commission on CIA Activities (Rockefeller Commission) in Washington, DC, on April 21, 1975. Box 32, Gerald R. Ford Library, Ann Arbor, Michigan. Declassified from Top Secret in 1996.

DB: *Do you remember specifically what, if anything, was discussed in any of those conversations?*

My recollection, which isn't too specific, is that this was a discussion of the desirability of developing such a capability within the CIA that presumably would be a small special unit and highly compartmented from the rest of the organization.

DB: *Did you have any feeling as to whether or not this was done with or without the knowledge or consent of the President?*

I had no specific feeling on that point, but I had a great deal of confidence that the two gentlemen whose names I have mentioned would not have discussed this with me or encouraged any course of action that they were not confident the President would approve.

DB: *Did you ever have any such discussions with any official in the Eisenhower Administration?*

Not to my recollection, and I think I am almost sure that I did not.

DB: *Now, apart from discussions of an Executive Action Capability, did you ever or were you ever aware of any development of plans inside of the Agency with a specific plan or goal of the assassination of any particular foreign leader?*

Yes, I was aware of investigation and planning to that end.

DB: *Will you please enumerate before the Commission which foreign leader or leaders were involved?*

There were three cases I remember. One of them would have involved Sukarno [the president of Indonesia], the second would have involved [the Congo's Patrice] Lumumba, and the third did involve [Cuba's] Castro. I am not giving that order chronologically. I don't remember what the chronology was, but those are the three cases I remember.

DB: *Could you please state for the Commission your entire knowledge with regard to the Sukarno matter?*

There was planning of such a possibility. I believe this was initiated in the Far Eastern Division of the CIA. The planning progressed as far as the identification of an asset [agent] whom it was felt might be recruited for this purpose. The plan was never reached, was never perfected to the point where it seemed feasible. The difficulty concerned the possibility of creating a situation in which the potential agent would have access to the target; and because the plan never reached that stage, it was never, so far as I am aware, discussed outside of the Agency with a view to obtaining approval or authorization.

DB: *So far as you are concerned with the Agency, this would have required such approval or authorization before they would have undertaken such a plan?*

They would.

DB: *Does that relate not just to Sukarno but with any other target?*

That is correct.

DB: *Now, what about Lumumba?*

The Lumumba case planning began, was initiated, within the Agency; and in that case, on my initiative, a case officer was directed to look into the possibilities. He reported back in a matter of weeks and convinced me that this was probably unfeasible, and probably an undesirable course of action, and he recommended instead that a quite different kind of operation, somewhat larger in scale, be attempted for the purpose of discrediting Lumumba and undermining his authority.

DB: *To the best of your knowledge, did the Agency, in any manner whatsoever, have anything to do with the death of Sukarno?*

Absolutely nothing.

DB: *Did the Agency have anything whatsoever to do with the death of Lumumba?*

Nothing.

DB: *All right, now, you said there was a third.*

The Castro case.

DB: *Could you tell the Commission the background of the Castro case? First, before you answer that, I will ask you the same question about Lumumba that I asked you with regard to Sukarno. Would there have been any operational plan put into effect without approval from the White House on that kind of a situation?*

No, there would not.

DB: *All right, now, let's turn to Castro. Could you tell the Commission about the Castro situation?*

I became aware—and the timing of this, I believe, was the very beginning of 1961—of the possibility that an assassination attempt might be planned using Mafia resources, or syndicate resources. My very uncertain recollection is that I first heard of this possibility from Shef [Sheffield] Edwards, who I think has testified here.

DB: *He has been interviewed by me.*

I see.

DB: *And for the record, he was the head of the Office of Security?*

That's correct.

DB: *During this period of time in the Agency, is that correct?*

That is correct. The Commission should also understand that this would have been a very different kind of an operation than anything that the Agency normally undertook in that it would not have been carried out . through DDP [the Directorate of Plans]; that is, Agency operational channels, or through any case officer in the Clandestine Service. The possibility that seemed to exist was that through several intermediaries, the Office of Security or the Director of Security could be, and indeed was, in touch with individuals in Las Vegas, who claimed they could make such an attempt using their own personnel. This possibility was discussed by me, again I think probably with Walt Rostow. It may possibly have been discussed directly with McGeorge Bundy, but I suspect that it was through Rostow, who was then Bundy's assistant and on his staff. My impression, but again I must emphasize that this is an uncertain impression, is that I was encouraged to go ahead with the investigation and planning of this operation, and by investigation I mean simply to find out what would be involved to make some assessment of the likelihood of success, and other aspects of the matter. Under the circumstances, this had to be and was the responsibility of Shef Edwards.

DB: *Again, I will ask with regard to this aspect of your testimony the same question I asked you concerning the Executive Action Capabilities. Did you have an opinion as to whether or not what you refer to as this encouragement had any authorization from the President, or that the President in any manner knew about this?*

I had no direct reason to believe that he did, but I will make the same answer, that I had a high degree of confidence that the gentlemen I was talking to in the White House, whom I have identified, would not have given such encouragement unless they were confident that it would meet with the President's approval.

DB: *Did you ever have any discussions with anyone in the Eisenhower Administration concerning any possible plan to assassinate Castro?*

I have no clear recollection of such a discussion, but there could have been. . . .

DB: *Do you know whether or not during the last few months of 1960, which would have been in the Eisenhower Administration, any plans were developed within the Technical Services Branch of the Agency to develop any kind of poison pills that might be used to assassinate Castro?*

I very much doubt if any such development was attempted with this or any other specific operation in view, but the Agency did have and does have an ongoing R & D [research and development] program, and I am quite certain that products of this sort were among those that it had available.

DB: *Do you have any other recollections concerning the Castro matter at this time?*

I am vague as to the final outcome of that attempt. I have no recollection of a specific authorization that it should go forward. I believe, however, that we probably did move to be in a position to carry it out, or to authorize it if authorization were received. One of the reasons, I believe, that my own recollection of the final stages of that plan is vague is that, as I have already explained, what it contemplated was furnishing probably some money and such items as pills or other devices through a number of cutouts or intermediaries to a group which we ourselves, of course, did not in any direct sense control. This was not an operation of such a character that the communications would run through Agency channels, or that authorization on the spot would be by Agency personnel, or that the Agency could precisely and tightly control it.

DB: *Did you ever call Mr. William Harvey, who was a CIA man, to eventually take over this operation within the latter part of '61 or early '62?*

Now, I did ask Mr. Harvey to take over a part of our reviving efforts against Castro and the Castro Administration. I probably urged him to look into this plan that had been active or that had been the subject of active attention nearly a year before. I have no recollection of authorizing him to revive it, except to look at it as a plan, or to proceed with any action along those lines.

DB: *Do you have any personal recollection as to whether or not the pills or pills of any kind, poison pills, were ever delivered into Cuba?*

I do not have any recollection of that.

DB: *One way or the other?*

One way or the other.

DB: *Do you have any recollection on any other facts relating to this matter?*

I don't believe so. . . .

JOHN CONNOR: *I have a question. At the time you had these discussions with either Mr. Walt Rostow or McGeorge Bundy or both, as you recall them, to whom in the Agency did you report?*

Allen Dulles, or Mr. [Charles Pearré] Cabell, his Deputy.

DB: *And did you ever have any discussions with them about this matter before you talked to the Director of Security?*

Well, as I have already testified, my impression is that the first time I heard about this was in my first conversation, at least, with the Director of Security, so that would have preceded any conversation with the Director. And my own belief is that matters took that [turn] because, I believe, the original approach was made to the Agency, that this was not a matter of the Agency seeking out the individuals with whom subsequently messages were exchanged.

CHAIRMAN NELSON ROCKEFELLER: *You mean, approached by the White House?*

No, approached by the syndicate interests that had their own very strong motivations for carrying out this.

JOSEPH KIRKLAND: *What was their price if they would cooperate?*

Well, they had, as I say, very strong motivations on their own. You remember that Castro had fairly recently come to power. They had been powerful under [Fulgencio] Batista in Cuba, and they had a very lucrative set of interests for the syndicates, and they had, in effect, been thrown out. There was still, of course, reasonably free travel, and so they had the strongest sort of reasons or anti-Castro sentiment on their own.

JK: *But did they want any specific quid pro quo from the Agency?*

I'm sure they wanted some money as well as technical help, but I don't remember exactly what.

JC: *Well, after you did learn about this from the CIA Director of Security and then had some White House discussion, did you thereafter have any discussions about it with Mr. Dulles or his Deputy?*

Yes, I am sure I did with Allen Dulles, simply that he should be aware that the planning was going forward. As a matter of fact, I believe the Director of Security had talked to Allen before I did on the matter.

JC: *So that the subsequent activity and planning was with at least his tacit understanding?*

Correct.

NR: *Through previous testimony I got the impression that there were two attempts: one through this syndicate, and then another one directly through agents.*

DB: *I think that the record basically is that in the first stage it was through the syndicate, and that in the second stage basically they used Cuban exiles . . . but the exiles who were being used were not necessarily CIA agents at the time so far as regular, full-time employees of the Agency.*

I don't have a recollection of that second one.

MARVIN GRAY: *You left the Agency when, sir?*

In February of 1962.

JK: *During this time that you were interested or this operation was under consideration, no one in a position of authority ever said flatly, no, kill it?*

To the best of my knowledge, that is correct.

JC: *Did you ever discuss it with the Attorney General, Robert Kennedy?*

I have no recollection of discussing it with him.

DB: *But you do have a recollection of discussing it with Allen Dulles?*

Yes.

DB: *If the records were to show, or if Mr. Edwards were to say, that rather than he contacting you that you contacted him concerning the Mafia, would you say that they are wrong, or would you say that perhaps your recollection is wrong?*

Well, it is possible that my recollection is wrong, but I think I will stand on that as my recollection, and it may be that Edwards and I simply have inconsistent recollections. But I seem to remember rather clearly that it was from him that I first learned of the possibility of this operation, and that he came to see me for this purpose rather than my sending for him. Now, could I just say that I had several conversations with Shef Edwards on this matter and it is very possible that, in a subsequent conversation, I did take the initiative and send for and discuss it with him. But there may be an inconsistency here.

NR: *Was there ever any question raised as to whether this violated any of the domestic statutes limiting CIA's activities within the United States?*

That question was never raised, to my knowledge.

DB: *Are there any other questions by members of the Commission?*

SOL CORBIN: *May I ask a question? You said that you did not discuss it with Attorney General Kennedy. So far as you know, did you have any information or believe that he was ever aware of the proposed plans here?*

I don't remember any conversations or incidents that would have constituted evidence to me that he was aware, but I would not have been in the least surprised if he were. He could have been aware from Bundy or Rostow and conceivably in other ways. If the President knew of this, then I think it highly likely that the Attorney General did, because the President was in the habit of talking over matters of concern to him with the Attorney General. . . .

NR: *Was there evidence, to your knowledge, that Castro was aware of this attempt [on his life] or became aware of it?*

I don't remember any evidence to that effect. I don't think that the actual attempt was ever made, although it is physically possible that the devices to be used, the poison pills, did reach Cuba, and it is perfectly possible that with some time lag Castro would have come on some evidence of this operation. But I don't remember ever seeing any report to that effect.

NR: *The operation wasn't under your direct management?*

Not really, indirectly but not directly. Within the Agency the key individual was Shef Edwards, yes.

JK: *Were there efforts during the period following the Bay of Pigs to land agents on the island?*

Excuse me, sir?

JK: *Were there efforts post-Bay of Pigs to land agents on the island?*

Well, there were none for awhile, and, I don't know, I would assume that such efforts have been made since then. But I think for a good many months after that it would not have been easy to recruit agents, and also there was absolutely no internal underground or resistance that could give any infiltrated agent support. So my guess is that no such efforts were made for at least a year or more.

DB: *Mr. Bissell, you were in charge, in a sense, of the Bay of Pigs operation with the Agency, were you not?*

I was.

DB: *Could this have been part of an overall Bay of Pigs operation as opposed to in any way being a direction from the White House? In other words, could this have been something that the Agency just developed internally as its overall Bay of Pigs operation?*

I don't think this . . . In fact, I am quite clear that this plan was not developed in that way. I don't think it was even known to many, if any, of the individuals within the Agency that were concerned with the planning and preparation for the Bay of Pigs.

JK: *Mr. Edwards was not involved in the Bay of Pigs?*

No, he was not.

SC: *I believe you testified that you discussed the establishment of the Executive Action Capability with either Mr. Bundy or Mr. Rostow. Did I understand that correctly?*

Correct.

SC: *Who was it that first raised this subject, as you recall it?*

I have no recollection of who first raised it. My belief is that this would have come up as a subject very probably in conversations between myself and Mr. Rostow, and the reason I give that as my belief is that I had on a number of occasions discussed with Mr. Rostow the various kinds of capabilities, and especially unconventional ones, that the Agency should or might develop. At a somewhat later stage, for instance, he asked me and I asked for a small interdepartmental group to examine the ways of improving our military capabilities, and his thinking ran along the lines of developing these tools of action. And I think, therefore, that it is very probable that this came up in conversations with him, but which one of us would have coined the phrase, for instance, I don't know.

SC: *So far as you recall it, were there any plans for such a capability being developed at the Agency when you had your first conversation with him?*

Oh, I'm reasonably certain the answer is negative to that.

JK: *There was no such capability in the Agency prior to that?*

There was no separate organization, identified capability of that sort.

DB: *Did you have any discussions with any people in the White House during either the Eisenhower Administration or the Kennedy Administration to the effect of why can't you do something about Castro?*

Well, it's possible. I don't remember a specific case, if there were any. When you asked earlier if there had been any discussions of this during the Eisenhower Administration, the reason I said that there could have been was just [that] that sort of remark might easily have been made in a meeting. You know, is there any way that you could remove Castro and do something much simpler than the Bay of Pigs operation—that sort of remark could have been made in, for instance, a meeting of the Special Group. I don't happen to remember such a remark having been made in the Eisenhower Administration.

DB: *Would President Eisenhower himself have made such a remark, or was he not a member of it?*

He did not attend the Special Groups.

JC: *This small group that was formed by Mr. Edwards after your discussions, how many people were involved within the Agency?*

Well, I don't know that he formed a group. I think he conducted probably with the help of one other man in the Security Office such communications as there were.

DB: *Mr. Olsen, I think, has several additional questions in this area.*

ROBERT OLSEN: *Howard Hunt has stated in several of his writings that in connection with his work in preparation for the Bay of Pigs, he recommended an assassination of Premier Castro be undertaken either to precede or to be contemporaneous with the Bay of Pigs operation. Now, Mr. Hunt was working under your direction?*

Right.

RO: *At that time, was he not?*

Yes, he was.

RO: *Did such a recommendation from E. Howard Hunt ever come to your attention?*

I wouldn't be at all surprised. I don't have a specific recollection. It is the kind of thing he could have said in a meeting orally, and I don't remember any written proposal to that effect originating from Headquarters.

RO: *Is it your testimony that you have absolutely no recollection of an oral recommendation from Mr. Hunt to that effect?*

I don't have any specific recollection, but that doesn't mean that it couldn't have happened.

RO: *Do you have a general impression that it happened?*

I would suspect that he is telling the truth when he said that he made this recommendation. Whether he would have made it in my presence or to me, or to Colonel [J. C.] King or others, I don't know.

RO: *Mr. Bissell, there has also been testimony that has been taken by the staff of the Commission to the effect that a Bernard Barker, a contract agent of the CIA, or employee of the CIA, I believe it was at that time, made contact with the person acting in the Cuban community down in the Miami area and asked him about this time whether he would be willing to undertake an assassination. Do you have any knowledge of that?*

I don't remember that.

RO: *Were you aware, Mr. Bissell, in the period 1961 [to] early 1962 of there being a great deal of talk among Cuban exiles in this country of a desire to kill Fidel Castro?*

Again, I have to say I have no specific recollection of reading newspaper stories to this effect, or hearing reports through CIA channels, but it seems to me highly likely, given the nature of the situation, that there would have been talk of that sort.

RO: *A great many of the Cuban exiles in Florida in particular and elsewhere in the southern part of the United States at that time were being, in effect, utilized through front organizations that were being sponsored by the Agency, were they not?*

I think that is true, yes.

JK: *Was their discussion of targets there confined to Fidel Castro, or would it include [Ernesto "Che"] Guevara and others?*

Exclusively Castro.

NR: *Were not most of those Cuban organizations penetrated by Castro representatives?*

They were, indeed.

NR: *So that it would be very easy for double agents to report back to Castro what was going on?*

That's right, exactly. I think our judgment at the time, as a matter of intelligence—and I am now talking about after the Bay of Pigs operation in particular, but the same applies, by the way, to most of the preparation—I think our belief was that Castro was extremely well informed on what was going on. I don't think that he penetrated, so far as we knew, parts of that preparatory activity that were under the Agency's direct control, but all of the exile groups in Miami, including the political groups that we attempted to form and did form as front organizations, I'm quite sure he knew what was going on.

NR: *Did CIA know, have any information to the effect that [Lee Harvey] Oswald was trying to penetrate some of those groups?*

I don't remember that, Mr. Chairman.

JC: *Did it ever come to your attention in any way that Oswald had any interest in the Cuban situation or was associated with it in any way?*

Never. I don't ever remember hearing any association, in anything that associated him with that.

JK: *You mean prior to the assassination [of John F. Kennedy]?*

Prior to the assassination.

NR: *Did Bill Pauly work for you during that period?*

Yes, in a sense. I mean, he served as a messenger, but for the most part that was in the final days of the Batista regime and he was used in an effort to persuade Batista to leave the country.

DB: *Mr. Olsen?*

RO: *After the assassination of President Kennedy, when it became well known that Lee Harvey Oswald had been active in attempting to penetrate anti-Castro groups and had engaged in kind of a one-man operation for the Fair Plan for Cuba Committee, did it not occur to you, Mr. Bissell, that there might have been some relationship between the assassination of President Kennedy in attitude, at least, that Oswald might have developed in connection with his Cuban contacts in New Orleans?*

Well, I think I can honestly say it didn't particularly occur to me at that time. I read the usual newspaper accounts of the assassination, but it wasn't until a good deal later that these facts about Oswald surfaced, and I will honestly say that really didn't occur to me, that there was a connection.

DB: *Any other questions by the Commissioners on this particular area? Now, let's turn to the question of [Rafael] Trujillo, and I am going to ask Mr. Gray to interrogate you in that area.*

MG: *Mr. Bissell, we have gone over the circumstances surrounding the death of Trujillo just before you testified; is that correct?*

Correct.

MG: *Incidentally, in the thirteen years or so since you left the Agency, have you had occasion to review the documents dealing with that?*

I have not, no.

MG: *Now, in early 1960 the records I reviewed indicate that the government was maintaining a policy of nonintervention toward the Trujillo regime, and that in the early months of that year Ambassador [Joseph] Farland, who was then our Ambassador in the Dominican Republic, suggested that that policy be changed. Do you recall Ambassador Farland?*

I don't remember whether I ever met him personally, but I do have some recollection of this recommendation of his.

MG: *And do you recall anything about his background?*

He had been, I believe, in the FBI at one time and he had an intense interest in intelligence matters, and I think he had worked very closely with the CIA Chief of Station in the Dominican Republic.

MG: *Incidentally, was that station declared to the Dominican government?*

I believe it was.

MG: *That would mean that the government, even though the people were under cover, would know who they were and what they were?*

At least who some of them were.

MG: *Now the records reflect that when Mr. Farland returned to Washington for consultations in May of 1960, he stated that he had been in contact with some internal dissidents in the Dominican Republic, that they needed support from the United States, and in particular that they needed a number of high-powered rifles with telescopic scopes; and the Agency records reflect in conversations at the Agency that he further went on to say that the Dominicans planned to remove Trujillo from the scene through use of some sort of explosive device. Do you recall conversations along these lines?*

My recollection is that on the occasion of this visit of his to Washington he did urge that some military equipment or guns or other devices be made available to the internal dissidents. I have a dim recollection that this was to include one or more rifles with telescopic sights. I wouldn't have remembered the number unless you had mentioned it from the records.

MG: *The records also reflect that at the end of June or the beginning of July you approved of the furnishing of such rifles to the Dominican dissidents on the basis of a memorandum from Colonel King, who was then Chief of the Western Hemisphere Division, stating he had received authorization from Mr. [R. Richard] Rubottom, who was then Assistant Secretary of State. Do you recall such approval?*

This is all consistent with my recollection.

MG: *Would you, yourself, be involved in any negotiations with the Department of State as a normal matter?*

As a normal matter I would not have been involved with meetings at the Assistant Secretary of State level. I would have been involved if and when this matter was discussed in the Special Group.

MG: *And do you have any recollection of whether or not you were involved in any discussions involving the furnishing of these rifles?*

I don't remember that.

MG: *Now the records pretty much petered out at this point. They don't show that either this plan was killed or that the rifles were actually sent. It could not be developed whether they were or not. Do you have any recollection why that change of course might have taken place?*

None whatsoever.

MG: *At the beginning of '60 and '61 you presented a proposal to the Special Group to work with the internal dissidents and at the same time work with exile groups for paramilitary capability and things of that sort. Am I correct?*

Correct.

MG: *At the January 12, 1961, meeting at the instance of the Department of State, the Special Group, which approved these covert operations, approved the provisions to the Dominican internal dissidents of limited supplies of small arms and some explosive devices, some explosives, I believe. Do you have any recollection on that?*

Such as it is, it would confirm what you state.

MG: *In your opinion, when they approved the provision of small arms, were they talking about assassination weapons, or were they talking about guerrilla supplies and things of that nature?*

I would have said definitely the latter. However, I think it was the understanding of everybody in Washington that if you provided weapons to internal dissidents, and especially in fairly small numbers, and were contemplating truly guerrilla-like activities as distinguished from something on the scale of the Bay of Pigs, that these might well include assassination attempts. But the concept that I seem to remember was that this was a plan for, in effect, the logistic support of the internal dissidents, and it did not contemplate that the Agency or the Station would be planning specific operations for them to carry out.

MG: *So, it would be their operations and the Agency furnishing the equipment?*

Right.

MG: *And you draw a distinction there, do you?*

I do partly because in situations like that the Agency really has very little effective control over the group that is supported once the support has been granted.

MG: *And with respect to the explosives which were authorized, the Agency had been in contact with these internal dissidents and was aware that they did plan to use a bomb to kill Trujillo?*

I imagine that's the case, yes. I don't specifically remember.

MG: *And you then, if you don't recall your own state of mind, do you have any recollection as to whether other members of the Special Group knew what the purpose of the explosives might be?*

I believe that they would have, yes.

MG: *You think they would have?*

I think they would have, yeah.

MG: *Now, the dissidents had difficulty coming up with a workable. . . . Oh, very important, the Special Group attached the condition that these weapons and explosives be delivered to the representatives of the dissidents outside of the Dominican Republic, is that correct?*

Correct.

NR: *Did this get the approval of the White House?*

MG: *The records that I have reviewed show it was approved by the Special Group.*

There was also a White House Representative on the Special Group.

NR: *And you said earlier that any assassination or assassination attempt would have to have the highest approval?*

That's correct.

NR: *From the President?*

That is correct.

MG: *Would [it] include this sort of instance of furnishing material to people knowing what they are going to use it for, but where the Agency itself is not directing the operation?*

Well, let me answer that question this way: this clearly required and received the Special Group approval. The procedure always in the Special Group was that the White House Representative was presumed to inform the President of whatever was brought up in that Group that in his opinion should be brought to the President's attention. And furthermore, it was presumed to obtain presidential assent to action in those cases where he believed the personal assent of the President was called for.

JC: *And who was the White House Representative sitting on the Special Group at that time?*

Gordon Gray. And, given that procedure, it was frequently the case that a proposal would be made at one meeting of the Special Group. It would be discussed but no action taken until the next meeting, in part to provide this opportunity for the White House Representative to consult with the President to the extent he believed necessary.

MG: *Now, the dissidents were never able to develop a capability to receive these goods, nor did they ever provide any persons to be trained in the techniques of explosives and detonators and so forth?*

[Witness nodded in the affirmative.]

MG: *In March the Station cabled the request of Mr. [Henry] Dearborn, who was then Consul General, Trujillo's relations having been severed, for three .38 police specials to be turned over to the dissidents as a show of good faith and material support. Now, do you recall a discussion of the pistols and sending pistols by [diplomatic] pouch and so forth?*

Yes, I think I do remember that discussion, and for that purpose you have identified.

MG: *The record also reflects that on the first couple of occasions such requests were made by the Station, the Agency refused them, stating that it was inconsistent with the limitations imposed by the Special Group. The last request was not responded to for a period of some days, approxi-*

mately a week, following which you approved it. It appears there was a meeting in the State Department between some State Department officials and Agency officials, and the State Department memorandum of that meeting is not in their files. Based on that statement of documents, would you say whether or not you think there would have been State Department approval of pouching those pistols?

I think there almost certainly would have been State Department approval because there had been a specific prohibition imposed by the Special Group, and the Agency would not on its own authority have considered it possible to violate that prohibition unless and until there had been consultation with the State Department and concurrence by the State Department.

MG: *Would such consultation normally have been at your level or on Colonel King's?*

I think probably Colonel King's.

MG: *Assuming the State Department agreed to waive the Special Group restrictions and the Agency felt this was appropriate, would you have felt it necessary to go back to the Special Group in any formal fashion?*

I think probably not, but I think the Special Group members would have been informed of this action at the next meeting.

MG: *As I stated, the record reflects that the pistols were sent to the Dominican Republic and were passed to the dissidents.*

DB: *When, Mr. Gray, does the record reflect that?*

MG: *I believe it was March 25th. I don't have my notes with me.*

DB: *Of what year?*

MG: *1961.*

DB: *When does the record reflect the rifles were shipped?*

MG: *The Springfield rifles, the ones that Ambassador Farland talked about?*

DB: *The first rifles that went down.*

MG: *As near as I can tell on the rifles that I spoke about earlier, they never went to the Dominican Republic. . . .*

NR: *I would like to ask Mr. Bissell whether there was any question of violations of statutes by sending these weapons to a group through the use of the diplomatic pouch in relation to either a direct assassination attempt, or implied or possible?*

Well, I am not aware of any. In any case, I think that consideration did not arise at the time, and it obviously didn't arise in the minds of the State Department or the Special Group members or the Agency.

MG: *Now, following the shipment of the pistols, the Station cabled back that they had discovered in the Consulate three carbines that had been left behind by departing Naval personnel and requested authority to pass those. Again, Headquarters delayed, and again there was a meeting with the State Department. There is a memorandum of this meeting and it doesn't reflect [that] this subject came up, but the same day your Deputy, Mr. [Tracy] Barnes, approved the passage of the carbines. Would you say that this would . . .*

I think almost certainly that the State Department would have been consulted.

MG: *Now, following this, the Station and the Consul requested or relayed the request to the dissidents for some so-called grease guns, M-3 submachines, and three or four such weapons were pouched to the Dominican Republic. But with the Bay of Pigs and unsettled conditions in the Caribbean area they were never passed. Do you have any further recollection of the events preceding the death of Generalissimo Trujillo?*

I really have none, no.

MG: *Do you recall discussing these matters with any one, let's say, of your superiors or anyone outside of the CIA?*

No special discussions, nothing other than those that would routinely occur in reviewing projects with Allen Dulles internally and any special reports to the Special Group.

DB: *Did the Special Group give or reaffirm its position to pouch the weapons that were actually shipped in the spring of 1961?*

I don't know whether they did or not. As you have just heard, there is the indication that this was cleared with the State Department, and I have said that the normal procedure would be that everything cleared with the State Department and the Special Group at least would have been informed of this at its next meeting, and presumably, therefore, it accepted that, or at any rate did not reverse the agreed-upon position between the Agency and the State Department. . . .

MG: *Mr. Bissell, one other aspect of the cable traffic I should call to your attention is that shortly after the shipment of the pistols and the authorization to pass the carbines, there are several cables between the Station and the Agency Headquarters reflecting some concern whether Consul Dearborn is going to mention these matters in his correspondence with the Department of State. Now, I suppose there could be two reasons for that: either nobody in the State Department knew it, or very few people in the State Department knew it. Would you have any opinion as to which of those situations existed?*

Yes, I am almost certain it would have been the latter. Operational information of this sort was supposed to be confined to the Assistant Secretary concerned and his Deputy. Quite often, matters of somewhat lesser sensitivity involved the Station Desk officer in the State Department, but it was supposed to be limited to two or three below the level of the Undersecretary and the Secretary.

JK: *Was the Ambassador back in the country?*

I believe the Ambassador was back in the country, but in this particular case where Farland had been the Ambassador and was succeeded by Dearborn, they were both kept completely informed of what was going on at all times. The reason I say "in this particular case" is that these were two men who, I mentioned earlier, were intensely interested in intelligence and covert activity or operations of this sort. It was Farland, as you have heard, who really initiated the policy of supporting the dissidents, and they were, to my recollection, very fully informed of what was done.

DB: *Again, you mentioned earlier that you felt that the Special Operations Group approved possibly a shipment of rifles in 1960 which evidently were not shipped. Do you have any specific recollection of that approval, or do you have any specific recollection that it was approved or not?*

I don't have a specific recollection, but I take it there is a record of that.

DB: *Are you assuming that if they were shipped, they were approved, and if they were not shipped, you don't know whether it was approved?*

I think that is what I am saying, yes, as you are stating.

DB: *And if the record shows there were weapons shipped in March or April of 1961, then is it your specific recollection or just that you are assuming that the Special Operations Group approved that?*

No. I have some recollection of that one, the shipment involving the three revolvers, and I particularly remember the case that was made by Dearborn for doing it, which was to be able to issue some weapons to the dissidents as evidence of our continued interest and good faith.

DB: *And would that approval of the Operations Group then have been in the spring of 1961 or the first part of 1961, or still going back?*

I'm quite certain it would have been the first part of 1961.

JK: *Following the death of Trujillo, did the Agency give any help or aid to the surviving executioners?*

I don't remember that specifically. It was a confused period, of course, and the Agency was very active there in the next few months in making contact with the various political groups and individuals that emerged, but I do not remember anything specific of the sort you speak of.

DB: *The records of the Agency show that Mr. [John] McCone was not briefed about either the Castro plan or the so-called Executive Action Capability until some period after he became DCI, which would have been in 1963 or so. Do you know any reason why he was not briefed about this?*

Well, I think by the time he took office, which, as I remember it, was late in 1961—I think it was about the first of December in 1961—any plan to develop an Executive Action Capability internally was in abeyance. I don't know whether it ever was revived, certainly not while I was there, and I think that's the reason that he was not briefed on that. The possible plan of a possible Castro assassination had aborted; and although an individual was designated by me just about that time to begin to look at the potential operations against the Castro regime, that designation would have occurred only a few weeks before I left, and I don't think anything ever came of that. Bill Harvey, who was put into that position, was active in planning for a time, but I know that after a fairly short tour of duty he was removed, and so I am assuming the reason McCone was not briefed about these was that really nothing was happening worth bringing to his attention.

DB: *Any other questions on the assassinations before we turn to one final area?*

MG: *I do have one other question. Mr. [Richard] Helms was your Deputy for a portion of this time?*

He was.

MG: *And ultimately your successor?*

Right.

MG: *Was he involved in any of these operations or planning that you have described?*

Well, he was generally informed about them because he saw copies of all of the cable traffic that came through and sat in meetings with the Director and things of this kind. He was not actively involved in the Bay of Pigs preparations when that was going on. It was nearly a full-time job for me, and I was handling much of the rest of the business of the CS [Clandestine Service]. There's a chance that he would have been involved in the Dominican activities, but to just what extent I don't remember.

JK: *I have one question. This group that carried out the assassination in the Dominican Republic were not initially sponsored by the CIA?*

That's correct, sir. They came into existence on their own, and, as you have heard, it was Ambassador Farland's recommendation that they be supported. And I do want to emphasize, as I have said, that this was regarded by the Agency as a logistics support operation, in full knowledge that it was giving them the capability for violence. But nevertheless there is quite a distinction, or at least there was in our minds, between supporting an operation and either initiating it, organizing it, running it, and controlling it.

JK: *And this was not too long after the Trujillo assassination of a President of a friendly state?*

Exactly.

EDWIN GRISWOLD: *Did anyone give consideration as to whether this was a wise thing to do or a legal thing to do?*

Well, I would presume, sir, that consideration was given in the State Department. And as you have heard, it was the Ambassador who first recommended that this support operation be undertaken. This was then approved by the Deputy Assistant Secretary of State He is the approver of record, but this must have also included Tom Mann, who was the Assistant Secretary of State. It was discussed in the Special Group where it was approved at the Undersecretary level, and by a White House Representative; and the general presumption in the way the Agency's covert action operations were run was that the policy considerations of the wisdom of the action were a matter for the State Department, the White House, and, in a sense, the National Security Council and the Pentagon wherever its interests were relevant, which was in many of these.

EG: *But the CIA didn't regard itself as having any responsibility for either wisdom or legality?*

I wouldn't say that. I would not say that it had no responsibility for wisdom. The CIA obviously was represented both at the Special Group and on occasion with the ad hoc meetings when operations of this kind were discussed, and CIA representatives were quite often not backward in giving their views about wisdom. But this was not the part of the Agency's charter. I think that was recognized at the time, and it was one of Allen Dulles's repeated exhortations that the CIA does not make policy. It is there as an agency in this capacity. It is there to carry out policy decisions.

Now, as to legality, I think there was a real effort in the years that I was in the Agency to restrict the Agency's operation within what was believed to be its charter. And in that sense, at least, there was a concern for legality. I have to say that I am unclear myself as to how the concept of legality can be applied to many covert activities.

JC: *Who was the Undersecretary of State in the Special Group at that time?*

Well, back in '60 it was Mr. [Robert] Murphy, and in '61 it was Chester Bowles who was the Undersecretary. He did not represent the Department very often on the Special Group, and I don't remember whom he used for that purpose.

MG: *Mr. [Livingstone] Merchant was there at that time?*

Yes, I think he was.

EDGAR SHANNON: *Staying on this matter of approval as to the wisdom, you assumed the State Department had covered this, and that would mean you assumed the Secretary of State was informed?*

Yes, sir.

NR: *Was [Richard] Goodwin involved in any of this stuff?*

Dick Goodwin became somewhat involved in the Bay of Pigs operation, but very late in the game. For the most part, only after it was over in the business of picking up the pieces. I suspect that he was involved a bit in the Dominican operation, and I believe that he would have been one of its supporters and very sympathetic to it.

NR: *How about the Castro assassination attempt?*

No, I am almost certain that he knew nothing of that.

DB: *At least not during the time that you were with the Agency?*

That is correct, yes. . . .

DB: *The final area of inquiry that I want to go into pertains to recommendations you might have concerning Agency operations, or based upon*

your experience in the Agency and your experience both before in gov-
ernment and after in the business world. Do you have any specific recom-
mendations as to how to improve the operations of the Agency?

Well, as I have mentioned to you, Mr. Belin, I had a few that are
rather scattered and to which I do not attach any very great importance. I
had occasion a few years ago to do a paper on this, and I am going to
supply Mr. Belin [with] a copy of this if it is of interest to him. The main
thrust of that—I will put it this way—is that most of the Agency's so-
called failures, and especially its more massive ones, have taken the form
of a compromise of operations, or operations have been deemed to be
failures largely because they were compromised. That is not true in all
cases, by any manner of means. I mean, the Bay of Pigs is a notable exception. But in general that is true, and that had led me to argue, or really
to remind any readers of this essay to which I have referred, that the prime
expertise the nation should seek in a foreign Clandestine Service is an
ability to keep things secret, and to perform operations in secret and without compromise. And in part because of my own failings and shortcomings, by the late '60s the Agency already had, I thought, a rather lamentable
record of not being able to do this.

Now in reviewing the whole range of different kinds of covert operations, they involved propaganda operations, paramilitary operations, political action operations, and the whole range. And, with respect to each
of these, the Clandestine Service is not the place where one would expect
to look for professional competence, military competence—one would
look to the Pentagon. [In] competence in political analysis and political
science he would expect that the most competent people in the nation
would be elsewhere, and he would not look there for competent economists as such. The professional competence that the Clandestine Service
should have is, as I said, the ability to plan and organize and carry out
operations, both intelligence collection and such covert action operations
as are authorized with high security, and hopefully avoiding compromise.

Given that as its role, given its poor record, I suppose the thrust of
this paper was that every effort should be made to improve this aspect of
the Agency's operations. I made one organizational recommendation. It
is just one way of doing it. It was to propose that there be a small internal
staff in the Agency, in the Clandestine Service but with the direct line to
the DCI, that should scrutinize every proposed new operation before it is
initiated, and at least once a year should scrutinize every ongoing operation from one standpoint solely that was the prospect of compromise, and
their change from year to year. My feeling is that in the years that I was in
the [Agency]—it was the DDP [Deputy Director for Plans] in particular—lacking this or any similar mechanism, a number of our mistakes

occurred because there was not a strong-enough voice raised internally in the councils of the Agency in favor of the precautions that would be required to maintain secrets.

JK: *Would that not be a function of the Counterintelligence Division?*

Well, it could be, but actually the CI staff or Division did not function in that way and did not really attempt to perform that role. It was attempting really to protect the Agency and other parts of the government from penetration—and I really had in mind not the compromise by classic penetration—but if you stop to think of it, it hasn't produced the great, dramatic revelations of recent years. It is the compromise from letting too many people become knowledgeable of an operation and still letting the operation go on, of having inadequate cutouts, and having inadequate compartmentation both within the Agency and elsewhere in the government.

DB: *Now, you contrasted that with the Inspector General's review, which was a review of operations that had already been completed as opposed to current operations?*

That is correct. I am talking about before-the-fact review, and, for this, the sole purpose really of what I have identified as security.

DB: *You also had a recommendation . . .*

JC: *Excuse me. You made an exception for the Bay of Pigs in that. Now, why would you say that that operation failed?*

Well, that operation not only was dramatically compromised, and indeed it is questionable whether that could have been avoided under any circumstances, but it was also a military failure, and it seems to me perfectly clear-cut that that is the case.

My reference to that was to contrast this with, for instance, the by-now much publicized support to the Student Association and support to labor groups overseas. These operations, in my opinion, were tested by what they accomplished up to the point of compromise, and could perhaps still have accomplished, were brilliantly successful; and what destroyed those operations was purely and simply compromise.

I also happen to think that they are examples, although perhaps I have not looked into them enough to be confident of this opinion, but I am afraid I think they became examples of very sloppy procedures. I think that anyone who had looked by the early '60s at that set of operations coldly, and somewhat at arm's length from the standpoint of security, would have said that they are absolutely doomed to compromise, and quite soon, if major changes were not made.

After all, the very fact that, for instance, in the Student Organization you had new officers every year and most of the officers were knowledgeable of the source of funding, it was absolutely inevitable that that would be brought up before long. And, indeed, a state of mind had developed, I think, that it really would not do much harm if it were blown. I think that state of mind was perhaps perfectly proper with regard to the radios because they really had been blown before, but there are instances in my view of operations that did achieve notable results, and which eventually failed and had to be ended for the reason of compromise.

DB: *You have also had some recommendations concerning the type of personnel that the Agency ought to recruit.*

I will mention, before touching on that, that I had one other specific one, which is really the subject of long-standing discussion inside of the Clandestine Service. I felt the Agency had come to rely much too heavily on official cover and was using its official cover again somewhat carelessly, and it is a very difficult job to build up unofficial cover, either governmental or nongovernmental. But I felt that far too little was being done about that. Mr. Belin refers to a quite unrelated recommendation of mind. I was fearful that the course the Agency was on was placing more and more reliance on staffing, on men and women brought in fairly young, in many cases right out of college or soon after college, trained in the Agency and then spending or planning to make life careers there, somewhat in the fashion of the military services and of the Foreign Service. I think that that is a perfectly appropriate pattern for those other services, but my own belief is that one of the great strengths of the Agency as a corps of individuals in, say, the mid-'50s under Allen Dulles was that it attracted men from all walks of life; and because it was such a new organization at that time, most of its officers and all of its senior people had had some other kind of professional experience and accomplishment before they came into the organization.

It had quite a scattering of men who had had military experience, it had some professionals like myself, it had lawyers—and Helms himself, before his OSS period, had been a journalist—and it had a wide range of skills. I do not mean those skills were important to be used. I never used economics in the Agency, and Helms I don't think ever used journalism. But my point is, I think when it [the Agency] is engaging in the kind of business it is, it is better to have a variety of backgrounds, and not to have more than perhaps half of its personnel men who were in there for lifelong careers.

This relates to my remarks about official cover and its overuse. The pattern that I think was developing by the beginning of the '60s in the Clandestine Service was that its members more and more thought of their careers as a little different in kind, and a little removed, from Foreign Service careers. They expected to spend a life doing tours of duty in every case under official cover, and usually identified to the host government. And, in short, to follow much the same career pattern as the Foreign Service.

I believe that this is not consistent, really, with the maintenance of the state of mind that ought to animate the Clandestine Service.

DB: *Any other questions by members of the Commission?*

RO: *I have one that I would like to get kind of on the record. Mr. Bissell, there have been people responsible or irresponsible who have suggested that because you and Allen Dulles and General Cabell were all terminated from the Agency, in effect, by President Kennedy within a fair period of time after the failure of the Bay of Pigs, that the three of you and other people in the Agency would have had a motive to retaliate against President Kennedy. Could you describe for us what you know of your relationship and that of General Cabell and Allen Dulles with President Kennedy after the termination of your respective periods of service with the Agency?*

I can't say very much about the other two gentlemen. I am sure that Allen on occasion saw the President, and I have every reason to believe that it was a friendly relationship. I rather doubt whether General Cabell had any direct contact with him after that.

I did have contact with him on perhaps two or three occasions. He asked me quite soon after I left the Agency to lend a helping hand to the then head of the rather new Alliance for Progress, and he also asked me to do a paper for him, that is, for the President, which I did do, on the question of what lessons from the Marshall Plan [for postwar European recovery] might have been applicable to the Alliance for Progress.

On another more lighthearted occasion, he got me to come over to the White House to give him some advice on cruising off the Maine coast. And I suppose the final time I saw him, which couldn't have been but very shortly before his death, was the award of a medal. I think I can honestly say that the relationship was an extremely friendly one in my case and, as far as I could judge, mutually so. I had quite a number of contacts with him in the roughly eight months that I was still in the Agency after the Bay of Pigs, and I can say the same of that period.

And finally, for the record, I perhaps should say that shortly before I did finally leave the Agency, John McCone, with the President's knowledge and concurrence, and also that of the then Attorney General, asked me to stay on in the Agency, but in a somewhat different position than that of the DDP. I thought it was wiser for me to leave.

LYMAN LEMNITZER: *I have a question. Don't you believe that in carrying on the covert operation of the magnitude of the Bay of Pigs, that compartmentation was one of the weaknesses? Compartmentation in a clandestine operation to maintain cover and security was absolutely essential, but on the other hand, on an operation of that size with military aspects involved, it seemed to me that compartmentation was a weakness in the preparation of carrying out the operation, not to mention the changing decisions that took place along the line as the operation unfolded.*

Well, I certainly agree with you, General Lemnitzer, in the change in decisions, and I probably would agree with you if you and I discuss specific examples of the compartmentation. I will say, however, that some of the compartmentation, I think to this day, was absolutely essential, and I will give you an example. We really could not allow the Cuban politicals in Miami, the exiled members of the political parties, to visit the brigades in training in Guatemala, and the reason for that was that the brigade was shaping into a disciplined and unified force, and the politicians were totally insecure and at odds with one another on almost everything. There was a great deal of intriguing in Miami because if one politician could become identified in the eyes of the brigade, and if the operation was then successful, he would have been the leader.

So there is an example of where I think we were right to enforce compartmentation. But I don't think that is the kind of thing you have in mind, and I think I would agree with what you have in mind.

LL: *Well, specifically I have in mind that within the Joint Chiefs of Staff at the time we could not find out what the diplomatic estimate of the situation was; that if this force did get ashore and up in an accessible place, that the Cuban people would rally to it; and, as a matter of fact, I have not found out yet what the diplomatic estimate of the situation was.*

Yes, I agree with you. That is an unfortunate example.

EG: *Let me ask you, did the Bay of Pigs operation have anything to do with the gathering of intelligence?*

No, sir. It was somewhat dependent on it, but it didn't have anything to do with it.

EG: *Then what business is it of the CIA to engage in operations which have nothing to do with the gathering of intelligence?*

NR: *Covert.*

Well, the category that came to be called covert action operations is justified under a much-quoted clause in the CIA's charter which refers to such other activities as the National Security Council directs.

EG: *Is there any evidence that the National Security Council directed this operation?*

There is a question of definition of exactly what constituted the National Security Council at the time of that operation, but I will say that the plans for the operation were repeatedly reviewed by a group that included the President of the United States, the Secretaries of State and Defense, and the Assistant Secretary of State who was involved, the Chairman of the Joint Chiefs, or the acting Chairman of the Joint Chiefs, and then [the] Army colonel, now general, I believe, who had been designated the chairman of a group of three officers by the JCS to review plans and preparations. So I would say that rarely has what started out as a clandestine operation been more intimately directed by a group, by those individuals who are, I believe, the members of the NSC.

NR: *Was that both President Eisenhower and President Kennedy?*

No, this was President Kennedy, and this began with the new Administration.

NR: *And did the brigades have reason to expect that if they were successful, they would get support from the U.S. military forces?*

No, [they] had no reason to believe that.

LL: *Isn't a part of the answer to this question the comment made by President Kennedy after the operation failed that he was responsible, that it was at his direction that this operation was carried out?*

Yes, I think that's true, General Lemnitzer, but you remember, I am sure, just as I do, the degree to which the group I have identified was repeatedly involved in review of plans and whatnot.

THOMAS SOAPES: *I believe you went to the CIA in about 1954?*

RICHARD BISSELL: Yes, I think January of '54, as I remember it.

And, I believe, from reading the Columbia [University Oral History] interview, your first major project was involved with the U-2 [reconnaissance aircraft]?

Yes, in a sense that's true. I was somewhat involved in the Guatemala operation . . . but the first major activity that I had charge of was the development of the U-2.

Conducted by Dr. Thomas Soapes in Farmington, Connecticut, on November 9, 1976. Oral History Interviews, Dwight D. Eisenhower Library, Abilene, Kansas.

What were the major problems in that project that you had to overcome?

Well, they need to be divided at the outset into two series. One included the technical problems of getting an aircraft designed, developed, built, getting its equipment to work, learning how to use it. The other set of problems had to do with organization, personnel, and training. I think the nature of the technical problems is pretty self-evident when you consider that we were trying to achieve performance in certain dimensions exceeding any that had been achieved before. And we were trying to do it very fast indeed, and in deep secrecy.

In terms of speed, was there a target date for completion?

Well, very early in the game, I would say within two weeks of the authorization, the go-ahead, which was at the beginning of December of '54—Kelly [Clarence L.] Johnson had established a date in August 1955 for the first flight of the aircraft. So he was allowing himself less than eight months to first flight, from a time when he had not yet finished his engineering drawings, which I think is very nearly unprecedented. I believe there were one or two new aircraft built that quickly during World War II, but I'm not sure that there were any done faster.

I had no technical background for this task and had to learn as I went along. The technical decisions were pretty largely left to the contractor, primarily Johnson, and, to a degree, to Pratt & Whitney Aircraft up here. I think the problems that took up most of my time, energy, and attention were those in the areas of organization, organizational relationships, and personnel. I found myself running an organization in which, broadly, there was about one-third Air Force personnel on active duty (but assigned to the Agency so that I was actually their commander for this purpose); about one-third Agency personnel (including people in the fields of finance, procurement, and also security and communications); and then in the field units about one-third contract employees (mainly Lockheed, but also some from Perkin-Elmer and a few from Hycon, another camera firm on the West Coast). I received a very liberal education in the difference with respect to their terms of employment, privileges, prerogatives, rights, and duties as between government civilians, military personnel, and civilian industrial employees. Forming harmonious teams of these groups took a surprising amount of time and attention. I think it was successfully accomplished, but one had to be very sure of equity in matters like rest-and-recreation leave, trips from Adan [Turkey] back to West Germany, and this kind of thing.

Basically personnel administration matters?

A lot of that, yes.

As opposed to the concept of the mission and that sort of thing? That wasn't . . .

Yes, there was no problem of that sort. First, a relationship had to be hammered out with the Air Force and then to be maintained. The hammering out was bureaucratically a moderately bloody affair, but that was accomplished by mid-'55. After that, the relationship with the Air Force really was very smooth. . . .

In terms of the origin of the project, were you involved in developing the concept from the beginning, or is this something just thrust upon you?

Definitely the latter.

So you are not in a position to give insight into the origins of the idea of the U-2?

Well, not very much, no. . . . But early in '54, nearly a year before the authorization to proceed with the U-2 project, the Air Force, on its own, had solicited proposals from four air-frame builders for very high-altitude reconnaissance aircraft. The proposals were simply in sketch form. They were design concepts, not what later came to be full-blown proposals. One of the submissions was by Lockheed, and it presented the technical concept of the U-2. Another one was a stripped-down Canberra-type bomber. There were four, although I don't remember the other two. The U-2 concept was one of the ones turned down by the Air Force. They did have a few of the lightweight Canberra configuration built and flown, and they did use them occasionally for high-altitude reconnaissance. So the technical concepts originated, really, in the Air Force and in the industry, whether identifiably for overflights or just as an invulnerable high-altitude rconnaissance aircraft I have no idea. Of course, the idea of the project as a major intelligence operation (and I'm sure this has all been documented) originated with the so-called Surprise Attack study, undertaken at the direction of President Eisenhower and under the chairmanship of James Killian by the so-called Technological Capabilities Panel of the President's Science Advisory Committee.* Specifically, it grew out of the work of the TCP's Intelligence Subcommittee, which was chaired by Edwin H. Land and had Ed Purcell and James Baker (the prominent astronomer) as members, as well as someone from A. D. Little and someone from Vanderbilt University. In any case, it's this group that I really credit with boring in on the concept of overflight as a means of obtaining intelligence. They got hold of these conceptual designs that had been sub-

---

*Editor's note: The report of this group was entitled, "Meeting the Threat of Surprise Attack."

mitted to the Air Force, decided that they were very interested in the U-2, and finally crystallized this into a specific proposal.

In the Columbia interview you indicated that Eisenhower kept very tight control over where the flights went, frequently disapproving certain proposals, approving others. As you were frequently present when he made those decisions, could you discern what his priorities and objectives were in approving and disapproving certain flights?

The approval and disapproval of proposed missions, I think, had to do very largely with time-dependent circumstances—more with that than with any details of the proposed mission plan. There would be periods—well, for instance, shortly after a mission had been flown—when he would be reluctant to authorize another. I think he would want to let the whole provocation cool off before risking it again. He would be influenced by whether there had been a diplomatic protest—as you probably know, there were at least two of those that I remember and there may have been a third—and by whether the mission had gone in part undetected or had been accurately tracked, and things of this kind. I think lots of other circumstances also influenced him and influenced [Secretary of State John] Foster Dulles to feel at one point that they could afford to allow a mission to be run at another point or that they couldn't. I suppose that the apparent sensitivity of the mission target or of the area to be covered by the flight may have influenced them a little, but I don't really think it did much.

As I've said, Eisenhower's first authorization to me was simply for a certain number of days, without specifying any number of missions authorized or anything to do with their geography. And I don't really believe that throughout the life of the project he was greatly influenced in the go-no-go decision about where a flight would be flown. I think he was influenced favorably in several cases by the possibility that we, hopefully, could fly missions from a Pakistan base with a much lower chance of being tracked by the Russians. But it was the possibility of greater anonymity rather than the geography covered that I think would have weighed in his decision. As to corrections in flight plans, when he had approved the mission for a particular date we would bring in the flight plan and show it to him. I don't know quite what influenced him. He would sometimes cut out particular legs or say, "Well, don't go from A to B to C, go from A to C." And I think probably it was a quick layman's effort to cut down exposure and risk more than anything else. Don't take in unnecessary targets. Don't expose yourself any more than you need to.

Of course, one question that was frequently raised about [Francis Gary] Powers's [U-2] flight was that it was so close to the Summit [in

Paris between Eisenhower and Khrushchev]. Do you recall any concern at that time about being so close to the Summit?

You perhaps remember better than I do now, that when the authorization for that flight was given, it was going to expire a certain number of days before the Summit. That obviously reflected a concern—I think, really, probably as much as anything on Foster Dulles's part—that there should not be a provocative act just before the Summit occurred. With hindsight, I've often wondered why that date wasn't put further in advance of the Summit meeting. But at the time the fact that a date had been set made it clear to me that the desire to avoid a provocation during such a meeting had been recognized and had been weighed and taken into account, and competent authority had fixed what they thought was an adequate safety margin. I certainly didn't question it.

You don't remember anyone else raising the issue?

I really don't, no. Before the fact, no.

In regard to Guatemala, . . . what were the concerns of the time that made Guatemala such an important country for such an important mission?

I think, really, nothing more than the fear that it would become the first, rather definitely Communist-influenced foothold in the Western Hemisphere. After all, it was years before Castro. But there was a great sensitivity about communism in all of Latin America. I think, really, the fact that this appeared to be the first country where the Communists might be able to achieve effective control is what focused the spotlight.

So there wasn't anything in particular about Guatemala that was important; it was just that any country in that situation might well have received the same attention?

I think so. I think perhaps in those days, the U.S. Government's sensitivity was greater about the whole Caribbean Basin than about southern South America. But that's the only possible qualification. . . .

What about in Indonesia? In '57, I believe that there was some activity in regard to Sukarno.

Well, I got quite involved in the Agency's support of the rebellion on Celebes and on Sumatra against Sukarno's central government. I did so, really, working with General [Charles Pearré] Cabell, who was the Deputy Director at that time. I don't know how much you've read about the Agency's involvement in that whole affair.

I've really not read too much at all.

It was, in effect, an uprising by small outlying garrisons. Certainly, no large number of regular Indonesian Army units was involved, only small groups in those two completely separated areas. My most recent refresher on that comes from having read a draft of a biography of Allen Dulles, which goes into it at a good deal of length. In that draft it is emphasized that Foster Dulles, among others, vigorously approved and urged Agency support of the rebels against Sukarno; and from the nature of the geography and everything else, the support had to be almost entirely by air, although there may have been a couple of small-boat operations. The form it took was the infiltration of communicators and of arms and ammunition and other equipment—all of this, however, on quite a modest scale.

The reason for my personal involvement was that the U-2 operation was fully operational at this point, and one thing that we did was to fly quite a lot of reconnaissance missions over that whole area of the world. But also with that organization and with the experience I had, Cabell relied on me to participate in some of the planning of the operation. Desmond FitzGerald was, I think, most actively in charge, and I suppose my involvement essentially would take the form of attending planning sessions in Cabell's office. The operation was, of course, a complete failure. The regular army landed on the south coast of Sumatra and moved inland with very little resistance. And also there was the embarrassment of a plane being shot down with, I think, one or two Agency or Air America [operated in the Far East by the CIA] air crew, who were then held for a number of years. But that's the nature of my involvement.

The assistance there was, then, military as opposed to political or economic-type of activity?

Yes, correct. The rebellion didn't last long enough for economic measures. Insofar as the assistance was political, it consisted really of the fostering of contacts. At least two years before the rebellion the Agency had been approached by representatives of some of the political parties in Indonesia, had given them some financial support, and had thus made contact with a number of political figures in the country. Almost all the people—I think it's fair to say all the people the Agency had dealt with—eventually ended up as opponents of Sukarno. So the background of the paramilitary activity was an essentially political-action kind of operation, through which some of the contacts had been developed, that then carried over to the military.

The charter for covert operations was the 5412 memorandum?

Correct.

Were you involved in the origins of that?

Not at all. I think it probably preceded my appearance in the Agency, and it certainly preceded my subsequent direct activity in the Clandestine Service.

One mechanical question I'd like to explore is, where did the ideas for clandestine operations begin?

Well, I suppose one could say that they would come from a number of different sources. On occasion, individuals in the Agency would be asked by State Department officers if they could accomplish a certain type of operation or accomplish some result by a clandestine operation. I'm inclined to think that some of the operations—if they involved the support of political parties (essentially the financial support of political parties) and sometimes covertly organized propaganda or information activities—originated in the State Department. Typically, however, the sequence of events would be that a CIA branch chief, country desk officer, division chief, or station chief overseas (or their colleagues) would conceive of the idea of a project, or we would perhaps encounter an opportunity. I would call it "an encounter" if someone in another country approached a representative of the Agency deliberately to solicit help in some kind of an operation. In short, I suspect that most ideas were generated from Agency personnel or from foreigners who were in contact with them, were then refined, and then, of course, brought in almost every case to the attention of State Department people.

The Church Committee [investigating the Intelligence Community] in its report said it was undecided whether or not Eisenhower really wanted Lumumba assassinated. What's your reaction to that conclusion?

I am not undecided at all. I think that's probably the one perfectly clear case, though I don't know whether the President ever said that in as many words. If he did, he presumably said it to Gordon Gray. Gordon Gray would have been the communication link here. But when Gordon Gray comes into the Committee meeting and says that his "associate" is very eager indeed that Lumumba be got rid of—and no doubt who the associate is, no doubt at all—the only ambiguity in my view might be in a phrase like "got rid of." Because, after all, nobody wanted to commit an assassination or to plan an assassination if there was some other way of getting rid of the individual.

My own belief, about which, as I said, there isn't any doubt in my mind, is that the President did want a man whom he regarded (as did lots of others, myself included) as a thorough scoundrel and a very dangerous one, got rid of. He would have preferred if it could be done in the nicest possible way, but he wanted it done and wasn't prepared to be too fussy about how it was done. I would really place heavy odds that that's the message he communicated to Gordon Gray and that Gordon Gray passed along.

So there were a range of options that could have been used to carry out Eisenhower's desire, but he was not ruling out assassination?

That is my view. That is my belief of what his position or instruction was, yes.

This question is, I suppose, more informed by our current state of mind and reaction to this sort of thing. How believable was it to you at that time that an order would come from the President of the United States to assassinate somebody?

It was quite believable. I would say it was pretty thoroughly believable.

Believable because of precedent or . . .

No, but at least as believable of the next President, who was a very different kind of person in age, background, training, and everything else. And if anything, more surprising to me coming from Eisenhower than from Kennedy.

The reason I raised the question was on the basis of my own background in military intelligence, where they taught us that when you get a piece of information or directive, you evaluate it on two scales: one, how reliable is your source; another one is how believable is the information. And that raises the question not only of how believable is it that the President would want someone assassinated, but also the line of communication to you from the President in terms of its reliability. Now your line of communication would be directly from Allen Dulles?

Yes. In this case the line of communication was a very clear one because it was from a Special Group, with the input to the Special Group being from Gordon Gray and the link from the Special Group to the Agency being Allen Dulles.

Now I'll tell you something that I don't think is in the Church Committee report but that I saw in the course of looking over some of the papers and cables that were sent. This is an anecdote, if you will, having to do with this matter that bears on the line of communication. There was one critical cable of instruction that went out at some point in the month of August, and I guess this would have been in 1960, wouldn't it? I'd have to check my memory as to the year, but it was the time when the assassination planning took place. It was a very vigorous cable indeed saying that every effort must be made to get rid of this individual,

Lumumba. The cable had been signed off, because I saw the copy, by Allen, so there's no doubt that it was sent on Allen's authority. Interestingly enough, I had not signed off on it and there's no indication that I had seen it, but my Deputy, Dick Helms, had.

Now that, in my mind, could not have happened if I'd been in town. Allen simply would not have played it that way. I think there was an indication that Allen, in fact, wrote the cable. But very often if he was himself writing an operational order of this kind, he would not have it sent until I had seen it or, in my absence, Dick Helms, although he obviously had the authority to do so. From this I did some reconstructing with diaries as best I could, and I'm pretty sure that it was a time when I was away on vacation, which would explain the absence of my initials. Here you have a quite explicit cable of instruction being, I think, drafted—I think there was evidence of that—and definitely signed by Allen and sent to the field. You have minutes of the Special Group that I think are quoted in the Church Committee report or at least were available to the Church Committee.

There's only the one major ambiguity that I've already referred to. It just makes every kind of sense to me that neither Eisenhower nor any other President ever said, "I want that man assassinated." What he would say was, "I want that man got rid of."

Obviously, if he could have been kidnapped and kept some place for four or five years incommunicado, probably everybody concerned, probably any President, would have been much happier with that. But also any President, and notably, I think, Mr. Eisenhower, would have realized that if you go out to kidnap a guy in the middle of Africa and he's your enemy, the chances of his ending up getting killed are very good indeed. People can't exercise that kind of detailed and precise control over events when they're working through layers of Agency, sub-Agency, and ally. So it never occurred to me that the President necessarily used the word "assassination," and it certainly never occurred to me that he preferred that means of solving the problem to others that would remove the character from the scene of action, but I have not the slightest doubt that he wanted Lumumba got rid of and he wanted it badly and promptly, as a matter of urgency and of very great importance. Allen's cable conveyed that sense of urgency and priority.

Looking at the other end of the line of communication, the Field Station officer, the Church Committee report quoted the station officer as saying that when he heard about the scheme that he called it a "wild scheme professionally." Was there normally a route for the station officer to communicate feelings like this back to Headquarters?

Oh, yes, he could have made that comment back if he didn't like the operational plan, and indeed he should have if he didn't like the operational plan. I don't remember enough about the operational plan to know. I must confess, I seem to remember having, myself, some doubts as to whether it was going to prove to be workable.

Was it possible—and here I'm talking generally about covert operations—for instructions to be given or operations to go on within the CIA without Allen Dulles knowing precisely what was happening? Was it a tightly administered Agency, or was there some degree of looseness?

I would say in general it was a pretty tightly administered Agency. Now, as you of course are aware, the number of activities that were classified as separate operations with operational names and, in the larger ones, the number of different phases of the operation or events comprised within it added up altogether to a formidable total. So obviously no one person could possibly have detailed knowledge of everything that was going on. However, I felt that it was a very tightly administered Agency in this sense, that up and down the line there was a pretty clear understanding of what operational decisions raised questions of policy requiring pretty senior-level decisions or senior-level authority and what ones did not raise questions of policy and therefore could safely be made at the level of the station chief or the case officer or what have you. And with a pretty clear understanding of that, I saw very few cases, I hardly remember any that I observed in the cable traffic (which, of course, was enormous) of subordinates on their own making decisions that they should have referred higher up. Well, occasionally you have to, that is, circumstances require that you act on your own authority when it would have been better to obtain approval. I suspect if Allen were alive and you asked him that question, he'd probably point the finger at me more than at any one person who ever worked for him. That's in one context and is perhaps in part facetious, but I really think that I did this very, very little with Allen.

There was one area of the Agency within which he knew comparatively little of what went on—almost nothing from day to day and week to week—and that was the U-2 operation. That was the most compartmented and self-contained activity within the Agency. It was the only part of the Agency that had its own operational cable traffic which did not go to Allen's office and of which he did not see any selection except cables that I personally took him. Now there was, in my view, a very good reason for this. The kinds of decisions that were involved and the subject matter of the cable traffic was heavily operational and even logistical. "Do we run a special flight of the C-54 from Wiesbaden to Turkey to carry such-and-such people back from leave and to carry such-and-such spare parts?" Well, that's the kind of thing that Allen Dulles really shouldn't have had anything to do with whatsoever. And because it was a kind of quasi-military operation (the U-2), most of the traffic had to do with, as I say, logistical matters, and a great deal of it was what I identified earlier, essentially personnel management.

The important decisions about the U-2 were ones that he always, of course, participated in. These were the go-no-go decisions. I don't mean the decision to go tonight as against tomorrow night, but I mean the decision that you've been granted authority to go if weather permits. Now having been granted authority to fly such-and-such a mission weather permitting, it was entirely my decision (which I never took to anybody else) when I looked at the weather to see whether the weather'd be good enough and whether I would authorize the flight. Again, in the preparations for and conduct at the Bay of Pigs operation, there were an awful lot of operational decisions that I couldn't possibly take back to Allen. But I would say it was a very tightly administered Agency.

What about coordination with the White House, State, and with DOD [Department of Defense]? Was there adequate information passed between all of those agencies and the Agency?

I think so. Most of the coordination was with the State Department, and that became, in the years that I was there (not because of me but it came to be in that period) a very tight coordinating relationship. There were few decisions made that weren't discussed at either division level or bureau level at least with opposite members in the State Department. Also while I was there the 5412 Committee (which has had so many other names since) became much more formal and, if you like, a more effective channel for coordination with the White House.

You would coordinate through Gray or [Andrew] Goodpaster?

Yes. Well, the U-2 operation was always through Goodpaster. The 5412 liaison was Gordon Gray as security advisor to the President. And then, of course, later it was McGeorge Bundy under Kennedy. I believe that was very adequate, and I think the individuals in question themselves felt that it was.

You never had complaints or complaints never came to your attention from Gray or Goodpaster or from State, DOD, saying we didn't know about this?

No. DOD was a little different. There was an Under Secretary present at this 5412 group, at Special Group meetings, and there was some coordination at the staff level, but the Pentagon was much less involved in most of the policy decisions that concerned Agency activities.

I'd like to turn in the last few minutes that we have here to Cuba. We've been told that Allen Dulles presented a plan to Eisenhower in early 1960 for the harassment of Castro by sabotaging sugar refineries and that Eisenhower's response to that was, "If you're going to do that, why not do something that will lead to his downfall?" and that Dulles then returned to the Agency and came up with a four-point plan. Do you recall that sequence of events?

I don't. There's no particular reason why I should except that, let's see, by '60 I had been the DDP [Deputy Director for Plans] for a year, I guess. And I think that after such an exchange Allen would certainly have communicated the results to me, not necessarily to me alone. He would probably have asked me to come in with J. C. King, who was the chief of the Western Hemisphere Division, and talked to us together, and he might have had somebody else in there as well. But I think it more probably would have been J. C. King and myself, and I'm really very surprised that it didn't proceed in that manner. To answer your question, I don't happen to remember any such session with Allen. Although I remember the plan that became the Bay of Pigs operation, the stage it was in early in 1960, I don't really remember the very earliest stages when the initial planning was being done in the WH [Western Hemisphere] Division.

Was it normal procedure that plans would not come to your direct attention until they were fairly well along in their planning stage, that something like the Western Hemisphere Division or similar divisions would begin them?

That could happen, yes. That could very easily happen, and quite often did. I would say, as I said to you earlier, the shaping up of a concept of an operation was much more apt to start in the Division or even in a station in the field than to start at my level and result in an instruction from me to the Division. What I don't remember about the beginning of the Bay of Pigs plan is an occasion when either Allen or I told the WH Division to get busy on a plan.

We've talked some about the administration of the Agency, and I really would like to know something about Allen Dulles as a personality, as a person to work with, as a supervisor. Could you give me some sort of a sketch of your remembrance of the man, Allen Dulles?

I suppose I'll start off by saying that I became extremely fond of him and a great admirer of his. I had known him for quite a few years, also Foster [Dulles] and their sister [Eleanor], when I joined the Agency. At the time that I joined it, however, I didn't know Allen very well, though I admired him. My first several months there were very inactive, rather dull. This didn't bother me; it had been apparent from the start that I wasn't going to fit into a pre-existing job in the Agency. But I saw a good deal of Allen; and then, of course, with the beginning of the U-2 project, which really totally absorbed me for quite a long time, I saw him very,

very frequently. He was basically a good delegator, notably in that project. He backed me up: he never interfered with me. He was just an ideal superior from my standpoint. I don't think he ever felt that he wasn't being adequately informed in the U-2 case. And, as I say, he didn't really have to exercise very much control. He relied quite heavily on Cabell with his Air Force background, and I saw Cabell constantly. As I've said, the kinds of decisions that Allen should have been and was concerned with on the U-2 were the policy decisions, which were fairly infrequent. Actually, they were made by Foster Dulles and the President really rather than Allen himself. Well, that's not a very responsive, partial answer, but let me continue.

When I became DDP, I became more vividly aware than I had been of a habit of Allen's which for the first time began to concern me quite directly: that of dealing with my subordinates directly. On one occasion I got quite angry and I think I probably wrote him an angry memorandum, but, in any case, I argued with Allen and he said firmly, "I am going to talk any time I want to, to anybody in this Agency about anything, and I'm not going to do it only through you." He added, "The rule is that any time I give an instruction to any subordinate of yours, that individual is supposed to clear it with you before carrying it out. If you don't agree with what I have told your subordinate to do, you can bring it back to me and we can talk it out. If your subordinates don't follow that rule, if they go and do things that I told them to do without checking with you, that's because you don't have proper discipline. It's your problem, not mine."

Well, I stewed over this for some days and Allen was completely uncompromising. He wasn't going to change and he wasn't going to discuss the matter any further. It was partly, I think, for that reason that Allen had the reputation in Washington—or at least I felt that he had the reputation—of being a bad administrator. That's one of those cliché characterizations and it was quite wrong. Allen was a somewhat untidy administrator, notably in the way that I have just illustrated. He didn't always go down the line of command, even though this Agency was a much more hierarchic organization than the State Department, for instance. It had overtones of a military organization about it still. Yet Allen would often go three echelons down to ask a question.

I became a complete convert to his way of operating after I'd lived with it for a few months. He never had done that, you understand, to the U-2 project because he couldn't get into that box. He didn't know what to ask: he didn't know who to ask. I'd kept that box closed. But he knew all the people in the Clandestine Service, notably the division chiefs, and I became convinced that one of Allen's greatest strengths as an executive was that he had, on a sample basis at least, a depth of knowledge of what was happening in the Agency and of the people in the Agency.

In the three years that I was DDP, whenever there were important personnel appointments or assignments to be made—a new chief or station, a new division chief, a new deputy division chief—these, of course, I had to talk over with Allen. He would have been most displeased, and rightly, if I had ever acted on these without talking to him. On quite a few occasions I came to Allen with a recommendation to appoint a specific individual to a specific job, and I would say that nearly half the time Allen disagreed. I will certainly say to you, I believe it's true, that in every single case where Allen disagreed with me and persuaded me, perhaps reluctantly, to do something else, I was convinced with hindsight [that] he was right and I was wrong. After a few experiences of that kind, I wouldn't have been willing to make any single appointment without consulting with him because I admired his judgment and it was proven in my eyes. It was thoughtful. He would frequently, in discussing such a matter, a personnel matter, bring up a consideration or an aspect of an individual's competence or an aspect of a job that I hadn't thought about. And I came greatly to value his position as a counselor in these matters.

On the substance of policy, I quite often disagreed with him. I was quite activist and he was, on the whole, I think, the wiser. I never counted these cases up in my mind in the same way, so I couldn't give you even a guess at how often when Allen didn't let me do what I wanted to, I concluded that he'd been right, and what percentage of the time I felt after the fact that I'd been right. But I'm sure I thought he'd been right a fair proportion of the time. Generally speaking, we didn't have very many disagreements; at least we didn't have many that we couldn't talk out. And our manner of working together was very seldom that of the recommendation and then concur or reject or modify or overrule. Obviously, I'd go in with things and talk to Allen about them. If I had a position, I would try to persuade him of it. And if he somewhat disagreed, he'd try to persuade me of his view. Obviously, in the end his view would prevail as the superior officer, as indeed it should. But I found that that whole relationship of talking over personnel matters I mentioned—talking over organizational matters with Allen, talking over most policy matters, talking over relationships with other agencies—was highly effective. It seems to me, in the vast majority of cases, I found the consultation with Allen and his role in the decision-making process one that ranged from being easy to live with to being extremely valuable to me, and I'm sure valuable to the Agency. He was fairly impatient of many aspects of organization. That's another reason he somewhat got the reputation of being a "bad administrator." I've heard that label put on other Washington figures, and they've usually been the men who were so concerned with substance that they didn't spend all their time on organization charts and budgets.

4

Samuel Halpern

F ROM HIS POST AS Teaching Fellow of History in the History Department at the City College of New York (CCNY) in 1943, Halpern
joined the Office of Strategic Services as a research analyst in Washington, DC. The next year he went abroad as part of OSS Detach-
ment 404 to Kandy, Ceylon, in the China-Burma-India Theater. He
was ordered back to Washington in early 1945 to help the Joint
War Planners in the office of the Joint Chiefs of Staff as they prepared for the coming invasion of Japan in Operation OLYMPIC (for
Kyushu) and Operation CORONET (for the Tokyo Plain).

Born in Brooklyn, New York, to Henoch and Edis Jagid Halpern,
recent immigrants from Galicia, Austria-Hungary, on February 23,
1922, young Sam later attended public schools in that city. He earned
his B.S. in social studies at CCNY in 1942 and then began a Master's
degree program at Columbia University before joining the OSS. Soon

after war's end, when the OSS disbanded, Halpern was transferred on paper with the rest of the Research and Analysis Branch to the State Department as a research analyst. The Central Intelligence Group was established in January 1946; and several months later, now a member of the Strategic Services Unit (SSU), Halpern transferred to the Unit as an operations officer. He moved into the newly formed Central Intelligence Agency in September 1947. In 1948 he married Kathryn Detreux of Philadelphia, and they would have two children.

In the CIA, Halpern continued in operations as a case officer, serving first in the Office of Special Operations and then in the Directorate of Plans, largely in the Far East Division. In early 1962 he transferred to Task Force W, the CIA component of the government-wide Operation MONGOOSE (the codename for the project to overthrow Fidel Castro), and contributed to the intelligence community's 1963 report to the President's Foreign Intelligence Advisory Board on the Soviet arms buildup in Cuba. In 1966 he became the executive assistant to the Deputy Director for Plans (DDP), who was responsible for worldwide operations relating to the collection of intelligence by clandestine means. The Directorate also prepared covert actions in support of U.S. foreign policy. Over the next seven years, Halpern served three directors: Desmond FitzGerald, Thomas Karamessines, and William Colby. Before retiring in late 1974, he served as deputy chief of the division responsible for collecting intelligence from knowledgeable and willing Americans who provided information on foreign affairs.

Since retiring from the CIA, Halpern pursues a very active consulting career involving foreign intelligence matters, including service on the board of directors of the Association of Former Intelligence Officers and the National Intelligence Study Center, and on the editorial boards of the *International Journal of Intelligence and Counterintelligence* and the *Foreign Intelligence Literary Scene.* As co-editor with Hayden B. Peake of *In the Name of Intelligence: Essays in Honor of Walter Pforzheimer* (Washington, DC, 1994), Halpern collected more than thirty essays by leading scholars of foreign intelligence. His lecture series at the Smithsonian Institution as well as his consulting work with television productions on foreign affairs offer accurate perspectives on the role of foreign intelligence in American society. He continues his research and writing at his home in Alexandria, Virginia.

RALPH WEBER: *You were in the Office of Strategic Services and when it was terminated by President Harry S. Truman in September 1945, what happened to your unit?*

Conducted by Ralph E. Weber, Arlington, Virginia, on November 11, 1995. Tape in editor's possession.

SAMUEL HALPERN: We stayed in the same building behind the same desks doing the same job, except we were called the Strategic Services Unit (SSU) and were part of the War Department, not part of the Joint Chiefs of Staff as we were in OSS. In January 1946 the President created the Central Intelligence Group, and SSU, over a period of months starting in the spring of 1946, was swept into CIG by General Hoyt Vandenberg and we would become the Office of Special Operations (OSO). And then we became part of the Central Intelligence Agency in September 1947. At my level we did not know [Adm. Sidney] Souers; however, we may have heard the name once or twice. With Vandenberg we began to feel that there was somebody up there doing something with us. We were still working with our counterparts in the other agencies around the city, such as the State Department and the military in the Pentagon. We knew it was important to have someone with political clout on the Hill [Capitol Hill, or Congress] because of Vandenberg's relationship with Senator [Arthur] Vandenberg, who was a good Republican on the Hill. But we never felt any real effect of the changes in Directors. All this time I was in the Far East Division.

In OSO we did collection and counterintelligence, and later covert action in the elections in France and Italy in 1947 and 1948 because we were the only people who had troops in the field. OPC [the Office of Policy Coordination] was created in 1948, and by the time the Korean War started in 1950 it really exploded in adding people. And they wanted to make their own mistakes; they took space, needed guidance but would not take advice from us, and they made mistakes. OPC was like a big vacuum cleaner—they would pull people off the streets, anybody with warm blood who could say yes or no or move arms and legs!

How difficult was collection during the Korean War?

It was tough because North Korea was a denied area, no one came from there, and no people traveled there. We were not successful in collection about North Korea. Most people forget this. In the *West Point Atlas of American Wars* [vol. 2, p. 9] it says the CIA failed to produce information about the forthcoming use of Chinese Communist troops in the Korean War. Well, it is wrong! Director [Adm. Roscoe] Hillenkoetter had a hard time trying to prove this on the Hill. We were able to collect information from the Chinese Nationalists. When the Chinese Nationalists left the mainland of China in 1949 and moved to Taiwan, they left a "stay behind" group of intelligence assets all up and down the China coast in preparation for the return of Jiang Jieshi [Chiang Kai-shek]. Some of the OPC people were enamored about this return and spent a lot of money trying to make it happen. The Chinese Nationalists were able to have their stay-behind people who were working in the Chinese Communist armed forces, particularly in the army, continue to report back to Taiwan.

Some people thought it was propaganda, and it may have been, but it sure had a lot of factual and accurate information. Their agents on the China mainland were reporting order of battle of Chinese Communist army units as they moved from south to north into Manchuria and over to Korea. So we were providing everybody with good order-of-battle information, but nobody wanted to believe it. They thought it was all Jiang Jieshi and his people making it up.

General [Douglas] MacArthur, who hated OSS and everything associated with it, would not look at it, but in the end General [Charles A.] Willoughby, his G-2, thought it was something he ought to look at. MacArthur did not believe it until the Chinese Communist troops moved into North Korea. CIA people had Chinese language-proficient officers from World War II who were actually debriefing Chinese Communist POWs [prisoners of war] in American POW holding areas. And they were talking to these guys, and they reported these are Chinese Communist troops, *not* North Korean troops, here. Willoughby and his people refused to accept that until finally it was obvious that there were Chinese Communist troops pouring in by the hundreds of thousands. So the *Atlas* is wrong. CIA did provide information but not for the first time and not for the last time: people who got the info did not like the info and refused to accept it. We gave the data to the military. In my professional experience, when we had doubtful info from doubtful sources, we let the reader know without exception. We never did try to hide the stuff as being honest-to-goodness information if we had any doubts at all. As a matter of fact, the old evaluation system for the reliability of sources was from A through F and the reliability of info was 1 through 6, with F being "cannot tell," 1 being "confirmed." C-3 was in the middle. We got this system from the British. The military did not want to believe our information. This is not unusual. In World War II, OSS reported that the famed Japanese Kwantung Army in Manchuria was no longer the army it was in Manchuria, that they had used a lot of its units down in the Philippine Islands, fighting in Manila. This was the army that everyone was afraid of. When the Russians went in, in 1945, they went through that army like a hot knife through butter.

What do you remember about General Walter Bedell Smith as Director of the Agency?

Bedell came aboard, and everyone in town knew he was Truman's hand-picked guy. And Truman, who usually hated military brass because of his experience in World War I as an artillery captain on the line, loved this guy. So whatever Smith wanted to do, he just did it. He did not hold meetings, he did not write lots of papers; and everybody knew if they went to Harry Truman to argue a case, they had three strikes on them before they entered the room. Truman might have listened, but no one wanted to take a chance. So the first thing Bedell did that I remember as a junior officer in 1950 is that he took one look at the OPC setup vis-à-vis CIA: OPC had basically been part of CIA only for quarters and rations and took its direct orders from the Secretary of State and the Secretary of Defense, not the CIA Director. In the early days, the DCI had nothing to say about OPC. Bedell suddenly said, "They're under my command," and just took over. Neither of the two Secretaries or anybody else said, "You can't do that." He did it, and he did it in the first seven days of his tenure as DCI. I don't think anyone was more surprised than a guy named Frank Wisner, who suddenly found he wasn't running his own little show anymore. He was now part of something called CIA, and Bedell Smith was going to have something to say about it.

Did Smith give a great deal of status to CIA?

He put CIA on the map. If it hadn't been for Bedell, I don't think there would be a CIA today. He made it what it is: he firmly established it as an important element of government, both on the Hill with Congress and in the Executive Branch, particularly in the Defense Department. He was only at CIA a relatively short time because when Eisenhower became President, he took Bedell away from CIA and made him Deputy Secretary of State.

Did Smith want to be moved to State?

No, he liked being DCI. But you don't say no to the President, particularly Eisenhower, who wanted Smith as John Foster Dulles's Deputy. Eisenhower had a very good impression of OSS during World War II: he got along with [William] Donovan, and OSS was very useful to him in the field in Europe. Eisenhower must have had a good reason for moving Smith.

What was the reaction in the Agency when Smith was moved?

We were all sorry to see him go, because he'd get done what he wanted done. Smith brooked no nonsense from anybody. Just before he became Director, most of his stomach had been removed; and he lived on crackers and warm mush, which he ate all day long to keep him going. He wasn't the easiest guy in the world to work for. I never had to report to him. The stories we heard about him were frightening, especially to junior and middle-level officers. When you talked to Smith, you had to be very careful to answer his questions the way he framed the question. I remember there was one very senior officer who was up there doing a briefing on some part of the Far East. When the officer came back, he was shaking like a leaf in the wind. He was a very senior guy who had been around a long time. Apparently, at some place in the briefing he made some remark about some particular event in the Far East which involved some numbers, and Bedell asked him some question about how many X, Y, and Zs were there. The officer gave him some kind of precise figure like 22 1/2. Bedell lowered the boom on him and said, "I asked you for an approximate figure, not a precise figure! Don't you hear well?" I can see why he was indispensable to Eisenhower in Europe for the invasion [of Normandy (D-Day) in June 1944], and later in SHAEF [Supreme Headquarters, Allied Expeditionary Forces].

I know of another case. A very good friend of mine, who was a former Air Force officer, joined CIA. He went out to brief an agent of his and he took some classified documents with him, which he shouldn't have done; some were as high as Top Secret. Somewhere along the way he lost the documents in a car or a taxi he used. He was smart enough to report it right away. This is in the early 1950s. It got to the Director. Bedell insisted the man be fired immediately or roughly within twenty-four hours. This fellow was well connected politically with lawyers in New York. His brother was close to Donovan, a member of the Donovan law firm. This brother got ahold of Donovan, who allegedly called Bedell Smith to argue the case, saying it was unfair to fire him in twenty-four hours, that the man had a good record, et cetera. Bedell listened to Donovan and said, "All right, I'll give him forty-eight hours." That's exactly what happened. Within forty-eight hours that man was out. No nonsense: he suffered fools in absolutely no way whatsoever. Everyone was allowed one mistake. This brings me to another Director, John McCone, who was the same way. One mistake, everyone is entitled to one mistake, but Lord help you if you make another one. It was no fun-and-games: it was tough. That kind of a reputation, when it gets down to the troops, people mind their Ps and Qs.

When Allen Dulles became Director, was there a different atmosphere?

Totally different. Allen was the first Deputy Director of Plans under Bedell before OPC and OSO finally merged in 1952. The best account of Bedell as DCI is the Ludwell Montague history of him [*General Walter Smith as Director of Central Intelligence*, 1992], because he writes well and he was part of the Agency and knew what he was writing about. It's a marvelous work.

Truman wrote a syndicated article in 1963 [Washington Post, December 22, 1963] denouncing the CIA, saying it changed from the original assignment he had given it of collecting intelligence reports and giving them to the President in their raw state, free of interpretations so he could do his own evaluation. Moreover, CIA had become a policymaking arm of the government. He had not thought the CIA would be involved in peace-

time covert operations, cloak-and-dagger operations. What do you think of this?

That's nonsense. Not only was he aware, he was the guy who put us into what I call the first paramilitary operation. My friends say it wasn't the first, it was the second or third which Truman himself put us into. Truman did not write the column; rather, a staff officer wrote it. As far as we know, Truman never saw it. Both [Lyman] Kirkpatrick and Larry Houston wrote a few years later that they visited Truman and talked to him about this, and it was quite clear Truman never had seen the column.

Let me tell you about an operation I know about in the Far East, the Li Mi operation. Li Mi was a Chinese Nationalist general from Yunnan Province. This is 1950, shortly after Bedell Smith becomes Director and the Chinese Communists move into the Korean War. Somebody in the Pentagon, I don't know who, it could have been Louis Johnson, or some officer, had the bright idea that the way to draw Chinese Communist forces away from Korea would be to attack China through the back door, as they called it: from Burma into Yunnan Province. Communist China would have to do something about this back-door attack. The Pentagon came up with this bright plan, as I understand it; at least, I was told this by my boss, Lloyd George, who was Chief of the Far East Division at the time. The plan was presented to Truman and the National Security Council, and Bedell Smith was there as intelligence advisor to the Council. They're talking about creating this army for the attack by using Chinese National-ist forces from Taiwan plus those who might have escaped out of China into Burma and into northern Thailand. We would support and ferry these Chinese Nationalists from Taiwan to Bangkok to the back door of China in Burma. We didn't ask the Burmese about this. In fact, Truman's orders to the Agency and the Defense Department were: "Don't tell the Ameri-can Ambassador in Rangoon what the hell is going on." That was Ambas-sador [David McKendree] Key. That Truman didn't know about covert operations is just wrong.

This back-door operation had Truman in the Chair of the National Security Council. When Bedell Smith was asked for his views as an intel-ligence officer, he said, "The Chinese Communists have so many troops they can't even count them all, so why would they worry about a little pinprick down in Yunnan Province when they're fighting a major war in Korea? They won't move a single, solitary soldier out. Don't do it." Ev-eryone listened and discussed this, and Truman went around the room to get everyone to vote. Smith had no vote, and neither did the Chairman of the Joint Chiefs. Everyone else said, "Yes, let's try it!" Truman looked at Bedell and said, "You've got your marching orders, General." "Yes, sir," said Bedell. So they created something called SEA Supply—South East

Asia Supply Corporation—which was a cover name for a huge OPC out-fit. Chinese Nationalist troops were flown from Taiwan, were regrouped, trained, and then we dropped them into Northern Burma. From there they invaded China. The Chinese Communists let them walk in and then destroyed them. It was a shambles. The OSO people were doing their proper counterintelligence job, and they discovered that the chief radio operator for the Li Mi troops happened to be a Chinese Communist agent. The OPC people refused to believe it, and they refused to accept the intelligence and couldn't imagine that one of the people they hired was working for Beijing. There was no love lost between OSO and OPC at that point, obviously, and this went on for years. The OSO would never let the OPC forget this mistake. Colonels Dick Stilwell and [William E.] DePuy were involved. Stilwell was chief of the OPC Far East Division, Bill DePuy was in charge of the China Desk for OPC; Desmond FitzGerald was Stilwell's executive officer.

Let me give you an example of why it was difficult to work with our military friends. Bill DePuy honestly believed Jiang Jieshi [Chiang Kai-shek] had a million guerrilla forces waiting on the China mainland to rise against the Chinese Communists. And that was another big operation they ran. They created Western Enterprises, which was a cover for a commercial company in Taiwan. They weren't fooling anyone, not the Chinese Communists, not the Chinese Nationalists, not the Taiwanese, not the Thais, not the French, not the Russians. When the OPC people like Bill DePuy were told by the OSO people, who were doing their counterintelligence job, that we have to penetrate the Chinese Nationalist forces on Taiwan in order to find out what they're up to and what they're going to do, Bill took this as a personal affront, a personal insult. "How dare you try to penetrate and spy on our friends and allies!" he said. Obviously, there was no meeting of the minds. All this nonsense about Harry Truman, that he didn't want this OPC activity, didn't want this covert activity, is not true. He knew exactly what was going on. Truman knew what he was doing.

What do people in the Agency think about having military officers such as Souers, Vandenberg, Hillenkoetter, and Smith as Directors of the Agency?

People in CIA felt that as long as Smith was around, the military would not be able to squash us completely. But not everyone agreed with Smith and what he was doing: for example, whether OSO and OPC should be merged. But they had to be merged. They were fighting in the field to get the same targeted secretary, the same waste basket! Counterintelligence, collecting intelligence, was OSO's job; OPC's job was to do something in terms of action—it was not a collection agency. Finally it was realized that you had to have a decent intelligence base for decent covert action. You have to know the players in the country, who's involved, and work through these players. When Allen Dulles took over, everyone had a high regard for him. His sense of security was almost nonexistent: he'd be on the telephone and knew it could be bugged, but he would talk to Frank Wisner about "our [English] cousins." Dulles came in with a good reputation for his work in World War II. He wasn't viewed as a great manager; however, people felt they could discuss with him, argue with him. For example, after an operation we had, we owed the military a goodly sized figure for the supplies they had given us. The military gave us a figure from their finance people to our finance people. They gave us what they called a "divisional slice," which means they started with the Secretary of Defense with 10 percent or 1 percent of his salary and worked down the line through the whole big structure called the Pentagon. And that's what you had to pay for.

Dulles wasn't going to pay that; we didn't have that kind of money. I had to see Allen, who had the figures in front of him. He took one look at the figures and said, "I'm not going to pay it!" I said, "Yes, sir." He was having a bad gout day, had his slippers on and was smoking his pipe. The more he smoked, the more he puffed, the tougher he got. "I'm not going to pay that, that's highway robbery! They should know better. They're part of the government, we're part of the government. We can't pay that. I think I know what I'm going to do. How about this figure?" and it was a small part of the total. "I'll pay that," and he told me to see the director of finance, who couldn't believe Dulles's low figure. The finance directors finally compromised. Allen could take this kind of position because he knew that Eisenhower had no great love for the Pentagon bureaucracy. That is why he turned the CORONA satellite project over to the Agency rather than the Pentagon.

Does the Agency get involved with Democratic or Republican politics?

No. Remember, our funds come from the Congress, not the President. We were pretty well wired in with both parties. If you look at the National Security Act of 1947 as originally drafted, you cannot find a word about espionage, counterintelligence, covert action. You didn't talk about this, although everyone knew what you were talking about. If you look at the testimony of Vandenberg and Hillenkcetter in the executive sessions, nobody wrote the words down, although they knew what was happening. Now if you look at the latest version, in the authorization act of 1993, the original act was changed. The text now talks about collection by human means for the very first time. We always had oversight. Committees on the Hill always were looking at us, but unfortunately they weren't interested in the kind of detail they're now looking at. A phrase I heard many times from my bosses after they came back from DCI staff meetings was: "I go up on the Hill and I want to talk about problems I'm having, but they don't want to talk about the problem. 'Do you have enough people, enough money? Then go and do your job. You're doing great, keep it up, you're doing fine.' "

Did Agency personnel worry about the transition when a newly elected President from the other political party came into office and might change Directors?

We always worried about who was going to be DCI. We worried in terms of personalities, not political parties. Jack Kennedy told Dulles to stay on.

In one of the oral histories at the John F. Kennedy Library it was noted that Bissell was led to believe he would take over in July 1961.

I was on a flight with Bissell from Hong Kong to Tokyo before the Bay of Pigs. We were chatting about the future, and it was clear from the questions Dick was asking me that he made no bones that his next job was going to be the DCI job. I believe Dick Bissell thought he'd be the next DCI. He had been very instrumental in the U-2 and CORONA projects and helping Wisner with the Guatemala show. He would have passed through Congress with no problems if the Bay of Pigs had worked out.

CIA officer Dave Phillips said that the successful overthrow of the government in Guatemala in 1954 provided confidence for carrying out the Bay of Pigs plan in April 1961. But did the failure in the Indonesia operation in 1957 and 1958 affect planning?

Nope, and I'll tell you why. I was put on as Deputy Chief on the Cuba Desk in October 1961 by Bissell after I came back from Saigon and Tokyo. In the office I opened a four-drawer safe, and in the bottom drawer I found a copy of the history report or study of the Indonesia operation. I found a bookmark about the second page of the first chapter. This indicated to me that no one had read beyond that point, and so they made some of the same mistakes we made in Indonesia. No one is interested in history! They ignored history. The person who put the bookmark there was one of the old Western Hemisphere hands who had a good reputation as a case officer. But no one reads history, so nobody learns what happened before. I found another folder in that same safe, the report by Kirkpatrick on the Bay of Pigs. It damns the hell out of Bissell and the rest of the others. I started to read it, and I got no farther than halfway into the first chapter before someone in the Agency recalled all copies of the report. I never saw it again.

I wish I could have read the Kirkpatrick report so we wouldn't make the same mistakes in Operation MONGOOSE, which was a government-wide operation under the direction of the Attorney General, Robert Kennedy, and the President, John F. Kennedy, "to get rid of Castro and the Castro regime" begun in late 1961 and lasting through the Cuban missile crisis in late 1962. If Kirkpatrick hadn't gotten polio, he would have been Deputy Director of Plans, and maybe even DCI eventually. I think he never forgave himself or the rest of the community for that. He was no longer a key player, although they kept him in senior jobs. But the minute Dick Helms became Deputy Director in 1965, Kirkpatrick left. Kirk got the polio on the trip in 1952 to Bangkok to prevent OPC and OSO from shooting live bullets at each other. OPC did the shooting: OSO did not. OPC kidnapped the OSO communicator thinking the OSO station would be incommunicado with Washington since it couldn't send messages. This was done by OPC guys in the field, it wasn't ordered by Washington. They forgot, or they didn't know, that the two guys at the OSO station were old United States Army communicators from World War II so they could communicate, and they told Washington what had happened.

Does the Agency change much when President John F. Kennedy becomes President? One observer thought there was administrative fragmentation during his first months in office.

In CIA there was a lack of unity or fragmentation from January 1961 to the time that McCone takes over. Some of this comes as a result of the Kennedy brothers handling business on a day-to-day basis. They didn't think anything of picking up the phone and calling XYZ Desk, and some poor Desk officer who may have been a GS [Government Service at rank] 13 or 14 or lower suddenly found himself talking to the President of the United States or the Attorney General, and wasn't sure what to say. No one likes to say "no" to a President, but I think that particular President would have accepted a "no" or a "don't know." The brothers were gadflies. When it came to Cuba, they were persons with a fixation. In my humble opinion, they couldn't care less about the United States of America and what it stood for. They were interested in one thing only, and that was clearing the blemish on the Kennedy escutcheon. They were getting blamed for the Bay of Pigs—partly it was their fault, partly it wasn't. There were errors on both sides.

In 1961 and 1962 the Kennedys wanted things done literally by mirrors, because they were screaming "sabotage, sabotage, sabotage, move 'em back, move 'em back," and nothing we did pleased them. And when we did have some success—I believe we blew up some small power plant or a generator—we got chewed out because the story about the explosion and damage made headlines in Cuba and in Florida, where it hit the front pages. Bobby Kennedy screamed at us and said, "I thought you guys did things in a secret way! What's the matter with you guys? Why all the publicity?" And we had to tell him in no uncertain terms that when you're going to blow something up, it's going to make noise, people are going to see it, it's going to be on television, and it's going to be in the newspapers. That's the kind of stupidity we were getting from the White House, from the President and his brother the Attorney General.

Does McCone intercede when he becomes DCI?

Yes, but that didn't stop the telephone calls directly down to the Desk. Poor Bill Harvey was getting the brunt of most of these things. It was awful. We thought the whole purpose of "boom and bang" was to scare Castro. McCone had enough presence and status to help us.

Some severe critics say McCone did not do enough to convince his superiors about a possible Soviet missile threat in Cuba, and that he should not have gone on his honeymoon during this time.

McCone was the only senior officer in town who believed there was a danger from the missiles in Cuba. The entire intelligence analytic community—all the DCI types in all the agencies, State, Defense, Commerce, Treasury—were convinced this was nonsense, that McCone was wrong. When McCone went to the French Riviera, he had secure communications for the so-called Honeymoon Cables. He could have been anywhere and made the points he wanted to make. But he had made the points, and he couldn't do more than repeat what he was saying, which was that you don't put in SAM [surface-to-air missile] sites, which are defense missiles, unless you want to defend something. What do you want to defend? It has to be bigger than the air defense missiles. Ted Shackley and his people down south were really worried. We were worried up here. And it was really Bill Harvey who talked to Ray Cline and got him to consider writing that special September estimate, the SNIE [Special National Intelligence Estimate], on which my friend Sherman Kent was so wrong. And Deputy Director [Marshall S.] Carter as Acting DCI signed off on the SNIE. McCone did not agree with Carter's approval of the SNIE and let him know it. McCone could not have done more to alert the intelligence community even if he had been in town.

Those Honeymoon Cables had an impact. Guys like Bill Harvey, Dick Helms, I, and others thought the boss was really onto something, but we couldn't back it up. That was part of the problem. Ted Shackley and his analysts in Miami came closer to the estimate of the number of Soviet troops in Cuba than anyone in the Community. The Community had figured about twenty-two thousand, but the Miami boys figured about forty-two thousand, and that's the figure the Soviets have used. One of Ted's agents sent a simple message back to us that the Soviet and Cuban military were moving everything out of an area between four little towns, and he named them. This was the only report from any source that named the towns and defined an area. We talked to one of our Operation MONGOOSE counterparts in the Defense Intelligence Agency [DIA], Colonel John Wright, and he came over to our war room and we marked the towns on the map. Someone suggested we send a plane over the area. Wright said DIA would request it. There followed ten days of fighting as to whether to fly over the area. The State Department refused to allow a flight *over* the island: all they wanted were peripheral flights with oblique cameras. They didn't want a U-2 shot down. State and [Dean] Rusk worried about this; and maybe this was a blessing because if we had gone over earlier, we might have missed the detail that we got in mid-October. Finally, pictures showed the threat.

Did McCone restore CIA morale after the Bay of Pigs disaster?

He did, but it took awhile. The number one priority had been Vietnam, but by the time I arrived back in Washington from Saigon in September 1961, Cuba had become the first priority. McCone instilled respect, with a capital R, and during the Cuban missile crisis review sessions I thought he was one tough Director. In retrospect, I put him second from the top as DCI. First is Bedell, who put us on the map. McCone made the Agency run extremely well. He established the Directorate of Science and Technology in 1963 by merging the Projects Development Division from the Directorate of Plans with the scientific offices from the Directorate of Intelligence and upgraded the Directorate of Research all into the new Directorate.

Why does President Lyndon Johnson replace McCone?

McCone said he had enough: he had lost Johnson's confidence, probably because of Vietnam. I recall that McCone listened to us. In April 1964, Shackley and his people in Miami and we here in Washington were screaming bloody murder about Cuba: let's stop all this sabotage nonsense. We were doing nothing. There was no end result. We convinced McCone, and he convinced the President. Cuba remained a problem but reduced in size, and money; we limited ourselves to collection. President Johnson hadn't been embarrassed! Vietnam became priority number one.

How effective was McCone's successor, Admiral William Raborn?

He began in April 1965, at the time the Dominican Republic crisis erupted. Richard Helms was his Deputy. Because of the crisis, we set up in the Cable Communications Section a "pit," a small office with one desk, a few tables, and chairs. We had two teleprinters hooked to the Santo Domingo Station. It was a really hectic time. Raborn came into the "pit" with Helms; Dave Phillips and I were there. Raborn saw all the info from the embassy, with reports from the Ambassador plus military attachés' messages. The communications office was handling all the messages. Raborn tore off some of the dispatches because he wanted to talk to Dean Rusk about some of the State messages. We were not supposed to be reading other peoples' messages, but this was an unusual time and a time of crisis and all messages were coming in on one machine. Helms somehow convinced Raborn not to call the principals since they hadn't received their messages yet!

The next time I saw Raborn was on a Sunday during the Dominican crisis. He had to send a page or somewhat longer memo to President Johnson on the crisis. So Raborn called Des FitzGerald, who was still Chief of the Western Hemisphere office to come to the Director's office; Des brought me along. Raborn began dictating to his secretary his version of the Dominican Republic situation, but you could not tell what country he was talking about! He finished, told his secretary to type up the memo and return with it. As the secretary stood up, Des signaled to me to go out with her and make some sense out of the memo. I rewrote the memo and when Raborn read and signed it, he said, "It's a good memo!" Raborn was a nice guy, but he was in the wrong job at the wrong time in the wrong place.

Was Helms the most experienced Director since Dulles?

He was second to Dulles. Dulles was older, both served abroad, both OSS, both served in Europe. Neither knew much about the Far East; they had to learn about it. We all had to learn about Africa and Latin America. Helms was a case officer; Dulles was partially a case officer.

Was President Johnson very much of a supporter of covert action?

Presidents don't know what the words "covert action" mean. They mean different things to different people at different times. Covert action could mean nothing more than giving money to someone to run an election or print pamphlets. Covert action may range from political action to paramilitary action. Most people equate covert action with paramilitary action, and that's not true. But since the time of the Church and Pike Committees that's become the equation. When the Agency gave money for political action in Italy and France in 1947 and 1948, paramilitary wasn't involved, just political support. We did something in Chile in 1963 under the Kennedys to get [Eduardo] Frei and the Christian Democrats elected.

The British always called it Special Political Action. They never called it covert action, it was SPA. The Brits are always better at this; they taught us in OSS. They have a much more quiet approach, a more professional approach. For example, at the end of the failed Indonesian operation, when this blew up in our faces (we ended it with [Allen] Pope being shot down in 1958), the British station commander was in my office and saw us running around. He said to me, "Why do your people get so excited when it's all over? In our case by that time it's much too late to do anything about it. Why get excited?" He added, "Just relax."

CIA was giving order-of-battle [OB] information on Vietnam which was different from the military figures. Was this a serious problem?

It's a tough subject and it's hard to explain OB to people, the numbers to people. The military had a vested interest in their numbers. Our analysts did not; none of our operators did. In Saigon, I went through a similar, though smaller, situation in 1961. After the French left Vietnam, the South Vietnam government kept the figure of ten thousand Viet Cong effectives during the period 1954 to 1961. Bill Colby had me look into these numbers. I got help from three Army majors, one of whom was an OB specialist. We looked into the numbers by putting maps of South Vietnam around all four walls of a secure vault we built in the old Embassy. We covered the maps with acetate and put numbers on them from all human and technical sources, and put the particular sources on file cards. We came up with twenty thousand instead of ten thousand! Colby didn't want to release the number. After several days of discussion, Colby said, "Let's take five thousand or three thousand or one thousand, and we'll call some construction battalions, some supply units, something else, and something else." I said, "What do we end up with?" And Colby said, "Eighteen thousand, is that okay?" I said that's okay if I can put some qualifier on it, saying maybe more are around. We agreed, and sent the figure out on our communication channels.

The colonel at the CINC [Commander in Chief] Desk in Honolulu, who had served with the French forces, fired a message back, saying he was coming on the next plane. He arrived, met the four of us, and I said, "Why don't you read the map and the file cards in the safe?" He did; and the next day he came into my office and said, "You fellows may have something. I think we must make changes." Later I learned that everything we knew, the enemy knew. The penetration of the GVN [Government of Viet Nam] was unbelievable at every level. Colby refused to develop counterintelligence operations to penetrate GVN in order to find out what the enemy was doing within the GVN. This was one of the big battles between Colby and Jim Angleton. I have no idea what the DCI thought about this. In 1961, Cuba becomes the number one priority.

When President Richard Nixon and Henry Kissinger came into office, was the Agency weakened?

No, strengthened, except for one area. Under Nixon and Kissinger, the DDI [Directorate of Intelligence] side of the house was downplayed.

Kissinger did his own analysis and the DDI felt ignored. The operations side was not ignored, and we were used much more than during the Johnson Administration. On the day after Nixon was sworn in in 1969, there was a meeting in the Cabinet Room at the White House with Nixon, Kissinger, John Mitchell, Helms, and Tom Karamessines. Nixon and Kissinger made it clear that they were going to use the Agency all over the world for all kinds of things. They wanted to know what assets, what capabilities, where, what can the Agency do. They did not ask about sources as such; they knew better than to ask. Nixon and Kissinger used us as they said they would.

Were you surprised and the Agency demoralized when Director Helms retired from the Agency in 1973?

Yes, we were all surprised; we didn't expect it. When Helms left the building, all the troops jammed the Headquarters Building entrance for his departure. There wasn't a dry eye in the house. Everyone knew we were in for a bad time after that. The grapevine was alive with what [James] Schlesinger had done when he was at Atomic Energy [Commission as chairman], and what he had done at the Bureau of the Budget as a deputy. Great apprehension! Many resigned. Everyone knew Colby had talked to Schlesinger even before the appointment, giving him all the stories. After Schlesinger went over to the Defense Department, the story is that he told people he went after the wrong Directorate, that he should have gone after the DDI side of the house rather than the DDP side. The DDI is the focal point for everything we do. Schlesinger thought he went after the wrong group.

Who was the most popular Director during your career?

Allen Dulles was probably the most popular among the troops, junior, middle, and senior. The most effective Director was Smith first, McCone second, then probably Helms and Dulles.

Which Director had the best press relations during those years?

Allen Dulles. In those days the press did not ask the silly questions they now ask. He knew how to massage people. He was different from Bill Casey, who didn't know how to glad-hand the guys in Congress. They didn't trust him, and he didn't trust them. Dulles and McCone worked well with Congress.

Which President was the most friendly to CIA?

Eisenhower is number one. He had good experiences with OSS. He knew the Agency could produce for him. Ike wanted the CORONA project done by the Agency in a clandestine operation. When this began in the late 1950s, the first twelve or thirteen attempts to launch the rockets were failures. Bissell had to report this to him. Ike said, try again, try again, and he pushed it. Congress didn't know about it; there was nothing in the newspapers. Ike said, we have to have this: the U-2 someday will stop flying.

Which Directors had the closest relations with the Presidents?

Bedell Smith and Truman, Allen Dulles and Eisenhower. I should add that I believe that unless the DCI is able to walk in to see the President at will, privately, except maybe for the secretary, just these persons—unless that's possible, you don't have a DCI

5

Lyman B. Kirkpatrick, Jr.

T HE SON OF BUSINESSMAN Lyman B. Kirkpatrick and his wife, Lyde Paull Kirkpatrick, Lyman, Jr., was born in Rochester, New York, on July 15, 1916. Soon after graduation from Princeton University in 1938, the six-foot, five-inch-tall Kirkpatrick joined the editorial staff of David Lawrence's Bureau of National Affairs, which published several business journals in Washington, DC. Marriage to Jeanne Courtney soon followed, and they later would have four children.

In May 1940, with war raging in Europe, Kirkpatrick applied for the Navy Air Corps; however, he failed the eye examination. Soon after the surprise attack on Pearl Harbor, he joined the recently formed office of the Coordinator of Information (COI) headed by William Donovan. He stayed on when the COI became the Office of Strategic Services. His first assignment abroad took him to London, where he served under his former political science preceptor at Princeton, William Maddox.

As a liaison officer with the British Secret Intelligence Service, and an analyst who studied the German order of battle, Lieutenant Kirkpatrick enjoyed sifting through intelligence data. Sent to Normandy in 1944 soon after the Allied invasion, he served with the G-2 Section under Col. Sheffield Edwards, who would subsequently become Director of Security in the Central Intelligence Agency. Moreover, his commanding general, Edwin L. Sibert, would become an Assistant Director of the Agency. As the battle lines moved east of Paris, Kirkpatrick acted as briefing officer for Gen. Omar Bradley.

After the surrender of Germany and Japan, and the dissolution of the OSS, Kirkpatrick rejoined Lawrence's Washington staff. A year later, Sibert recruited him for the newly formed Central Intelligence Group. Following passage of the monumental National Security Act in the summer of 1947 that established the CIA, National Security Council, Department of Defense, Joint Chiefs of Staff, and Air Force, Kirkpatrick helped the intelligence agency develop better relations with other U.S. intelligence groups. Finally appointed a division chief by CIA Director Roscoe Hillenkoetter (who at first feared he was too young at age thirty-one), he established special liaison arrangements with other organizations and individuals who might serve in collecting intelligence.

Soon after Gen. Walter Bedell Smith became Director in late 1950, Kirkpatrick was named his executive assistant. Smith, a brilliant leader and manager, moved the CIA into the first rank of the world's intelligence organizations. Smith and his staff, especially with Richard Helms, shaped the Agency by combining the Office of Policy Coordination and the Office of Special Operations, reorganizing the analytical sections, and demanding professional competence. And most important, Smith had the unquestioned support of President Harry Truman.

In July 1952, stricken with polio overseas, Kirkpatrick spent the next eight months in hospitals undergoing painful rehabilitation before returning to the Agency as Inspector General under Director Allen Dulles. In this post, the wheelchair-bound officer reviewed covert operations planning and major personnel complaints. His office also served as the Agency's special contact with the President's Board of Consultants on Foreign Intelligence Activities, established by President Dwight Eisenhower. Despite his physical disability, Kirkpatrick visited Agency offices throughout Latin America, Western Europe, Africa, and Southeast Asia.

During several confidential missions to Cuba in the 1950s, Kirkpatrick urged Fulgencio Batista and his government to investigate the growing Communist menace, and with dismay he witnessed the increasing support given by the Cuban people to Fidel Castro because of the Batista regime's brutalities. In January 1959, Castro gained control of Cuba, and the United States accorded him recognition. As evidence of Castro's Communist affiliations mounted, President Eisenhower in early 1960 approved a covert CIA plan for his overthrow. This liberation plan eventually grew into the Bay of Pigs operation devised by Richard Bissell and Allen Dulles.

After the failed invasion, Kirkpatrick, in a public postmortem (his in-house critique was suppressed before 1998) written several years later, argued that the liberation effort was doomed "not because of the CIA, but despite what was available in the CIA. . . . The men in charge of the project chose to operate outside the organizational structure of both the CIA and the intelligence system and consequently forfeited a considerable amount of expertise and judgment available in Washington" (The Real CIA [New York, 1968], 204). In addition, he emphasized that the most important lesson to be learned from the failure is that it is rarely possible for the United States to achieve by covert paramilitary means what it is unwilling to do either by diplomacy or direct military action.

A few months after John McCone became Director in late 1961, Kirkpatrick became Executive Director-Comptroller of the Agency, a post he held until he retired in 1965. In the following years he taught at Brown University and the U.S. Naval War College and wrote four books on intelligence operations. He died at Middleburg, Virginia, on March 6, 1995.

LYMAN KIRKPATRICK: I don't recall ever having met President Kennedy before he took office. I did know his father, Joseph P. Kennedy, when he was on President Eisenhower's Foreign Intelligence Board. President Eisenhower tried to keep a Democrat on that Board at all times, and Ambassador Kennedy was the first Democrat. He resigned from it, if I recall correctly, sometime during the 1956 [National Democratic] Convention or just before, when it looked as though Senator Kennedy might be a candidate for Vice President. He wasn't very happy on the Board anyway because he didn't feel that boards like that were very constructive or could do very much.

JOSEPH O'CONNOR: *Did he participate very fully on this?*

Oh, yes, while he was on it, he participated completely; and part of my job, in addition to being the CIA focal point with the President's Board, was when members of the Board wanted special briefings or to be advised about anything, I usually laid them on. And I recall one rather amusing anecdote about the Ambassador. He was there one Friday and decided

Conducted by Joseph E. O'Connor in Providence, Rhode Island, on April 26, 1967. Oral History Interviews, John F. Kennedy Library, Boston, Massachusetts.

to stay for lunch, and fortunately my secretary remembered that the CIA executive mess didn't always serve fish on Friday, so she had them go out and make sure that they had some fish for him.

But as far as President Kennedy was concerned, indirectly, I remember Ambassador Kennedy saying to me on more than one occasion how he bemoaned the fact that all of his sons were so interested in public life that he had nobody to run the family business. [Laughter.]

That's contrary to all past reports.

So he was very active while he was on it, and I had the distinct impression, because he generally was going out to Bobby Kennedy's after these sessions and also going up to the Senator's office, that he probably informed them to a degree about what was going on.

I met the President, I think, the first time when John McCone was sworn in as Director, and, if you'll remember, McCone came to Washington and was sworn in and then went home and brought his wife back after the swearing-in, and his wife died one day later. So it was a very hectic period as far as both McCone and the Agency were concerned. But McCone took the senior officers of the CIA over with him to the swearing-in, and I particularly remember the President's comments, "Welcome to the bull's eye," which I'm sure are in the record somewhere, or if it isn't, it should be. I don't know whether it was taken down verbatim or not, but President Kennedy's remarks were very pertinent there. And then I also remember that the President walked around the room after the swearing-in and spoke to every one of us that was there and said something about the work we were doing, which was, I'm sure, appreciated, certainly by the hired hands.

Did you have any feelings, during the campaign, for example, or can you speak for other members of the Central Intelligence Agency, as far as preference is concerned? I mean specifically as far as the operations of the CIA are concerned, did you prefer that John F. Kennedy or Richard Nixon become President, or didn't it make any difference?

Well, as far as I'm personally concerned, I don't recall analyzing the two candidates in that particular category. Nixon, of course, had been known for his work at the time of the Whittaker Chambers case [an American Communist charged with espionage for the Soviet Union] when he was a member of Congress and was probably better known to most of us in the Agency than Senator Kennedy was. But I think the feelings of the Agency weren't so much as to what the candidates might do in regard to operations as they were based upon the political beliefs. And the CIA as an organization has the same spectrum of political beliefs, I guess, as the country does, or fairly close to it, because you've got the conservatives and you've got the liberals, and obviously all the liberals were heartily in favor of Mr. Kennedy.

I thought there might be some particular feeling; I didn't have any . . .

I don't recall any specific feeling about what they might do as far as operations were concerned, and my personal instinct would have been that their reactions would have probably been fairly close in this regard because it seems that with a security or an intelligence agency that politics sort of goes out the window when that becomes involved.

Okay, we could move on then to the Bay of Pigs operation. Were you involved in it at all before you became the man in charge of the CIA's investigation of it?

No.

Were you aware of it, I should say?

Oh, I was aware of it; we were all aware of it, you see. I should say probably here that I was Inspector General of CIA from 1953 until 1961, and as Inspector General it was my responsibility to see that my staff investigated everything the Agency did. This was a constant rotational type of investigation to all of the units to see how they were operating.

Now the Bay of Pigs was an operation which was conducted outside of the normal structure. Mr. [Allen W.] Dulles and General [Charles Pearré] Cabell and Richard Bissell set up a unit for this one operation, and consequently it was outside of the normal operating divisions or the support units of the CIA. But I did propose at one course during the mounting of the operation to Mr. Dulles that I be permitted to put one or two inspectors in this unit to currently follow what was going on rather than waiting for its ultimate conclusion. And this was turned down, so we had nothing to do with it whatsoever. It was handled completely outside of our jurisdiction. It was only after the operation was over that we were brought it.

Can you tell us something about the beginning of the operation or the investigation itself? Who decided that the investigation should take place?

Mr. Dulles decided that an investigation should take place. This was a very dramatic period, of course, that week in April when the operation was launched and then collapsed. And it happened that on Friday of that week—the operation by then was over, it had failed—I had to be in the Agency training area, which is a bit of a distance from Washington, to give some training lectures, and I didn't get back to Washington until Saturday. And I went into the office Saturday morning and happened to coincide with Mr. Dulles, who was coming into the office, and we rode up in the elevator together. He asked me where I'd been, and I told him where I'd been. And he said, "I've been trying to get ahold of you. I'm very anxious to talk to you about the Bay of Pigs operation, and I want you to start immediately to investigate it and find out what went wrong." And he said, "Let me get through with the letters on my desk, and then I'll give you a buzz and come down and see me."

So he buzzed me that morning, and I went down, and we talked about the investigation and how it should be conducted. It is my recollection that we agreed that it should deal only with the CIA and the CIA role in it because I think by then President Kennedy had established the Board with Mr. Dulles and Attorney General Kennedy and Maxwell Taylor and Admiral [Arleigh] Burke, and they were going to deal with the externals of it. So I set out immediately to put three of my best men on this, and this was the start of our investigation.

We worked from that last week in April, and we finally got the report written—I think it was well into November before we finally got the report written. Now we tried to talk to every Agency employee who had been involved in the operation. We obviously talked to all of the senior officials in Agency units who had not been involved but were supporting it in some way or the other; by that, I mean the logistics office, which had put a lot of people into it, communications office, and so on. We didn't talk to any Cubans. We stayed away from them because we thought this would be a little sensitive; and, certainly, we weren't too certain we would get very objective comments from them in the height of the emotional aftermath which they were . . .

Was that your decision?

Yes. And we had access, of course, to all of the files that were available and, in addition, to the minutes of the Taylor group. They had a secretariat, and they kept a daily record of who talked to them and what they said, and those were made available to me so that we could see what was there. But in writing the report, when we came down to it, the report was tailored quite specifically to just what CIA had done and how it had done it, and we avoided any political decisions that might have been made in the White House or the Pentagon or in the State Department or Congress because we were tailoring our report strictly to CIA successes or failures.

And I would add that when the report was finished, it was a very, very difficult decision on my part as to what to do with it and how to do it because it couldn't but help but be a highly critical report of the Agency's operations. Mr. Dulles by then had announced his retirement; the President had appointed John McCone; and I probably handled it the wrong way, in retrospect, after the six years, nearly six years that have passed. I decided to show it to John McCone first (he was within a week of being sworn in as Director) and asked him how he thought I should handle it. And I handed it to him Thanksgiving week, and he was going out to California, and he said he was going to take it with him and read it there. And he called me the next morning from California, having apparently read the report through on the plane, and said, "I think you better hand this to Mr. Dulles immediately." I had told him when I gave it to him that I realized that this would both shock and hurt Allen Dulles because it did indicate such very serious failings in the Agency's operation: poor organization, poor use of personnel, overoptimism of the success of the operation, failure to use the intelligence side of the Agency—the intelligence side, I mean the Research and Analysis Directorate.

And so I did hand it to Mr. Dulles, handed him a copy and General Cabell a copy the very next day, and they were both exceedingly shocked and upset, irritated and annoyed and mad and everything else because Mr. Dulles, I believe, used the term to McCone when he saw him that it was a hatchet job. And McCone talked to me and said, "Mr. Dulles thinks this was a hatchet job. I want you to reread it and write me a memorandum as to what you think now, looking at it again." This was about, oh, either December of '61 or January of '62. And I reread it, and I wrote a one-paragraph memorandum to Mr. McCone, saying, "On rereading it several months after the report was finished, it's my observation that, if anything, this is a moderate report and is not as severe as it should be."

But Allen Dulles was so upset by the report—I learned later, indirectly—that he had told John McCone, when McCone had been named Director, in talking about the personnel in the Agency that there was nothing in the Agency that I couldn't do and do well because I had been on all sides of it, and General Cabell had said about the same thing. After the Bay of Pigs report, I understand they both went back to McCone and reversed their positions on that. McCone, however apparently wasn't impressed, because he promoted me to Executive Director after that.

Now I want to talk about the report itself because, seeing this is a part of history that has never been recorded, I think it's important. The report itself, as I say, dealt solely with CIA and CIA's omissions and faults in operation. What it boiled down to, in simple terms, in a report that ran about a hundred and fifty pages, was that by trying to do it in a compartmented unit outside the regular structure of the Agency, it had failed to take advantage of the best talent in the Agency. Richard Helms, the present Director of CIA who was the Chief of Operations and was Bissell's Deputy, was never consulted about the operation and never brought into it; and, because he was never brought into it, he wisely kept out of it, as I did as Inspector General. The chief of the counterespionage staff, one of the most talented men in the Agency, was never brought in or consulted in that particular area, which was quite important. The Board of National Estimates, Sherman Kent's board, was never brought in, never asked to do an estimate on the possibilities of success. So there was a very broad spectrum of the Agency that was never consulted or brought in, and the operation was handled on a very close basis with Dulles and Cabell and Bissell and Tracy Barnes and the immediate operators that were running it, including the Marine colonel who had come over to run the specific military operations.

Do you know who it was that made the decision that it would be handled this way rather than . . .

Well, I think it was Dick Bissell, with the approval of Dulles and Cabell, because that was the way they were operating. Now as a result of this, we discovered that the problems in even such basic things as communications about airdrops were manifold, and the CIA certainly had all the expertise and talent to lay on successful airdrops. We had a very large number of personnel who had been in OSS and in other types of intelligence operations in World War II when we were both dropping teams of agents and supplies to resistance groups in France and Burma and other parts of the world, and they had generally been highly successful.

The airdrops over Cuba were highly unsuccessful in nearly every respect, and there had been some fantastic blunders made in this category, speaking mainly now about airdrops. We were told of one operation where they were asked to drop in some supplies of arms and equipment which were to be dropped on a fairly sizable estate of one of the anti-Castro people in Cuba, and a decision, I think made by General Cabell, was to also drop some supplies of food, rather heavy supplies of food, and that this man was so thoroughly irritated by what he considered this jeopardy to his security that he came out of Cuba himself and said he didn't want to be involved any further with this, if this was the way the operation was going to be run.

And we found that this was fairly typical of the general failure in the area of support and supply of the resistance groups, which, of course, in turn related to the decision to change the whole nature of the operation from building up guerrilla units in various parts of the country to the brigade landing, which was, of course, a complete change in the concept and quite a different type of operation. And probably when that change was made—and perhaps I say this with hindsight and if so, why, I accept that—to change it from building up guerrilla groups to a brigade landing, somebody realistically should have said, "Well, this ends the covert aspects of this because a brigade landing is not covert, never could be."

Our investigation also showed such things that despite the fact that Allen Dulles, by his orders, had directed the operational side of the house to put the best men, the best personnel on this operation, that all we had to do was to examine the rosters of ratings which the Agency has, competitive ratings in all grades by categories of personnel—this is used for the competitive promotion system that they have—and we found, rather than getting the top men in the organization, they had generally, with some exceptions, the bottom third in ratings.

That's incredible.

It is incredible, but that is exactly what the case was.

In investigating this, did you attempt to find out why this was so or in talking with the men who perhaps were . . .

Yes, we did. We investigated and tried to find out in great detail why this was so, and our conclusion was that the people running the operation had not been sufficiently insistent in getting the best men, that they accepted the second- and third-raters. Now this is not to say that the people they got weren't hard-working and honest and diligent, but the real operational talent was probably for the only natural human reaction—that good supervisors don't like to let good men go. And unless somebody came—and this, I think, would have primarily been Tracy Barnes's responsibility—and said, "Look, you've got to let this guy go for this operation because it's absolutely vital, it's the most important thing we're doing," they probably wouldn't have. Now, in due fairness to the people running the operation, it is quite true they were trying to hold this very closely, so they probably weren't too willing to go and say, "Well, this is the most important thing the Agency's doing," and evoking curiosity about it. . . .

There's one other aspect that's important from many points of view. The post-operation criticism tended to concentrate fairly heavily on the fact that the Joint Chiefs of Staff should also be to blame. Now that, I think, is extremely unjustified and uncalled for. The role of the Joint Chiefs of Staff in this operation was to evaluate the training of the unit and to pass upon the feasibility of the operation; those were basically its two principal roles. And you will recall, I'm sure—it's been recorded, it's in all of the books about this operation—that the original concept, when it was decided to make a landing in some force, was to take the town of Trinidad on the south coast of Cuba, but the State Department objected that this would cause too much noise level, and therefore they switched to the Bay of Pigs. The Joint Chiefs reviewed both of these plans and passed upon their feasibility, indicating the possibility of making a landing and so on. And they also sent an evaluation team down to Guatemala to the training camps to look at the quality of the training and how the Cubans looked, and they looked very good from the point of view of their evaluation. They were well trained and motivated and very heavily armed for a group of this size. But to afterwards say that there was some failure on their part, I just never felt was justified in any respect or in any regard.

There was one episode which I think indicates this to a very important degree. Colonel—what was his name, the Marine that commanded
it?

*Colonel Frank? That's all that I'm aware of, that it was a Marine
colonel.*

Well, at any rate, he was the Marine that was . . .

Training them at Guatemala?

No, this was in Washington. He was the chief, the operational chief
of this, and I talked to him for three hours afterwards—in fact, recorded
it, the three-hour discussion with him and the other chief operators—on
why the operation had failed. And on the night that the decision was made
not to do the H-hour air strike—which I think was a Sunday night, if I
remember, April 16th—he had gone out to dinner with his wife; he had
not been home for several days and he told her he would take her to dinner that night, feeling there would be a lull between the operation going
off and the landing. And when he left, he had turned to the men that were
staying behind in operational headquarters and said, "Don't let them do
anything to this operation." By "them" he meant the policymakers. While
he was gone, McGeorge Bundy had called Bissell, and Bissell and Cabell
had gone over and talked to [Dean] Rusk and gotten the decision that
there would be no H-hour air strike. When this fellow came back, Cabell
was in the operational headquarters and made the announcement. This
fellow slammed the desk in front of this four-star general and said, "This
is criminally negligent!" But, of course, none of this seeped back up because—it just didn't get back, I know, to the Presidential level or to the
Secretarial level that the operators felt that condemned the operation to
failure.

*This is, in effect, a key point, why this never did get up to the point at
which the decision was made.*

Well, I think the point there is that General Cabell and the others felt
that they were the senior men running the operation. They would make
the decisions, and they made the decisions ignoring the advice of what
the men doing the nuts and bolts of the operation said.

And there's one other interesting aspect to this. One of the men running this operation, who was a very able man and had been brought in on
it—in this conversation that I had with the three of them, the top three
men at the operational level—reported that after Cabell had come back
and told them that the H-hour air strike was cancelled, he called, I believe, Major General [David W.] Gray from the Pentagon, who was the

liaison man to the operations (this is about one o'clock Monday morning or something like that), got him out of bed, and told him to come down and talk about it. And they talked about it, and Cabell is reported to have said to Gray, "Now I want you to think up things that your people can do to help us." And they talked about what could be done: however, all present were well aware, I believe, of the fact that President Kennedy had said that no U.S. forces would be involved, no U.S. personnel would go to the beach with the Cubans.

So they were operating in that structure of command, and this officer reported to me that after this conference he escorted General Gray to the door; and Gray turned to him as they were going down the hall, and he said, "Surely, Cabell realizes that this means this operation is doomed to failure." So this is the general structure of the fact that at the operating level, once this H-hour strike was eliminated, the general reaction was it couldn't succeed. They went ahead with it on the presumption that they had a chance, but only a chance, and even before that, the general attitude of the operators was that this was an operation on a very, very thin margin, something which I am quite convinced in my mind was never communicated to President Kennedy. [Interruption.]

But the impression I get is that even when the H-Four strike was cancelled, General Cabell and Mr. Bissell attempted to convince the men who had actually cancelled the strike—in other words, the President, the Secretary of State, McGeorge Bundy—to re-lay on the strike

Isn't it true—this is my understanding; I may be in error—that when Secretary Rusk informed Cabell and Bissell that the strike had been cancelled, he said, "The President is at Glen Ora, and if you wish to appeal it, you may." But I understand no phone call was made to Glen Ora.

That's right, not at that point. I was under the impression that a little bit later, perhaps as these men regained their courage or I don't know what, that an attempt, a direct appeal to the President was made.

Later that night?

Yes.

Well, it may be, but I never heard that.

I see. Well, why wasn't an appeal made? Do you think that the importance of this strike was not realized, or that these men simply decided not to attempt to buck their political superior, or what?

I don't know, quite frankly, and I would be speaking more from this role reaction there than from anything else. I had a feeling of antipathy between Cabell and the President, and I don't know why, but there was some feeling there, I'm quite sure. And I don't know whether you could get any facts on this or not, but whether this was what restrained them. Now, Dick Bissell, of course, was a personal friend of the Kennedys, of President Kennedy, and I know that they used to converse on a personal basis quite frequently. In fact, it was Bissell that the President called to get the signs down that pointed to the CIA building. I don't know whether you've gotten that or not . . .

No, I didn't realize that.

But that's a fascinating anecdote. And what inhibited them I just don't know. Now they surely couldn't have underestimated the importance of this strike because by then the U-2 photography showed that Castro had moved all of his remaining aircraft that hadn't been destroyed in the first strike into two air fields and that he had his tanks at Camp Libertad lined up bumper to bumper. And the air strike would have been just perfect from the point of view of trying to disable those tanks, and with napalm they could have probably all been put out of operation; and they should have been able to have gotten the rest of the Castro air force, including the five jets that made the difference. So I just don't know why. And, of course, Mr. Dulles was not there; Mr. Dulles was in Puerto Rico giving a speech.

Oh, it is true, though, that General Cabell did later convince the President to provide air cover the following morning, American air cover, not an air strike, but jet cover. Isn't that so?

Was it jet cover, or was it simply two jets from the carrier *Essex* to appear without any permission for engagement?

Well, I was under the impression that the permission for engagement had not been granted, and yet the jets were to be above the B-26s, and therefore, if the B-26s happened to be attacked, the jets could return the fire. In other words, it was air cover without saying it was air cover. This is the impression I had had.

I'm not sure that they had permission to fire. As I understood it, the two jets were to be there at the time the 26s hit, but simply as a show of force without actually being permitted to engage. Now, I'm sure you can check this with the Navy because they must have it in their files. In fact, I talked to somebody at the Naval War College just a couple of weeks ago about it, and he said, "We had permission to be there, but not to engage." And, of course, they missed it because of the time difference. There was a one-hour time difference. They showed up an hour late, and it was all over.

But the importance of this that I was trying to bring out was not so much that the airplanes could or could not fire but that General Cabell had apparently approached the President again to try to restate his case.

I think that's probably true. But by then, of course, after the H-hour strike had gone to the board, and after, of course, all of the tanks had moved out of Camp Libertad and the jets were unloosed on the landing force.

Getting back to this business about the part that the Joint Chiefs of Staff played in it, and I realize that you did not investigate the problem from the Joint Chiefs of Staff point of view, but you did mention that the Joint Chiefs of Staff were responsible for commenting on the feasibility of the operation. Well, by this I would understand you to mean the military fragility of the plan.

Right.

Well, it then was the Joint Chiefs of Staff's responsibility to advise that one aspect or another aspect or the entire plan was, from a military standpoint, very fragile. Is this correct?

Yes, it's correct, but then I think the question immediately arises as to how far behind the plan did they go. Were they going to re-review the intelligence that went into making up the plan, were they going to study the intelligence accuracy and make their own assessment of it? And it's my understanding that was not part of it, because it's my conviction now, both from my investigation then and from the studies that I've done more recently, that the key to the failure of the operation, in addition to the operational failures of CIA, was an intelligence failure: (1) there was an underestimation of the fighting ability of the Castro forces—they were not considered to be as good as they turned out to be; (2) there was an overestimation of the number of defections that would take place from the Castro militia and from the Castro army—they felt that once the fighting got intense that Castro's militia and troops would drop their arms and come over and surrender; and (3) there was a complete error in anticipating what could be expected from resistance inside Cuba, because if they were going to put ashore a brigade to secure a beachhead, regardless of what anybody says, the intention must have been to get a beachhead which could be elbowed out in size to which Cubans would come over, from which they could fly their Free Cuba flag and ask for assistance.

Well, to say that they didn't expect any people to come over, as I believe Mr. Dulles has recently, I just don't think is consistent with the facts. They must have expected people to come over. Yet you'll recall that President Kennedy, I think about ten days before the Bay of Pigs, had said the United States would never intervene in Cuba. And about a week before—or I don't know the exact day, I don't have it in mind, but somewhere in that general time category—Castro had rounded up about a hundred thousand Cubans and put them in concentration camps. Now, both of these were very important factors on this operation because: (1) who's going to risk a firing squad when the President of the United States has said the United States will not intervene, because it meant they were fighting completely on their own, none but Cubans, and I don't think people inside Cuba would have anticipated their exiled brothers and cousins were going to be that effective; and (2) it seems to me that the operation should have been cancelled immediately when Castro picked up all of what was remaining of the resistance inside Cuba.

There were other indicators, too, because I recall having lunch with Ambassador Earl Smith and several operators in about February or March of 1961. This was all related to Cuba, and the question came up as to the degree of resistance inside Cuba, and the Chief of the Western Hemisphere Division—who incidentally was also not involved in this operation, even though he was a man who had spent his entire life in Latin America and was running the Division—reported that resistance units in the Escambray mountains were starving to death because the peasants wouldn't feed them. Well, this, for anybody who's ever been involved in guerrilla operations, is a complete clue to the fact that they're terrified and that they just don't have a chance of surviving. You can't build a guerrilla unit unless they can live off the land.

So there were many indicators beforehand, and I think that if the Joint Chiefs had done a thorough review of the precise situation in Cuba, I don't understand how they could have done an analysis of the success of the operation. That's why I used the words "military feasibility." I think what they passed on was their impression as to whether this brigade of fourteen hundred and fifty men could land there and secure a beachhead, and they said they thought it was feasible with the size and the strength and the arms that they had.

And yet there still seem to be many points, many very, very weak points, that could have been cleared by military experts.

That's right.

People point to the landing craft, to the reef that was suddenly discovered, to various other things that one would think military experts could have seen. Now I understand that the criticism of the CIA was that there were not experts with experience in amphibious operations doing this operation, controlling or planning this job, but I should have thought that this would have been the military's responsibility to check on this.

It would have been the military's responsibility. That was another aspect of our report about the inadequacy of the maritime capability in the vetting of adequate maritime personnel. By "maritime," I mean people skilled in small-boat operations and experience in that area. And again, it was a case of not asking for it, because the military has always supported CIA to the hilt.

I remember in 1951, when [Walter] Bedell Smith was Director, he sent me over to see Anna Rosenberg in the Defense Department, and I negotiated that day with the three chiefs of personnel—or the four chiefs of personnel, the Marines were also in for support of CIA with military personnel—and ever since that day the Agency's gotten whatever they asked for. If we want a small-boat expert from the Navy or if we want a cargo drop expert from the Air Force, they were always forthcoming. And the services would go out of their way to make them available; they would recall them from foreign duty and things like that. So it isn't a case of not being there, but I think this type of analysis just was not being made, because I'm quite confident in saying the Joint Chiefs were not asked to come in and review the operation in progress. They were asked to review the plans of the operation. If they had, if the Joint Chiefs had sent, say, a couple of their inspectors from one of the service IG [Inspector General] staffs around, I think they would have come up with the same conclusions we did ex post facto.

This was not my impression, from public sources, at any rate, of the role that the Joint Chiefs of Staff had. I thought they were . . .

Now, I'm sure you will talk to Bissell at length on this, because Dick was the man running this operation. He's a brilliant man with tremendous talents, and he may have a different version than I do; but based upon our study of it, that was our impression of what it did. And then I certainly would hope you'd see some of the men that were in the Joint Chiefs at the time and talk to them about it.

Well, this has been done already to a certain extent. We're not, by any means, finished talking with people.

On the rest of this investigation. I think I sort of summarized the more important points that the study made. The way it was handled was that Mr. Dulles read it, wrote a very brief comment on it; General Cabell read it, wrote a very brief comment on it; both of them, in effect, rejecting it as being prejudiced. The operational side of the Agency under Tracy Barnes studied it, wrote a rebuttal to it which was longer than the original report. The President's Foreign Intelligence Advisory Board—the same one that Ambassador Kennedy had been on but which President Kennedy re-established after the Bay of Pigs operation—held hearings on it, at which I testified. And they read my report plus the rebuttal and the other comments, and then Barnes and Bissell testified before it. And then on McCone's direction, the entire package was bound together—my report, the comments on it—and placed in the executive registry in the Agency with the instructions it would never be released except with the Director's personal permission. And the only time it has been released, to my knowledge, was in . . . well, it was before the President's death. I'm quite sure Mac Bundy wanted to see it. [Interruption.]

You were talking about the way the investigation was handled, or the way the report was handled.

Oh, yes, at any rate, I took this over. McCone called me and said, "I want you personally to carry this over to Mac Bundy." And I did and handed it to him. And he said, "Where can I find what I'm looking for?" And I said, "Well, I don't know really what you're looking for, but if you turn to"—I think it was page 148—"you'll see the conclusions and recommendations." And so he turned and looked at them, and his eyebrows went up a bit. He said, "Well, this casts quite a different light on things," and then asked if he could keep it and read it in full, which he did. I didn't go back and talk to him about it. I don't know what his reaction was after reading it, which also is related to a comment that McCone made to me in January of 1962.

He had set up a board composed of myself as chairman and General Cortlandt Schuyler and Patrick Coyne to look at the Agency's work and particularly his job and how he should relate to the President, other departments and agencies. The three of us were meeting with him at his house one night for conversation, and sort of as an aside, I think, the Bay of Pigs had come up. And he turned to me, and he said, "I thought Charlie [Charles J. V.] Murphy's article in *Fortune* was the authoritative version, until I saw your report."

So that's where the report is today. The recommendations, however, I think have been implemented to a degree. I'm not sure I would consider them satisfactory—maybe Dick Helms will change them a bit—but the most important of the recommendations that we made was that in any operation of this sort there should be an advisory and review board composed of military, State, CIA, USIA [U.S. Information Agency], and others that would be involved, high-level, fully cleared, and fully briefed on all details, who could review it without any operational attachment. You know, in intelligence work the operator falls in love with his operation—I don't care who it is or what his level is, whether it's Allen Dulles or a subordinate officer. And it's very difficult to be objective about your operation and say, "We'd better drop it; it's not going to succeed."

So that was our most important recommendation; and the second of which was that we felt that the Agency had been a little narrow in not using all the Agency facilities for supporting this operation, because it would have had so much broader a base to operate from and so much better advice and guidance. And we pointed out that everybody in the Agency is cleared through Top Secret so that they could be trusted on an operation like that. The whole Board of Estimates should have been in on it. Bob Amory, I believe, has said publicly that he was never brought in on it, which is quite true. So that some of the most senior talent of the Agency was excluded from it by direction.

You mentioned that some gaps in intelligence led to various failures, for example, in connection with the line of resistance or the effectiveness of resistance within Cuba itself. Well, if the intelligence side of the CIA, Robert Amory's side, had been involved in this or had been made aware of this operation, do you think this would have changed this? Did the intelligence information they were gathering give sufficient information to permit a different decision on this area?

Well, this is something that's going to be one of those "ifs" of history. You would never know whether they would have said, "No, you're too optimistic; there isn't that much resistance in Cuba, and you aren't going to get that much defection." And I suppose that if archives were ever made available, what somebody would have to do is go back and read what intelligence was receiving as distinct from what the operators were receiving.

Now this operation combines some of the classics of what people worry about in intelligence—mainly, the fact that the same organization that was collecting a lot of intelligence, the same organization which was dealing with refugees, was also mounting the operation. And it's terribly hard to remain objective and dispassionate under those conditions, particularly when the refugees themselves are all gung-ho to go and liberate their country and are obviously going to picture everything in the most optimistic possible light.

This, incidentally, of course, is related to that very key political question that came up afterwards, and that is whether the CIA training officers had implied or said that U.S. military support would be behind the Cubans. And we went into this most thoroughly, and our conclusion was that the CIA training officers probably didn't say anything more than any training officer would say under similar circumstances. In other words, they certainly weren't going to say, "Look, you're on your own, and if you miss, why, you're through." They probably said, "We're all for you, and get in there and do it, and you can win." But we were not able to ascertain that anybody ever said, "The Marines are right there, and they're going to come in behind you." Everybody that was knowledgeable knew that that wasn't true.

Haynes Johnson in his book about it [Bay of Pigs (1964)] says at one point that the leaders leading the training in Guatemala told the Cuban people there, the Cuban invasion force, that if too much opposition arose in Washington, they should put in the local prison the American advisors and go ahead and carry out the operation itself by themselves. Did you hear anything about that, do you know? You found that simply wasn't so, or . . .

No, I didn't find any evidence of that.

Okay, I have a series of other questions here. There has been much talk of communication gaps between the CIA and the Joint Chiefs of Staff, and the CIA and the White House in connection with this operation. At the same time there has been criticism leveled at the Kennedy Adminis-tration for, in the early stages of the Administration, eliminating various links between various agencies without reimposing new communication links. Did you find that this played any role in this, or did this come under the area of your investigation?

I don't think there were any communications links which were miss-ing because of some presidential order or some higher decision. The links were available if they wanted to be created or used. No, I wouldn't say that that affected the operation at all, because CIA has hundreds of daily contacts with the Pentagon and the same with the State Department, so the channels have always been open and were not inhibited. They may not have been the same formal-type channels. . . .

A number of people have pointed out that this Bay of Pigs failure tended to destroy the President's confidence in the CIA organization as a whole, and I wondered if you found that was so or not. Do you have any comments on that?

I think that the President's confidence was severely shaken in the CIA and also in the government. I think it was broader than just CIA, from my distant observation. But I don't think his confidence remained shaken for long. From what I've read in the various "S"-type memoirs and others, the President apparently blamed himself for taking the advice of people he considered experts without sufficient review. But if this con-fidence was shaken, it didn't last for long because—I am not precise about my dates, but I think it was '62; it might have been in early '63—I men-tioned to Mr. McCone that we did not have an official portrait of the President in the CIA building and asked his permission if I could call the military attaché, Ted [Chester V.] Clifton. At any rate, I called him and said, "You know, we haven't got an official portrait of the President. Do you think you can do anything about it?" And he said, "Sure, I'll be in touch with you."

About a month passed and I didn't hear anything, and he called me up on the phone, and he said, "The picture you asked for is on its way over. Call me when you get it." So the picture arrived, and it was, I imagine, the President's favorite picture of himself. And it was inscribed, "To CIA, with esteem, John F. Kennedy." So I called Clifton back and said, "This is far more than we asked for. I certainly appreciate it." He said, "Well, you'll be interested in the story of this. I told the President that you wanted it, and he said, 'I'll inscribe it.'" And he said, "There was another one of the assistants standing nearby, and when he wrote, 'To CIA, with esteem,' he said, 'Well, Mr. President, if you write that to CIA, you've got to do it to the rest of the government.' And he [Kennedy] said, 'Well, maybe I don't hold the rest of the government in esteem!'" So I think this indicates how his attitude had changed from the shock and disappointment of the Bay of Pigs.

The other anecdote that also indicates a rather amusing side of the President was the business of the signs of the CIA building. When he took over as President, the building was just nearing completion. We started moving in in 1961, and there were big signs on Route 123 near Bobby Kennedy's house, great big six-by-four signs, "CIA (arrow) That Way." And then coming out George Washington Memorial Parkway there were signs periodically "To CIA," and at the entrance there was a sign "To CIA." Incidentally, I suppose it's known that Memorial Parkway was extended as a part of the CIA building bill. Congress said, "You can't build a building till the Parkway's finished."

Mr. Dulles was at the White House for a meeting sometime in this period before the building was finished, and President Kennedy said to him, "Mr. Dulles, do you really think you should have signs to your building? It doesn't seem consistent with the character of your organization." And as I understood the story, Mr. Dulles said, "Oh, Mr. President, we've got to have it. If we didn't have the signs, they probably couldn't get the building built; the workers wouldn't find their way." He sort of laughed and left. A week or two passed, and Mr. Dulles was over at the White House for another meeting. And the conversation, I am told, went something like this, "Allen, I really think you ought to take those signs down at the CIA building. They attract attention, and your Agency is one that shouldn't attract attention." And Mr. Dulles again said, "Oh, Mr. President, I think that we do have a large research side, and it is overt, and if we take the signs down, it would probably cause more comment than not." So another day passed, and Richard Bissell got a phone call, and a very familiar voice said, "Who in the hell do I have to talk to to get those signs down?" They were down the next day.

The President did make some effort, as I understand it, at the failure of the Bay of Pigs to appoint a committee or to resurrect a committee to supervise a little bit more thoroughly the operations of the CIA.

This is correct. This is the President's Foreign Intelligence Advisory Board. Now to make it different from Eisenhower's Board, they added the word "Advisory," but Pat Coyne and I worked on the charter or the Presidential letter setting up the new one in 1961, and, basically speaking, it was charged with the same thing. But I think President Kennedy wanted to make sure that they reported to him more frequently than the previous Board had. The Eisenhower Board was required to report to the President not less often than semi-annually, and the Kennedy Board, I think, was asked to report at least every other month, whether there was a specific reporting date.

And he named Dr. [James R.] Killian to be the first head of that, and put people on it like Clark Clifford and Gordon Gray and Robert Murphy and Jim [James H.] Doolittle, a very distinguished group of people. I think their first series of meetings were in July 1961, if I remember it, or at least they met with the President, I know, in July of 1961. This, of course, was simultaneous with the Taylor group on the Bay of Pigs operation itself. And they met very frequently during the rest of President Kennedy's Administration. In fact, they still meet very frequently, the same group with a few additions and deletions. And their responsibility was to look at everything the Agency did and, in fact, everything the other intelligence agencies did too, and report to the President, make recommendations for changes, and so on. I think it's a very constructive body. I think it's unfortunate it doesn't advertise more.

Was this control more effective than the control of the group under Eisenhower?

Well, I don't know whether you could really compare them one way or the other. It's an advisory body purely. They make recommendations to the President, and then it's up to the Director of Central Intelligence as to what to do about it. And if the Director goes along, why, something happens, and if he resists . . .

Arthur Schlesinger mentions at one point that Robert Kennedy had become very much interested in the supervision of the CIA after the Bay of Pigs and that he himself took a more active role. Were you aware of this?

Oh, yes.

Can you tell us how he did it?

Oh, yes, very much so. He took a much more active role on a personal basis, from the point of view that he and Mr. McCone became very close friends, saw a great deal of each other. It wasn't at all unusual for the Attorney General to stop in the building on his way to work. It's only about two hundred yards from his house. And he and Mr. McCone discussed a great number of things quite frequently. So he was very active, and I think he perhaps felt a custodianship here, that he was handling . . .

Because he was geographically so close?

. . . this account well, and also this account for his brother, and also for the fact that the President felt so strongly about the failure of the Bay of Pigs. And the Attorney General probably wanted to make sure this didn't happen again.

Another thing that happened and that I thought might be an aftermath or a part of the aftermath was that, in May 1961, President Kennedy is said to have attempted to reassert control by the embassies in various countries over the operations of the CIA within those countries. Now that had been attempted before; that had been attempted under President Eisenhower, or at least a statement had gone out to that effect. Were there any more teeth in the statement? Was this a stronger attempt to bring this about?

Well, I would like to put this in context. Every President, I believe, if you examine the record since the proliferation of our foreign relations and the addition of new organizations in foreign affairs, whether it was agricultural attachés, commercial attachés, et cetera, has periodically reiterated the primacy of the State Department in foreign relations. Eisenhower did it, President Kennedy did it, and others. There were more teeth in the Kennedy effort from the point of view that one of the previously announced or advertised efforts of the Administration was to restore the State Department to its role as the director of U.S. foreign relations. There was a great deal of talk, including testimony before Congress, about alleged interference of CIA and other agencies in embassies and so on. This is probably one of those reiterations that's required in government periodically to ensure that everybody knows who is the boss in an embassy and who does this. Yes, I think it probably accomplished something.

On the other hand, I would say that certainly in the last decade or so there has never been any question, certainly not in the minds of CIA, as to who the boss was in any embassy. The discipline there is quite tight. The Ambassador is head man, and he is supposed to be privileged to what CIA is doing. And if he disagrees with what CIA is doing, he has not only permission but the responsibility to advise the State Department in Washington that he doesn't like it. Then State would advise CIA to stop it if they agreed with it. If they didn't, why, they'd probably say they thought it was necessary. But where the CIA station chief and an Ambassador disagree on something, then they both go back by their own channels to get a decision. Presumably the station chief would stop doing it until he got a decision.

They said that when John McCone came to the CIA that he, in effect, repaired relations between the CIA and the State Department. Do you agree with that, or do you think relations were in need of repairs?

I would find it difficult to believe that relations were in need of repairs when brothers [Allen Dulles and John Foster Dulles] had been heading the two agencies up until very few years beforehand, and Mr. [Allen] Dulles and Christian Herter were two exceedingly close friends. I think there it's talking more about atmosphere than anything else, because Mr. Dulles had said to me in 1957, "You know, while Foster and I are around, we should do our best to make sure that the relations between the CIA and the Department are put on the best possible footing." And what he was talking about was that there is a basic incompatibility between CIA and the State Department. CIA is covert, secret, clandestine; it has even a different type of personality working for it. The State Department is overt, diplomatic, gregarious, dealing with indigenous people. There is this incompatibility, plus an almost automatic competition that exists. The CIA's got money to use clandestinely to obtain information. The young Foreign Service officer thinks that's buying reports away from him. And the older Foreign Service officer, who grew up in a nonintelligence atmosphere, is occasionally terribly suspicious of the CIA people. So that there is an incompatibility there that will always exist as long as you have a legitimate Foreign Service and a distinct intelligence service. The Russians don't have the problem because they don't have any legitimate Foreign Service.

I should have thought, though, that after the death of John Foster Dulles and the period between his death and the Bay of Pigs operation, there were certain specific items which did destroy the relations, the Bay of Pigs being one, because I understood that Secretary Rusk was, in effect, opposed basically to the Bay of Pigs operation. Number two, there were conflicts in Laos and in . . .

Well, I think that's right. But you take an Ambassador like Winthrop Brown, who was very heavily involved in Laos, he was one of the Agency's greatest supporters. And it is probably true that Rusk was worried about Dulles. I just think it comes down simply to that. Now to McCone's credit, he used to have a meeting with Rusk every Sunday. They met every single Sunday practically, unless one of them was away. And this provided an opportunity to go down and say, "Well, what problems have we got, and what do we do to straighten them out?" McCone was superb in his interpersonal relations with his opposite numbers.

At the same time it is said that Mr. McCone repaired relations with the State Department, it is said that he could not repair relations with the Pentagon. Do you understand what is meant by that?

This may be a factor in how long this particular section will be kept in the files, because there was a great deal of talk in Washington in 1964 and 1965 about CIA versus the Pentagon and McCone versus [Secretary of Defense Robert S.] McNamara. And I suppose there is some merit to the argument that McCone and McNamara were fundamentally competitive in nature because they are both very strong-minded men and very able men and very aggressive men. But quite frankly, on the intelligence-level liaison, I thought relations with the Pentagon in most of the fundamental areas were excellent. Our relations with the Defense Intelligence Agency, I felt, were very, very good. All the top men in that were men that had grown up in intelligence. Rufus Taylor, who was the Deputy Director there, is now the Deputy Director of the CIA. Joe [Joseph F.] Carroll I've known since his FBI days, and our relations, I thought, were very fine.

Occasionally there were differences in two major areas: (1) intelligence interpretation, and this was particularly pertinent to Vietnam; and (2) as to CIA's activities in overhead reconnaissance, which the Air Force thought should be theirs. Even though they didn't want to build a U-2, they still resented anybody else's overhead reconnaissance. And the key to it, I think, was the fact that McCone was always pessimistic about Vietnam and McNamara was always optimistic, and consequently they were putting in contrary reports to the President. So I would think it did revolve a great deal around that area, because I think John McCone would still be in Washington if he had been asked to stay.

Okay, you said there was something you wanted to mention about your impressions at the time of the President's death, and I wondered if you had . . .

Well, I thought this would be of interest from a historical point of view because the day that the President was killed, the Foreign Intelligence Advisory Board was meeting. And John McCone had planned to go out to California that afternoon; he practically commuted to his home and business out there. And he and I left the Foreign Intelligence Board at about noon, and he said, "What are you doing for lunch?" And I said, "I have no plans." And he said, "Well, let's get some of the others, and we'll have lunch together in my dining room before I leave." So we did; in fact, we had lunch in his outer office because his dining room was being refurbished at that particular time. And there were about six of us present at that: Sherman Kent, myself, a couple of others.

It was while we were sitting there that McCone's assistant came in, and he said, "There's been a flash on the radio that the President's been shot." And McCone turned on the television right there in the room we were eating in, and we all watched and listened. And then he went and got the White House phone and called Bobby Kennedy and went over to Hickory Hill. I think it has been reported that he was walking in the yard with the Attorney General when the final news came through.

But then, of course, we had to move into fairly high gear intelligence-wise to make sure that the Russians didn't use this period for any adventures. So when Mr. McCone came back from the Attorney General's house, he called an Executive Committee meeting and issued orders for all stations to be on the alert and to watch out for all movement of Russian personnel, particularly Russian intelligence personnel, and any indications of any activity on their part to take advantage of the situation.

And we moved then into the phase of the funeral, which caused us very serious concern. And the State Department asked to borrow and did borrow about a hundred CIA security officers to assist them in the security considerations. McCone went down to be in the funeral, and General Carter, the Deputy Director, went to the church, and I stayed in the building to monitor anything that came in which might bear on it. And after McCone had left for the White House, we got a report from the French saying that there was an OAS [(Algerian) Secret Army Organization] threat to assassinate [French President Charles] de Gaulle and that he should not march in the parade. So I called McCone and got him on the phone at the White House and told him this and said, "You'd better tell General de Gaulle that we have this report and see what he wants to do," which he did.

De Gaulle wasn't bothered by this?

Not bothered a bit. They missed him before; I guess they missed him again.

6

Robert Amory, Jr.

I N 1953, ROBERT AMORY BECAME the CIA's second Deputy Director of Intelligence and served almost ten years in that post under Director Allen Dulles. In many ways, Amory's earlier military career had prepared him for paramilitary operations in the Agency. Enlisting in the U.S. Army as a private in 1941, he served with the Army Corps of Engineers and won promotion to colonel as a combat officer during twenty-six assault landings in the South and Southwest Pacific region. With Reuben M. Waterman he wrote a regimental history of the amphibious operations, entitled *Surf and Sand*, published in 1947. Awarded the Silver Star, Bronze Star, and the Legion of Merit, Amory continued in the National Guard during the rest of the 1940s.

Young Robert, Jr., was born on March 2, 1915, to Robert and Leonore Cobb Amory in Boston. He attended school in the city, then graduated from Milton Academy. At Harvard he earned an A.B. degree in politics and government and also was elected to Phi Beta Kappa in 1936. He continued his studies at Harvard Law School, earning his LL.B. degree in 1938, and he married Mary Armstrong several days after graduation. Two sons, Robert III and Daniel, would complete the Amory family. Practicing law with the firm of Cahill and Gordon in New York City, Amory also became president of the New York Young Republicans' Club.

After World War II, Amory taught law and accounting at Harvard from 1946 to 1952 and wrote *Materials on Accounting*, published in 1949. With enthusiasm, he joined Dulles's new intelligence team in Washington during the Eisenhower Administration. However, the wide gulf between Agency operations and analysis continued during the 1950s. This serious problem became most evident in the planning for the Cuban Bay of Pigs invasion. Hints and fragments of information reached Amory; however, Dulles, Richard Bissell, and other operations managers blanketed this operation with silence. After the failed invasion, John McCone replaced Dulles as Director and brought the Intelligence Directorate largely into covert planning.

In 1962, Amory moved from the CIA to the Bureau of the Budget, serving there as assistant director until 1965 when he joined, as a partner, the Washington law firm of Corcoran, Foley, Youngman, and Rowe. Seven years later, in 1972, he became secretary and general counsel for the National Gallery of Art until his retirement in 1980. He died in Washington in April 1989.

JOSEPH O'CONNOR: *We can go on to any later contacts you had [with President Kennedy]—you mentioned a few of them—on up to 1961.*

ROBERT AMORY: This first little contact was rather interesting in showing how Kennedy was testing the organization that he inherited. The day of his Inaugural, Mrs. [Eugene] Meyer sent him a long and thoughtful letter urging that because of the obvious famine conditions in China, he start off with a great gesture of American wheat to the Chinese people, not to the Chinese administration. And, as I recall, Inauguration was a Friday. Anyway, early Saturday morning, I was called over to the White House by Ralph Dungan and handed this piece of paper which had marked on the corner of it in Kennedy's writing, which I knew, "Ask Chet [Chester Bowles] and Bob Amory what they think of this." So I got the piece of paper and went back and spent the whole weekend writing an analysis of the problem seven or eight pages long and showed it to Allen Dulles Sun-

Conducted by Joseph E. O'Connor in Washington, DC, on February 9 and 17, 1966. Oral History Interviews, John F. Kennedy Library, Boston, Massachusetts.

day morning. He said, "Oh, this is a policy question. We can't get into this. We're intelligence people." I said, "Goddamn it, Allen, it's a new President. He's going to do things differently. He's asked for this. Now our first response can't be a bureaucratic 'No, somebody else.' " And Allen said, "Well, all right. Dungan's asking for it. Take it over to Dungan and let him read it, but get it back. I don't want that kind of a paper in the White House files."

So I went over and showed it to Dungan, and Dungan read it. Somebody later said it was a very good paper. Though it didn't come out firmly one way or the other, it showed the arguments pro and con—what he'd have to consider, what the likely reaction of the Chinese regime would be. It predicted the reaction of the Chinese, essentially, if you made such a gesture. I said, "Now may I have the paper back?" And Dungan says "No," in his rather charming and tough manner. So I said, "All right," and came home and didn't say anything about it. I saw no need in worrying Allen; I'd get the paper back in due course and get to it.

Well, the next week was the National Security Council meeting, and I think it was Kennedy's first—it must have been. And everybody was very new and fresh and sort of introducing each other and their subordinates. Allen introduced me to [Robert S.] McNamara and things like that, and I sat in the back of the room as I was accustomed to doing while Allen made his briefing. Immediately at the end of the briefing, Kennedy raised this subject. To Allen's horror and to [Dean] Rusk's and Bowles's obvious annoyance, he raised the issue and said, "Now, Bob Amory, I understand you think this is probably not too good an idea, but that it just might work. Is that right? And Chet, I asked your views of it, but I haven't gotten them yet." And it went on, otherwise inconsequentially, but it showed how directly he was going to operate. It was an early example he wasn't going to fool around with chain of command or logistical places; he was going to go to human beings on problems.

Of course, the Agency developed thereafter a very good, what we call quick response to the whims or any other desires of the President, and that built it up in those first few months, until Cuba, very favorably. I know from Mac Bundy of other little things. The President was quoted, not directly, to me as saying, "By gosh, I don't care what it is, but if I need some material fast or an idea fast, CIA is the place I have to go. The State Department is four or five days to answer a simple yes or no." And so on. So we tried very hard to live up to his high views of us. I don't mean just at the high level. This had a very good morale effect all down the line in the analytical side of the CIA establishment. People were willing to work long hours and to come in at three o'clock in the morning because they knew damn well that what they produced was read personally by the President immediately upon its delivery to the White House.

What was Allen Dulles's attitude toward this?

Well, he gradually came around. You see, he'd had to be so careful in the days when he and Foster [John Foster Dulles] were together in the thing not to one-up on his brother, and time and again I've heard him respond to Eisenhower, "Yes, Mr. President, that's a tough question, but really it's up to the Secretary of State to answer it." And Eisenhower would accept that. He'd say, "All right, Foster, well, what do you think?" And I think he had conditioned himself that way. Allen was very pleased to have been immediately reappointed. You remember, right after the election, in Hyannis Port, he and J. Edgar Hoover were the first confirmed appointments, announced appointments. . . . As is natural, a guy young enough to be his son, virtually—it wasn't quite true, but certainly another generation in the Presidency—he didn't really feel comfortable with him.

I know he liked him and had seen a lot more of him as a Senator than I had. They used to go to neighboring estates. The Kennedy and the [Charles] Wrightsman estates adjoin each other in Palm Beach, and Allen was always a very regular visitor to the Wrightsman estate. They'd swim and play tennis and other things together. And he saw a lot of Kennedy in that worst winter he had when he nearly died. He used to go over and chat with him and pay his respects. So Kennedy, I think, was genuinely fond of him. Kennedy also was extremely fond of Dick Bissell, had a very high regard for him. I think he regarded Dick as probably one of the four or five brightest guys in the whole Administration.

Do you know what this was based on? Was this prior to 1960?

Yes, I don't know what it is . . . but, anyway, there was a good feeling, a good rapport between the Agency and the President. I would say, just sort of by hunch, that this had a lot to do with Kennedy's relatively unquestioning acceptances of the Bay of Pigs proposal and so on. He got off on a good start, but it was only a very few weeks later, by the end of February, early March, that you started to have the nut-cutting sessions on the Bay of Pigs.

We also worked very hard to be sure we understood the White House staff arrangement. After all, it was commented on by many people that Kennedy didn't have a cohesive staff. He had a lot of able staff officers who worked directly for him or in small groups, like the Bundy-[Theodore C.] Sorensen team and so on. And very early in the Administration—this date would be easily available, I would say the first week in February—Allen took the Alibi Club, a private dining club of some fame, and he had, I would say, the ten top people in CIA and ten, or it may have been twelve, of the White House Staff: Sorensen . . . I remember I sat beside [Lawrence F.] O'Brien. It was a pleasant three-cocktail dinner, but then a serious discussion went on until one o'clock in the morning in which, first, each of us in the Agency described briefly—not a Pentagon formal briefing but sort of a *New Yorker*-ish type of précis—just what did we do, and what are our problems, and what did we see as the important things the White House should be interested in in our work. Then they asked questions on it. Why did we get in such a mess in Indonesia in 1958 and that kind of thing. But it was a good hair-down thing, and everybody got pleasantly acquainted.

From then on out, there was nobody in the key White House staff I couldn't pick up the phone and say, "Hey, Larry," or something like that, "This is Bob." It was, again, a very sensible thing for Allen to have done and, I think, sat well with the people. This came as sort of a head start on State, which is a bad thing in a way to state it that baldly. But it was State's own damn fault. State is so full of the need for everything to be cross-checked in the legal area or the policy area, and they just can't move their papers as fast as they should. We had the same problem with being sure that if we're talking about French North Africa, the African specialists as well as the French specialists had their views in it. But we did it in an hour instead of three days of putting papers out in a messenger car. [Pause.]

Well, to continue on first with the sort of more direct contacts that I had with him [President Kennedy], I was, as Arthur Schlesinger accurately says, not privy to the Bay of Pigs, officially. On the other hand, I had all the photo interpretation in the Agency under my command, and my head photo interpreter, Art [Arthur C.] Lundahl, kept me advised on what they were taking pictures of, so I knew informally what was going on. But I was never in on any of the consultations, either inside the Agency or otherwise. I think it was foolish, not because I would have decided it any differently, but at least on paper I knew more about amphibious warfare than anyone in the Agency. I had made twenty-six assault landings in the South Pacific—Southwest Pacific and so on—of about the size, many of them, as the Bay of Pigs, whereas the Marine they had advising them had made one in his whole goddamn life, and that was Iwo Jima, which was three divisions abreast. He was a very able soldier and Marine, but he just didn't know beans about what a small self-contained beachhead would be like.

Who was that man?

Again, my memory is not good enough. It was a simple name [Hawkins] like Williams or Harris or something like that. But he was the Marine that was seconded to the Agency by the Joint Chiefs of Staff. He's either retired or he's a general now, because he was that degree of seniority; he was a colonel then. And he was seconded by the Joint Chiefs of Staff to Bissell at Bissell's request. So there was no question but a bunch of Ivy League amateurs, Corinthians [men-about-town], weren't making military logistical decisions which, of course, the press later charged.

So I want to jump from there right on to the days after the fiasco, in which the Bobby Kennedy-Max Taylor-[Arleigh A.] Burke-Dulles committee was sitting. There was an awful lot of rehashing going on, and I had some contact then in larger meetings with Bobby and the President as to where we should go from there. I felt the President was genuinely floundering thereafter, and I don't blame him. We haven't done any good anywhere in Cuba since. But he certainly was taking full responsibility for the thing. There were no recriminations. I mean, I know there were none publicly; he stood straight on that. But even in private he treated Allen with the greatest cordiality and almost affectionate loyalty, which was the highest type of esprit-building thing, that kind of loyalty down in trouble.

Bobby was convinced that we could upset Castro by a long campaign of meddling, infiltration, and so on. The first time I came into those discussions, I was always negative on that. I said that I don't think this will work; this will just provoke sympathy in the rest of Latin America. The thing to do now is to isolate Castro and treat him like an inoculation. The body is the whole of Latin America; this is the sore arm that's been scratched and poisoned with the thing, but the rest of the body will develop antibodies because of it—much propaganda to show up the thing. Take the Cuban refugees, get them the hell out of Florida. Get all the young ones in universities in Central America and Venezuela and Colombia where they can talk as Latinos about the horror of the thing, instead of the Yankee Colossus del Norte talking about how dangerous it is to have a little island in the hands of communism. And I felt that I didn't get very far with this. I had a lot of allies on it in the State Department, but . . .

Can you name some of those allies?

Oh, yes, Henry Owen . . .

Or was there anybody else saying the same thing that Bobby Kennedy was saying?

Almost everybody was saying the same thing Bobby Kennedy was saying. Tom Mann was. Of course, Tom Mann was in Mexico City then in those days. He'd left, I think. I've forgotten who took his place—[Robert F.] Woodward or [R. Richard] Rubottom, I've forgotten which. They weren't terribly active. They don't come through very vividly in my recollection as to what they did say. But, anyway, again I played a relatively minor role in that, but it was quite a different role from the February and March one, which was as a cipher.

The rest of the routine developed during the summer that every other day I or my Deputy would be the one to bring a special morning briefing to the President. It was a damned early hour. I got out to the Agency at 5:30 in the morning, let's say, three mornings a week. A guy who'd been there all night would have a draft of what he thought the thing ought to be, and we'd finalize it and run it rapidly through a typewriter and a little offset printer, take it in, and talk to Max Taylor, Bundy, and Ted [Chester V.] Clifton.

Then very occasionally I would go to the President's office with them. I would say only twice it happened. Otherwise they, after cross-examining me, would go up to the President with the book. I would wait, and they'd come back and say, "Well, the President wants an amplification of this." Or he would even charge us with action: "He wants you to get hold of the Secretary of State, or the Assistant Secretary of State, and be sure that that message is answered by noon," or little trivial, ministerial odd things. But you did get this strong impression that his first interest in the morning was the world of intelligence, that he really focused on it, that nothing would stand in the way of his grasping everything from the smallest detail that was going on and being very interested in it. . . .

On Laos I saw a lot of [W. Averell] Harriman and a little of Bundy and others and had something to do with Chet [Chester L.] Cooper's being put on the delegation to the Geneva meeting there that ultimately settled the Laotian thing. I thought the President showed great skill and restraint in not falling for the contingent plan of putting twenty-five or forty thousand American troops in Laos. And there the Agency was very badly split. The activists in the DDP [Directorate of Plans] side were all for a war in Laos. They thought that was a great place to have a war and then did run a good little small-bore, bush-league war with their Meo tribesmen, which was their responsibility, and they felt a very little more force would turn the thing round, and we could stabilize the situation there. But I felt it was just an impossible logistics problem and that the people of Laos . . .

As I've said, the interesting thing about the Laotian war is there still is yet to be the first casualty by a bayonet. Those people just don't like to stick each other. They love mortars, but they fire them from this side of the hill around the other side of the hill, and they say, "We're not killing anybody. The great god Buddha's deciding where the mortar shell falls." You just can't think in terms of making these guys a Prussia of the Far East. And Kennedy, two or three times in my presence, showed an instinctive grasp of what that thing was and loyally backed Harriman in getting this kind of sloppy peace we have out there as his military advisors and everybody—I won't say everybody, but lots of people in the State and Defense Departments—were pushing for more aggressive action.

Various people have commented on the difference between the CIA attitude in Laos, and the State Department and Defense Department. Particularly, they contrast Defense and CIA people with Ambassador [Winthrop G.] Brown, who was there at the time. Now, will you comment on this conflict?

Well, actually we had several people—I can't remember their dates and things—who were our Chiefs of Station in Laos, and some of them were activists, to use a simple phrase, and backed Phoumi [Nosovan] very hard. But by the time Win was there, our man out there—his name escapes me—was very much on Win's side. And essentially it was Embassy Vientiane, including its military and CIA people, who were in favor of [Premier] Souvanna Phouma and against Phoumi, and it was back here [J. Graham] Parsons, before he went to Sweden, and his successor . . . Who preceded [Roger] Hilsman?

I'd have to look that up.

Assistant Secretary for the Far East. Who the hell was he? I can't think. There was a short time, then, before Harriman took over the job. But anyway, that guy and the characters from ISA [International Security Affairs] in Defense, General [Victor] Krulak and Paul Nitze and Bill [William P.] Bundy. It's long before Bill went over there. Bill was Paul's assistant in ISA of Defense, and they were urging more action. In other words, the people ten thousand miles away from the thing were the aggressive ones; the ones on the spot just said this wouldn't work. Harriman was the one guy back here, with a small assist from me. . . . By this time I guess we're getting on into the [John A.] McCone stage. McCone was a terrific activist on it. So I'm talking early '62 now. And then, of course, before that all got settled, I left the Agency in . . .

March of 1962, wasn't it?

Exactly, end of March 1962, and went over to the Bureau [of the Budget] where I stopped having any direct influence, you know, other than over coffee in the White House mess and that kind of thing. . . .

[What about] Vietnam, the [Ngo Dinh] Diem crisis—the Diem fall, really?

The Diem fall, I had absolutely nothing to do with it. And you're perfectly right. You know, I read the cables in the back room from time to time, and I bumped into Fritz [Frederick E., Jr.] Nolting from time to time socially but never went to one of the meetings.

Well, backing off, you know who first put Ngo Dinh Diem in power? Very interesting. I do have something, but this goes way back to 1954. I was at an after-theater party in Martin Agronsky's house—pleasant, a couple of Scotches and some canapés—and got off in a corner with Mr. Justice [William O.] Douglas, and Douglas said, "Do you know who's the guy to fix you up in Vietnam? He's here in this country, and that's Ngo Dinh Diem." Well, I wrote it down in my notebook on the way out as, you know, Z-I-M Z-I-M. I came back and asked the biographic boys the next morning, "Dig me up anything you've got on this guy." "We ain't got anything on this guy." And at the next morning meeting I said to Allen Dulles and Frank Wisner, "A suggestion out of the blue . . ." But Wisner picked it up and looked at the thing. And that's how "Ngo Zim Zim" became our man in Indochina. [Laughter.] The long hand of Mr. Justice Douglas. But as to his fall, I know nothing other than . . .

Yes, you were in the Bureau at that time.

Bureau at that time, and by that time in the fall we were up to our ears in hearings and so on and so forth.

You know, when I started trying to think of questions to ask you after you were in the CIA, when you were in the Bureau, I wasn't really sure what your office dealt with. It was the international office of the Bureau of the Budget, but I didn't quite know what you did.

Essentially, we oversaw all the agencies of the government primarily involved abroad: Peace Corps, AID [Agency for International Development], USIA [U.S. Information Agency], Food for Peace, State Department, CIA, and the military assistance program part of the Pentagon, and the military intelligence part of the program. The real reason I was sent there . . . Well, let me back off and tell you what is relevant to why I should be doing any talking, why I moved during the Kennedy Administration.

I was going to ask you about that.

I wrote in my June 1961 25th Reunion Report that I had the best job in the world that I know of outside of the President of the United States, or something like that. It was a fascinating job, and I just couldn't have been more happy. And that was even after the Bay of Pigs. Then when Allen was obviously due to go, I was not at all happy with McCone as a selection. In fact, I protested vigorously to Mac Bundy, and Pete [Herbert F.] Scoville and I both threatened to resign. I thought this appointment was just the wrong thing; this was just a cheap political move to put a prominent Republican in so the heat could be taken off the Bay. We would no longer be part of the Kennedy New Frontier; we would be something that was an incubus that he'd inherited, and so on and so forth. And I thought it was a very bad show, and I intended this to go back to him. Let me see, I'm getting out of order here. No, that's when he was first moving around; that is the right order. Then, very shortly, Kennedy made up his mind and firmly announced McCone.

And at that time, by coincidence, they were having trouble with Elvis Stahr, and I was approached by Nitze as to whether I would be interested in being Secretary of the Army. Well, I was just delighted with that. I had started as a private and come out as a colonel; I thought it would be nice if I could wind up as Secretary. [Laughter.] But I had no particular qualification for it except I knew a lot. I had served in every combat branch in the Army. You know, I could be a good regimental commander. Whether I could be a good Secretary was another question. And McNamara said, no, he'd like to have me on the team, but he wouldn't put me on at that high level at first. Why didn't I come over and be a deputy to Paul [Nitze] for awhile? He needed two deputies—one to run Berlin and NATO, and the other to run the rest of the thing; and I would take over the Berlin-NATO part of Defense.

I had lunch with Paul at the Metropolitan Club—I could find out in my red book if it's all that significant, but anyway it was about in that time, I would say, of October '61—and agreed to go and told Allen about it and told Mac. And Mac said, "Well, you know I think I'd just better check it out with the President because he's interested in you," and so on. And to my surprise, I got called over to Mac's office, and Mac said, "Bob, it won't wash. The President asks you as a personal favor to give up the idea because there is criticism among scientists and others of McCone's appointment, and if you leave now with your university background, they'll sort of say, 'Well, all the liberals are leaving.'" He said, "You don't think so, but you have a nationwide reputation; you're known to readers of *Time* and others for a few things." A lot of applesauce. Anyway, at the personal request of the President there's nothing you can do. It was his Administration. I couldn't say, "Screw you," because he'd just call up Nitze and say to Nitze, "Don't take him." So I bided my time.

And then I thought I had a fair chance for the number two job, and McCone talked to me in those terms when he first came in. I immediately decided I had been wrong. I didn't know McCone well; I had met him about ten or twelve times before. But anyway, in the first sessions he obviously grasped things awfully fast and was not a reactionary, and was obviously going to work with the staff he'd got. And so I knew I was in consideration for that. But when he came up for confirmation, Dick [Richard B.] Russell and Lev Saltonstall—to my knowledge, Saltonstall had been a good backer of mine on the little things that I needed his help on—without anything to do with me personally, said, "Well, of course, you're going on with the thing of having a military deputy." McCone said, "Well, I haven't really made up my mind on that." And they said, "Well, it's our opinion, Mr. McCone, that though the statute explicitly only requires that both not be military, the implicit sense of the Senate and the House was that if one is a civilian, the other should be military, and vice versa." So McCone worried about his confirmation. He did wind up with twelve adverse votes and, of course, that hurt his feelings a lot. No question he wasn't going to make it, but he then said, "Well, if that's your feeling, Mr. Chairman (and Russell, of course, was tremendously powerful), I will be guided by it." So that fed me up.

And I figured then that I'd been ten years Deputy Director, and I was forty-seven. Did I want to go on for another fifteen years doing the same thing? I didn't want to go overseas. I was willing to go overseas; my wife was perfectly happy, but we weren't pressing for a big London or Bonn or Tokyo or one of those jobs there. So then I started to look around again. But I was very casual about the whole thing until Elmer Staats came over to me one day and said, "You know, we've really got this problem of intelligence. It's just not working, because neither McCone nor Dulles has taken control of the thing from the top, and we think the Bureau's got to get into the act." This sort of inspired me. And he said, "I want to create and readjust and take out of the Military Division of the Bureau everything to do with military intelligence, put it in one subdivision along with the other international things, and have you head that."

[David] Bell [President Kennedy's assistant] and he and I had lunch at the Cosmos Club in February, I would guess, and that just plain intrigued me. I knew I was stale, and I was annoyed. You know, you felt passed over. I didn't dislike Marshall Carter; I got to know him and like him very much as years went on. But I was just intrigued by that. So I talked to Bundy, and Bundy talked to the President. The President said, "Well, McCone's all settled in now. If Bob really feels he'd be happier over there, the Bureau of the Budget's very close to me." Pleasantly, not wildly enthusiastic about the idea, but he said, "Fine." I had been having mild troubles with McCone. He wanted to break up my part of the empire. You see, the empire had really three satrapies, or whatever you want to call them: mine, which was all analysis and overt collection; Bissell's, which was all covert collection and covert action; and then they had a large, what the Army would call a G-1, G-4 Administrative Support Communications Group. And he wanted to create a fourth one called a Scientific Group, which would pull out of Bissell's shop research and development and making of U-2s and satellites and pull out of my shop the scientific analysis. I said that both of them are a crazy idea. And Bissell quit more or less on that account. He was in my mood, also. And that was the issue with which I broke with McCone.

Is there a unity, a cohesive and sensible unit to be made of research and development in secret inks and appraisals as to where scientific education is going in the Soviet Union? I felt there wasn't. And we won on this for awhile, and then we lost. At the time I just said, "Well, let's activate this Bureau of the Budget opportunity." So I called Dave and said I'd come. . . .

On November 3, 1961, I have down "White House, twelve o'clock, running about an hour," and I think that's the one that was the dry run for the meeting with [West German Chancellor Konrad] Adenauer. . . . But that's easy for you to check, because it would show Adenauer meeting the next day or later that afternoon or something like that. And that was essentially the presentation of an argument to him from both the intelligence point of view and the American military capability point of view on November 3, 1961, that the Russian armies on the ground in Germany and their potential reinforcements were not invincible in a conventional war, and that their divisions were much smaller than ours—the strength of many of their so-called divisions were really little more than cadres—and that Europe had the capacity to build itself up to where it didn't have to quiver and quake at the thought of the Russians running all the way to the English Channel. Adenauer was skeptical. His attitude was that, well, maybe they wouldn't run all the way to the English Channel, but what would happen if they just took Hamburg and then just sat down there and said, "Okay, now, we want to settle for that"? This was his fear; and, as you know, this has persisted in German-American relations ever since. But we have at least gotten away from the early Dulles-Eisenhower views or the [French] President [Charles] de Gaulle view that if anything happened at all and one platoon came across, we'd drop all the bombs in the arsenal. Now if that isn't the right date, this can be just applied to a different date, because I do remember very clearly that thing.

Now, other dates not on here. There was a meeting shortly after the Bay of Pigs in which Bobby Kennedy took a very prominent part and which I attended, which essentially reviewed what we could do to harass and trouble Castro, admitting that we couldn't and wouldn't go in and drive him out with the Marines and the Army. That led to the setting up of a special task force under Bobby and, I think, including the famous [Gen.] Ed Lansdale, who is now in Saigon. . . .

You, during your years in CIA, apparently were working on interpretations or estimations of Soviet military strength, among other things, certainly. I wondered if you were involved in the estimates of Soviet missile strength—in other words, the missile gap?

Yes, very much. I can tell you a little about that. We started at the very beginning, as I think I may have told you, estimating when they would develop just the rawest capacity to get one missile to travel several thousand miles, and we predicted these things with some accuracy. We had to help us both communications intelligence and overflights—U-2s after 1956—over their missile test range in Tyura-Tam. And as we saw them coming along, we began to get (a few of us, Bill Bundy and myself, particularly) increasingly fed up with adjectives—have a "substantial capability" or something like that—because we felt everybody was using the words with different numbers in their mind. So I suggested that we stop talking in adjectival terms and focus on the dates when they would have, first, a ten-missile capability, second, a hundred-missile capability, and third, five hundred—the idea being we're just substituting numbers for an initial capability. The first significant capability would be a hundred. And they could do a lot of damage even if 50 percent of them didn't work and so on and so forth. And five hundred would be a major change in the balance of power. When they orbited their first . . . [Telephone call.]

So the estimates then, and they varied, were on dates when these things would come about. Naturally, once the Russians orbited their first missile, the computation was based on our industrial experts' opinions of Russian missile industry. We tended to give them fairly near dates for when they could, if they froze the design at the very first missile, have these various numbers. And that's what led to the rather alarming predictions that got into the hands of the Symington Defense Preparedness Subcommittee. Taking our earliest estimate of when they could have five hundred and then comparing that with the known projection of American strengths, which were none of our business, you came up with a *potential* missile gap—everybody struck the word "potential" in getting excited about it. And Kennedy quite reasonably as a politician used the thing to belabor the Republicans, and when he got into office and saw the real estimates and the actual state of the thing, he realized that there was no gap.

Now there could have been a gap. This wasn't bad intelligence; as I said, this was a potential. But, in fact, what the Russians did was concentrate not on intercontinental ballistic missiles; they concentrated on intermediate range . . . [Buzzer.] . . . on a missile that was a threat primarily to continental Europe. From this we had concluded—we rapidly were aware of this—that they were not satisfied with their first intercontinental ballistic missiles, and they went from the SS-6 through the 7, and 8, and I think now the 9. . . . And even so they have been rather slow to build up a capacity. I don't know what the exact estimate is right now, but it's a few hundred, nothing like ours. But this is very parallel to what they did with the airplane. In 1954 they flew by the Bison, the big four-engine jet like our B-52. And everybody jumped to the conclusion—[Air Force Gen. Curtis E.] LeMay and others—that they would have hundreds and thousands of those and present a threat to the United States, when, in fact, they built sixteen hundred two-engine ones that were a threat to Europe. They never built over a hundred, or about a hundred, of the big ones, thus showing that their basic strategy was founded on an accurate estimate that if they held Western Europe hostage, it was just as good in restraining us, as a deterrent to our deterrent, as if they'd held Chicago, because no American President was going to lightly demolish Paris and Brussels and Rome, not to speak of London and Liverpool, just to save a situation in Iran or something like that. I think it was a very sophisticated analysis on the part of the Soviets, and we were very unsophisticated in not realizing it for so long. . . .

Another thing we didn't talk about the last time was the CIA role in the reemphasis of counterinsurgency forces in the early part of Kennedy's Administration. I wondered if any CIA people were particularly prominent in pressing for emphasis on counterinsurgency forces? The name Bissell was mentioned frequently.

Yes, Bissell should certainly be questioned on this. Another guy who should certainly be questioned on it is FitzGerald.

Dr. Dennis Fitzgerald?

Desmond FitzGerald, who's now got Bissell's old job in the Agency as Deputy Director of Planning and so forth. I'm not a particularly good witness on that. Actually, counterinsurgency became almost a ridiculous battle cry. It meant so many different things to so many different people. The extreme kind of reaction to Bobby Kennedy's insistence that everybody get gung-ho about it was that word went out from the Chief of Staff of the Army that every school in the Army would devote a minimum of 20 percent of its time to counterinsurgency. Well, this reached the Finance School and the Cooks and Bakers School, so they were talking about how to wire typewriters to explode in the face of things or how to make apple pies with hand grenades inside them. It just really was a ridiculous thing in that way. But, on the other hand, to the extent that it really meant that one should look at the real causes of discontent in a place and prepare a rounded program to meet them, not just helicopters and machine guns and so on, it was very sensible.

Where CIA figures primarily on that is helping develop internal police forces, which is a dangerous ground because you can get to Gestapo-type tactics and so on and so forth, but essentially bringing to bear good police methods—good filing systems, good fingerprinting systems, good systems of riot control such as using dye so when you get the ringleaders, they can't wash the dye off their clothes, without having a riot squad that picks up a lot of innocent people who just happen to be caught on a street corner. They worked very closely with AID on this. It's a program called 1290-D, which could be a very good subject of a Ph.D. monograph sometime, which involved who was responsible in this police thing, and it fell back and forth between AID and CIA.

Finally, under Bob [Robert] Komer's leadership on the White House Staff, a task force was set up under Alexis Johnson. I happened to sit on it, and we solved the problem in a rather rude but practical fashion by saying, "By God, AID will be responsible for it, but the brains are in CIA, so we'll move those brains over to AID." So we just took the CIA men and gave them the mission of training police forces using American police forces occasionally as sort of sponsors, using the Michigan State University School of Police Work, which is the best in the country, and a lot of excellent work has been done there. . . . In some respects the groundwork done there, in Indonesia, may have been responsible for the speed with which this coup of last September, or whenever it was, was wrapped up. . . .

In some of the early meetings on Laos, General [Lyman] Lemnitzer comes out as advocating many military blunders in Laos, advocating stronger military force. I wonder if you were involved in all that or any of it.

That was the so-called Plan Five? Yes. Well, I was on the edge of the scene there, and all I would do would be to sort of point out that if we put American forces there and they decided to play chess with us, they could build up much more rapidly than we could. I thought it was a very bad basic strategy, that our line of communications was long and roundabout and insecure while theirs was difficult in terms of jungle trails and so on, but they'd shown us in the French days that they could move a large number of people over trails and supply them. And I was always very much against it. But the others in CIA . . . FitzGerald was very strong for it, Bissell and McCone were strong for it.

I tried to point out to these people how empty the damn country is. I wrote part of a speech that Kennedy gave to the nation very early in his Administration where he used three maps of Laos—I think it was in February 1961—and I put in it that everybody talked about "little Laos." Laos is actually as big—and you can see it on that map there—as Italy. But whereas Italy has forty-five or fifty million people in it, Laos has two million. There are more tigers and water buffalo in Laos than there are people. So it's a great empty land; you've got to think in those terms. It isn't a nice "little" place. And Kennedy changed the analogy to three times as big as Austria. He wanted to pick a neutral country, he told me. And you know, his expertise of style, just what will be dramatic, and you pick what is a fair simile or metaphor or figure of speech, and he had a better one.

You mentioned there were some activists in CIA eager also to put troops in Laos.

Yes, FitzGerald is the key guy I'm talking about.

Do you know of anybody in the State Department who was also of this opinion? Are you aware of any particular people?

Oh, I think—what's his name?—[William H.] Sullivan who's now the Ambassador out there.

How about William Bundy?

Bill Bundy wasn't there then. Bill Bundy was in Defense, and I wouldn't want to characterize Bill's views. He was under Paul Nitze there, and I don't remember his taking a particularly prominent part in the argument. Mac was very cautious about it.

It is said that when McCone came in, he repaired relations with the State Department and the Congress but not with the Defense Department. Do you know what is meant by this?

Yes, a very long, complex story. And this may be one thing you might make a note of, that what I say here might be better classified for awhile. He, I think, did very well in the Congress. There were less demands on his time for Congressional oversight committees, and he went out of his way to brief people over and above the actual select committees to keep them happy. With State I don't think it was so much McCone repairing relations as Kennedy making it perfectly clear in his general policies that State and the Ambassadors had primacy, and there were going to be no rivals to them. So McCone was just a good executor of Kennedy's policy there. With respect to Defense, everything was by and large in good shape except for one major rivalry, and that is the rivalry in satellite reconnaissance. This goes way, way back.

When we first heard of the Russian missile center in 1952, or about then, at Kaputsin Yar on the Volga, we demanded that we get photographs of it. "We just can't ignore it. This is going to be a major new thing, this whole missile development, and we've got to get on top of it in the beginning and judge it." And [Nathan] Twining—I guess it was Twining—said it couldn't be done. The British actually did it for us with the Canberra all the way from Germany to the Volga and down into Persia, a risky thing, but they got some fair pictures. And then we said, "Well, this is fine." But the British said, "God, never again," so to speak; the whole of Russia had been alerted to the thing, and it damn near created a major international incident, but it never made the papers. Then we went to Twining and said, "You've just got to develop a plane that will do this, that will be high enough so it will go over their radar." And the damned Air Force insisted that every plane be an all-purpose plane. In other words, it had to have some fighter ability, it had to have some maneuverability, and so on.

At that point a guy who really deserves a great deal of credit from his countrymen named Brigadier General Philip Strong, a retired Marine who worked for us, a friend of Kelly Johnson's, went out on his own hook to Lockheed and said, "Kelly, what could you do if all you were trying to do was get as high as you could, get moderate speed but not too great speed, but just sit above their air defense?" Kelly said, "Jesus, I've got just the thing for you. I'd take the Lockheed such-and-such; I'd give it wings like a tent." And so on. And that was the U-2. Bissell was put in charge of the project with Kelly Johnson. And, essentially, the Air Force's eye was wiped in you-know-what. And they resented that from the beginning.

Then when the U-2 started in 1956, everybody knew it had a limited life. The Russian radar would improve; their fighters and interceptors and other things like their surface-to-air missiles would improve. And a precisely accurate prediction was made of about a four-year life. So immediately the CIA started, secretly, work on a missile system. Meanwhile, the Air Force had a publicly classified, but not very covertly held, missile system called . . . Oh God, I forget the code name [SAMOS]. It will come back to me. This was a system which would set up cameras in the sky and would take pictures and televise them down to the ground. And hundreds of millions and billions of dollars were spent on it, but the bloody thing never was workable. Meanwhile, CIA, working again independently and with the closest of tight security, produced the Corona missile and camera, with [Edwin] Land working on the camera at Polaroid, and I think Lockheed's Agena was the booster rocket. They put it on any major base. I think they used Atlases at first and now Thors. And this thing was ready to fly and did fly and got pictures in August 1960, less than four months after the U-2 was shot down over Sverdlovsk. Well, again the Air Force was just horrified. . . . All through until today, still today, there is a bloody running war between the Agency and its contractors and the Air Force and its contractors on it. And Scoville quit on account of this business. . . .

McCone fought with [Cyrus R.] Vance, McNamara, and particularly Brock [Brockway] McMillan, who was the Under Secretary to the Air Force, on that thing, and Kennedy and Bundy tried to arbitrate from time to time. They'd think they'd get a settlement. They'd arrange kinds of partnership deals where the National Reconnaissance Authority was created in which the joint responsibility was held by McNamara and McCone, but the executive directorship was held by Brock McMillan of the Air Force with the CIA scientist as his Deputy. Well, it just was patchwork, and it didn't work. They went along their various rival ways. Actually, CIA produced the best general search capability—in other words, the broad coverage to find out new things. The Air Force came up with a camera that produced very high-precision photography. So if you knew what you wanted and turned the camera on in the right place, you could get the best pictures. So actually the country hasn't suffered too much by it.

Where the thing stands now . . . I'm six months out of touch with it and no longer hold clearances for it. But when I left, the problem was who would control the next phase of development, which would be a camera system good enough to get . . . Well, let me put it this way. The Air Force wanted to go ahead on two systems—again, a general search and a precision. CIA felt that the modern techniques would enable you to do the general search with such precision, down to a one-foot resolution, that you didn't need any more. The Air Force time and again moved in to block off CIA and said, "The time has come now to make this entirely a 'blue-suited' operation." And that's where it was when McCone left. It never was settled in his day, and whether [William F.] Raborn's been able to settle it or not, I don't know.

All right, that answers the question.

Well, that's the big issue about Defense.

Let's move into the question of the Bay of Pigs. Why weren't you told about it?

It was traditional in CIA that operational matters were strictly the business of the DDP—that is, most operational matters had been relatively small clandestine things in which the less number of people who knew, the better. And the patterns were essentially a one-man operation against [Iran's Mohammed] Mossadegh by Kim [Kermit] Roosevelt, [and] a larger but nonetheless small American involvement in Guatemala. And that pattern set the sort of style of the thing. Bissell, also, though he's a good personal friend of mine—we see a lot of each other socially as well as business-wise—was a very naturally spookish guy, and I think he just wanted all the reins in his own hands. He particularly didn't want me, as a coordinate officer, involved. He didn't mind using some of my people, but he'd personally select them and then brief them into his thing and sort of co-opt them. And my knowledge, as I think I said in the last interview, of the thing was not negligible because these guys were also loyal to me; and though they'd sworn to Bissell they wouldn't, they would tell me in a way what was going on.

But the extreme example came the Sunday before the Bay of Pigs was launched on a Monday morning. That Sunday I was the duty officer. You remember we'd already had the bombing and the trouble at the UN with Adlai [E. Stevenson] and stuff. And that was the famous night with JFK at Glen Ora when Bissell tried to get the air strike re-laid on and didn't. Saturday, Allen Dulles left for Puerto Rico as part of the cover plan to sort of show that he was out of town to make a speech. As he was leaving, alone with him in the office, I said, "You know, I've got the duty tomorrow, and whether you know it or not, I know what's going on. Now what should I do if anything comes up?" And he just said rather abruptly, "You have nothing to do with that at all. General [Charles Pearré] Cabell will take care of any of that." So I came in and opened the cables from Uruguay and Nigeria and so on and so forth and went home and played five sets of tennis. I said, "Screw 'em."

Okay, the CIA comes out very badly in the reports and investigations after the Bay of Pigs. Do you have any comments on that?

Yes. An investigation was made by several people, but probably the most damaging one was made by our own Inspector General, General Lyman Kirkpatrick—he recently resigned and is now a professor at Brown who should, incidentally, also be on this project. I'm sure he would be. His basic charge is that despite Dulles's and other people's injunctions that the very best of everything CIA had available be brought to bear on this in the way of human resources, actually they were a bunch of guys who were otherwise not needed. They were a strange bunch of people with German experience, Arabic experience, and other things like that. And most of them had no knowledge of Spanish—they'd have to deal through interpreters or through juniors who had had some Spanish—and absolutely no sense or feel about the political sensitivities of these people, you know, who were all the way from moderate right to strong leftists. Of course, they kept the straight-out Batistas out of it. But the guys like Miro Cardona and Manuel Ray and others never had any confidence in the CIA people.

Now at the top level, Tracy [Barnes] and Dick did have some sense of this, but the people they sent to Miami were just pretty much roughnecks, and they were pretty goddamned good at blowing up barns and power stations. I think that that's really the worst fault of the thing, that if they had realized that this was the biggest thing that the Agency ever tried to do and sat down carefully with the Director of Personnel and Allen and Dick and myself and said, "All right, where's the best? If we pull this guy out of Buenos Aires and this guy out of Mexico City and this guy out of Madrid for our political section, and Amory out of DDI because he knows something about amphibious warfare, and somebody else out of it because he knows something about paratroop jumps and so on and so forth," I think we could have had an A team instead of being a C-minus team. I don't think it was a D team. The thing failed, but it would have failed even so.

But I don't think it would have been as abysmal a failure, and there've been so many chances to say it never would have worked because if this had been improved, the other mess would have happened. But, you know, I never investigated it myself. I know most of what I know from the standard talk that went on all over the place and from reading everything that's been written on it, good, bad, and indifferent. So I don't want to be used. I'm just really quoting Kirkpatrick here, and I'm not adding anything to say that I know that to be true, too. But you asked what the basis was, and I think that's the most solid basis.

Yes, we're interested in your opinions as well.

Yes, but I think one of the things that ought to be in the files of the Kennedy Institute is the actual Kirkpatrick report. And one final thing that that did lead to was from then on out, once McCone got in, nothing went on in the way of operational things of any size—I don't mean just splitting a mailbox or something like that, but anything that involved a political overthrow or a major guerrilla-type raid—without my people including myself, in the DDI [Directorate of Intelligence] being called upon in McCone's office for our comments. We'd be able to ask, "All right, how many assets have you really got in that country?" And then we would give them an appreciation of whether if all those people rose at once, the country government could be overthrown.

Now the charge was leveled at the CIA—and I'd like to have your opinion on this, if you don't mind—that the CIA was deceptive in a sense because they didn't let the President become aware of the real risks involved in the operation.

Oh, I don't think that's fair at all. I think that is mixing up the fact that Rusk didn't say anything, that Schlesinger kept his mouth shut until the very end, that Bowles was suppressed by Rusk, that the machinery of government over and above CIA did not do its part. A child would know that a failure in this would be a disaster. You can't say that fifteen hundred Cubans got together in a sort of Michael Mullins Marching and Chowder Society and acquired aircraft and ships and ammunition and radios and so on and set forth all by their little selves. The American hand would clearly show in it.

I'm sure had Kennedy been in office a year and a half and the team shaken down instead of a very few months—that's the gravamen of Schlesinger's book—it never would have gone that way. But one of the things that may have led to this was the CIA estimate, which I was responsible for—actually, it was written by Sherman Kent and his people, and concurred in by the State Department and the Defense Department—that Castro's hold on Cuba was getting increasingly strong, that time was running out. And this Bissell used time and again to the President. He said, "You can't *mañana* this thing." You can cancel it, in which case you've got a problem of disposal. What will we do with these fifteen hundred people? They'll all run amok in Central Park or something like that. But anyway, "it's now or never" was the theme. And that put the President in this awful bind.

Here was something the great General Eisenhower had begun. He may not have been the world's greatest President in Kennedy's mind, but prestige-wise, as Kennedy admitted, he would have been licked if Eisenhower had run for a third term. The American people would have felt, "Well, God, he cancelled something that Eisenhower'd set in train which would have liberated Cuba." And therefore the total political risk, undoubtedly balanced in his mind, was a very close one. And certainly there would have been leaks. The Senator [Kenneth] Keatings and the somebody elses would have come out in due course and said, "Well, Kennedy got in and just settled with Castro rather than drive him out as Ike would have done."

Well, do you agree then that, as some people have said, Kennedy was a little bit trapped in this operation?

Yes.

Were there any men in the CIA that you were aware of that opposed this operation before it came up? There wasn't much opposition to it anywhere else.

I would say I know of none. But it doesn't mean there weren't some on the DDP side that I don't know about. And basically the DDI side, as I said, except for a few technical experts, wasn't aware of the thing.

It's often said also that this helped to destroy John F. Kennedy's confidence in the CIA. You had pointed out in the last interview that his confidence seemed to be pretty great in the CIA initially because of the quick response CIA was able to give him.

Yes, it certainly hurt him. Of course, in that quick-response stuff I was talking more about my side of the house, the analytical side. That didn't suffer too much. And his personal confidence in Bissell was extremely high, and that never went down. His feeling about Dulles was well put in the Schlesinger book, that it was an inability to understand the guy. He'd gotten so used to dealing with guys like [Theodore] Sorensen, [Kenneth] O'Donnell, and others over the years that he knew exactly what they meant by a shrug of their shoulders or the way they phrased a sentence. With Dulles, it was something brand-new to him, and he just felt he had to get somebody who was more on his wavelength than Dulles had been. But obviously, you know, I think he'd made up his mind to look for a successor then, but he wasn't in such a state that he wanted to tear the place apart. And certainly he approved of McCone's essentially keeping everybody who was there. After all, though Arthur's taken it out of his book, I would say that Rusk and the State Department were as much hurt by it, by their failure to have done their part of warning him in it, as the CIA was in his.

The 5412 Committee is a committee that comes up periodically as a kind of a control committee of the CIA. What was its role during the Bay of Pigs? Do you have anything to say on that?

Ah . . .

I mean, was it as effective a control agency as it was intended to be? Or was it intended to be that?

It was in general, but I think the Bay of Pigs thing was raised to a higher level than it. And my limited knowledge would indicate to me that it was probably not even cleared for it, all the members of it.

It can't be considered an effective control commission at all with regard to CIA?

With regard to that particular operation. Of course, it was since strengthened in this Special Group countersubversion setup under Harriman afterwards. But on all other things the 5412 group has been an effective thing. It may be that CIA sells its wares too easily in the 5412 group, but the fact that a senior officer of Defense and a senior officer of State and a representative of the President have to be advised of and have to give their sanction to every operational thing is a fact of life which most of the public doesn't realize. Incidentally, 5412 means it's the twelfth National Security Action of 1954, but, before it, the thing was called the 10/2 Committee, and it really runs back into Truman's days.

All right. Bobby Kennedy became sort of a watchdog of CIA after that, I'm told. Do you have any opinions of this? And what was your reaction?

I think that he sat on the Special Committee for Countersubversion and was very active on that. I don't think he was a control mechanism so much as a gadfly to get them to do more and to build up more capabilities and to be more aggressive in places like Algeria and other places where things were going to hell in a hat. And again his personal affection for Dick Bissell was never shaken. I know that from several long talks with Bobby after his brother died. . . .

There was also reference to a circular letter by John Kennedy really putting CIA, in effect, under the local ambassadors.

It put everybody under the local ambassador, and CIA wanted an exception to it, and Kennedy refused to put it in. That letter is in public print. It's been printed by Senator [Henry M.] Jackson's committee.

But I wondered if there was much irritation or opposition to this within the CIA.

Among the pros, yes, only in the sense, and the legitimate sense, that many of the CIA operations are third-country operations. In other words, let's say in Denmark the CIA guy contacts a Russian seaman who's on his way back into Leningrad and sees if he can recruit him as a spy. Is there any legitimate need for the Ambassador to Denmark to know that? And our answer is no. And I think the pros are right on this—that just gets too many people involved. Take a thing like the [Oleg] Penkovsky case, a marvelous operation. And yet, secure as it was, it finally broke not, we know, of any leak on our side, but nonetheless when you've got something going like that, you want the case officer and nobody [else] to know the actual identity. . . .

I wondered if you can say anything about Penkovsky.

Well, all I can say is he provided us with uniquely valuable stuff that beautifully complemented the material we were getting from photographs. In other words, it gave us the detail and enabled us then to interpret our photographs better, and the photographs gave us the things to ask him as questions that he could put to his technical friends. And a combination of a highly placed spy and this capacity to look down on the whole Soviet Union put us in the securest possible position and had an awful lot to do with the 1962 missile crisis. Never before in history have two great powers come together on a collision course like that and one power knowing exactly what the other had. In other words, this is so different from 1914, where everybody was wondering who was mobilizing, what was going on, and so on. But Kennedy knew minute by minute what was going on and exactly what the Soviets could do and the fact that they weren't taking the covers off their missile silos, and so on and so forth. And I think the assurance with which he played his hand, and the whole Executive Committee with him, would not have been there if you took away this solid intelligence. If we came back in what we were talking about earlier this morning, the missile gap stage, where you wondered whether the Soviets had ten missiles or five hundred or a hundred versus five hundred, everything would have been at sixes and sevens. But it wasn't.

I was once told that the decision or the critical point in the Cuban missile crisis—and this may be completely false—was when we discovered that they were bringing in nuclear warheads. They had put them on ships and were sending a nuclear warhead to Cuba. Do you know whether that's true or false? Did you ever hear that?

I don't think it's true. . . . I think that the warhead is something that we couldn't tell; we couldn't see. They could be in the hold. After all, they're not very big. What we saw were these medium-range missiles and even a couple of the two-thousand-mile missiles that could have reached all the way to the Chicago-Duluth area, or whatever the President said. And we just assumed they wouldn't send the missiles without the warheads. I wouldn't separate the two; I wouldn't make a particular hinging point on them.

7

Ray S. Cline

THIS CENTRAL INTELLIGENCE AGENCY OFFICER who would combine a life of scholarship with a life of government service—the world of thought with the world of action—was born in Anderson Township, Illinois, on June 4, 1918, to Charles and Ina May Steiner Cline. After attending public school in Terre Haute, Indiana, Ray Cline won a prized scholarship to Harvard University in 1935. Traveling to Boston on a freight train, the bright young man looked forward with some anxiety to four years of rigorous studies among classmates who were largely graduates of eastern prep schools. In 1939, awarded an A.B. degree, he won another prestigious scholarship for study at Balliol College at Oxford University in England. Leaving from Montreal, he sailed on the *Prins Willem*, a Dutch freighter bound for London, as German submarines prowled the sea-lanes in search of British and French ships. Cline first learned about clandestine tactics during the four-week voyage when he helped the ship's captain falsify the manifest in order to hide the cargo of scrap iron, then considered contraband.

After a year's study, and shortly after the fall of France to invading German troops, he enrolled again at Harvard for graduate studies. His experiences in England during wartime convinced him that America must intervene and support Great Britain. As a member of Harvard's Society of Fellows, Cline continued his studies to earn a Master's degree (in 1941) and Ph.D. (in 1949). In 1941 he married Marjorie Wilson; they later would have two daughters. In August 1942, Ray and his wife joined the U.S. Navy's Japan code-breaking unit in Washington, DC, for six months followed by service in the Research and Analysis Unit of the Office of Strategic Services. Pleased to be associated again with many Harvard friends, he soon became Chief of Current Intelligence under Gen. John Magruder for the remainder of the war.

Peacetime offered new opportunities. Cline became chief historian for the compilation of an Army Operations Division history; and for over three years he researched World War II top-secret documents and interviewed the Army's high command. His subsequent book, *Washington Command Post*, published in 1951, became the standard reference on U.S. military planning during the war. Cline also recruited and organized the staff who prepared the ninety-nine-volume series on the U.S. Army in World War II.

In the early summer of 1949, Cline, lured by former OSS colleague R. Jack Smith, joined the Central Intelligence Agency's Office of Research and Estimates. He quickly became editor of the monthly "Estimate of the World Situation" under the guidance of Ludwell Lee Montague. With the outbreak of the Korean War in June 1950, Cline and the other Agency analysts finally gained access for the first time to all source collection data, especially signals intelligence.

Several months after the Korean War began, President Harry S. Truman granted Adm. Roscoe H. Hillenkoetter's request for a return to fleet duty and appointed Gen. Walter Bedell Smith the CIA's Director. Widespread reformation began as Smith brought historian William Langer, the former OSS Research and Analysis chief, to the Agency to organize the Office of National Estimates. Langer in turn recruited the thirty-two-year-old Cline to become the first chief of the estimates staff, responsible for producing drafts of the National Intelligence Estimates for the intelligence board. For the first time, the Agency had complete responsibility for preparing authentic interagency estimates based on data from all information sources and thoroughly evaluated by skilled analysts.

Offered a CIA overseas assignment in late 1951, Cline went back to England for a two-year tour in London, after which he returned to Washington in the Estimates Section, which focused on Soviet capabilities and intentions. In 1955 he became chief of the

Sino-Soviet Section's analytical staff in the Office of Current Intelligence. Another overseas assignment took him in 1958 to Taiwan, where he became Chief of Station. Over the next five years, he became fascinated by Chinese culture, especially by its emphasis on family and personal obligations. Here, with fleets of planes and boats for agent airdrops and penetrations, he practiced clandestine collection and covert operations. Threats of war with the People's Republic of China over the Quemoy and Matsu islands in the Taiwan Strait challenged Cline's analytical skills as he sought accurate estimates for the defense capabilities of the Chinese Nationalist armies in the late 1950s.

Soon after becoming Director of Central Intelligence in November 1961, John McCone selected Cline in early 1962 to manage the Directorate of Intelligence in a CIA weakened by the Bay of Pigs disaster. This year would mark a renaissance as the Agency regained prestige and status during the Cuban missile crisis. Often briefing President John F. Kennedy, his staff, and the National Security Council, Cline played a major role during these critical days of October 1962. Also, Cline's Directorate of Intelligence, consisting of research, estimates, and analysis, budgeted at $50 to $60 million per year, prepared approximately fifty annual national intelligence estimates on key contemporary strategic issues facing the United States.

When McCone resigned in April 1965, he recommended to President Lyndon Johnson that Richard Helms, Lyman Kirkpatrick, or Cline succeed him. Instead, returning the Agency's leadership to the military, Johnson chose Adm. William Raborn. One year later, his energies and morale at low points, Cline requested overseas duty. He became special advisor to the U.S. Ambassador—first George McGhee, later Kenneth Rush—in Bonn, Germany.

In late 1969, Cline returned to the United States and became director of three hundred analysts in the State Department's Bureau of Intelligence and Research. He would serve four years, even though he soon realized that Foreign Service officers had little enthusiasm for a research and analysis unit in the State Department. In late 1973 he retired from the federal government and spent the next two decades as a strong advocate for the intelligence profession while heading the National Intelligence Study Center in Washington. He died in Arlington, Virginia, on March 15, 1996.

RAY CLINE: I suspect that I have a few vivid impressions of President Johnson that might be of interest to you that are not so much associated with a particular historical event, but I would think that some beginning anecdotes might help give you an impression of my awareness of the President.

Conducted by Ted Gittinger in Washington, DC, on March 21 and May 31, 1983. Oral History Interviews, Lyndon Baines Johnson Library, Austin, Texas.

Actually, my first contact with him was when he was Vice President and he made a visit to Taipei, which would have been in 1961, I believe. He made a celebrated swing through Southeast Asia and came up to Taipei from Saigon. I was [CIA] station chief in Taipei and a quite public figure, because I was also advisor to the Ambassador, and it was such a friendly country and we had such an elaborate intelligence liaison operation at that time that I was treated as a regular official in the country team. Accordingly, I was instructed from Washington to get out and meet the Vice President when he arrived and to brief him on any recent intelligence about the area, particularly about the Taiwan Strait, that he might be interested in. And as usual they send you a package of stuff from Washington; it's some trading material to impress the VIPs. But my vivid recollection about it is based on this anecdote.

When I met the Vice President at the airport, I said to him that I had a message for him from Washington, that I was the local representative of the Central Intelligence Agency, still Mr. [Allen] Dulles at that time, and that I would like to follow him to the hotel and see him in private to give it to him. And he was pleased with that. You could tell he thought this was the way the government ought to operate, you know. He loved all that protocol business and special channels and so forth. Well, I did follow him in the motorcade, and when I got to the Grand Hotel and was able to speak to him privately, I handed him some messages and chitchatted a little bit. But I introduced one subject which I was not instructed to that I've often laughed about since. I told him that not too long before, in 1960, President Eisenhower had come through on a very similar visit; this was his trip which was supposed to take him to Japan when he was cancelled out by the peace demonstrations in Tokyo, and he didn't ever go. But he had a very warm and fascinating visit to Taipei, which he loved very much. And I had met him at the airport in the same way, although in that case I had known Eisenhower, having worked for him before he became President.

So I told Lyndon Johnson that I'd served the same function for President Eisenhower, giving him some messages. But I said, "You know, on that occasion it was rather exciting because the Chinese Communists announced that they resented the appearance of the American President on Chinese soil and they fired a hundred and forty thousand rounds against Quemoy, against Chinmen." Usually by that time they were just firing token rounds of propaganda shells, which they kept up for many years.

Well, this really caught Johnson's imagination. He said, "You mean they just did that to show their contempt and disapproval of our President?" I said, "Yes. I don't know whether they'll do the same for you, but I thought you perhaps should be warned that there could be a little thing like that, so you wouldn't be surprised if you hear it." Well, that was the wrong thing to say, because he was so hopeful that they would fire a hundred and forty thousand rounds at Quemoy in his honor, and of course they didn't do a damn thing. They didn't say anything; they didn't do anything. And he said to me, "That's marvelous. I'm glad you're in touch with me and you're going to keep me informed [of] anything from Washington that happens and anything here. And if they fire at Quemoy, I want to know it immediately." I said, "Yes, sir." He said. "Now, have you got instant communications with my motorcade and everything?" I said, "That can be hooked up." I, in fact, had not intended to be wired right in. But he said, "Get yourself a communications Jeep or something. I want to be sure that I can get through and you can get through in case there's any important intelligence for me." So, by golly, he called me up at least four or five times in the very short period of time he was there: "What are they doing out in Quemoy?" [Laughter.] And I had to tell him each time that, well, so far we didn't have any sign of any activity. But it was clearly a disappointment to him; he would have loved the same treatment as President Eisenhower.

That gave me an impression of him that I've never forgotten, as a fascinating man, very attentive to what you were going to say, but extremely interested in the dramatics and the theatrical qualities of leadership. . . .

TED GITTINGER: *Let's do a couple of things on background here, and then we'll launch into the main body of this. I've heard it said, or read, that you worked on the question of the Sino-Soviet split a good deal in the 1950s. . . .*

My interest in the Sino-Soviet split does go back to the mid-fifties. I recommended to Dulles and to Bob Amory, who was the Deputy Director for Intelligence, that in terms of current intelligence reporting and analysis on China and Russia, we should do something to bring these two giant countries into a relationship to one another in our studies. Until about 1954 or 1955 the tradition was just like the State Department's. You know, Asia has got China in it, Europe's got Russia in it, and you've got a big bureaucracy on both and that's the way they're handled. But without making any predictions about the relationships, I said, well, I had been studying the Soviet Union for a long time but I am also keenly interested in China, and I think it would be a great idea to put some kind of a staff together to study them both, or put the whole staff together because that would stimulate people. And much to my amazement, they decided to do that for an intelligence office, and they asked me to go down and take charge of it.

Why were you amazed?

Well, people don't take suggestions in the bureaucracy very often, and you should learn not to suggest things, because then you are volunteering. When this occurred, I was back in ONE [Office of National Estimates] writing the Soviet estimate and having a very fascinating time. As I recall, it was then that I was doing the net estimate with the JCS [Joint Chiefs of Staff] on the Soviet threat to this country, a special enterprise that was set up under Dulles and [Arthur] Radford and ended up in that year, 1954 I think it was, in my writing the whole paper and getting it cleared through both the JCS and the CIA. And it ended up being briefed not by me personally but with me present to the President in a big, extended National Security Council group. That net estimate business was a fascinating one.

At any rate, shortly after that I became chief of the Sino-Soviet area of the Office of Current Intelligence. Having taken charge of the work on these two countries for that purpose of reporting in our current publications, I did become fascinated with this issue: how close can these two so-different countries be? They have the same ideology and then, as you recall, the political belief was very firmly held that there was a new bloc, a new Axis, that was tightly bound, as it was in theory, by treaties and common ideology. The people who studied the two countries obviously accepted that, but when you really talked to them, they didn't see much cultural affinity. So what I did was set up a very small group, I think four or five people initially, to study *only* the relationship between the two countries from a strategic and long-range political viewpoint. I didn't know what we would find.

But that probably happened in 1955. At any rate, in 1956 when the Hungarian explosion [of revolutionaries against the Communist regime] took place, the very first quite clear evidences of a different approach of Mao [Ze-dong], and I guess it was already [Nikita] Khrushchev, to first the Polish crisis, then the Hungarian crisis, appeared to the public. If you look at these things seriously, you had to say that there was some kind of ideological difference. So I began to pay very close attention to it at that time, and I had this very small staff just devoting themselves to seeing how the two countries viewed the world and each other. As soon as you do that, of course, once you set up a special lens to focus on something, you find out all sorts of fascinating things. Their speeches didn't agree in many different ways that had not come to attention particularly, because they weren't very exceptional speeches and they weren't very interesting anyway and, you know, people just shut them off. But if you had your mind [on] to what extent are these two drummers beating the same tune, very early in 1956 and 1957 I was convinced that there was a major difference between the two.

Now, that precipitated a great fight in the CIA, of course, and the old Soviet hands especially all denied it because they thought that probably it wasn't true. However, the DDI [Directorate of Intelligence] analysts were at least flexible and open-minded, whereas—oh, dear, who was the head of the Soviet division in what we now call the DDO [Directorate of Operations], or the DDP [Directorate of Plans] at that time?

I can't go that far back.

Well, I can identify him easily. [His name was Dana Durand.] I'd known him from Harvard days. . . . He came down to Washington and somewhat accidentally became a Soviet expert, but he was in the clandestine side, trying to penetrate the Soviet Union in those early days in the fifties when we thought there might be still a chance. . . .

He never came to believe in the [Sino-Soviet] split?

No.

Did James Angleton ever come to believe in the split?

No, he was James Angleton's right-hand man in all this. The two of them—it was the Chief of Counterintelligence and the Chief of Soviet Operations—were in agreement, whereas by the time I was DDI [Deputy Director for Intelligence], the whole position had changed, and we still had to fight with those two guys but not much of anybody else. Once I was DDI I had pretty much a free hand to propagate our view, as the senior analyst . . .

Dana Durand! I knew if I talked about it enough, I'd come to it. Very bright, intelligent, rational fellow, a perfect example of the intellectual errors of becoming totally identified with a body of knowledge and a viewpoint. He just could not believe that these two Communist nations would split when that was against their interests from our point of view. Jim Angleton believed the same thing as Durand; and, as far as I know, Jim still believes that they are getting back together. Of course, Jim's going to turn out to be right. They are getting back together to a certain extent. [Laughter.]

If you hold a view long enough, it will come true.

It will come around, yes. So I'm sure Jim is going to be saying, "Hey, look, you guys told me they split. Now twenty years later, here they are getting closer again. What are you going to say to that?" Well, you know, I never said they would have a war against one another or that they'd be eternally totally alienated.

Anyway, as a result of that early work in OCI [Office of Current Intelligence], I did become keenly interested in this issue. And in part that's why I was willing to accept an assignment overseas in the Far East, which I had never been to until quite recently before I went to Taipei.

Before we come to Taipei, let me interrupt you just a second. Now, you mentioned speeches. What is the story of the famous Khrushchev speech in 1956?

Well, that's an Angleton story, you know, because Angleton had connections in his liaison with counterintelligence agencies which were very special and very clandestine. And out of those came the speech. Jim will never go on the record saying what it is. My impression—and this is just fuzzy memory and lack of clarity even at the time—is that the people who handed him the speech were the Israelis, with whom he worked very closely and operationally, and that they got it from an agent of theirs in some East European country, probably Poland. It was passed along as a contribution to our common interests. All I know is that I said in my book [*Secrets, Spies, and Scholars* (1977)] that CIA had looked for it and had spent a lot of money trying to find it out, and Jim jumped on me and made a press statement, of all things, and said, "We didn't spend any money; we got it free." I said, "Hell, Jim, I didn't mean that you paid your friends to get it. It's obvious to me that we spent a lot of money on operations over many months trying to get it." "Well, it sounded like I had to pay my contact." Jim's a real stickler for his special interests and things. But it was procured, as I described briefly in the book.

It was a document which suddenly hit them, and Angleton very much wanted to keep it secret so that he could feed it out piecemeal here and there as he wished, probably occasionally misinterpreting as well as interpreting it for psychological effect on Communists in Eastern Europe and the USSR. He, I suspect, still believes that had he been able to do that, he could have used it to such advantage that he would have discombobulated the Russians and their security services and perhaps have used some of these émigré groups that we still at that time hoped to activate, and liberate the Ukraine or something of a general political nature. I never was very much a part of that operation, not in on the planning, and I certainly didn't agree with the thinking behind it. I just didn't think you could do it. That's why we had this difference of opinion.

Allen Dulles, who by then knew me fairly well, suggested that Frank Wisner have me read the speech, because I was then chief of the Sino-Soviet staff. It was a perfectly appropriate thing, and I knew a lot of the players in the operational side, so I read it. What they wanted was for me to say, "Yes, this is Khrushchev himself speaking," and I did. Because as you probably know, the speech started out as if it had been written with a lot of boilerplate. Somebody had drafted it. Then it began to launch into these emotional personal stories. I had read a lot of Khrushchev's speeches and I just felt sure this is Khrushchev speaking, so I didn't hesitate to endorse it. I couldn't vouch for every word of it, of course, but I said, "It is a fantastic revelation of what undoubtedly are the true feelings of all these guys who had to work under that old bastard Stalin for many years. For God's sake, let's get it out. This is great."

And, by golly, Wisner and Angleton didn't want to do it, and that's why I told the story in the book, that I succeeded only when I talked to Dulles personally and told him how I felt about it. I can still see the old man. He put his carpet slippers up on the desk; he had gout and he wore carpet slippers in his office. He leaned back and pushed his glasses on his head and said, "I think I'll make a policy decision." [Laughter.] I never forgot that, funniest thing I'd ever heard. The only time I ever knew when anybody thought they were making a policy decision; usually, Presidents and everybody else don't know when they've made a policy decision. And he flipped the switch and talked on the squawk box [intercom] to Frank as if he were alone—he did not admit he was sitting there with me—and kind of coyly talked Frank into a position where Frank could not disagree with releasing it, and using the same kind of arguments that I had, that it was a great historical chance to, as I think I told him to say, indict the whole Soviet system by its own chief. I said, "What more could you have, citing the crimes of the chief who ran it for so many years and gave it its coloration?" So he got Frank reluctantly to say we could release it, and he immediately called his brother [John Foster Dulles] over in the State Department and said, "I'm going to send you over something, and I think we ought to get it out." It was in the [New York] *Times* the next Monday; this was a Saturday, I recall, because the following Monday was my birthday. The 4th of June was the day it appeared, if I remember right.

But that handling of the speech was where the drama was in the Agency. I didn't have anything to do with getting it, naturally. But my operational friends gave me the impression that Jim was the person who ended up with it in his hands, that he got it from the Israelis and its place of origin clearly was a version prepared for Eastern Europeans, and that the place most likely to have been penetrated was Poland, though it could have—you know, we had agents, and the Israelis had agents, in nearly all of these countries—come from any of them. It did not come from inside the USSR, and some people thought therefore that it might not be totally accurate because it was prepared to explain the situation to party members outside the USSR. But I have never seen any evidence that it was not quite accurate, and all the suspicions about the CIA having fiddled with it are totally untrue, as far as I know. As I say, I think Jim Angleton would have loved to have fiddled with it, and there was some business about floating false ideas of where it came from. I've forgotten the details now, but there were some spurious versions of the speech that were floating around, and at one point they surfaced in Italy. Whether that was something the CIA did or some other entrepreneur was working on it, I don't know.

James Angleton was associated with Italy, too, in his past, wasn't he?

Yes . . . I think there may have been something about him wanting to cover the trail by letting some of it, and not quite the same thing, surface in Italy. I've really forgotten that now. But the central story was the case of the historical-minded analyst overcoming the native instinct of the operator, and particularly the counterintelligence operator, to use all intelligence to confuse the enemy rather than to triumph.

Well, the only thing I want to end up on, to go back just for a moment to the Sino-Soviet split, was that I had a pretty good idea that there was a difference of view between Mao and Khrushchev when I went to the Far East. But once I got in Taipei and began getting the much more intimate feedback of radio broadcasts and talking to people who knew all these Communists—you see, much to my amazement Taiwan was a fascinating place. I was sent out there with a briefing that it was a very fragile political establishment and the intelligence people were all just as tough and mean as the Russians and so on, a very hostile kind of attitude about the Republic of China at that time which we've, I guess, never completely gotten away from, but it's certainly different now. I was amazed how intelligent these people were and how well-informed they were about their own people on the Mainland. Naturally, you should not have been surprised and yet we were, because there was a lot of mythology. At any rate, by the time I had served there a number of years, there was no question in my mind that the Chinese and the Russians were going in a diametrically opposed view direction, not necessarily forever, but for a period.

So when I would come home, as I did about every six months on TDY [temporary duty], I would needle both the analysts and the operators about getting on with getting the Agency onto a firm position. If there was a Sino-Soviet split, I said, gosh, after Mao came out for the communes and said China was going to leapfrog Russia in developing socialism and communism, there wasn't any question about it. In fact, I always considered, and still consider, the Quemoy crisis of 1958—when they fired those hundreds of artillery shells, not the hundred and forty thousand rounds [for Eisenhower], but when they really were firing them in anger for several months in the fall of 1958—to be the turning point in the Sino-Soviet relationship.

We now know from Khrushchev's memoirs that he had a secret trip to China—I think we knew it at the time—and that he and Mao had discussed war and that Mao had said it didn't matter if we had a war, that the socialists would win, there'd be a lot more surviving Chinese than Americans, and so on. It's hard to believe this discussion, but it was very frightening; it clearly frightened Khrushchev. Shortly afterwards—maybe he also knew they were going off on this ideological tangent—he broke the agreement to give them nuclear weapons. They could not agree on the stationing of Soviet communications and intelligence people on the coast of China, even as a backup to the Taiwan war. In effect, they just did bloody nothing to help the Chinese in this very symbolic little fight over Chinmen. So I date the definitive split as at that time, with Mao pressing for military aid but not wanting any Soviet troops on his shores, and clearly Khrushchev thinking, "I've got to control this old devil. If I'm going to give him nuclear weapons, I've got to be sure I can keep him in hand. The way he's talking about nuclear weapons being a paper tiger and how the best thing that could happen to the socialist world would be to start a nuclear war, I can't do that."

Sure enough, then, before I came back to be DDI [Deputy Director of Intelligence], there were much more open and clear-cut indications of a split, especially their returning the Soviet advisors and stopping Soviet economic aid in 1960. But still, every time I came back to Washington, I found there was a cultural lag, that that stuff which was so vivid—and this is one of the things about being a CIA operator in the field, the details and the personality data you have and the coloration of events are so impressive that you know what is happening beyond just having the evidence in your hand. You go back to Washington and, God, the paper mill's still turning out, and people are still fighting over the arguments they had five years before, and old Dana Durand was still fighting as if it was all a fraud, and Jim Angleton, too. That really, I think, didn't get resolved until it simply became resolved, in a fashion, by my becoming the DDI and adopting the point of view which I had always tended toward and which I felt absolutely clear about. It's an interesting example of the way intelligence appreciations are made. They're made by people, and I think it was my unusual combination of experience of a longtime analyst of China and the Soviet Union plus that field experience in Taiwan that made it happen. Well, that's a lot on that one subject.

Oh, that's all right.

We can't go on like this on all these subjects.

Can we talk about your field experience in Taiwan as it relates to Southeast Asia at least?

Well . . .

Did you have responsibilities to support operations in Southeast Asia?

In a sense. We all had delimited local responsibilities, but Headquarters could assign you anything. And since my main job was getting intelligence on the whole of the Mainland, I did move around to the different stations to see what could be done to get agents through Burma, Laos, Cambodia, anywhere, into the Mainland and clear up to Japan and Korea.

As the war clouds began to develop in Southeast Asia, I followed that region very closely and was instructed by Washington to be helpful to—I think it was Bill Colby originally in the area. I went down to see Bill at least once, twice in that period; I didn't want to get in his hair too much. Station chiefs are like ambassadors, you know—they don't like to get into each other's territory intrusively—but Bill and I were good friends and got along well.

At any rate, the Chinese were asked through my channels if they would assist the South Vietnamese in methods for collecting intelligence, including signals interception and the flying of clandestine missions behind enemy lines. All of that was a technical science which we had developed with the Chinese. It was their science and their business and their responsibility in Taiwan as well as in Southeast Asia.

But one of my achievements as station chief was working with the now-President, Chiang Ching-kuo, who was then the chief of the National Security Bureau, the intelligence-coordinating outfit, to send substantial personnel and administrative and financial assistance down to the South Vietnamese. I cannot go into detail about what they were doing, but they did in effect put the South Vietnamese quickly into the professional business of signals collection and clandestine air operations. I think they coached and they trained and they flew some missions and they set up operations for them, to get them started. It was a kind of on-the-job training business with them. I think that was a very important contribution to some of the early achievements of the South Vietnamese.

Did you ever get any feedback on the success, or lack of it, that the South Vietnamese were able to make?

Well, a little bit. But you know, I think the collection of military operational intelligence was pretty good from intercepting messages, and certainly many were intercepted. As they went on in time, I think they got to be pretty professional themselves. But the Chinese helped them for a long time. They just did it at our request. It's a perfect example of having an ally that wants to do things rather than one that doesn't. We were having a hell of a time, and Lyndon Johnson was very preoccupied with the fact that other friends of ours weren't very keen on doing anything in Vietnam. I know he used to talk about that a lot. But all I had to do was mention it to Chiang Ching-kuo and to the old Gimo [Generalissimo Chiang Kai-shek], and, boy, the sky was the limit. They would have deployed their whole army down there, although the Gimo—incidentally, this is a matter that's in the record but very arcanely, I suspect—talked to me many hours about not getting bogged down in Vietnam. He said, "Don't put many American forces down there. You Americans don't know how to fight that kind of war. You'll be in trouble. You'll just spend countless resources which you don't want to waste down there. If you want to fight a war, go fight it on the Mainland and get rid of the regime that's causing you the trouble in Southeast Asia."

He was eloquent on that and really just spent hours telling me about his viewpoints, which I reported back to Washington. But everybody assumed that he was just trying to get the Americans to fight his battle, and he was, of course, to some extent. But I think he was very sincere in saying that we were making a mistake in getting our own forces deeply involved in a military situation unless we were prepared to fight right through to Peking [Beijing] and stop the resistance. I mean, he would have agreed heartily with the Cambodian operation and he would have suggested we go to North Vietnam and squelch them, but as he said, "You won't do any of that. I mean, you won't do it right. You'll just get in trouble and lose your resources and your money and your manpower, and God knows what will happen." Boy, as I look back on it, he was so right about all those things! I argued with him that we had plenty of power, which we did, plenty of determination, and at least the key men knew what they wanted to do. But the protracted battles, he was correct, we should have stayed out or we should have taken a much more direct military approach to stopping the source of the problems.

So I think that's about all the detail I should give, but the Chinese support, particularly in these early days, the early sixties, you see, I think it advanced the timetable of the South Vietnamese being able to field security forces and build up their own armies and so on by a great deal.

Was there ever any problem with the fact that these advisors were Chinese helping Vietnamese, in view of their long history of hostility?

No, and I tell you, those Chinese forces from Taiwan, I dealt with many of them in their operations. We set up U-2 operations later over the Mainland, and we sent these specially picked communications experts to many parts of Asia to do odd jobs. They were so disciplined and so tightly controlled, it was a fantastic facility. Of course, I often had to remind people back in Washington that it was not surprising that the Chinese understood the Chinese language better than our ninety-day wonders from our own training programs. As I pointed out, some of the guys who listened, say, a radio connected with air units, he'd been listening to them for ten, fifteen, twenty years. He knew the tone of voice, he knew the style of communicating, whether they used old-fashioned keys with fingerprints and so on. It was a totally different thing from running any kind of normal military intercept station, which I observed, an American one. These guys could be put into a foreign country, they were under tight military discipline, they were doing these intelligence tasks but they did them as if it was the most dangerous operation in the battlefield, and they would just disappear. There was no community problem, there was no difficulty with having them stay for months under deep cover and reappear, never having caught . . .

Of course, there was a Chinese community in Saigon, I guess. They didn't need that?

They didn't touch it, at least not to my knowledge. Maybe a few of them were clever enough to collect a Chinese girlfriend, but that was not the way they played the game. They stayed out of sight, out of touch. It was just as if you'd put them in a fur-lined foxhole and pulled the cover over them. They stayed there and did their job until they were relieved and brought home.

Kind of a monastic existence.

It was terrific, yes. I've seen it in other areas that I shouldn't designate, but it was always amazing to me how they could find these guys to go for six months, nine months, and do interesting but very confining intelligence work and live black for all that time, had no contact with the civilization around them. And they were able to do it, if we protected them. I suppose at that time still one of the real incentives was a lot of good food and good treatment and relatively pleasant living conditions. But, you know, we couldn't get our people to do anything like that.

So they did make, I think, a real contribution to the security of the South Vietnamese armed forces at a time when neither the Americans nor the South Vietnamese knew a hell of a lot about what was going on in the Viet Cong and North Vietnamese operations. And especially when they were able to find out what the Chinese were doing to provide weapons and transportation and things. As you know, the Chinese Communists had nearly forty thousand troops in North Vietnam at one time, and they were providing a lot of logistic assistance to the Vietnamese right up till the end of the war. It was the Russians who gave them the heavy hardware that crushed the South Vietnamese, but the small arms and a lot of railway battalion experts in logistics and that sort of thing were Chinese throughout the war. Of course, our friends in Taiwan were the ideal people to figure this out, sort it all out as to what they were doing and how it was showing up in the way of Vietnamese operations.

You made some admiring comments about the dedication of Nationalist U-2 pilots in your book, that they would destroy themselves rather than allow themselves to be captured.

Yes, that's right. I tell you, the ability of the Chinese to produce patriotic and dedicated people in their armed forces was fantastic, at that period at any rate. I presume it was the result of good political education in the armed forces and the fact that this army, these military people, had relatively good American equipment finally, after many years of being poorly equipped and in trouble on the Mainland. They got to Taiwan and we began giving them the chance to organize themselves in a sensible military way. It was exhilarating to them. And when they would get a new piece of American equipment, they were just like kids in a candy store; they loved it. But there was no doubt in my mind about this being a highly motivated people out of necessity. They knew that if they lost the battle of Chinmen, they would lose the battle of Taiwan; if they lost the battle of Taiwan, they were all going to be gone, dead or Red or both. They were pretty emotional about all that. So they were highly spooked up on the ideological as well as the military conflict. But more than that, the present president, Chiang Ching-kuo, and his immediate assistants, whom I knew in the air force, which did a lot of this stuff. It was General I Fu-en. . . .

He was a very brash Americanized type of air force officer, had spent a lot of time in the States, and was full of dash and adventure. When he undertook one of these things, like organizing the U-2 squadron, he was very, very energetic about selecting the cream of the crop. He interviewed everybody and he got undoubtedly superior young men to do it.

But they did that in all of their intelligence activities. Anybody that they were going to permit to do work on behalf of or in association with the Americans, they wanted them to be A1 people; that was a policy. It paid off, I think, in that gradually in the five years I was there, 1958 to 1962, nearly five years, the whole attitude in Washington toward the Chinese Nationalists changed. It was very skeptical to begin with. They sort of thought that was the end of the line and they would eventually collapse. But they did fight at Quemoy, as I predicted they would, and with a little logistic help from us they held the islands. That was their first real victory against the Communists for many years, you know, and it gave them a tremendous shot in the arm and turned them toward the philosophy that this little island could become a laboratory and an experiment in economic development and political security. . . .

There were stories at the time in 1960 that Francis Gary Powers was supposed to have done what the Nationalist U-2 pilots in fact did, and that he found a way around it.

Yes.

Can you comment on that?

Well, I think it was fair to assume that a red-blooded American boy is a lot less likely to pull a self-destruct button than these Chinese, carefully selected, patriotic, dedicated types I've been trying to describe to you in Taiwan. However, what I was told at the time by the people who were in charge of missions like the Gary Powers flight, and apparently what he told them when he was interrogated, was that he was unable to activate the destruct mechanism because it required him to reach somewhere in the cockpit, and that when his plane started spinning down, the gravity forces simply made him unable to do anything if he was going to get out of there. Now, exactly how specifically incapacitating that was, I don't know, but I can easily imagine that psychologically if you felt your plane was going to take you down shortly and that your only chance was to get out quickly, you would not worry very much about destruction, you would try to live. He was supposed to have destroyed the plane, but he was not supposed to destroy himself if he didn't have to. He made a choice, to save himself and let the plane go undestroyed.

That's fair enough.

That's the way I understand it, and I suspect that's literally true. I'm sure he was not under instructions, nor were our Chinese pilots, to kill themselves. But as I think I said to somebody, one of them said to me, "You don't need to worry about what happens to us, like Gary Powers. If we go down, everything goes with us."

We did furnish them the option in some fashion or other?

No. Well, those guys all carry some way of destroying themselves, but we didn't ever talk about it. That was left to the Chinese, and I don't know how they briefed them. See, we only set up the unit; we did not command it. It was a Chinese operation, and all we did was make it possible for them to get the airplanes, which they could not have purchased otherwise, and nominally they purchased them from Lockheed. So it was a Chinese operation, a regular squadron. I've still got the shoulder patch of the squadron; it's a black cat with enormous yellow eyes. I had it on a flight jacket they gave me so I could get on the flight line. I lost part of it and I've still got that one patch. So they told them what to do, but all the pilot was saying in effect was that he would destroy that goddamn plane; he was not going to let them catch him alive. What he meant was that he was going to drive it into the ground, which they all did.

But his fate in the hands of the Chinese Communists would not have been a happy one, I suppose.

No, that's right. Well, in a way I suppose if he'd been willing to bargain a little bit and say the right things that he might have come out of it okay, but he had no intention of that. Now, you know, when they defect a pilot, they give him thirty million dollars or something and marry him off to a beautiful movie star immediately. It's pretty tempting.

Especially if he's got a brand-new airplane.

And the Chinese in Taiwan do it to their people. They just got a good one recently.

So the main thing, I felt, was that in that period Taiwan provided two crucial elements which I helped get the U.S. Government to appreciate, though I don't know if they entirely appreciated it. One, it was a very trustworthy and reliable partner in operations—military, clandestine, or whatever—that were in the American interests in Asia, because they thought anything that was in the American interest was in their interest. As I say, the Gimo would have preferred we'd just head directly into destroying the Chinese Communist regime, but he knew we weren't going to do that, so he just wanted us to be in Asia and be working with them. And that was a tremendous asset, particularly in the intelligence field.

But more important than that, and I think in the long run it will be very crucial in the history of East Asia—and this was a revelation to me, I knew the intelligence capabilities when I went out there—was the ability of these dedicated people, with their American-oriented education, to create a dynamic Asian society that would eventually be threatening to outproduce the Japanese and the Americans and everybody else simply by their technical skill and their ability to turf up a very hard-working labor force. . . .

I just came to admire their ability to think out and focus on the key elements of economic development. By the time I left, they had all got the message: showcase of democracy, showcase of economic growth, showcase of at least a constitutional government. They aren't hooked on all the aspects of the electoral process that we are, but they've picked up most of those by now. In any case, they've always had a legal and representative form of government according to a written constitution, dated 1946. And they believe that they will create, are creating, a society that has many of the best features of the Confucian society, the Chinese-style, self-regulated, disciplined social system plus the dynamic of a free-enterprise economic system and a really quite open society. You can get in trouble for saying the wrong things in Free China but not very easily. It's a comparatively open system whereby the people can do about what they want to do as long as they don't give the impression they are going to overthrow the government. They don't approve of overthrowing governments.

Tell me about Mrs. [Anna] Chennault. What was your contact with her?

Well, as I say, it was purely social. My wife knows her better than I do, but I discovered she knew a lot about Asia and China when I was in Taipei so I kept in touch with her very intermittently. What Tommy is reporting . . .

This is Tommy Corcoran?

Tommy Corcoran, who, as you know, became her sort of protector and guardian. He was her legal advisor; he was the legal advisor of [Gen.] Claire Chennault, her husband. When Chennault died, Tommy really took her over and almost raised her as a child, and [it] became a sort of family relationship, very close, I think. Tommy came to see me once—and I didn't know Tommy before, though I knew about him—after I was Deputy Director, and said, "You know, this woman, Mrs. Chennault, has a fantastic acquaintance with Asians, not only in Taiwan but even more in Vietnam and Korea. I just think somebody who really understands the area and understands high-level politics of the area ought to talk to her once in awhile, so that the U.S. Government gets the benefit of what she knows. Would you do that?" I said, "Well, gee, that's not my bag. I'm sort of supposed to be running the analysis here now. But of course if she wants to talk to somebody, I'd be glad to once in awhile."

So what it amounted to was about every six weeks or so we'd find some occasion to have lunch, or [we'd] see each other at a party or something. It was never very formal. And she'd tell me what she thought about Asian politics. It was very casual in many ways. But I told John McCone that I would do it if he thought it was okay and if he thought it might be useful. I sometimes made a little memo of things she told me, mostly it was just exchanging ideas on policy. . . .

As DDI, I had dozens of people with whom I had these open, perfectly overt contacts to exchange ideas and interpretations, not information. [They included] a lot of newspapermen; [columnist] Joe Alsop was one of my designated contacts.

General Alsop, as Lyndon Johnson called him.

I had thousands of lunches, hundreds of lunches with Joe. Mostly I listened to his tirades. I finally got pretty ticked off at him. We disagreed over Vietnam. He was big on the generals after [Ngo Dinh] Diem. I told him he'd probably set us back three years in the war. He felt he overthrew Diem personally, and I think to some extent he did. He and [Averell] Harriman and those guys really did a great deal of damage. And that's a place, I think, where Lyndon Johnson agreed with me, because he was pretty pissed off with them when he came back.

Were you consulted about Diem's viability?

Yes, I was very much involved from the CIA point of view in that whole period. Of course, McCone was the one who was able to inject policy views as to what we ought to do, but I helped him write memos. And our general attitude, and the attitude, of course, of the CIA station chief, was that we couldn't do any better than the Diem brothers and that you couldn't have one of them without the other. The State Department view was that you could get rid of brother [Ngo Dinh] Nhu and the dragon lady [Madame Nhu] and then you might have a chastened Ngo Dinh Diem. I never believed that, and McCone and . . . the station chief at the time was Richardson, I think, wasn't it?

John Richardson. Do you know where he is these days?

No, I don't. Both argued against it. And, of course, Richardson got shipped out as a result and in effect we were overridden, though I don't think Kennedy ever quite understood what Harriman and [Roger] Hilsman and General Alsop and old Cabot Lodge—Henry Cabot Lodge, who became the Ambassador—were doing. They just felt they had a mandate to get rid of Diem.

Did you go to any of those policy meetings that were going on in August and September [1963] when Ambassador [Frederick] Nolting came back?

I was in some of them, yes. My intervention in these things was always very sporadic; it was when they decided they needed a working-level analytical type or when McCone would say, "Come along, you know more about this than I do." He was always very good to me on that. He loved to get me into these arguments because he figured I could stir up the dust.

Did Ambassador Nolting get much input? I've heard conflicting stories on this.

From CIA?

No, I mean, did he get a chance to express his view?

Oh, a chance to make an input. No, not too much. Nolting was a little gentle fellow, too dignified and easygoing to deal with these types like Averell Harriman. The old crocodile would eat him up. You know, we forget how rough those days were. I guess the Watergate was worse maybe, but—and there were some awful good guys involved—people did get eaten up in that period, and this was a real showdown. Overthrowing Diem was pretty much the State Department staging a coup against the advice of CIA, which is a curious inversion of the way you really think of it. But there's no question about it, if McCone and I had [had] our advice followed, we would have kept Diem in power and we would not have been —although there was never any real discussion of this—surprised, as both Kennedy and Mac [McGeorge] Bundy claim to be, when Diem was killed. We knew you played for keeps out there and that once that empire crumbled, it was gone. And they just couldn't bring themselves to understand that this was the kind of thing they were talking about. I'm sure none of them meant for Diem to get killed. They wanted him to be saved, but they wanted him to sort of step down the way Eisenhower had turned over to Kennedy. They just didn't understand the difference.

Some journalists on the spot reported at the time that the CIA establishment in Vietnam was not at all unanimous on the viability of the Diem regime.

That's probably true, yes. But the station chief was, and, of course, he was the one who was feeding money to brother Nhu and therefore was considered sort of the enemy by the State Department and that's why he got sent out. I don't know who the opposition might have been, but, oh, hell, CIA Headquarters are always riven with controversy of this kind, except usually they keep it inside the family and don't fight quite so publicly as a lot of people. . . . [Interruption.]

I was pretty close to Des [Desmond] FitzGerald, the Deputy for Operations when I was DDI. And, of course, he and I had worked together on Asia previously when I was station chief [in Taiwan] and he was division chief for Asia. I think that Des had a genius for developing operational programs that had a clandestine quality but showed a real understanding of the culture of the people you were trying to organize to do something in their own benefit and let them develop it in a way that did respond to their own cultural values. Now, this takes great attention to people and the plans and a slow evolution of thinking under essentially an educational atmosphere. I remember talking at length with Des about his plans for various types of teams to operate in South Vietnam in the villages to find out what the local views were, to protect the villagers against the Viet Cong. Some of those teams had very heavy artillery; they could fight a whole battalion of Viet Cong. But essentially they were to make contact with the minds and wishes of the people. So when you talk about winning the minds and hearts, you know, this was imbued in the Vietnamese teams who went out after, I think, almost a nine-month period of training and indoctrination.

These are the RD [rural development] teams; is that what they were called?

Yes, then there were some called census, too. I forget—there were two or three types of teams, a real big, heavy-armed hit team to protect an area that was being covered.

The RD team was a fifty-nine-man team in its final . . .

I think that may have been the one. But then they had one called census teams, and normally they just went into a village to count people and find out who was there. And incidentally to find out if they had any problems, like digging a well and all that. They were terrific—that was a great idea. Then there was a light-armed indoctrination team.

Armed propaganda team.

Yes. To tell them how to protect themselves and what to do in case the Viet Cong were around. Anyway, Des was very ingenious about dreaming up these things, and I think they were very successful in a limited way in the first. . . . [Interruption.]

Soon it was decided to turn all of that kind of thing over to MACV [Military Assistance Command, Vietnam], to the military. What happened, I recall, and it drove FitzGerald up the wall, was that all of those carefully trained cadres, a few hundred of them, who had the finesse to operate in a true counterguerrilla, counterinsurgency fashion, got mopped up and put into training operations to turn out a thousand more of them, you know, in a few months so that MACV could have a big record of thirty or forty thousand people all of a sudden. And I think the thing fell apart at that point because you can't replicate that kind of training in a ninety-day-wonder course, and you do tend to chew up all the personnel you've got trained by trying to have them teach people something that they had just barely been able to learn themselves. It's not the right way to do it. But it was what happened, and I think that was one of the real failures of the war, which came from beginning to turn it into a conventional military operation, even though they still were stressing the same counterinsurgency concepts.

[To turn from Vietnam to Cuba,] I'm sure you recollect the timing and the formal definitions of the MONGOOSE operation better than I do, but as I recall it, it was a persistent theme in national security circles' thinking about Cuba that we ought to be able to overthrow Castro, or get rid of Castro as people tended loosely to say, in other ways than by invading his island, as we sort of did in the Bay of Pigs, or trying to murder him, as later on we all discovered that a few people had had in mind for some time.

Just for the historical record, in case it makes any difference, the existence of the formal plan to assassinate Castro is the only operational program of any consequence that I know of that I might have been exposed to and was not. Dick Helms never mentioned it to me. I learned later that he didn't mention it to John McCone for a long time, too, so I guess I shouldn't have my feelings hurt, and I'm sure he was trying to keep it covered up for many good reasons.

But at any rate, after the Bay of Pigs and even after the Cuban missile crisis, I know that the Kennedys and John McCone, who talked to me about it almost as soon as I came back to Washington in the spring of 1962 to become Deputy Director for Intelligence, were preoccupied with the Cuban threat, the affront of having a Soviet-oriented Communist regime in the Western Hemisphere. In those days, people still spoke about the Monroe Doctrine as being a concept which ought to underlie our policy and ought to justify rather strenuous measures, if we felt they were necessary, to prevent the importation to this hemisphere of what they used to call an alien form of government. Of course, the original alien form of government was monarchy, and this is the Communist dictatorship. But, as I say, that idea that the United States had a kind of responsibility to prevent the form of government which was viewed as alien to our institutions, very correctly, I think, from taking hold in Cuba was occasionally discussed. At least the idea struck responsive chords whenever it was touched on. Now, MONGOOSE, as I understand it, was the operational plan, which seemed to me to be very amorphous, to bring this about after the Bay of Pigs failed. As far as I recall, it stayed on as a program up till the time of [John F.] Kennedy's death. I'm not even sure whether it ever got wiped out, but it certainly got called off eventually.

Were your analysts ever asked to evaluate the plan?

No. As far as I can remember, I was authorized to discuss this with some of my analysts in terms of the problem, the issues; and my opinion on MONGOOSE was very specifically asked for by McCone. But no formal papers were ever written that I remember, nor, I suppose, would they want any of the desk-level analysts to know that it was an approved project. However, John McCone was always more relaxed about some of these things than other people in the Clandestine Service might have been, and he talked to me regularly about it, not telling me everything he was thinking and doing, I am sure, but asking my opinion on many subjects and saying, in accordance with the understanding which we had in general, that I would be a kind of cutout between the Clandestine Service, for whom I had worked some, and the Directorate of Intelligence, which I then headed. So I could formulate the questions knowing full well the operational problem in a way which would elicit the information needed from the analysts without necessarily, and preferably without, giving the analysts the detailed picture of where the policymakers were going. That was the concept. I used to say I was supposed to be a permeable membrane between the analytical and the operational sides of CIA.

You let some things through and others you prevented?

And I took that very conscientiously and would indeed call in key analysts and say, "Just thinking out loud, if you were asked the following questions, what would you say?" And they were pretty savvy and may have guessed pretty well what I had in mind, but we observed the proprieties and did not surface the operations. I'm sure MONGOOSE wasn't known to very many people. In fact, I don't recall until long afterward seeing any very formal paper on it myself, but I wrote down suggestions for McCone. Chet Cooper, who was my assistant or Deputy part of that time and was working into the White House in a staff circle to which he, I think, eventually went full-time, was involved in some of that planning and he wrote memos for McCone, as I recall it. We certainly discussed what, as far as I could figure out, had to be essentially a program of economic warfare. Now, there was an operational side to it in that some of the teams that had been prepared for infiltration of Cuba for various purposes, to collect intelligence or organize a resistance group or anti-Castro resistance group or whatever, were infiltrated to do what I would call superficial economic sabotage. They tried to cause trouble for the economy of Cuba. That was the angle, at any rate, of MONGOOSE that I worked on and commented on and may have written some papers, though I don't remember anymore as to exactly what they were.

But McCone's thought, and he was very deadly serious about all this, was that it was crucial to have Cuban communism a failure. That if we couldn't destroy it, as he would have liked to at the time of the Cuban missile crisis, directly by military means, we ought to make it as unattractive as possible by making it a poor show economically for the Cuban people. He was not around as CIA Director at the time of the Bay of Pigs, but he certainly espoused the "surgical air attack" in 1962. And I think that economic discrediting was the main thrust of the operational planning in this sort of thing after mid-1961. The ideas discussed were so vague, and different people knew different things about what was in hand, that I was never absolutely sure whether something more ambitious was in train, and evidently now I know that for a number of years they were hoping some Cuban agent would shoot Castro and make Castroism definitively a failure. But that was not discussed with me.

We had this concept of two concentric purposes within the MONGOOSE context. One was to make sure that Castro was not able to export the revolution and communism to other countries, and we were very much onto watching for arms shipments and all that. There were a bunch of crises over it and a bunch of occasions when assistance was given to other Latin American countries in internal security. And all that leading eventually to Che Guevara's death was a side of our operational program in Central America and the Caribbean. But MONGOOSE, as I understood it, was aimed at Cuba proper and it was to prevent the economy from being successful. I know that the Agency sent out lots of operational instructions, and they were still going out years later when I was station chief in Germany, which wasn't till 1966. We continued to get messages occasionally saying, go do something to interfere with or damage a shipment of economic supplies of some kind to Cuba in Western Europe; and the justification was, without being very explicit, that this implied economic warfare against the government of Cuba.

I know, and it certainly has been revealed since, that there were lots of little gimmicks like spoiling the bearings in certain kinds of machinery, putting flat bearings in instead of ball bearings, trying to adulterate petrol supplies with sugar and various contaminants. All of that was part of it, as well as direct attack on certain facilities in Cuba. I don't remember any one target specifically now, but I think it was some kind of mining installations. I think they actually assaulted and tried to blow them up or something.

That's what I understood MONGOOSE to be, though, to be a mainly economic harassment war against Castro to destroy him without a direct military assault. Is that right? Is that your impression?

Yes, that's right. Do you recall the comments that you were asked to give and what you had to say?

Well, not very clearly. I believe that this concept of the tightening economic noose was one that Chet Cooper and I put together in 1962, because I think McCone asked me to pay some attention to it fairly soon after I came back, saying in effect, you know, that they screwed up at the Bay of Pigs and nobody's got any very good idea of what we ought to be doing, but we've got to do something. This is still a serious situation. We cannot tolerate the spread of Castro-type communism in Latin America. And after the Bay of Pigs it seemed obvious that no direct military assault was going to take place, and I felt that the Cuban motivation was not very ideological or very strong and that Castro would be viewed as a success if he improved the standard of living of the Cubans and be viewed as a failure if he didn't.

So I certainly urged this economic strangulation concept, recognizing, though, that it was not likely to bring the economy to a standstill, was not likely to prevent him from being in rigid control of the country, but that it could make the system unpopular, could make it more difficult for him to take steps both inside and outside the country that we would oppose, and generally move him into measures for his own internal security that would be unpopular with the Cubans and make it harder for him to operate. So we were in a sense doing what the Russians do so well and using much smaller assets than we had in Cuba, as they do in other countries, to force the regime on the defensive and to use its economic resources unwisely and to experience some sabotage of them.

So I can't say a great deal for this concept except that it was in the ballpark and it was assigned somewhere between outright war and surrender, and that was Operation MONGOOSE, a sort of classical covert-action program supported by the government, as far as I can know, fairly enthusiastically for a time and probably unrealistically enthusiastically on the part of some of the politicians. We never saw it, as I said, the people I talked to in the DDI, nor did I ever hear the operators in DDO wax very optimistic about its being totally successful. But the feeling was, well, we're supposed to make life tough for Castro. Bobby Kennedy certainly wanted it, [so did] Jack Kennedy, while he was alive, and there isn't much else you can do except take targets of opportunity. The only thing I remember that really still impresses me was the fact that John McCone, who was a businessman, felt that this could have a distinctly deleterious effect on the Cuban economy, and he was relentless in pursuing it. He was the one who would say, "Have you reminded the station chiefs everywhere in the world that if they know that some transaction involving trade to Cuba is taking place, try to do something about it? Try to make it unsuccessful?" So he was committed to it perhaps more than almost anyone else, and maybe under other circumstances it might have been more successful. But I think it suffered from two things: first, in 1962 the success of the Cuban missile crisis kind of eased the feeling that we had to do something about Castro though it didn't change the basic analysis, and then of course Jack Kennedy's death in 1963 changed all the bidding in terms of government policymaking generally.

Would it be misleading to say that the vendetta sort of ended with Kennedy's death?

Well, yes, I guess you could say that. I think the very bitter personal feeling that both Jack and Bobby had—I called it an obsession once in writing and Arthur Schlesinger jumped down my throat—and Mac Bundy, for saying that the President was obsessed, but whatever, he was certainly very determined to try to get even with Castro for what he thought of as a humiliation at the Bay of Pigs. I think that did end and it was unique. On the other hand, I think Lyndon Johnson was just as concerned about the problem. I feel that Johnson tried to pick up exactly where Kennedy left off on all these matters. He certainly was not enthusiastic about the prospects of getting involved in the Vietnam War, but he never questioned that the nation had to do it, and I think he felt the same way about Castro. Whatever it was we were doing that was anti-Castro, he would continue to support, and it probably took him awhile to find out what we were doing. So I don't think there was a big change in policy, but after Jack's death the spirit was just a little different.

Less intense.

Yes.

Did you have any contact with Ed Lansdale on MONGOOSE?

A little bit but not a great deal. He was the central planner in this kind of operation, but I had a somewhat unusual position, I think, in that I had met Lansdale and met nearly everybody in the clandestine business when I was station chief in Taiwan before I was Deputy Director. So nearly all the operators trusted me and told me things that technically and in the old days the DDI was never cut in on. So I would sort of float in and out of these things. It often was not my business to write papers or comment on operational programs, but every once in awhile McCone would say, "Come on along with me to this meeting. I'm going to the White House," you know.

So I would get into some of the clandestine planning more than I really wanted to. And McCone, I think, was—well, he used to say, "As far as I'm concerned, you're my China specialist no matter what happens." Anything on China he would ask me about, and to some extent, for not very good reasons, I think, he felt that everybody had screwed up on Cuba, so he kind of tried me out on Cuba once in awhile, too. But that was pretty much at the pleasure of the Director and I never pushed it any farther than he insisted, because I wasn't altogether comfortable sometimes with making proposals and suggestions in the clandestine field when I simply didn't have time or opportunity to do my homework. I know that in the clandestine operational field if you don't know all the details, you're likely to make a mistake; and that's the whole point of those operations, to be meticulous in handling every possible source of difficulty before it comes up. And since I couldn't do that, I tended to stay with the general analysis, which I thought was useful from the DDI but not determinative in the operational sense.

One hears in the literature allegations that the operational side of the CIA did not benefit from the comments of the analysts as much as they perhaps should have.

Yes.

What's your comment on that?

Well, I don't know. Maybe I have said something like this before, but let me just briefly say that I feel that the operational mind or the operational personality is different from the analytical mind or personality. It does not mean they're totally different, but it's like a spectrum in which one side tends towards one end of the spectrum and one towards the other. A good analyst obviously overlaps with the preoccupations of a good operator and vice versa. Ideally, they would be the same. They would cover the whole spectrum; they'd think all the abstract thoughts and all the possible generalizations and yet get down to all the nitty-gritty of what you can do and how you do it and what sort of personalities you can manipulate and so on.

But basically I would say, in oversimplifying, your analyst is trying to abstract general frameworks of ideas out of any issue he's studying so as to predict what's going to happen next and see patterns of past and future situations, whereas the operator has some such framework in his mind, and the more conscious he is of what it is, probably the more successful he'll be. But the operator's job is not to tinker with the subtlety of the framework but to manipulate the people and the events, and generally speaking it all boils down to manipulating people. So the personality of a good operator will normally be a hands-on manipulator of people, because that's the way he manipulates events and gets things to happen and finds out things. Many DDI analysts have many of those same skills. God knows, in Washington you have to manipulate people all the time in any walk of life in order to keep alive. But it is a distinction between the end product, which is for the analyst a coherent and articulate set of concepts, and for the operator either data or events taking place that you can report on and describe. So one is more analytical and one is more descriptive; one is more thoughtful and the other more manipulative.

Now, I think if you take those definitions not too seriously but indicating the slant towards which the ordinary employee in CIA would lean, one or the other, it's not surprising that communication is imperfect. I don't think that it was as bad as often is suggested. I know that when circumstances permitted, there often grew up a real love feast between various analysts and operators in a given field where they clearly exchanged a great deal of information and analysis and where the two sides of the house felt benefited from it. It was certainly the policy under, first, Des [Desmond] FitzGerald and then—no, first Helms and then Des FitzGerald, when I was DDI—to encourage a cross-fertilization of talents and information with due regard for sensitive security data.

But that worked both ways. You see, the analysts were very sensitive at that time about divulging photographic intelligence and signals intelligence for which relatively few DDO operators were cleared, just as the DDO people were sensitive about human source plans and operations that they were afraid might be blown. So usually a good operator and a good analyst established a rapport; they each knew the things that they probably would not want to go into fully with the other, but there was an enormous overlap where they could help each other, and they did. The extent to which this happened, as I say, usually sort of depended on the extent to which the DDs [Deputy Directors] pushed it, which was a good bit when I was around, or the accident of some people being thrown together on some specific project and striking up a personal relationship, which then almost invariably could go on without anybody ever suggesting it shouldn't, although the tradition was that the two sides of the house stay separate.

Were there instances where people went back and forth across the lines, operators and analysts and vice versa?

Oh, yes. Well, of course, I guess my career is the most outstanding, going back and forth several times. But we had a conscious policy, at least when I was DDI, of encouraging that, and of course I had a sort of Foreign Service in the DDI which I had built up very consciously, saying that the DDI needed the kind of field experience for its own analytical background that you could get in foreign assignments. So we would set up a post to which DDI people were assigned, but in practice in an overseas station if this guy didn't get up to his elbows in operations, it was because he and the station chief didn't hit it off. Because you couldn't live in a station without being exposed to a lot of the operational atmosphere and interest, and if the guy was good from the DDI side, he was usually welcomed and exploited and sent out on what otherwise would be clandestine operations. In other words, the difference between being a clandestine operator and a diplomatic or a scholarly operator is very slight in the initial stages of doing anything. You really just kind of get acquainted with people in finding out what they know, and the DDI people were very good at that. That's one of the ways I used to sell station chiefs that they would find it valuable to have a DDI operator there going around asking big, dumb, academic questions and finding out who knew what and so on.

So I guess I was probably the first DDI analyst to go overseas, back in 1951. I went to London to set up the exchange of NIEs, the National Intelligence Estimates, which were new then, with the British Joint Intelligence Committee. And the British were so anxious to know what the hell we were doing that they took me into their bosom, although I observed the very rigid lines between the operators and the analysts and didn't presume to get into any operations because there were some rather classical, old-fashioned CIA types in charge. The younger people in the operational side used to come to me and get acquainted with me personally and get me to help them find out what the British were thinking about this and that, because it helped them in their liaison, so I always felt that was quite useful. I don't believe there was anybody else doing this particular thing, the analyst overseas. But when I was DDI, I think we had almost fifty of them scattered around the world. So it clearly was a useful thing, certainly useful for the DDI people, and the brighter, the more imaginative operators soon discovered that in effect they were getting a free hand who had a good bit of academic training that was relevant to the area concerned.

Well, I mention that only to say that the Agency and, in my view, the more imaginative people on both the analytical and operational sides did do a good bit of cross-fertilization, but it did not break down completely by any means the cultural tradition, the cultural myth that the two sides of the house were totally separate. And I suspect, though I can't prove this, that my time in the Directorate of Intelligence was the heyday of pretty free exchange. The reason I say that is that whereas I had the feeling that Helms and FitzGerald were always very open with me and would answer any reasonable question and put people together at my suggestion if I felt there was some benefit in it for either side, Tom Karamessines, who succeeded and was DDO for a long time, was one of the more rigid, classical compartmentation types, and he never really felt the advantages of this kind of cross-information outweighed the possible security advantages that theoretically could be jeopardized.

It may interest you in this context—this is getting more into the folklore of intelligence than anything else—but I remember being amused and impressed when I was selected by Allen Dulles to go to Taiwan as station chief in 1957. I went to see Frank Wisner, who I'm sure would not have selected me particularly, although we got along well personally. It just wouldn't have occurred to him to take a senior analyst and do this. He said, "Well, I have a high regard for you and if the boss wants to send you out there, it's fine with me. However," he said, "you know, we have some pride in our traditions in the Clandestine Service just as you do in the analytical and scholarly world, and I'd like to ask you if you're willing, even though you are a GS-16"—or whatever I was, and [I] had been around long before any of the testing systems ever got started—"to take the short ops course, so that it can't be said that you don't know what the people working for you know." And I said, "That's great. I think that's a hell of a good idea. I think it would be probably too wasteful to take the long course," which I think was almost a year. But they had a sixteen-week course, I think, several months, and I did take it. I've forgotten how long it was, but it was quite awhile and involved going down to the operational training center and going through the whole bit, from night landings and safe-picking [on] up.

Did you get your wings?

I don't know what I got, but I had an awfully good time. I believe I passed the course with high marks! I enjoyed it thoroughly, wore Army fatigues all the time and slept in the bunkhouse down there and got a lot of exercise. It was a hell of a lot better than sitting around at your desk doing the normal [routine], you know. And knowing I was going to be going overseas soon, it was a nice transition period.

But what I started to say about this was that I brought the instruction to a halt at one point just by snorting. Although we were not supposed to know who each other were, at least nine-tenths of the people in this class knew who I was. A lecturer, who had obviously been giving this lecture for a long time, was stressing compartmentation of the security: "Don't tell anybody anything." And he had some rhetorical flourish about "You never know who the enemy is. The enemy is the Defense Department. The enemy is the State Department. The enemy is the DDI." Then he looked up and I snorted, and they had to stop the class and start over again. [Laughter.]

That myth was very much alive, and yet in practice, as I say, whenever two people saw a common interest, it usually broke down and they pursued it very effectively together. That was certainly what I encouraged, because I always found that it was useful. I never saw a situation—and I usually observed that analysts were extremely secure because they also, as I say, had their heads beaten all the time about the sanctity of SIGINT [Signals Intelligence] and COMINT [Communications Intelligence] and all that, and particularly photography, which was new and very sensitive in those days, nobody ever dared talk about U-2s and satellites—I never saw a situation in which any security was endangered, and I saw many in which the two people representing the two different traditions unraveled things and made faster progress and produced better results than they would have otherwise. And they usually felt that and were very enthusiastic about it.

Did anybody come to the DDI and say, "Will this work? We're thinking about committing combat troops in Vietnam. Run this through the mill and tell us what . . ."

Well, that's a little broad kind of a question to get asked, I think, but when I was DDI we did a great many informal memos, DDI memos, we called them. They were printed and circulated in limited copies. And in particular we did a number of SNIEs, Special National Intelligence Estimates, which were very operational. If they were interagency like a SNIE, as we called them, there was some effort to disguise the motivation by starting the estimate off with a bunch of hypotheses or assumptions—assuming the United States is in a war in Southeast Asia, assuming this, that, and the other. So you didn't have to guess exactly what the situation was or analyze it, but we would try to make those assumptions so that the analyst was clear enough [on] what he was dealing with that he would then be asked to spell out the probable consequences of certain developments in that context. And they would be very practical things like extending the bombing from a fourth of North Vietnam to all of Vietnam, what would be the probable consequences. Most of these SNIEs had "probable consequences of" as their title. So there was a lot of that. And a good bit of it, the same sort of thing, [was] done informally inside the Agency either by the DDO or the Director coming to me and saying, "Could you get a couple of your smart guys to answer these questions?" They didn't care how I went about it, and occasionally they'd say, "Don't tell anybody what we're really thinking of, but formulate something so you can give us your best judgment."

So my answer to your question is "yes," but not routinely and not as a matter of course. It was probably when somebody was disagreeing with a view that they would decide maybe this is a good one to try out on the analysts and see what they think.

Well, in the spring of 1964, as I recall, the contingency that we might have to use air power to get the North to cease and desist was being bandied about pretty freely, wasn't it?

Oh, yes.

Were you asked to comment on that possibility?

Yes, we were involved always a little elliptically. In other words, I was always involved in that kind of planning, either as advisory to the DDO or to the Director, mostly to McCone himself. But I had lots of conversations on those things and we nearly always wrote memos expressing what we concluded after discussion. I remember very clearly— let's see, I was going to say I remember clearly, now I can't remember the date. Just before Bill Bundy became Assistant Secretary of State for East Asia, Bill was in the Pentagon as ISA, International Security Affairs, senior officer. Bill, you know, had worked with me and took my job when I went to London to set up this exchange of estimates with the British, so I had known him some time and knew Mac, his brother, much better from our Harvard days. So whenever it was that Bill had just been selected, I presume, or was about to be selected, to go from Defense to State, I remember having a dinner seminar in the Agency. This is something Chet Cooper and I tried on; we had several of them where we invited about twenty people from all the agencies for a nonoperational but no-holds-barred discussion. I remember John Vogt, who became a general officer, one of the principal planners in Vietnam in the Pentagon, generally was one of the group. Johnny Foster, I think, was there; I may be wrong about that. I knew Foster.

General Anthis?

Probably. Buck [Rollen] Anthis, yes. We set up what I guess you could call a sort of shadow NSC for nonofficial, nonoperational purposes, and we discussed Vietnam one night for hours, I remember. We served dinner out at CIA. I'm sure this didn't happen too often, probably had trouble getting it through the admin office later, but at any rate I did it and nobody stopped me. But what I recall is the seriousness of that discussion and the way we went through all the hard questions. And these guys mostly knew what was happening and had seen OP 34A, or whatever that operational plan that was being worked up was. My recollection, though, is that this was in the spring of 1964.

That fits.

Does that fit? Was that when Bundy went over?

I think so, and the term 34A I don't think antedates December 1963 [inaudible].

I think that's about right. It was just being formulated. Whether we knew the name or whether anybody used it, I don't know. But I do remember thinking and have often thought since that evening, in about a four-hour conversation with everybody pitching in very strong with their views, we covered every problem that came up in Vietnam later on. And there wasn't anything that didn't come up. We covered all these questions: how far do you go, from helping the South Vietnamese harass the trails and the shore a little bit with motorboat raids, patrol boat raids, up to—and certainly it was a school of thought that the last items on the 34A would be where you would end up. You'd send in three to five divisions into the narrow neck of North Vietnam.

We discussed all those possibilities. We discussed the relevance of the North to the South. And I'm sure we discussed whether either the Administration or the public had the staying power to take on a burden like this. As so often is the case, people seem to think that no intelligent analysis and speculation take place when something happens in our government. In my experience that is seldom true. Now, it may well be that it never gets up into the mind of the President and the Secretary of State and the people who make the final decisions, it's filtered through so many layers. We were definitely at the Assistant Secretary level there, which was a high level for having this kind of discussion. But I know, going home that night and many times afterwards I thought, well, I can't think of anything that you'd have to take into account in tackling this problem that wasn't brought up there. And there were a few who thought we would lose if we went into it. There's no way the staying power—as I say, I think we tended to blame it on the politicians more than the public, but at any rate it probably was both—would take the long struggle. At least I know one of my points always in that period was "We're not talking about a one-year problem; we're talking about changing a society in the South, and that's a five-to-ten-year proposition." I always used to say "five to ten" when I was giving briefings, and of course nobody would blink an eye at that, but nobody really counted up the cost and identified the strategic goals of the kind of military operations that we ran for five years. If they had, I think they might have come out differently.

I may have told you last time, but I want to be sure to tell you [now]—there are two things about the Johnson era that I'm not sure are in the public record anywhere. One is that it was sometime after that meeting in the late summer of 1964, I believe, that Mac Bundy called me, as he often did, and said, "I want you to do something for me and not show it to anybody." I always at that point said, "Well, I've got to show it to John McCone." And he said, "All right, but, you know, don't let it out of hand." He said, "The President has just asked me for the best-informed opinion I could get on whether the losses in security and political stability in South Vietnam"—which set in, you remember, with the death of [Ngo Dinh] Diem in 1963 and were pretty bad there in the early part of 1964—"could result in an irretrievable loss of South Vietnam before Election Day in November," or whatever the date of the election was that year, before November 1964. "Old friend, you can understand I don't want anybody to know this question ever got asked." I said, "Well, okay, I'll talk to some people without letting them know why and I'll write you my opinion." And as I remember, I wrote a memo, a rather simple memo, saying the trend was down, it was very negative, but that taking into account all of the factors we could then foresee in what was, I think, only a few months—four, six at the most—nothing was going to happen which would make it irretrievable. That what would make it irretrievable would be just going on doing what we were doing, and that if we had a major, bold program to save Vietnam, it would be in the nick of time after the election but would be—

Johnson was asking, if I interpret you right, "Do I have to do anything before the election?"

Before the election. And you remember he was whacking away at [Republican presidential candidate Barry] Goldwater on the ground Goldwater would put our boys into combat, and some pretty dirty political TV shots were involved. So that's what he was asking. Now, I say I don't know if that's in the public record any place; it may well be. But I'm sure I wrote a little paper on it, and the thrust of it was "No, you don't have to, but be aware that if you don't do anything between now and then, you're going to have your back to the wall." And I think that probably was correct.

The other thing, though, that I remember that I think shows—I might have mentioned it—a lot about Johnson [is that] as I say, I think in a way he just sort of incorporated wholesale the attitudes that he inherited intact from the Kennedys but didn't for a long time question in any depth. It was revealed, I suspect, shortly after the election, though it could have been a little earlier when he asked for this memo. At any rate, sometime there, I think at the latter part of 1964, he had a meeting at the White House which I attended and a lot of people attended; I was probably there just supporting McCone. But I have one of those vivid impressions of going around the table the way he sometimes made them do, saying what they thought was happening in Vietnam and how bad it was. And it was bad at the time he was doing it. And everybody kept explaining it, but once or twice somebody—and I think, if I remember, [it was] somebody from the Pentagon—stressed the fact that this war is all redeemable if we put our backs into it, but it's going down the drain. And the real question—and this guy put it in a very skillful, precise way, though I can't remember those precise words—the real question is if we do what is necessary to win this war by building up the South Vietnamese army and government and making it a more attractive system, doing what we called nation-building in those days, and stop the North Vietnamese, will the process stretch out so long that the American public will not support it emotionally and financially?

Well, that kind of kept coming up, you could see that. And as I say, it made me remember that evening seminar. We discussed all those same things, and the general attitude was, yes, all these things are manageable in their own way if you'll put the effort into it, *but* do the American people want to put the effort into it? That was the [question].

And that's a political decision.

And I remember that when that surfaced clearly after kind of being skirted about—that's not the sort of thing you usually say in a White House meeting, but I think some military person finally pretty well said it—Johnson fired up and in his usual profane way said something [like], "Listen, you sons of bitches, don't tell me what the American people will stand for. That's my responsibility. I want to know whether we can win this war or not. Can we do what we have to do?" Nail the old coonskin to the barn door, as he used to say sometimes. "It's my job to assess the public opinion and get the Congressional support." Well, I always remember that statement, because I rather applauded him at the time. I thought, yes, he's right, it is his job. But in later years I came to feel that he put his thumb right on it: it was his job and he didn't do it. He didn't want to make the emergency appeals, the tough statements that would enable him to say, "This is a vital, strategic matter for the United States and we've got to sacrifice to do it." As you know, he used to say, "We can have guns and butter both. It isn't necessary . . ."

I'm sure a lot of the troubles came because the Pentagon always wanted to mobilize some forces. I remember Jack Kennedy called some reserves up over Berlin, and the Pentagon, I think, felt, "Gee, if we're going in this deep, we really ought to have some new troops called up and then we'll get some more money and we can handle things better." But Johnson never wanted to go onto an emergency basis, and in a sense he was right, you didn't have to, to do most of the things he approved doing, but he stretched the whole thing out so damn long and left the feeling this was a minor problem that ought to be able to be handled fairly easily. And if it wasn't handled fairly easily, probably we shouldn't be messing with it in the first place. It was just the wrong psychological framework for dealing with what turned out to be one of the decisive wars of the twentieth century, in my opinion.

So I go back to the feeling that Johnson's personality and his ways of doing things were critical in that whole process, that his ways were those of a Congressman who was accustomed to dealing in broad generalities and then building a voting base on any kind of system you could. You know, you threaten somebody and you build a new highway in somebody else's constituency and generally you keep the support. And he was a master at that, as everybody knows. He did it on the domestic programs initially, and then when he got to dealing with Vietnam he kept doing it. He kept saying, "We're fighting for freedom and we'll never let our friends down," and he felt strongly about all those things. It wasn't that he was double-crossing people; it was that, in my view, he kept deluding himself that it would all be easier than it was. He never wanted to bite the bullet of going downtown and telling his Congressional cronies, "I'm sorry, you guys, I got you into a situation here where you've got to do some unpopular things—we've got to do them."

I can see [President Ronald] Reagan doing that; he's beginning to do it a little bit right now. But Johnson didn't do it, and yet he knew it was his responsibility. And I think if he's to be criticized, it is for taking that responsibility on himself and telling all of us NSC types to stay the hell out of it, that domestic opinion was his bag, and then eventually letting it get so strong against what he was doing that he himself lost his nerve and gave up. I still think essentially the withdrawal from Vietnam was a misfortune in that it came from Johnson being persuaded that he would probably be so unpopular that he couldn't be reelected so he wouldn't run. And since he wasn't going to run, he'd just turn it over to somebody else and let them get out of it as well as they could, that he had misjudged it. I think it was a guilt feeling on his part there in 1968 that wound the whole thing down.

Let's move back to the summer of 1964 now, which, of course, is an interesting period if for no other reason than in August we got the Gulf of Tonkin [incident]. Were you asked what the North Vietnamese were thinking about when they sent those PT boats out there [to attack without provocation U.S. destroyers stationed in its Gulf]?

No, but I volunteered some opinions. This is one where—and I've spoken about this from time to time to people working on the problem—I got very worried during the flow of intelligence that we were possibly misinterpreting some of the messages. It all happened so fast that I've never gotten a chance, and I don't think any of us ever got a chance, to say very much about it.

But it was only a few days after the incident that the PFIAB [President's Foreign Intelligence Advisory Board] had a meeting and interviewed a lot of people, and, as they always did, they wanted to know all about the current crisis, flap, whatever it was. It wasn't too clear why they got into these things, but they always did. I remember being called over to the OEOB [Old Executive Office Building] and being given quite a going-over as to what I thought had happened. So they asked all the questions, and of course I was trying to be as loyal and reassuring as I could because what in effect had happened is that somebody from the Pentagon, I suppose it was [Robert] McNamara, had taken over raw SIGINT and [had] shown the President what they thought was evidence of a second attack on a [U.S.] naval vessel. And it was just what Johnson was looking for. I've read very detailed accounts by people who had gone into it much more than I was able to at that time, but it fitted what I remember from that time of how they just were dying to get those air attacks off and did finally send them off with a pretty fuzzy understanding of what had really happened. Well, I told the PFIAB, I'm quite sure, what I believed from then on, and later when I was in the State Department's INR [Intelligence and Research], I looked up the file to see if the State Department handling had anything different and found they had the same misgivings I did, really. I guess it was Roger Hilsman.

At any rate, the crucial point was that, as you remember, there was a PT boat episode on one night and some boats were damaged and there were some casualties. Then either the next night or two nights later, I forget which, the *Turner Joy* I think it was, they'd sent another ship up and it was patrolling in the same area; it was the area where they had been collecting SIGINT at the time of the South Vietnamese PT boat attacks on the shore station. When the North Vietnamese boats attacked—or, yes, I'm sure they attacked, at least made a firing pass at one of our destroyers—they got hit, I don't know, probably by aircraft, and there was a whole flood of reporting about what essentially are after-action reports. Many of those after-action reports were coming in to Washington still at the same time that we began to get reports of a second engagement. And as far as I can tell, the second alleged attack by North Vietnamese PT boats on our destroyers was inaccurate; it was a mistake. Undoubtedly there were PT boats there, undoubtedly they were running around, and you can't blame anybody for being nervous. But all the after-action reports I ever saw going on up into the seventies—as I say, I looked it up later to see if I had misread it—either were based on very flimsy sightings of torpedo wakes or something by inexperienced sailors who had no other evidence that they saw anything except phosphorescence or something, or the receipt of messages the date/time groups of which made it very hard to tell what the hell was going on but which sounded like there had been another engagement right then. And there was some firing, [but] as far as I can tell, that second night nobody got hit with anything and no [Vietnamese] boats came very close to the [U.S.] destroyers.

But I felt confident that the date/time groups were such that we couldn't have gotten back that fast, and therefore guessed what I later pretty well confirmed: practically all the ones that sounded like there was an intent to attack and perhaps some casualties due to the exchange of fire took place on the first night and nothing of that sort took place on the second night, though I am sure the President and McNamara and everybody reading them thought they were talking about something that was going on right at that moment.

Was this the unimpeachable intelligence source that McNamara testified to?

Yes.

That "one of our ships had been lost," when in fact a destroyer had been attacked two days before?

Yes, that's it. There's been a good bit of public writing on this so I think it's nothing secret anymore, but I tried to tip them off. The way I put it to the PFIAB was that I thought the intelligence circumstances of the second attack were really quite obscure, and I wouldn't want to guarantee that there had been a second attack. But I said, "Something happened the first night, so if you're saying, 'Was there an attack on an American vessel in international waters?' the answer is yes." The presupposition on which the Tonkin Gulf Resolution was extracted was correct, but I was trying to say to them, don't push it too far, because it's probably just a technicality. And I never heard any more about it from them. I don't know whether they reported it to the President. I doubt if they did. . . .

So I think that was a case, again, not criminal in my view, but a case where policymakers wanted an intelligence result that in the confusion of the use of raw material and very rapid transmission of information in the White House, practically everybody jumped to the wrong conclusion. And by the time a little more analytical process had taken place, it was too late to make any difference: the President had stuck his neck out publicly, the planes had been launched, and the Congress had passed this resolution [authorizing military defense of U.S. and allies' forces in Southeast Asia]. And Johnson never tired of carrying that resolution around; I've seen him pull it out of his pocket a dozen times.

He called it the [J. William] Fulbright Resolution.

Yes. And it was very valuable and, as I say, it's really a Shakespearean or Greek tragedy kind of play. You could deal with it as a tragic flaw in a heroic action. It may be that what Johnson wanted to do was the right thing. It may be that if the retaliation hadn't taken place, something worse would have happened in the war out there, all kinds of possibilities. But as a technical intelligence job, the intelligence people were not given the time to do a good job. That's the way I felt.

At the time, before you had gone to INR and [inaudible], what kind of doubts did you have? You said that you told the PFIAB that you knew there was an incident, that it was in international waters, and if you want to retaliate, it seems to me you've got a basis . . .

Yes, you've got a legal basis for doing it, but I think that the evidence about the second attack is fuzzy and inconclusive.

But it was the second attack that precipitated this. Had there not been a second attack, no planes would have flown and all that.

That's right, that's right. That's why—and I don't know how emphatic I was, but I was clear in my own mind at that time, which, of course, was after the U.S. retaliatory attack took place, though not nearly so clear as I was later—that it was hard to say that any of those messages that we had at the time related to a second attack. Now, I saw much less SIGINT, of course, at the time. The DDI gets only a sampling of stuff, and I mainly heard what my guys were saying when they were putting together the current daily bulletins and things. But I remember I formed a negative opinion that if I were asked to stand up and say did a second attack take place, I would say I cannot prove that it did, though I knew how important it was in their thinking. And I managed, I'm sure, to get that quietly in the record without upsetting the policy applecart, which I didn't feel I was being asked to do.

This, [it] seems to me, would have caused you to hold your breath a few times as the years passed. When McNamara was called to testify before the Fulbright Committee, for example.

Yes. Well, I, of course, never had a lot of confidence in Bob McNamara's judgment about intelligence. I think, like many policymakers, he was too persuaded of his own ability to analyze things correctly and he didn't feel that intelligence officers were very likely to tell him anything he didn't already know. Now, this is a congenital disease among high-level policymakers. They've heard it all and they know that the technicians tend to quibble and make reservations and so on, and there may be good reasons for their attitude. But it does not surprise me that McNamara went off half-cocked and that the President took the ball and ran with it. As I say, I don't have even a particularly moral feeling about that. I just think it's regrettable that you can't slow people down a little bit in order to take a second look. Like a cutting physician, you know, [if] your surgeon wants to operate, I would nearly always want a second opinion. But if he says, "Well, the guy's going to die on the table," you'd have to let somebody make that decision. As I say, at the time what I was aware of was a negative—it was that I could not convince myself from what I had seen that the second attack actually involved any firing that struck any destroyers or caused them to do any damage to the attacking vessel. But then you're always operating, even as a Deputy Director, on a selected bunch of traffic, and I couldn't go back and screen it all out either. So I wouldn't have been willing to say that it didn't take place at that time, so I took what was probably the diplomatic position that if what they were driving at was "did an attack take place," yes, but did it take place on two nearly successive nights, I was not at all sure.

And they didn't go much further than that into it. They were interested in it, but I didn't feel the PFIAB had a slant of any kind. I don't know what their view was. They were always rather mysterious about the way they operated, and the different members of the group always had different opinions. So it was very hard when you were talking to them to know what conclusion they were looking to draw. My impression was that they had called me in just routinely, and that because this incident had just taken place, they asked me to give them a full briefing on it, and I probably had more of the files and more of the data at hand than anybody else who had briefed them. So I gave them a pretty thorough rundown, but no very clear conclusion probably emerged from it that I know [of]. It was only later that I got, as I say, [to] feeling uneasy about this rush to take action, and frankly I didn't have a lot of confidence that any of them, either McNamara or Johnson, would not act with insufficient intelligence if he felt that what he was doing was right and he wanted to do it. They wanted to have intelligence support, but they were not very demanding. They would be perfectly happy to go off with something that met their criteria and wouldn't necessarily meet mine. I think that's pretty likely.

I don't know, I've argued with such people over the years about it, and some of them I had great respect for. I remember arguing with Chip [Charles] Bohlen once about U-2s when I went to the White House in early 1961 or 1962—I don't know, being a historian I get hesitant every time I start to mention a date because I know how often you remember them wrong. At any rate, I went to the White House, with Allen Dulles's approval in the early 1960s when I was in Taiwan still, to get a U-2 program set up against China after they were called off in Russia. I said, "You know, there's going to be a narrow window here when we can take a lot of pictures in China before they can shoot the plane down, and we need it; we don't know anything about China, practically. Let's do it." It was very useful, I think. But I had to carry that ball personally up to the

President; nobody else wanted to do it. The arguments leading up to it led me to have a scrap with Chip Bohlen, who was arguing that the U-2 had caused all this trouble in Russia, hence God knows it would cause trouble elsewhere. And I remember sitting in the corner of the White House while we were debating those things, him saying to me, "You know, there's just an awful lot of intelligence that you guys can get, such as photography, that I'm happy to have if it's free, but I'd rather do without it than have any additional international trouble over it. Because fundamentally, you know, we old diplomats, old Foreign Service officers, have to depend on our intuition and judgment about situations, and the evidence the intelligence people give us seldom makes much difference."

He was saying this when?

It was 1961 or 1962.

Well, it must have been before the Cuban missile crisis.

Yes, it was. No, I always felt the Cuban missile crisis vindicated the old bird, but he was in the doghouse from May 1960 when what's-his-name [Francis Gary Powers] was shot down until [then]. And it [the U-2] didn't fly for awhile and then they put it back on in Cuba and China. Right away I started urging it to be used in China, and there was a lot of resistance, probably from State. As I say, I remember being told up and down the line, "Look, we're for you, but we aren't going to carry the ball. If you want to carry this ball, come back and do it yourself." [Laughter.] So I went right on up and ended up talking to Jack Kennedy himself about it, who said, "Yes, that's a good idea. Go ahead and do it." You know, that's the way these things happen. But that was the time at which I had that fight with Chip. It was a fight, but I just said, "Jesus, that's a narrow-minded goddamn attitude." He said, "Well, you know, my experience is that fundamentally what we know from our background and our judgment of the people we are talking to is what really determines the policy we will take, and all the detail you add to it, we like it. I'm not running down your profession, but don't cause us any trouble to get it, because I would rather do without it than to have [trouble]."

You were making unnecessary waves for the diplomats?

That's right, that's right. Well, you see, he had been there with Eisenhower at the May [1960] showdown with Khrushchev, and it must have been pretty unpleasant.

Yes, apparently it was. Ike was furious.

Yes. Well, Khrushchev was impossible. He was posturing all the time, you know, but that's what happened.

8

John A. McCone

CONSTRUCTION ENGINEER, SHIPBUILDER, AND BUSINESSMAN John McCone, a Republican, was appointed by Harry Truman to the President's Air Policy Commission in 1947; and, as special deputy to Secretary of Defense James V. Forrestal, he prepared the first two years' budget for the new Defense Department. Trusted by four presidents and attracted to federal government administrative positions for the next two decades, McCone brought brilliance and superb management skills to several agencies, especially the Central Intelligence Agency.

Upon his birth in San Francisco on January 4, 1902, to Alexander J. and Margaret Enright McCone, John joined a West Coast family of engineers and manufacturers. Following his graduation from Los Angeles High School, he enrolled in the University of California at Berkeley and earned an engineering degree in 1922. An iron works firm in Los Angeles hired him as a construction engineer. When the firm merged with the Consolidated Steel Corporation, he would later become executive vice president and director.

In 1937, eager to establish his own business, he organized Bechtel-McCone, an engineering and construction company that built power plants and petroleum refineries in North and South America and Arabia. In 1938 he married Rosemary Cooper. During World War II his plant in Birmingham, Alabama, modified military aircraft; his California Shipbuilding Corporation produced more than four hundred vessels. With the war's end, McCone bought a California iron works, which operated a fleet of cargo ships and tankers in the Pacific Basin; and in 1948 he became chairman of the Pacific Far East Line. Because of his wartime skills, President Truman turned to this millionaire administrator for guidance in establishing the new Air Force. As deputy to Forrestal and later as Under Secretary of the Air Force, McCone would supervise the doubling of military aircraft production between 1951 and 1952. Although he also recommended a massive program for developing guided missiles before his resignation and return to private business, such a program was not implemented.

In 1954, John Foster Dulles asked McCone to serve on a committee to modernize the State Department's Foreign Service. Soon after the Soviet Union launched *Sputnik* in 1957, McCone renewed calls for a larger American space program as President Dwight Eisenhower created the National Aeronautics and Space Administration. In 1958, Eisenhower nominated McCone to administer the troubled Atomic Energy Commission, and in this post he won support from Democrats and Republicans in Congress on the Joint Committee on Atomic Energy.

McCone's return to private business in January 1961 proved to be brief because President John F. Kennedy asked him to take over the Central Intelligence Agency, then weakened by the Bay of Pigs disaster. He was named by Kennedy to replace Allen Dulles in September and sworn in as a recess appointee in late November. A few days later his wife died, and he was unsure about continuing in the post. Despite his tragic loss, McCone accepted this major responsibility and was confirmed by the Senate in January 1962 and sworn in as DCI in February. As the first Agency Director to come out of the business world, McCone rebuilt morale and confidence. Moreover, Kennedy gave him unqualified support as director of all elements in the Intelligence Community. His credentials as an anti-Communist were impeccable.

With much more emphasis on intelligence analysis and estimates together with stronger control over covert action and better resources for technical collection, McCone charted a new course for the Agency. He believed that the Intelligence Directorate should have been involved in the Bay of Pigs planning. Also, Kennedy's selection of a Republican and proven manager won respect in Congress, the Cabinet, and among White House advisors. Like Walter Bedell Smith, McCone had little patience for incompetence and inefficiency. He surrounded himself with talented deputies such as Ray Cline, Richard Helms, and Robert Bannerman, and he also took counsel from intelligence veterans such as John Bross, Lyman Kirkpatrick, Jr., Larry Houston, Sherman Kent, and Desmond Fitz-Gerald. Convinced about the need for expanding the technical collection of intelligence, he established the Directorate of Science and Technology. As Ray Cline wrote, McCone was "deadly serious most of the time, but he recounted his adventures at the White House level in detail with great skill, which frequently occasioned a little humor. He enjoyed the laughs if they did not get in the way of dispatching the day's business. As I got to know him better, I learned that he had a warm and sentimental side beneath the stern Scots exterior, although it surfaced only from time to time and usually when we were away from the daily grind at an NSC meeting or on a foreign trip" (*Secrets, Spies, and Scholars* [Washington, DC, 1976], 194).

McCone's close relationship in weekly meetings with Kennedy proved beneficial, especially before and during the Cuban missile crisis in October 1962. The Director had suspected that the Soviet Union would place offensive weapons in Cuba. The Agency's clandestine and technical collection data on Soviet missiles during the crisis enhanced media and government appraisals of the CIA. Several months after President Kennedy was assassinated in November 1963, McCone recognized that his rapport with President Lyndon Johnson lacked the closeness he had had with Eisenhower and Kennedy. Thus, in June 1964, McCone alerted Johnson to his plans to retire, but when he was asked to stay through the election that fall, he agreed.

William Raborn replaced McCone in late April 1965. Returning again to California and resuming his business interests, McCone was soon pressed into government service when Governor Pat Brown, in the aftermath of the Watts riots in Los Angeles, asked him to study and analyze racial strife and violence. His report focused on ghetto problems and suggestions for amelioration. In the decades after resigning from the CIA, McCone continued to defend the intelligence organizations, especially during the Congressional investigations in 1975. He died in Pebble Beach, California, on February 14, 1991.

JOE FRANTZ: *In the first week of January in the new Administration in 1961, you resigned as chairman [of the Atomic Energy Commission, or AEC]. I presume you planned to return to civilian life and stay there?*

Conducted by Joe B. Frantz in Los Angeles, California, on August 19, 1970. Oral History Interviews, Lyndon Baines Johnson Library, Austin, Texas.

JOHN MCCONE: I left on January 20 with the Eisenhower Administration, and returned to private life and intended to stay.

How did you happen to come back in then as Director of the CIA in September?

Well, the story there was this. Between the time I left in January and the time I went back, several requests were made by members of the Joint Committee that I sit down with the President and discuss the test moratorium which was continuing, because the Joint Committee shared my views and the Commission's views—the alarm and the concern. I refused to do that for the reason that I said that President Kennedy was fairly familiar with my views [in opposition to a moratorium], and a meeting which would be known to the press could not possibly bring any constructive result. He couldn't accept my views, and I wasn't ready to change my views. Therefore, about all that would come of such a meeting would be just to report to the press that we had a nice meeting but disagreed on a very important subject. So I felt, and I learned from others who discussed a meeting with him that he felt the same way and for exactly the same reason.

However, in the first few days of September 1961 the Soviets broke the moratorium by exploding a hydrogen bomb or two. Then he sent for me. He asked me to prepare a brief report on the consequences of the testing, indicating that he had a divergence of opinion between the AEC, on the one hand, and the State Department, on the other, as to the course of action that the United States should take. I spent about two weeks preparing such a report. When I called on him to submit it, it was then that he approached me and asked me to become Director of Central Intelligence.

You had at this time a discredited Agency, in one sense, with the Bay of Pigs problem?

Yes. It had come under very serious public criticism, more so I think than it deserved, although I think it was entitled to its full share of criticism. I think President Kennedy expressed the situation very accurately when he said, "There is room in this matter for criticism for everybody. The CIA must not be asked to accept all of the criticism." This was a very broad position for the President to take. He took it.

The organization, CIA, was suffering from the criticism. Morale was pretty well shattered. It was somewhat similar to the morale in the AEC when I took over after the years of difficulty with the Joint Committee because of the problems between Lewis Strauss [the AEC's chairman] and the members of the committee I've mentioned. So my first problem was to try and rebuild confidence. It wasn't very hard to do because that's such an extremely competent organization.

Being Director of the CIA also meant that you were Director of the U.S. Intelligence Board.

Yes. President Kennedy's letter to me asked me to assume the directorship of the Central Intelligence Agency and a responsibility over the entire Intelligence Community. I sat as chairman of the United States Intelligence Board. My first act was to put my Deputy, as the representative of the Central Intelligence Agency, on the Intelligence Board so I could sit and so far as possible remove myself from the Agency and represent the President as chairman of the Board, which is the way it should be. There are some people that claim that it's impossible for a person to wear two hats like that. Of course, you know the argument about the Joint Chiefs, whether they can act as Chief of Staff of their respective Services and then objectively view the totality of the Defense establishment as a member of the Joint Chiefs. But I did my best to wear the two hats, and the records will show that on any number of occasions I reversed the position of the representative of the Central Intelligence Agency on the United States Intelligence Board.

At the time of your nomination to the Directorship there was some criticism in the liberal press that you would not recognize sufficiently that the CIA is a branch of the government and is not sort of a semi-autonomous agency. Anything justifiable in that criticism?

I know that there was some criticism. I think the criticism was not only the liberal press but some of the liberal members of the Congress. Whether justified or not, I don't know. There were fifteen members of the Senate that voted against my confirmation for differing reasons, some of them because they thought I was too stiff-necked in my views on the threat of communism, and for that reason my estimates and evaluations might be slanted.

But most of the votes were internal to the Senate itself who were criticizing the lack of control on the part of the Senate over the Central Intelligence Agency. I thought it was quite significant that Senator [J. William] Fulbright, who voted against me, in doing so made a speech on the floor of the Senate that he would very probably vote to confirm me as Secretary of State, but he wouldn't vote for me as Director of Central Intelligence because what he was doing was moving against the manner in which the Senate handled its control of the CIA. I had taken the position that that was a matter of concern in the Senate and for them to lay down the ground rules and I would abide by them, whatever they were.

What sort of controls are exerted on the CIA? This is something that people talk about with very little knowledge.

Well, there has been a good deal written on it. The Senate had a small Select Committee, representatives of the Armed Services Committee and the Finance Committee—there were four or five of them, and chaired by Senator [Richard B.] Russell in my day. The House had a similar committee from the Armed Forces Committee and the Appropriations Committee, chaired by Mr. [Carl] Vinson in my day. He would meet with them quite frequently and review our programs, and be guided by their judgment on a great many matters. I would consult individually with both Mr. Vinson and Mr. Russell on matters which I felt they should be informed on.

Now the Senate Foreign Relations Committee and the Foreign Affairs Committee in the House were not represented on those committees. Senator Fulbright resented that very much. Congressman [Thomas] Morgan, chairman of the House committee, didn't express himself as violently as Senator Fulbright did. Since then, after I left, those committees have been expanded a little bit is my understanding; and two members of the Foreign Relations Committee sit on that committee, and two members of the House Foreign Affairs Committee sit on that committee on the House side. So there's adequate control, in my opinion.

Is it possible for the CIA to engage in some sort of clandestine operation without the approval of either the National Security Council or the Executive Branch?

No, it is not, under the controls that existed during my time.

In other words, you do not have an independent situation in which the CIA can make its own policy?

At no time. The Executive Branch of the government, represented by a representative of the White House and the State Department, Defense Department, and the CIA, discussed and reviewed all operational matters.

If you were getting into some sort of operation, you would always coordinate with State and Defense?

Yes, that was always done.

So that you would then deny the charge that the CIA is another U.S. Government operating abroad?

Certainly, as far as during my time, and I'm sure since, this is a charge that can be honestly denied.

You, of course, very quickly—well, within a year—got caught up in the Cuban missile crisis. You had the problem there of intelligence, which

I judge you had some difficulty at first getting anyone to believe, that missiles were being set up in Cuba.

Yes. That's a long story. I was persuaded myself that there was a danger that the Soviets might be tempted to put some missiles in Cuba. The majority opinion in the Intelligence Community, as well as State and Defense, was that this would be so out of character with the Soviets that they would not do so. They had never placed an offensive missile outside the Soviets' own territory. They had never placed an offensive missile in any satellite area. I pointed out that Cuba was the only piece of real estate that they had indirect control of where a missile could reach Washington or New York and not reach Moscow. So the situation was somewhat different.

Furthermore, the bulk of opinion was that what we were witnessing in the buildup in the summer of 1962 was purely defensive—the location of surface-to-air missiles such as the Egyptians are now putting along the Suez [Canal]. I was not persuaded about that because Cuba, being an island, such a defense mechanism could be destroyed momentarily by low-flying airplanes that could come in under radar, and with a very few well-directed rockets could destroy the very intricate radar-control mechanism of a surface-to-air missile site.

I reasoned that they were putting the surface-to-air missiles in as a means of stopping our U-2 [aerial] surveillance. Once they did that, then we wouldn't know what went on in the interior of Cuba, and they could safely put in some missiles. This was exactly what they planned to do. They got a little out of phase, and they didn't get their surface-to-air missile sites all operating before their offensive missiles began to arrive, and that's how we discovered it. Fortunately, we did.

Did you have much trouble persuading the National Security Council that there were missiles there?

Yes, I did, for the reason that the intelligence that we had up to the point when those very dramatic photographs revealed the presence of missiles was not really solid intelligence. We had lots of reports from informers, mysterious-looking large objects would be hauled through the streets at night, and things of this kind.

It was difficult to gauge . . .

Exactly how big they were. Sometimes there were delays in the transmission of this information because sometimes the information would have to go to Mexico, [and] then there were delays in getting that information through. Some of it had to find its way by way of a traveler going to Mexico and coming out. There wasn't a great deal of instant communication because of the restraints of travel and communication and so forth.

So we didn't have the hard information that a constant aerial surveillance would have revealed.

It happened that during the month of September I was away until the 25th or 26th. I found that during my absence—I was on a wedding trip, incidentally—surveillance had come to a stop. I insisted upon its resumption. Then there was a delay of a week or ten days for two reasons—one, bad weather: there was a tropical storm that swept through that made U-2 photography impossible, and secondly, a fear that if a U-2 plane operated by a civilian pilot from the CIA was shot down, it would create one kind of a problem. If operated by the military, it would be a different problem. Therefore the decision was made to transfer the surveillance responsibility over to the Air Force, and this took several days to check out the pilots and familiarize them with the equipment, which was very complicated.

These were the same type missiles that had shot down [Francis] Gary Powers over Russia?

That's right. And you'll recall one plane was shot down over Cuba. But in any event, these things cleared up so that a flight was flown on October 10, I believe, or some time in early October—I've forgotten the exact date. When those pictures were developed and analyzed, there were the missiles. Now, in some ways, it was providential that we didn't fly the flight the week before, because they might not have been there; and then it might not have been necessary . . .

Might have relaxed.

We might have relaxed a little bit. So it was just the right days. So maybe God was good to us, causing these delays, which were very aggravating at the time. In any event, once the indisputable evidence was placed before the responsible people in government, not only in the Administration but in the Congress, it was apparent that action must be taken. I must say that a very, very fine job of tactics was followed by the Kennedy Administration.

Was there ever very serious consideration of the quid pro quo with Russia to give up our Turkey bases if they'd take the missiles back, or was this just talk?

I think that was just talk.

Didn't get beyond that stage, really?

Nobody ever thought the missiles in Turkey were worth anything anyway, or those in Italy either. They never should have been put there in the first place. I opposed them. I wanted them taken out a couple of years before.

What do you do—get a sort of mentality where once you get an installation you just feel you have to defend it?

I have my own personal opinions of why those were put in, and I don't think I should express them, because they're just opinions. Sometimes, you know, when you spend a few billion dollars developing something, you've got to do something with it.

Did Vice President Johnson take any active part in these deliberations? I know he met with the National Security Council during this missile crisis. Or did he stay pretty much in the background?

In the first place, I saw to it that he was informed. I briefed him personally so that he knew what was going on. We developed our policy through an Executive Committee that President Kennedy established. That committee met practically day and night for days, as you know. Vice President Johnson appeared with that committee and on one or perhaps two occasions expressed his views and, of course, was tremendously concerned. The records of that committee, which I presume are available to you, revealed his position, but his position was a strong one.

There was no contention between him and other members of the committee? I'm thinking particularly of Bobby Kennedy.

Not that I know of, no.

Did you get the feeling that this blunted Castro's subversion in Latin America?

Unquestionably it weakened Castro's stature throughout Latin America. Whether it blunted his subversion efforts or whether other things did, I don't know.

But you think it did place him in a sort of puppet role?

It put him in a puppet role. It had very serious consequences for him.

Did the fact that Mexico refused to go along with the quarantine of Cuba give you any great problems? Or did it actually open up a listening post?

I, personally, wasn't concerned. There were people in the Administration who were very disappointed that Mexico would not go along, but in fact there were some pluses as well as minuses. You mentioned one; it did give a listening post that proved valuable.

What were other pluses?

Well, it gave a source of transportation in and out of Cuba that permitted some people that wanted to get out to get out that otherwise could not have done so. It permitted people from third countries, who were authorized to go in, to find a convenient way to get in there. It was very important.

In '63 the First Secretary to the British Embassy, H. A. R. [or Kim] Philby, was disclosed—that is, he had been First Secretary back in '49 to '51—as the Russian [double] agent who had warned [defectors Guy] Burgess and [Donald] Maclean that they were being closed in on. I rather gather the CIA was the one who made the disclosure. Also, there are rumors—which you can confirm, deny, or ignore—that you and Bobby Kennedy pretty well forced the hand of the British in making public the defection of Burgess and Maclean.

I didn't. I know of no activity whatsoever on the part of Bobby Kennedy forcing the public . . . The whole chronology of that Philby thing, and the fact that his role was uncovered and that there was a little delay in getting him out of Beirut, and during that delay he escaped behind the Iron Curtain, has been written up and is all rather blurred in my mind. Authority sources are much better sources than I am for that.

There were also in '63 rumors of a policy rift in Viet Nam between Ambassador [Henry Cabot] Lodge and the CIA chief in Viet Nam. Can you lend credence to that, or is this again in the rumor stage?

There were two schools of thought throughout government with respect to the [Ngo Dinh] Diem administration. There was one school of thought that Diem was a liability to the country, a liability to the goals that the United States sought. This prevailed in many sections of the White House and the State Department and in certain sections of Defense and some sections of the Agency.

The other school of thought was that there was really no apparent replacement for Diem, that the greatest of pressures should be brought on him to revise some of his policies, to improve his relationship with the people at large in South Viet Nam, and to improve his image throughout the world and most particularly in the United States. He was being bitterly criticized by the more liberal press at that time.

Now, I was very much in favor of this latter course for the reason that, after analyzing all of the potential leaders of Viet Nam, I could see no one on the horizon that could say, "Well, if the focal authority was transferred from Diem to this man, then conditions would immediately improve." Ambassador Lodge, I felt, was not aggressive enough in pressing his views on Diem. However, with the passage of time after his arrival in late August up to November, he had several meetings. I guess the differences were a matter of degree. He did have some sharp differences of opinion with John Richardson, who was our man over there; we withdrew Richardson because of those differences. To that extent the fact that there was a problem was not rumor; it was fact.

The CIA had warned both Ambassador Lodge and President Kennedy of the impending coup?

Oh, yes, coup rumors were frequent, and we had warned about it. I had also warned President Kennedy personally that removal of Diem would result in not one coup, but several coups—political turmoil that might extend over several years—and that's exactly what happened.

Shortly after the overthrow of President Diem, of course, you had the assassination of President Kennedy in Dallas. What did this do to you and your organization besides the fact that you had to sit out another group of rumors that you were somehow involved and [that Kennedy's alleged assassin Lee Harvey] Oswald was an agent?

I couldn't understand you.

You know there were those wild rumors that CIA was somehow involved in the assassination. There were the rumors that Oswald was a CIA agent, and so on, which you took care of by ignoring [them].

I never heard of any rumors that Oswald was a CIA agent.

His mother charged that at one time.

There were rumors that Oswald was an agent of either [Fidel] Castro or Moscow and that the CIA had such information in its files, which we did not have. We knew of his movements, but we knew of no activities of his that would lead us to believe that he was an agent of either.

After Johnson became President then, when did you see him first?

I saw him almost immediately upon his arrival in Washington. I think he arrived, as I remember it . . .

He arrived late evening on Friday.

Late evening, and I think I saw him at his home that night.

What was his mood like at that time?

Well, his mood was one of deep distress over the tragedy, and grave concern over how to get his arms around the problems that confronted him—some concern over how to properly handle the men in the organization whose competence he recognized but also whose allegiance to

President Kennedy . . . And, of course, you know the background of issues that arose that dated way back to the [1960 Democratic National] Convention here in Los Angeles and even before. However, he decided to work with the organization and to win its support, and he did so very successfully. Many men who were determined to leave the next morning stayed on and served him very loyally and very well, and some to the end of his Administration.

Did the sudden coming of a new Administration like this make any changes in CIA procedure or organization?

No. We pretty well followed the pattern of dissemination of information as we had with President Kennedy. I think the only real difference [was that] President Kennedy used to insist that he sit down with me alone for an hour or so a week to review a lot of things, both current and prospective. He was always very anxious to know what we thought might be the danger spot down the road in six months or a year. Was trouble going to erupt in Cyprus, or Suez, or in the Philippines, or what? He was always very interested in that. President Johnson—each man has to organize himself differently—only wanted to see me when I had something particular I wanted to tell him. His door was always open, but he wasn't inclined to want to sit for a general review.

To sort of have a philosophical talk, in a sense. Did the fact that the French had refused to sign the Nuclear Test Ban Treaty give any particular disturbance, either to President Kennedy or to President Johnson, that would have affected the CIA? Did you keep a special eye on the French after that?

No, we knew pretty well what the French were doing. When I was chairman of the Atomic Energy Commission I made several trips to France—official trips—and their people to the United States. We knew the state of the art, the state as far as they were concerned. We had a good measure of the competence of their organization and the people that were involved in their program. We had a reasonable estimate of their production of [nuclear] fissionable materials and could translate that into a weapon arsenal. Of course, what we didn't know was how fast they could bring about a successful atomic and, finally, hydrogen bomb. And the time has been much longer than we expected for the reason that it has been halted a couple of times because of fiscal problems, political problems, within France itself. So we were regretful but not surprised that they have failed to go along.

Incidentally, I can say at this time that I've been asked frequently why I supported the Test Ban Treaty in 1963 when I was so adamant against the Test Ban Treaty in 1959 and '60. The reason is simply this:

during the period we had so developed our efforts of detection of a violation that I was satisfied that our detection devices would reveal any violation of the Treaty, regardless of where it was done. The Joint Committee on Atomic Energy, after I went over that with them very thoroughly, agreed with this. It was for that reason that I was able to support the Treaty.

I know the CIA forecast the Chinese explosion of the nuclear bomb.

Very accurately.

Was this on intelligence, or was this on a detection system?

It was on hard intelligence. We knew what they were doing, and we predicted that they'd explode a bomb within thirty to sixty days of a particular date. I went to Europe and briefed the North Atlantic Treaty Council on the status of their development and said they'd explode a bomb within thirty to sixty days, and on the thirty-first day they exploded the bomb.

They made a prophet out of you.

Yes, they made a prophet out of me.

Early in the Johnson Administration in late January of '64, after he had come in at the end of November, you went to Spain to confer with [Francisco] Franco. The subject of this meeting was never revealed. Was that at Presidential direction, or was that on your own?

I went to . . .

There were talks of rumors again. The CIA, as you know, travels in rumor because of its secretiveness, but there were rumors of upcoming Spain-USSR talks that the press was . . .

That wasn't the purpose of the trip. I made a trip to Europe at that time. The fact is I made two trips, and I went to all the principal capitals, including Spain. My purpose was to give a thorough background briefing on a status of the weapon developments and the military posture of the Soviet Union and of the Chinese Communists. I found Franco very receptive, very interested, and very appreciative of the briefing. I didn't go only to Spain. I went to all the capitals and briefed either the head of government or the head of state.

Later that spring you were named to a committee to study the feasibility and desirability of the supersonic transport. Did the President give any directions to that committee, or did he just want the committee to come up with the facts?

He wanted the committee to come up with the facts and a recommendation as to what he should do. We worked for about three years on that. [Secretary of Defense Robert] McNamara was the chairman of it: the Secretary of the Treasury, and the Director of NASA [National Aeronautics and Space Administration], and the Director of FAA [Federal Aviation Administration], and then there were three non-government people. I, at first, as Director of the CIA—that really was not my role, but the President asked me to do it because of my business experience. Then, when I resigned, he asked me to stay on the committee as one of the three non-government people.

You really went on as an engineer and a builder.

An engineer and a builder and a person familiar with the field who just happened to be the Director of CIA. If someone who hadn't had the technical background that I had the good fortune to have had been the Director of CIA, he wouldn't have asked him to be on it.

Later in the year, in the fall of '64, [Nikita] Khrushchev was ousted, and you made the statement that this surprised the CIA. What happened to intelligence in that case?

We had no advance notice of it. I don't think that anybody had any advance notice of it. I learned about it by a telephone call from Moscow telling me that Khrushchev was going to be removed the following day, or later that very day. Now, in analyzing it, we felt this: there was a good deal of dissatisfaction that had grown up in Soviet higher circles over Khrushchev's conduct, some of his statements—principally the missiles of Cuba and some of the things that had gone on in the UAR [United Arab Republic], plus some of his domestic policies. Now, a two-day meeting of the Politburo, or some segment of it, was held and Khrushchev was not attending. He was down at his vacation resort on the Black Sea. Apparently when they gathered, they found that this criticism was so general that they had the strength to do something about it, and did. But looking back, there was no movement . . .

It had almost the spur-of-the-moment quality about it.

There was no discernible movement. These various factors all had to come together and then they found they were all thinking the same thing, and so they decided to act. So they sent for him, and he said, well, he was down there and he wasn't coming up. And they said, "Well, you'd better come up. There's a plane on the way to get you." It was just about as simple as that. I know of no intelligence resource that could have told the outside world what was forthcoming.

In '65 in April you retired from the CIA. Did President Johnson try to get you to stay on?

Yes. I told President Johnson in June of '64 that I wanted to return to private life, that I felt that I was getting to the point in age that I was getting too old to run a large department in government and I thought that the larger departments in government should be run by a younger man. He complained about that. I said, "Well, you have to remember that my age now is where you'll be after your third term quite a ways from now." So he said, "Well, all right, but not until after the 1964 election." He said that would be all right.

Then after the 1964 election, he never refused to accept my resignation, but he would never give consideration to the appointment of a successor. So I finally submitted a list to him and set a date when I would have to leave, because I found that I would have to leave. I submitted a list of men who I thought should be considered. Shortly before April 30, he called me and talked to me about Admiral [William F.] Raborn. Then when he had made that choice, Raborn came up and I took him around to the various Senators who would be involved in his confirmation. We got that lined up so it went through without any trouble.

Now, your and President Johnson's relations were always cooperative and harmonious, I gather, as much as any two men who have to think out policy matters together can be. Admiral Raborn had been a great man with the Polaris atomic sub program, but was not generally considered to be too successful with the CIA. What do you think the difference was?

I think Admiral Raborn was a hard-driving, technical man, and I think the CIA requires a different kind of mentality. You have an operational responsibility on the one hand, and you have several thousand academicians on the other, and you have to be kind of an operational manager and play somewhat the role of a college president on the other hand.

Sort of a fractious faculty on your hands.

Yes, so I think that the appointment of Admiral Raborn was an unfortunate choice. Here was a man who had a most distinguished and successful career, and he was thrown into a job that he wasn't really equipped for. I think he drew a lot of criticism that was unfortunate and unfair. I think a great deal of Admiral Raborn, but at no time would I have considered him for that post. I would have considered him for a lot of other posts, but not that one.

Is the CIA's role somewhat exaggerated by the press and public and Congress?

I think it is. I think that the press and various books that are written place total emphasis on the clandestine operations of CIA. This makes good reading. Everybody is fond of James Bond, and so forth. Really, CIA gathers important intelligence. There are such activities.

Really, the important contribution the CIA makes to the country is in their estimative and analytical capacity. They can take the great volume of intelligence that comes from all sources—from the military, from the State Department, from the National Security Agency, and from CIA itself—and put it all together and figure out just what it means with respect to the intentions and policies of others, and how it might affect our own policies. I have always felt that that was really the very important contribution that the Central Intelligence Agency makes, although their gathering of information upon which the basic estimate [is made] is important, but that gathering is done by others as well. It's just too bad that this side of the CIA isn't given more publicity, more importance. But it's kind of dull, you know. It isn't exciting, and therefore it doesn't make very good reading.

After you left the CIA, some time afterwards, there came that exposure, if you want to call it that, of CIA support of National Students Association and some publications. I presume this goes back to the period in which you were associated with the CIA?

And before, I think.

Had you assayed the consequences when disclosure should be made?

The chronology of that whole thing is kind of dim in my mind. There were several Communist-organized student meetings held throughout the world. There was one in Vienna; there was one down in Brazil.

Youth congresses and peace meetings.

The Youth Congress. The National Student Association itself became somewhat concerned that these were dominated by Communist spokesmen, and it was they themselves that wanted to be sure that the other side of the story was told. And the CIA arranged so that it would be told, arranged the resources so that they . . . And the great majority of people involved were past officers and presidents of the National Student Association.

Now the involvement was picked up and totally distorted, because it was a very, very successful operation. One or two of those youth congresses found at the end of the second of a three-day congress [that] the Communist spokesmen had been so totally discredited—I mean, somebody that was there that was willing and strong enough to get up and say the truth—that they adjourned the congress. Now I never have been apologetic for one minute for the role.

I wondered—this is, then, in the guessing realm—if our government shouldn't have been more aggressive in saying, "We did it, and we'd do it again. We think it's a good idea."

Well, we were in a period then when there was sort of an inclination, if an accusation was made about the CIA, not to analyze it at all but to crawl under the table and hope that it goes by. I thought it was wrong at the time. I was inclined to speak out, myself. The whole thing, you know, was developed by these two fellows that ran this *Ramparts* Magazine [a radical, left-wing publication] up here who were inclined to produce the sensational rather than the accurate account.

They're not very long on balance.

No. . . .

In 1965, Major General Edward Lansdale of the U.S. Air Force and Colonel Napoleón Valeriano of the Armed Forces of the Philippines went to Viet Nam to head a special team. I would rather gather that they were trying to utilize the techniques that the Filipinos had used to defeat the Huks. I'm wondering two things: what sort of results did they have, and did the CIA in effect sponsor them?

I can't answer that, because that was after my time. You have to realize that Lansdale did a great job in the Philippines. He also had a lot of experience in South Viet Nam in the early days. I would imagine that he was leaning on both of his experiences dealing with the Huks as well as his earlier experiences in Viet Nam. Just exactly [what was] the purpose of his mission, who supported it and so forth, I don't know. That was after my time.

What is the CIA relationship to Air America [an airline operated by the CIA in the Far East]?

I don't know.

There's a close relationship between the CIA in Viet Nam or CAS [Civil Action Support cadres], I believe it's called, and the U.S. forces there. The CIA, I presume, provides valuable intelligence to our Armed Services there. I've wondered how these working relationships have stood up over the years, and what are the major areas of controversy or overlap that you've had to work with?

I think the relationship has been, so far as I know of the CIA organization in Viet Nam, of both military and the Embassy, very good. I know that throughout my experience, and from all I have learned since, that the closest of liaison exists between the Ambassador and the Chief of Station as well as the military organization and the Chief of Station. The fact is there are times when the offices were almost adjoining one another. The only difficulty was that incident with Richardson which we took care of, not because we necessarily thought Richardson was wrong, but sometimes it's best to kind of move the players around a little bit rather than . . .

Was this to some extent a conflict of personalities?

It probably was a conflict of personalities. I've always felt that there was a very satisfactory relationship, and that the CIA, or the Chief of Mission over there, was able to provide both the Ambassador and the military with some very valuable intelligence and also to provide them with great assistance in interpreting the importance of recovered documents and interrogation of prisoners, and so forth. There have been many changes in the role of CIA—I won't go into the history of them, because they're relatively unimportant—but I think the fact that the man that was most important in CIA's affairs in South Viet Nam for the last ten years [William Colby] is now Ambassador over there in charge of the civilian side of the Vietnamization program is evidence in itself of the intimacy of the relationship—of the fact that [first] the relationship was satisfactory, and secondly that it was greatly respected.

Where does the CIA fit in with the concept of the country team?

Well, in every country, there is a country team headed by the Ambassador. The members of it are the head of the AID [Agency for International Development] mission, the MAAG [Military Assistance Advisory Group], and head of the information service—

USIA [U.S. Information Agency].

USIA, and the CIA. The country team's direct policy—obviously not all operational matters are brought to the attention of the country team, but operational matters must conform to policy. Operational matters are reviewed with the Ambassador if he wants them. There are some Ambassadors who prefer not to have them.

But ostensibly the CIA head in a country is under the direction of the Ambassador and cannot run an independent policy to the Ambassador?

That's right.

Do you have a formal link with British, French, German, and other friendly nations, or their equivalent organizations, where you exchange information?

No, it's informal. There is a great deal of exchange of information.

There is a great deal of cooperation?

There's a great deal of cooperation, but it's informal.

One final question, and that is in the decisions in '63–'64–'65 to increase our troop commitments in Viet Nam. How much of a role did the CIA play in those recommendations?

Those were policy decisions, and that was beyond the province of the CIA.

In other words, you provided the intelligence . .

Provided the intelligence, and it was up to the President and the Secretary of State and the Secretary of Defense to make the decisions. Now occasionally the President would call upon me for my personal judgment on a policy decision, and when I would give it, I would qualify it by saying that [in] doing so, it was beyond my competence as Director of Central Intelligence. In other words, I didn't want to get in the position where somebody might suspect that our intelligence reports were slanted because I might have a particular personal view on a policy matter.

You more or less laid out a raw report and someone else had to arrive at conclusions?

Yes. The difference arose in 1964—Mr. McNamara and [General] Maxwell Taylor and Mr. [McGeorge] Bundy, in the absence of Mr. Rusk, and I went to review the Viet Nam situation. This was shortly after President Johnson took over. He asked us to give a report. I had to take a dissent from the report. Mr. McNamara gave a very optimistic view that things were pretty good. I had to take the position that as long as the Ho Chi Minh Trail was open and supplies and convoys of people could come pouring in there without interruption, that we couldn't say that things were so good. This caused quite a sharp difference. But this was an intelligence appraisal.

Now, Mr. McNamara made several recommendations, or this group did, of the things that should be done which I thought weren't enough and therefore I added some more. I later withdrew those additional recommendations because they were policy matters, but the position that we took on the enemy potential because of the open road to access was an intelligence appraisal, which I couldn't withdraw. This became a sharp difference, and that dissent is recorded in the report.

Again, in the Dominican intervention, you would have had the Administration making its policy decision with a good base on the intelligence that the CIA had provided, but without any CIA recommendations for intervention.

I don't know that one, because I wasn't there.

Again, this is after you've left.

It was the day I left.

9

Richard M. Helms

RICHARD HELMS WAS BORN IN St. Davids, Pennsylvania, on March 30, 1913, to Herman and Marion McGarrah Helms. The oldest of four sons, he grew up in South Orange, New Jersey. When his father, an executive with the Aluminum Company of America, retired, the family moved to Europe, and Richard continued the last two years of his secondary school education in Germany and Switzerland. Returning to the United States, he attended Williams College, and his talents in journalism brought him the editor's post on the student newspaper and senior yearbook. Elected to Phi Beta Kappa, he was president of his class before graduating with a B.A. degree in 1935.

Eager to develop a career in journalism, he moved to London and became a European correspondent for United Press. He covered the Olympics in Berlin in 1936 and had a private interview with

Adolf Hitler (Allen Dulles had had an interview with Hitler three years earlier). Late in 1937 he returned to the United States and worked for the Indianapolis *Times*, where he soon became its national advertising director. He married Julia Bretzman Shields in 1939, and they had one son.

Commissioned an officer in the U.S. Navy in 1942, Helms served in New York City and then transferred in 1943 to the Secret Intelligence (SI) unit of the Office of Strategic Services (OSS). After espionage training in Maryland and assignments in New York and Washington, DC, he was sent to London, and soon after V-E Day he joined Dulles in Germany. When the OSS was disbanded in September 1945, five hundred Research and Analysis members under Dr. William Langer were assigned to the State Department: the SI and other operations branches with eight hundred members became the Strategic Services Unit (SSU) under John Magruder in the War Department. Helms and Dulles briefly served under General Magruder.

Discharged from the military with the rank of lieutenant commander in 1946, Helms continued in the SSU. His field station collected both open and clandestine data for the Central Intelligence Group, established by President Harry Truman in 1946. Helms's SI group would become the Office of Special Operations (OSO) and was merged into the CIA in 1947. In mid-1952, CIA Director Walter Bedell Smith created a Directorate of Plans by merging the smaller OSO with the glamorous covert-action Office of Policy Coordination (OPC), which had been established by the National Security Council in 1948. Although the OPC was under the Defense and State Department Secretaries, it was staffed and financed by the Central Intelligence Agency.

Frank Wisner, who had managed the OPC, became the head of Smith's new Directorate with the title of Deputy Director for Plans; and Helms, from the OSO, was named his deputy and chief of staff with the title of Chief of Operations, first on an acting basis and then in his own right in February 1963. However, Helms isolated himself from involvement in Operation PBSUCCESS, the 1954 overthrow of the Arbenz regime in Guatemala. He would run clandestine intelligence agents, not covert paramilitary operations. His friend Ray Cline wrote that Helms "was the perfect model of the cool, well-informed professional manager of agent networks and case officers. . . . Helms knew this arcane world [of clandestine collection], especially in Europe, better than anyone else except Allen Dulles himself" (*Secrets, Spies, and Scholars* [1976], 161).

When Wisner's mental breakdown occurred in the summer of 1958, Director Dulles bypassed Helms and asked his technology assistant, Richard Bissell, to become Deputy Director for Plans. Tensions between Helms and Bissell festered. While Helms continued to run agents and collect secret information, Bissell managed several ongoing covert operations such as training Dalai Lama forces for guerrilla warfare in Tibet, and also for attacks on Chinese mainland targets. The Dulles-Bissell covert plan for overthrowing Fidel Castro proceeded without Helms's counsel or support. In fact, he distanced himself and his friends from the project. The failed invasion at the Bay of Pigs in Cuba dimmed the Dulles-Bissell luster, especially in the White House and among the military.

President John F. Kennedy chose Republican businessman John McCone to succeed Dulles in the aftermath of the Bay of Pigs disaster. Cautious and conservative, McCone asked Helms to become Deputy Director for Plans because of his skills in running agents rather than in designing covert operations. Irritated and embarrassed by the Cuban fiasco, Kennedy moved planning and control of some covert operations into the White House under his brother Robert, the Attorney General. During the McCone years, Helms emphasized human source collection and analysis. And above all, he believed that sound judgment must surround technical intelligence collection, whether by U-2 photoreconnaissance aircraft or by computers.

President Lyndon Johnson's management style differed greatly from the Kennedy-McCone design. When Johnson cut back the number of his foreign policy advisors, McCone was not on the short list. In April 1965, McCone resigned, and William F. Raborn took on the assignment with Helms as the Deputy Director of Intelligence. The President told Helms at the time that Admiral Raborn's appointment was a temporary measure and he planned to make Helms the Director in the future. A year later he revealed to Helms that the Raborn tour gave the relatively unknown Helms time to acquire status with Congress, the media, and the public. However, Helms first learned of his appointment as Director in June 1966 from members of the news media who contacted him! Within a space of twelve days he was confirmed by the U.S. Senate and sworn in.

During his years as Director under Johnson, Helms faced difficult daily decisions in rebuilding Agency morale and in reporting the downside of the Vietnam War to the President. He succeeded in convincing Johnson and his advisors that he was "on the team." Moreover, he became a member of Johnson's famous Tuesday luncheon group of close advisors (which seldom met on Tuesdays). With Helms's support, Agency analysts predicted that no amount of bombing would force Hanoi to surrender or end the war; furthermore, they maintained that the war was not winnable, nor was the Cold War-era "domino theory" valid. (If one nation fell to communism, then its neighbors would do so in succession, like a stack of dominoes.) Johnson's decision that he would not stand for reelection and that the United States would attempt to end the war reduced White House-Agency stresses.

Following the 1968 election, Richard M. Nixon, as had President Kennedy with Dulles, kept the CIA Director in office. However, tensions mounted quickly as National Security Advisor Henry

Kissinger, along with Secretary of Defense Melvin Laird, vehemently disagreed with CIA estimates on Soviet missile technology. The White House, and especially Nixon, distrusted Ivy League liberals in the CIA. Kissinger and Nixon often served as their own intelligence analysts and used the National Security Council as their personal CIA when evaluating raw intelligence data.

In 1970, Nixon ordered Helms to prevent by covert means the election of Marxist Salvador Allende as president of Chile. Estimating chances of success as one in ten, Helms and the Agency tried and failed. Overall White House discontent with the CIA as well as Helms's refusal of Nixon's request to help block the Justice Department's investigation of the Watergate break-in in June 1972 led to the appointment of a new Director. Soon after the 1972 election, Nixon called for Helms's resignation; and in February 1973 James R. Schlesinger became Director. Helms accepted the post of Ambassador to Iran, where he served for four years. Since 1977 he has been a consultant on international affairs in Washington, DC.

PAIGE MULHOLLAN: *Let's begin by letting you simply identify yourself and your position.*

RICHARD HELMS: My title is Director of Central Intelligence, not Director of the Central Intelligence Agency. When the Agency was established by law under the National Security Act of 1947, the individual who held my job at that time was given the title of Director of Central Intelligence. This obviously includes his capacity as Director of the Central Intelligence Agency, but it is intended to give him a wider responsibility—in this case, Chairman of the Intelligence Community. This is manifested by the other hat that I wear as Chairman of the United States Intelligence Board. As Chairman of the United States Intelligence Board, I have no command authority over other elements of the Intelligence Community, but I have a coordinating responsibility. Therefore, the title of Director of Central Intelligence was, as I understand it, picked to indicate that the man holding this position had these two jobs, which I have already enumerated: one as Director of the Agency, and the other as the coordinator of the Intelligence Community.

It is indeed true that I have been with the Central Intelligence Agency since its inception in 1947. I was the Deputy to the Deputy Director for Plans for several years until 1962, when I was made Deputy Director for Plans, which is the title given to that element of the Agency which deals with its secret overseas operations.

Conducted by Paige Mulhollan in Washington, DC, on April 4, 1969. Oral History Interviews, Lyndon Baines Johnson Library, Austin, Texas.

In 1965 I was appointed in April by President Johnson as the Deputy Director of Central Intelligence on the same day that Admiral [William] Raborn was made the Director of Central Intelligence. Then in June of 1966 after Admiral Raborn had resigned, I was made the Director of Central Intelligence.

That clears it up in an exact way. That's what we want, fine. Also, for the record here, you had no close contact with Mr. [Lyndon] Johnson when he was a Senator and you were simply a member of the Agency here, nor very close contact while he was Vice President, you said.

No. As a matter of fact, I have a rather vivid recollection of the first time I ever met Mr. Johnson. It was under the most casual circumstances at what was then, as I recall the name, the Congressional Women's Club, or something of that kind, which was located just off 16th Street [in Washington, DC]. I happened to go there one evening with Congressman [Alfred D.] Sieminski from Jersey City because my son and his daughter were attending a dance. As we walked up to the dance floor, which was on the second floor of the building, I recall Congressman Sieminski introducing me to Senator Johnson. We walked very slowly up to the second floor because it was just after Senator Johnson had recovered from his heart attack. And although I don't remember the year or the month, I remember that he was compelled to walk very slowly even when walking on the level.

That was the only time that I recall seeing him or speaking with him until, in point of fact, I attended a meeting with him just prior to the time when he was Vice President that the problem arose about President [Ngo Dinh] Diem's administration in Viet Nam, and the problem existing at the time that had been created domestically in the United States by the fact that several Buddhists had immolated themselves in Saigon. Following two or three meetings in one week which the Vice President then attended, I do not recall having seen him or spoken to him until I was taken by Mr. John McCone, who was then the Director of Central Intelligence, to see President Johnson. Then, I think it must have been some time in the winter in 1965.

This was just as Mr. McCone was resigning?

Mr. McCone had indicated that he had wanted to leave government. I had been taken there to be introduced to President Johnson, I can only assume, because maybe someone had the idea that I was a possible candidate for one of the top jobs in the Agency. I had a brief conversation with President Johnson, and then I went in as an observer to a National Security Council meeting. That was the last time I saw him until I received a call in April from Marvin Watson asking me if I was the Richard Helms who had seen the President some days before. I said that I was. He then said, "Would you please come down to the White House right away? Don't tell anybody you're coming."

So I did go down to the White House, and Marvin Watson ushered me into the President's office. I sat beside his desk, and he told me that he had decided that he wanted me to be the Deputy Director of Central Intelligence, and that the Director of Central Intelligence, whom he was going to appoint, was Admiral Raborn. We then entered into a discussion of what the job entailed and how he would go about announcing it.

It has been frequently assumed that there was at least an informal understanding that Mr. Raborn's tenure would be short and that you would succeed him. Was that explicitly understood at the time?

President Johnson said to me that he wanted me to come in as Deputy Director, that I was not very well known, that he really had it in mind that if all went well and there weren't any undue problems that he'd asked Admiral Raborn to come back from civilian life, that Admiral Raborn had had a heart attack and that he didn't want him to strain himself and make too great a sacrifice physically to undertake this job, and that he did not know how long Admiral Raborn would stay, but probably only for a limited period of time—and that all else being equal, I might move up to the job. It's of historical interest to say that that was the first and last conversation we ever had on the subject until totally to my surprise, in 1966, he announced at a press conference that he had just appointed me Director, although he had not communicated with me about it, at any time in the interim.

He liked to make his appointments with unusual circumstances like that. You mean, he didn't talk to you at all?

Not a word. That was the first and last word we had on the subject.

Had you known that Admiral Raborn was leaving?

He told me that he was going to resign, but I had heard nothing about what the President had decided to do. He had been in office for fourteen months, and since I had heard no word, I didn't know whether he intended to go ahead with this or not. He obviously assumed, which I learned about President Johnson later, that when he told you something, he meant it. Although he had a reputation sometimes for saying something and then taking it back, I never found in my relationship with him that this was ever the case. When he announced my appointment, totally to my surprise at this press conference, (a) I didn't know he was going to announce it, and (b) he didn't tell me he was going to announce it.

That's remarkable. This, in spite of the fact that your actual meetings had become more frequent during that period when you were Deputy.

Well, during this period that I was Deputy I attended all of the National Security Council meetings with Admiral Raborn. In fact, the President had made it clear that he wanted me to come to both of these things because he wanted me to get some exposure and some experience in these meetings of the various kinds. So I had seen him with quite some regularity during that period.

And still he hadn't seen fit to call it to your attention again.

No.

This is really a very subjective kind of evaluation, but what kind of man is Mr. Johnson to work for in a close way as you did?

I found that Mr. Johnson was, in the first place, in my opinion, a first-class boss. I had had some experience in the outside world from the time I graduated from college until the time that I went into the Navy during the war and went on and stayed in intelligence, and [I] had worked for a variety of bosses not only outside the government but inside the government. It was one of my observations that a good boss was a man who made it clear what he wanted you to do, and when you did it, then he was generally satisfied with your performance. In this respect I found Mr. Johnson absolutely first-class. From the time we entered into this relationship, particularly when I was Director, but even when I was Deputy Director, whenever he asked me to do anything, he made it explicit what he wanted. When I had produced what he'd asked for, that was fine with him. I know of no instance during this period when we had any differences over this. In that sense I felt that I knew where I stood with him.

In addition, I found him an excellent executive in the sense that an executive is an individual who runs and deals with his subordinates in a way that makes it clear what is expected of them. He never went behind my back in the Agency or in the Intelligence Community. When he wanted something, he asked me for it and expected me to get it. He never told me how to run the Agency. I simply assumed that he wanted me to run it. He had so indicated, and I took him at his word. I did run it, and I dealt with my responsibilities in the Community as best [as] I knew how. I was never criticized by him for it. He never asked me to make an accounting of how I was spending my time or where I was spending it or on what I was spending it. I found that in that sense I was no exception in government; that he dealt through his Cabinet officers, and he dealt through the heads of agencies; that he did not do what President Kennedy used to do, of going behind these people to lower-down individuals whom he either knew or had some regard for their technical competence or something of this kind.

Interestingly enough, Mr. Johnson gave me such a free hand, if you want to put it that way—and I don't mean free in the sense of permitting me to overplay it—but such a free hand that I do not believe that he really had the faintest idea how the Central Intelligence Agency was organized, or how the Intelligence Community was organized. He expected me to produce the goods. When I produced them, which I think I did with regularity, he never asked any questions about where they came from.

We had hoped to get him out to the Agency on our twentieth anniversary, which occurred in 1967, but at the last moment, because of a crisis which had arisen in the domestic field, he was not able to come. So he sent a congratulatory letter instead. I was disappointed at this because, at least during my tenure here, he never had an opportunity to visit the Agency.

Another aspect of my relationship with him: he clearly understood that I was not a part of the policymaking aspect of his Administration. In fact, I am not sure how keenly aware of this he was, but I am sure he was somewhat aware that the Congress—Senators and Congressmen—do not like the Director of Central Intelligence to be involved in policymaking in any way. He, too, was not keen on this. The net result is that on no occasion in all the meetings I attended with him did he ever ask me to give my opinion about what policy ought to be pursued by the government. He asked for information about the facts in the case, what was happening in the overseas area under consideration, what I thought the opposition might do, what I thought the people might do in other countries, but he never asked me to make a statement about what he ought to do as President or what policy the Administration ought to follow. Even during the most intense decisions and difficult decisions over Viet Nam and other problems, he never deviated from this.

I have often thought that once he had focused—I use that word because I can't think of a better one at the moment—on what intelligence could do for him, he then realized that I probably had a role to play at various meetings that were held in seeing to it that—and I'm not attempting to use a phrase which in any way characterizes anyone or is an unpleasant phrase, it's simply a descriptive one—I helped to keep the game honest. Those individuals in government who have policies to espouse, policies to pursue, policies to defend, have a tendency as all human beings do to kind of fudge the facts in an effort to support these policies; and having the government's intelligence officer there who knows these facts just as well as they do and who can correct them at the proper time or draw attention to a series of facts that have been overlooked, or something of this kind, does indeed help to keep the game honest. Although

President Johnson never said anything about this to me, I rather got the impression that this was what he wanted from me; that he wanted to be sure that what he was hearing was the truth, and the more detailed the information, and the more information he had, the better he was able to make his decisions. In fact, I heard him say on many occasions that the decisions that a President made were no better than the information he had on which he made them. So this, I think, was a role which he felt was important: that the fact man, if you want to put it that way, was sitting at his elbow and that he was dealing with the right sets of facts.

It has been published, for example, that he was less interested in intelligence, generally speaking, than President Kennedy had been. Do you think that's inaccurate, based on what you've just said?

No, I think this is true. From the time that he took over as President, he started off by having John McCone brief him every day. I think that lasted for about ten days immediately after he became President, and then it was stopped. As John McCone told me on more than one occasion, one of the reasons that he left the government was that he was dissatisfied with his relationship with President Johnson. He didn't get to see him enough, and he didn't feel that he had any impact and he didn't have sufficient influence. This just didn't suit John McCone's way of life or interest, and this was why he left as Director.

But to answer your question in more precise terms, I think that President Johnson came to understand what intelligence could do for him during the events leading up to the [Arab-Israeli] June War of 1967.

That late?

I'm sure that he had been reading the information on Viet Nam and other things prior to this, and I don't mean that he'c rot been reading his intelligence publications, because, as you know, President Johnson didn't like to be briefed very much. He did not like to be talked at very much. He much preferred to read his intelligence. From my standpoint I thought this was infinitely preferable because a written document can be a much better balanced document than anything an individual can give orally. It can be more closely reasoned. Subtleties can be identified, which is very hard to do in a conversation. Last, but not least, for better or for worse, President Johnson, when he had something on his mind, simply wasn't listening to what one had to say to him. You could tell this from a variety of signs, and if he wasn't talking to you about some other subject, he wasn't listening to what you were saying. But when he read, he read carefully, and he hoisted aboard what he read. So during the time that I was Deputy Director and principally since I've been Director, I saw to it that he got the right publications put in his nighttime reading. I could tell from the questions he asked later that he did read it and read it very carefully. That was the way I communicated with him in the intelligence field. In my opinion this was absolutely fundamental—that if we had not had this system of ensuring that he read the intelligence on Viet Nam, on the Middle East, on a variety of other subjects, that he would not have been well served. But he was far better served by having the written word than he would have been if I had come down there every day. And I am quite satisfied with this.

I put this in at this point for this reason. I was constantly asked, particularly during the first year that I was Director, "How often do you see the President?" because there is a feeling loose in the land that unless you're in the President's presence a good deal, you don't have any influence on him. It was my distinct impression that the influence that I had with President Johnson was the right kind of influence, i.e., not my personal influence [but] the influence of the publications and the written documents and the intelligence reports, analyses, and estimates which I sent to him, and which he read. That was the right kind of influence to have, and it was influence applied in the right way. He could make intelligence judgments about them. He had time to study them. He could later ask questions about them, and they were closely, well-written documents all the way from the President's daily brief, which he got every night and which gave him a quick rundown on important things in the world which he should know, through the longer studies and periodicals and so on. So I was quite satisfied with my relationship with the President in this respect. Put another way, the President of the United States paid attention to what his intelligence officer gave him to read, and this is the most important relationship you can have, in my opinion.

Rather than paying attention to the intelligence officer as a man.

Who's a man, and whose personality inevitably gets involved in these issues when he's sitting there. I've heard all kinds of opinions on this, but I have my own opinion. I hold to this quite firmly, that there is a tendency in life for the human personality to unduly influence what is being said, and this can be very misleading to the President. It may not make so much difference with the Secretary of State or Secretary of Defense, but the President, who has to make the ultimate decision, should be dealing with a set of, if not solid facts, at least conceptions which he understands; and with a man like President Johnson, one communicated with him much better through the written word.

This more or less answers one of the questions way down the list here regarding how you keep your intelligence estimates from being policy-advised. This is, I assume, one way—what you're saying is that you keep the human element out of it here.

That is right, and he has a chance to see that this is an estimate. It's labeled as such. When those important documents. particularly on the Soviet strategic offensive forces and strategic defensive forces and general purpose forces—those three major National Intelligence Estimates—are produced each fall, they are clearly labeled on the cover sheet "National Intelligence Estimates." No one is under any illusion as to what they are designed to do. They are our best effort in the Intelligence Community to tell the President of the United States and the Secretary of Defense, "Here's what the Soviet Union has as a military force. This is what you have to deal with." Now, they're estimates, because we do not know with precision every single tank, every single plane, every single submarine, every single missile. But we believe this to be the case, and we believe this is the direction in which they're going, and we believe this is what it's going to look like two years from now, or three years from now, or five years from now. So he has every opportunity to deal with this problem in the proper context.

This also avoids, I take it, any highs and lows of personal being-in-favor or out-of-favor that might influence judgment.

That is right, plus the fact that anyone who ever watched President Johnson spend his day realized that this was an enormously active and restless man who had many contacts that he was making, whether by telephone or personally or through his assistants, and that the world around him was the world of action and of motion. Attempting to stop that action and motion to get him to listen with great precision to a long disquisition on some subtlety of Soviet weaponry was more than one could expect.

And you're quite right about the personality aspects of it, that in human relationships inevitably one has one's good days and one's bad days. There are certain days when you like a certain individual and certain other days when you'd prefer not to have to see him And the Presidency of the United States, being the peculiar office that it is—and I say peculiar because all the power in the Executive Branch derives from the Presidency; Cabinet officers don't have any power, heads of independent agencies don't have any power except what the President allows them to have at any given point in time. I think Secretary [of State Dean] Rusk described this as being the flow through government of the President's interests, which is another way of saying, "He's permitting you today to run your business," or, "He's not permitting you to run your business." But in and of yourself you have almost no power at all. And since the President is also a human being, the more one can do to permit him to deal with concepts, facts, policies, if you like, separated from the man who's espousing them, the better chance there is that he will come up with an answer which is satisfactory to him personally, which after all is the object of the exercise.

He's accused quite a lot of being volatile and of having tantrums when someone crosses him. Did you find this in your particular relationship to happen occasionally, or ever?

No, I can't say that I ever did. There were times when I, in meetings, was obliged to give him the results and studies or analyses that we had made which did not conform with his opinion. At these times he obviously challenged me, and we might have an exchange back and forth. But I invariably found that he had a remarkable ability, in my opinion, when he finally realized that the facts were right and had been accurately presented and that his conception was wrong, to simply swallow and accept what you had told him and not refer to it anymore—simply go on about his business, having changed his view about what this series of events either portended or what had happened.

This happened, for example, in connection with the amount of damage that the air bombardment of North Viet Nam was accomplishing. On two or three occasions he felt that we were unduly pessimistic, or—to put it another way around because I don't like the word "pessimistic," it doesn't convey anything—that our analyses of what was actually happening were short of the actual facts. But when he finally became convinced that we had the information and he was simply dealing with what he believed to be the case, he never made any problems about it at all.

I found this about him, that when he taxed one with having done something or not having done something and the facts were different, that it behooved one to go right back at him, and go back at him forcefully and without any undue amount of kid-glove work so that he clearly understood your side of the case. President Johnson did not like being opposed, but I think he liked far less any individual for whom he didn't have any regard and whom he didn't think could stand up for his side. So when he attacked, if you had reason to counterattack, one [had] better counterattack right there and then so that it was clear to him that you heard what he said and that you didn't agree with him, that the facts were different and you were giving them right back to him. On such occasions when this may have occurred, he never held it against me; he listened to what I had to say. He may have shrugged his shoulders, he may not have agreed, but this never got into any personal pique on his part. He never ostracized me; he never said anything to me that indicated that he wanted to avoid me; and I just felt that from this standpoint that one got along much better with him if you were a man and stood up to it and took it as it came, because I think he, like every human being I've ever known, liked to be agreed with. But I think that he had a very great disdain for people who held other views but still agreed just because they didn't want to cross him. . . .

What about an instance like when you first became Director, you got into the press with an episode regarding the [J. William] Fulbright letter in the paper? Did he then respond by calling you up and saying, "Watch out; don't do that anymore," or this type of thing?

I never discussed the Fulbright letter with him, ever! When the trouble came on the floor of the Senate one afternoon—it was as I recall a Thursday afternoon that Senator [Eugene] McCarthy got up and drew attention to the fact that this letter had been published in the St. Louis *Globe-Democrat*—quite a ruckus started on the Senate floor. I called various people in the course of the afternoon to get some advice as to how I should deal with the problem. I called Bill Moyers; I called Dean Rusk; I called Nick Katzenbach; I called J. Edgar Hoover—two of them, Katzenbach and Hoover, because I had had an indication from Moyers that it would be a good idea to get in touch with them and get their advice. I assumed from the way he put it that he'd talked to the President about it, and this was what the President was suggesting.

Katzenbach was still in the Justice Department?

He was then the Attorney General. But I never spoke to the President about it, and he never spoke to me about it personally. Since this question will obviously arise in your mind, I will go onto another episode.

When the problem of the National Student Association arose in February of 1967, I happened to be out in Albuquerque. I was doing something in conjunction with the Atomic Energy Commission, and I got a message from Walt Rostow saying that the President thought that since this thing was about to break that I ought to be back in Washington. So I returned to Washington within two or three hours. But from that time to this, the President never called me, and I never had any conversation with him about the whole episode. My testimony in the Congress, my dealings with the problem in the context of the Katzenbach-Gardner-Helms committee, and all the rest of it—I never had any conversation with the President about this. A period of three or four weeks must have gone by, and one day he called me on the telephone. I thought, "Well, he's calling up about all this trouble that the Agency has had in the last few weeks." When he got me on the phone, he said, "Dick, I need a paper on Viet Nam, and I'll tell you what I want included in it." When he finished telling me what he wanted, he said, "Thank you very much," and hung up.

And that was that.

So there was no discussion of the student business of the covert funding or anything else—absolutely no discussion at all. He left this entirely to me to deal with. Obviously, in appointing the Katzenbach committee to deal with the matter, to try and come up with some recommendations, et cetera, that was his action but he did not discuss the action with me. He simply established the group, and we went to work.

He didn't give it a specific charge as to what . . .

Well, he gave it a charge, but he gave the charge to Katzenbach, not to me. When we came up with a report and went and discussed it with him, I had a disagreement about one aspect of the report, and I presented to him in writing my disagreement with it. But he never called me back. He had Harry McPherson talk to me about it. I'm not, in this sense, saying that he *should* have called me back. I don't think necessarily that he should have. I simply had the feeling when the episode was all over that he wanted me—and obviously I had his backing, otherwise he would have said something about it—to make my own way and establish my own foundation under me, and to get through this thing as best I could because that was going to be much better for me and for him in the end than if he told me how to run it.

Do you think that perhaps he might have taken this too far sometimes and perhaps there was a problem of accessibility ever?

No, I can't say there was ever a problem of accessibility. If I had wanted to talk to him, I'm sure he would have talked to me, but I did not ask to talk to him.

Were there any long-run results of that that hampered the Agency's operation from those disclosures?

Certainly, in closing down some of these operations and changing the financing of others and so forth, that made problems for the Agency. They may have stopped some activities which were desirable activities. But the Agency was fortunate, lived through this thing without any trouble, and I think as of 1969 one hears very little conversation about the problem anymore at all. I think that it simply has passed over. I have to say, in connection with the way the President dealt with this, that in retrospect I think it was the right way, because I never had any conversation with him about how he dealt with human beings, or why he did one thing in one case and another thing in another. But I had the distinct impression that he, having been in Washington as many years as he had been here, had learned that either a man can make his way by himself with [the] proper kind of support in the background, or he can't, and that one had better find that out fairly soon.

You mentioned the second of your jobs as Chairman of the National Intelligence Board. Is that an adequate means of coordinating the Intelli-

gence Community to avoid interagency competition and strife that are typical of some of the domestic agencies, for example?

This is such a complicated problem that I don't think that it would be terribly useful to include it in this interview. My reason for saying this is this: the Intelligence Community is made up of a variety of agencies. Several of them are under control of the Secretary of Defense; others, such as the Federal Bureau of Investigation, which has its internal security arm, which in effect does intelligence work; the Atomic Energy Commission, which has an intelligence side to it; the State Department, which has its intelligence entity. The relationship among all of these is quite manageable in the current context. The work can be coordinated; it's a collaborative effort these days. During the period that I've been Director I can simply say that this has been a harmonious relationship, and I'm not in any sense making a self-serving statement here. After all, I inherited the work of a great many individuals. But at this period in history that aspect of government is working rather smoothly.

But when you ask me, "Is this coordinating authority enough to run the Intelligence Community?" I have to answer that it's far more complicated than that. I don't run it all that well. As I pointed out originally, I don't have any command authority. There are other ways that one might organize this which might make it run, if not more effectively, perhaps more cheaply. I don't know, but these are ongoing problems that are going to be with us for some years, and I don't think they really have any part in the historical record.

I suppose what I'm really meaning there is in regard to the Johnson Administration. Did it frequently occur that different members of the Intelligence Community made estimates that were considerably at variance? You mentioned, for example, your estimates regarding the effectiveness of the bombing sometimes being different and . . .

Well, most of those estimates that were made then were made jointly between the Agency and the Defense Intelligence Agency, and therefore they were joint estimates. I know it was played up in the newspapers that there were differences between the Pentagon and the Agency, and so forth, on these matters. These differences were minimal. From time to time there were differences on certain intelligence matters between the military command in Saigon and the Agency, but I think that one can play those up to a point where they not only will become exaggerated, but they would give a false impression of what was influencing the President. Those differences, such as they were, were not permitted by me to loom large in the President's mind, because when these questions came up, I told him what the disagreements were and what the possibilities for error were, what the dimensions of the problem were, so that if he wanted to, he could take the worst case any time. So I think this had no influence on his making of policy. . . .

Does the control mechanism allow proper Executive understanding of what the Agency is doing? For example, the committee that authorized the NSA [National Student Association] things is what comes to mind here—the Undersecretary of State, the Deputy Secretary of Defense, and yourself, which ten or fifteen years ago instituted the policy. How is the information about those policies broadcast into the proper Executive channels over time?

What you're referring to, I think, is what at one time was known as the Special Group. Then when that term appeared in a book—I think it was [David Wise and Thomas B. Ross's 1964] *The Invisible Government*—the name of the committee was changed to the 303 Committee. That name simply derived from the fact that McGeorge Bundy issued a NSAM [National Security Action Memorandum] which established this committee "de novo," and the number of the NSAM was 303, so it became known as the 303 Committee. And that was composed of the Special Assistant to the President for National Security Affairs as the chairman, the Deputy Undersecretary of State for Political Affairs as the Secretary of State's representative, the Deputy Secretary of Defense, and the Director of Central Intelligence. And it was indeed that Committee which has the responsibility for passing on or approving not only the covert action operations of this Agency, but, starting in 1961 in the early days of the Kennedy Administration, it also took on the responsibility for approving reconnaissance activities, whether by the Navy or the Air Force or whoever might be conducting them. In that context, it was that committee which would have passed on the *Pueblo* mission [a U.S. intelligence ship seized off North Korea in 1968].

But are there techniques for . . . like Mr. Johnson comes into power suddenly, he can be apprised of past authorizations by that group? Is there a means of doing this so that he knows what was authorized in 1958 or '59 and has been ongoing, [so that he] doesn't get surprised by something like the NSA disclosures?

I see what you mean. In an imperfect world it is always possible that something has been approved that someone omits or overlooks to report to a new President. In the case of the NSA business, Mr. Johnson was forewarned that this was coming over the horizon well before it did, because we had indications that this was going to create a problem. He was briefed about it, and he was informed about it, so he was indeed ready for the trouble when it began.

That was the point I was driving at, perhaps not very clearly.

But in retrospect, after the initial shock and publicity in the newspapers and so on, the thing that quieted that storm down, particularly in the Congress, and which in my opinion caused it to blow out to sea, was when Senator Richard Russell made a public statement that he had known about these things and that he'd seen nothing wrong with it and that it seemed to him that there was a great deal of fuss and fury about something that was useful, and so on. Then a few days later, Senator Kennedy, who was up on Long Island, I think, on this particular occasion . . .

This was Robert Kennedy?

Robert Kennedy. He, having been Attorney General for a time and therefore had known about the deliberations of this 303 Committee, had known about our relationships with student organizations, youth organizations, and certainly others, made in effect a statement that he had known about these things and that they had gone on since the early days of the Eisenhower Administration, and that they'd been approved by each President as he had come to office. When both of these individuals, the elderly Russell and the young Kennedy, had both come out with this—after all, they knew about these things—it immediately stopped the Congressional attacks. I mean, within a matter of hours almost, one ceased to hear anything about it. . . .

How frequently did you attend the Tuesday lunch sessions during the time you were Director?

Whenever I was invited.

How often were you invited, then?

I can only give this as an impression because—well, I will come to that because there's a point I want to make about the whole Tuesday lunch operation—it was my impression that starting in the summer of 1967 that I was at the Tuesday lunch when there was a Tuesday lunch or the corresponding equivalent. In other words, at that point I started to be invited. Admiral Raborn, I think, went only once or twice, so that the man in this job became a regular attendee at these meetings, starting about in the summer of 1967.

Since we're on the subject of the Tuesday lunch let me give you my impression of this. And in giving you my impression, I am literally talking from my personal point of view, and I'm not being influenced by what I've read in various documents or magazine stories or books and elsewhere. I'm simply talking about what I observed and what I drew from those observations. However, the Tuesday luncheons may have gotten started . . . as time went on I had the impression that President Johnson liked this as a mechanism for dealing with national security affairs, which encompassed foreign affairs and military affairs, because he was able, by inviting individuals to lunch, to limit attendance in the way that he wanted to limit it. To put this in another way, the National Security Council by statute has certain members. They are stated in the law: the President, the Vice President, the Secretary of State, Secretary of Defense, the Director of the Office of Emergency Planning—it's now Preparedness, but in those days it was Emergency Planning. In addition, the Chairman of the Joint Chiefs of Staff and the Director of Central Intelligence regularly attended as advisors in their respective capacities. Through the years other individuals have been invited and, if you want to put it this way, got used to attending. In the Johnson Administration the Secretary of the Treasury was usually invited, the Director of the United States Information Agency was usually invited.

Now, a man with President Johnson's preoccupations not only with security but with leaks—in other words, he liked to be able to discuss a matter with a group of his advisors in whom he had confidence and trust, (a) that they would not leak stories about it, but (b), and I think even more important, that they were not interested in using anything they heard there for selfish purposes, in other words, purposes that would in any way do him harm. I'm sorry. I believe that that's a slightly awkward way to state it, but I think it's an accurate way to state it.

In any event, if he invited individuals to come to lunch with him, this was something to which no one could possibly object, because they couldn't at that point say, "Well, I've got a right to be there. The law says . . ." So he didn't call it the National Security Council, but what he had there invariably was that part of the National Security Council which he wanted and which had something to contribute to his deliberations because the normal attendees were the Secretary of State, Mr. Rusk; the Secretary of Defense, Mr. [Robert] McNamara, then Mr. [Clark] Clifford; the Chairman of the Joint Chiefs of Staff, who during all this period was General [Earle] Wheeler; Walt Rostow as his Special Assistant for National Security Affairs; George Christian as his press secretary; Tom Johnson, the assistant press secretary. But Tom Johnson was really there to take the notes.

I was going to say, did Mr. Johnson keep, so far as you know, fairly complete . . .

Yes, he did. Let me come back to that. The other person was myself. So that this, interestingly enough, was human beings that were invited there; it was not people with certain jobs. If, on occasion, Secretary Rusk was away, Katzenbach might attend; and if General Wheeler was away, maybe General [John P.] McConnell would attend, or General [Harold K.] Johnson, depending on who was senior in the Joint Chiefs of Staff. But frequently I noticed the meetings would be cancelled if one or the other principal participants were not in town, because the President didn't want to just have a meeting; he wanted to have certain human beings there. So the regular people were the ones I've enumerated: the President, Rusk, McNamara or Clifford, Wheeler. Rostow, Christian, Tom Johnson, and Helms.

Now I didn't during this period attempt ever to send anybody else or suggest that Admiral [Rufus] Taylor, who was my Deputy, be invited, because I stayed in town during the period that I've been Director simply because I had the distinct impression that this is where I could do my job best. When President Johnson reached for his intelligence officer, he was reaching for me. He was not, I don't think, ever particularly good at dealing with people he didn't know. He didn't like to, for some reason; I think he felt uncomfortable. I don't know whether he felt uncomfortable, but anyway he didn't know that fellow and he didn't know what he stood for. Therefore he didn't know whether he could say certain things or wanted to say certain things.

That's consistent with why you say he liked the Tuesday lunch. He knew the people.

Yes. So that I just stayed in town and did not travel during these years, because I felt I could serve him best that way.

During all the time that I attended the Tuesday lunches, the detailed notes were kept by Tom Johnson, and that's why he was there. He, in fact, had a secretarial pad, and the minute he sat down at the table he started to write. I know from what he told me that he had those notes typed up and that there is a detailed file somewhere in the Johnson Library of the minutes and remarks and general conversational topics of all of those Tuesday lunches that I attended. What went on before this, I don't know.

Now you get down to the question of the decision-making at these lunches, or at the National Security Council, or the Cabinet, or wherever the case might be. One of the things that impressed me, starting in this summer of 1967 and going through to the end of the Johnson Administration, was that I had not understood really the way government operates before. But it did dawn on me during this period—I'm not using a self-denigrating phrase, I mean it did take a little time for this to sink in, if I may put it that way—that a President of the United States does not make his important decisions in an orderly way or the way the political scientists say they should be done or the way the organization experts would like to see them done or, in fact, the way 99 percent of the American people understand that they are done. This is a highly personal affair. A

President may sit at the Tuesday lunch, and a matter may be posed and he may reply and say, "We'll do this," and he has made a decision.

President Johnson might listen to a debate at the table over perhaps the bombing of some target in Viet Nam and then not make any decision at all. He would get up from the table and then at some point he would make a decision. But I never knew whether the debate that went on at the lunch decided him in his mind as to what he was going to do, or whether he had talked to six other people on the telephone in the course of the next two or three days, or had consulted Mrs. Johnson, or talked six more times to the Secretary of Defense, or read two or three intelligence papers, or what were the final sum of ingredients that went into the decision. All one knew was that when something had happened, he had made up his mind that this is what was going to happen.

This is the thing that is simply not understood about the Presidency, in my opinion, and that is that this man is in the constant process of deciding things, but that no man likes to be forced into a straightjacket as to where he has got to decide something. And President Kennedy, whom I worked with, and President Johnson just refused to be buckled into this. Therefore you never knew when you went to lunch whether any decision was going to be made, or seven decisions were going to be made, or twelve decisions were going to be made. The Secretary of State would raise a matter—I've heard President Johnson say, "Well, what do you want to do?" "I want to do this." "Well, let's think about it." I assume that at some point he finally decided the matter, but it was certainly not decided at that luncheon. On other occasions a question is raised; a little discussion has been held; he says, "All right, fine, let's do it."

That is a clear decision.

That's a clear decision. I've seen situations in which the Secretary of State and the Secretary of Defense disagreed. When he'd heard enough of it, he would say, "Now, look, you fellows go off and talk about that and see if you can't get this agreed and come back to me and tell me what you want to do." It was very clear over the years that President Johnson did not like to make decisions when he had to decide between one or the other of his Cabinet officers. He wanted them to agree and give the decision to him, which was jointly endorsed, and then he would make up his mind whether he wanted to follow it or not. But he did not like to choose up sides, and he did not like to cut the Gordian knot when there was a disagreement. He invariably sent the subject back for further examination, further study, or further discussion away from him!

Did the Tuesday lunch, being so personalized, perhaps encourage— not Mr. Johnson, but the participants who were there regularly—to perhaps disagree less with one another than they might have?

No, I think it encouraged frank talk; it encouraged saying what was on one's mind. One could afford there to disagree without being impolite or indicating to the world that there was this disagreement. That was encouraged. Everyone was encouraged to say what was on their mind, and I think within reasonable and human limits they did. I would think that this [was] one of the reasons that he liked the discussions there, because he was keenly aware that the people were very careful what they said in his presence or in the presence of each other because this gets out in the newspapers and there's trouble. It's impolite, and there is the sense that maybe one is being rude and so on. It was made very clear by him that he didn't want people to hold back for any reasons of that kind. When he saw that there was a disagreement, he just didn't want to decide the disagreement. He didn't like to do it that way. He liked a consensus. He always liked a consensus, and he liked his Cabinet officers to agree about these things.

There was a question later about what had been decided, and the way you describe it that would not be a problem, it would seem.

There has been a contention in the government that these Tuesday lunches were bad because the working level in the government, the Assistant Secretaries of State and so on, really didn't know what was decided, how much was discussed, what was decided, what was said. So therefore they felt that they were not able to do their jobs properly, and they were very critical of these lunches. Well, I know why they were critical, because the principals involved—and I'm not being critical here, I'm simply citing what I know to be a fact—were such busy men that when they got back to their departments, they didn't adequately report to their subordinates what had happened.

I remember that Walt Rostow used to go downstairs and call up Ben Read in the State Department and give him his rundown of what had gone on at the meeting. But that is not the same thing as hearing directly from the Secretary of State, if you're the Assistant Secretary, exactly what the Secretary says that the President wants you to do. They're two quite different things. This is influence, innuendo, and so on. I think that particularly the State Department, where these things tend to be slightly more complicated and more ephemeral, had difficulty with Dean Rusk on this score because he was so busy dashing from one meeting to another that I don't think he really adequately reported what had gone on. It was for this reason rather than the fact that I was sitting there and knew what had gone on, I knew what had been decided. I didn't have any trouble with this. So I think that was unfortunate in the sense that the flowback from the meeting was inadequate. It wasn't because there was any lack of clarity. And when there was a lack of clarity, you knew why there was a lack of clarity.

This could give rise to their beliefs sometimes that the White House NSC staff, the Rostow shop, was giving the orders too, sometimes.

That's right, I think that was indeed true.

You indicated that was not a problem with your Agency.

I never had any problems as far as the Agency was concerned, because, after all, I was sitting there, and I have a very different situation in this Agency than most people have. In the first place, there weren't all that number of matters that came up that were of direct interest to the Agency. But even when there were, this Agency was constructed originally on a kind of vertical arrangement so that the whole Agency is geared to have very direct and quick communications with the Director and back and forth. So I have no trouble in communicating with my organization. But I'm lucky in that respect—fortunate, rather.

So you didn't have the general relations with the White House NSC staff then that some of the other agencies had where orders were relayed frequently and sometimes to lower echelons and this type of thing?

They called me.

Some of the charges, particularly by some of Mr. Johnson's critics, have been that his staff constantly sought only the best face of things—I don't want to use "optimistic" since you said you don't like "pessimistic," but for want of a better word—only the optimistic side of the intelligence picture.

I've heard the criticism, but I never made it, and I never paid any attention to it. I had an arrangement with Walt Rostow that if I put the President's name on a publication and sent it down to him, he would send it to the President without any question; he would exercise no veto of any kind, which was all I wanted—to be sure that something that I wanted to get to the President went to the President. A lot of other stuff went.

But you are confident . . .

But I'm confident of that, and I could see later that the President had indeed seen these things. So whatever Rostow may have done to help the President to reinforce his impressions with facts, figures, statistics, and so forth, they weren't necessarily mine, and mine were not kept from the President. And I didn't care who was giving him a rosy picture. I gave him what I thought were the facts and what this Agency thought were the facts, and there was no problem about this. The newspapers tried to make a problem out of it, but I am convinced there was none.

I've never seen any decision that President Johnson made that he made because he had the wrong facts or the wrong set of facts. Maybe he did interpret things overly optimistically. But I used to notice that before he made the major decisions, he spent hours going over the facts and getting opinions and impressions and talking with all kinds of people that you never heard of and finally, in some strange way, coming to his decision. But anybody who says that they were battling for the mind of the President and finally won as a human being, I've always thought was talking the worst kind of twaddle, because President Johnson had a complicated mind, an enormously intelligent mind, a great capacity to grasp facts. And when he had an important decision to make, he talked to scores and scores of people, I know. And he went over and over and over the facts again until you were exhausted!

And he did master the details?

He mastered the details down to the last riffle, no question about this. So if there's any conclusion that could come out of this part of our discussion, it is simply that whether you agree or disagree with the decision that President Johnson made on an important matter, you could rely on the fact that he had exhausted all the existing sources, information, and so forth, and that the decision was made because that was where he came out, not because he did it quickly, that he skirted it, that he was unconscientious, that he didn't pay attention, that he didn't talk to the right people. He exhausted the subject. I've never seen such a careful man.

The other side of that coin is the charge that's also made occasionally, that the Agency and other members of the Intelligence Community were more or less given the conclusions that the staff or somebody in the White House wanted and told to go produce the intelligence to support it.

Absolute nonsense! I was never given any conclusions about anything, never! I would have been so offended if anybody had done that that I would have told them what they could do with it. Because there was nothing about the relationship between President Johnson and me as his Director of Central Intelligence that had loaded into it anything except the fact that I was here to do this job. He never intimated to me by word, gesture, or deed that he wanted me to knuckle under, that he wanted to get involved in policy, . . . that he wanted me to do any of those things. He wanted me to stand my ground and give him the best facts I had, and he made that clear. And I had carte blanche on this. There was no problem about that. Nobody would have told me what to do, and never did.

That's well to get on the record too in the light of some of the claims that have been made.

Never did!

The final thing I have down here that I think you're mentioned in connection with, in public print anyway, are the events leading up to the March 31st decision to institute a partial bombing halt [in Viet Nam]. You're mentioned as one of the participants in those meetings. Can you shed any light on the circumstances that did lead to that? Were there new intelligence estimates that played a major role, for example?

I talked to Walt Rostow not long ago on the telephone and told him that I had seen all of these articles; that I had been importuned by various newspapermen to contribute to them and that I had not done so, and that I had not permitted anybody in the Agency to do so, principally because I don't believe in instant history but also because I really don't know what led President Johnson to come to the conclusion that he came to. It seems to me that this is the case that we've been talking about, or that I've been talking about just a few moments ago: that this man went through weeks of work on this problem. What it was in the end that decided him to go in this direction rather than that direction, I don't know. And until he comes out with his own explanation of this, I wouldn't accept anybody's, because I don't think that there's anybody that knows. I assume that these articles are generated by certain individuals who wanted to get their side of the story on the record and out in the public domain for whatever self-serving purpose this might have. But I could not accept these as being the truth.

When I say to you that I don't know what went into President Johnson's major considerations, I say this because I believe there were many people who influenced his decisions while he was in the White House that did not sit in the Cabinet, that did not sit in the National Security Council, that did not attend the Tuesday lunch. There were people whom he trusted, whose advice he valued, and all of this was weighed in the scales. And that this—I come back to it because I think it's the most important point of all—that a President certainly has to have some kind of mechanics or machinery to organize his government, to bring the various and appropriate people to bear on a given problem. But in the end he decides it himself. And I don't think very many people ever know just exactly what decided him to do it.

Now, there may be one President who depended on his Secretary of State to a very great extent; there may be another President who didn't. I don't know. All I'm talking about is President Johnson. And that is that I had the distinct impression that he was extremely careful not to allow any particular individual, outside of his family, to have undue influence on his decisions, and that he did not look to anybody as his prime advisor; that he heard this from all the proper people, gave due weight when it was the Secretary of State, due weight when it was the Secretary of Defense, due weight when it was intelligence to his Director of Central Intelligence, but that what made him decide to finally do it, only he knew.

All of these accounts do sort of put the political scientist's simplicity of organized decision making on the thing . . .

They do, indeed. And there just isn't any question about it. Let me give you, while we're talking about this decision-making thing, another example of a decision that I saw made that is the kind of decision that one seldom thinks about but does occur. On the Saturday morning at the end of the [Arab-Israeli] Six Day War in June 1967, [Soviet Premier Aleksey] Kosygin came on the hot line. I don't have a precise recollection of the entire message, but the message that came along was to the general effect that unless the United States made its influence with Israel felt and weighed in to stop this war, to bring about a cease-fire, that the Soviet Union was going to have to take whatever actions it had within its capacities, including military actions.

Well, it was a rather somber group that was sitting down in the Situation Room of the White House. The President was eating his breakfast, and McNamara was there. Clifford had been brought in as an advisor on this crisis. McGeorge Bundy was there, Katzenbach was there for awhile, Dean Rusk was out of town. Ambassador [Llewellyn] Thompson, who was our Ambassador to the Soviet Union who happened to be back in Washington, was there. Let me change that. I am not sure whether Ambassador Thompson at that point was Ambassador to the Soviet Union yet or not. But if he was not, he at least was Ambassador-at-Large in the State Department working on Soviet affairs.

In any event, a message was sent back, and the morning wore along and everybody was speaking in a very low tone of voice, and the Russian text was examined very carefully to be sure that the Soviets did say that they intended to take any actions within their capacity, including military—and sure enough, the word was "military" when translated by Thompson and everybody else. After this had been going on for an hour or so, the President finished his breakfast and excused himself for some reason, went out of the room. While he was out of the room, McNamara—Katzenbach had gone off to the State Department to see the Israeli Ambassador—turned to Thompson and said, and everybody was speaking in a low voice, "Don't you think it might be useful if the Sixth Fleet, which is simply orbiting around Sicily" (you know, they go so many miles in this direction, so many miles in that; I mean, that's the way they cruised in those days), "that in light of this Russian threat and so forth, that we sort of make it clear to them that we don't intend to take this and take it lying down? Wouldn't it be a good idea to simply turn the Sixth Fleet and head those two aircraft carriers and their accompanying ships to the Eastern Mediterranean?"

Thompson said, yes, as a matter of fact he thought that would probably be a very desirable thing under the circumstances.

I said, "Well, the Soviets will get the message right away because they've got some fleet units in the Mediterranean, and they're sure watching that Sixth Fleet like a hawk with their various electronic devices and others. Once they line up and start to go in that direction, the message is going to get back to Moscow in a hurry."

Both Thompson and McNamara certainly agreed with that. So when the President came back in the room, McNamara said, "We've been talking about this and we'd like to recommend that we head the fleet toward the Eastern Mediterranean."

The President smiled and said, "That's a good idea."

So McNamara went to the telephone, and the fleet got headed for the Eastern Mediterranean.

A momentous decision made in thirty seconds . . .

A momentous decision made in a very short space of time, so that the might of the United States was headed in a very assertive direction. I mean, there was a decision that was made literally from one minute to the next. There were no papers, there was no direct organization, there was no estimate, there was no contingency plan; there was nothing!

That would drive a political scientist crazy.

But I think this is interesting.

Yes, it is. That, as you noticed, has exhausted the list I had here. I don't want to cut you off by any matter or means, if there are areas of . . .

As a matter of fact, I really think that I've covered everything I had down here except for perhaps a little bit more on the Middle East war, and the only reason I put the June 1967 war down here and I adverted to it earlier was that we made an estimate about the capacity of the Israelis to withstand a combined attack of the Arabs if war were to break out. This was about ten days before the war finally did break out. It was quite clear that this estimate was at variance with what the State Department thought. At that time it was clear that the Israelis were attempting to get from President Johnson some kind of a public statement of identification with their cause. He obviously didn't want to give this if he didn't have to. Our intelligence estimates, of which we wrote several in this period of time under his aegis: "Are you sure about that? Have you really studied it?" So these estimates were quite firm on this point. In fact, we predicted almost within the day of how long the war would last if it began.

Your estimates were the accurate ones.

And these turned out to be absolutely accurate. I think the President was sufficiently impressed with what intelligence could do for him in a situation of this kind that from that time on he paid more attention to it.

DAVID FROST: *As you look back over your long career in the CIA, what would you say was the high point, the greatest moment, and what was the lowest or the saddest?*

RICHARD HELMS: Well, it is a little difficult to say what was the greatest moment, because there was some success that was not manifest, perhaps, to the public. I think that one of the high points was the time that we predicted beforehand how long the Six Day War would last almost within a matter of hours. In other words, before the war began, we told President Johnson that it wouldn't last more than seven days no matter what combination of forces was brought to bear by the Arabs. When you come as close as that in the intelligence business, it has to be regarded pretty much as a triumph.

I think the lowest point came after I had left, when in 1975, during the investigations, I saw what was happening to the Agency and heard the charges being brought against it and saw the amount of material pushed into the public domain at the time. I think that was probably the lowest point. It was not while I was in the Agency itself.

If you'd known at the outset what you know now, how many things would you have done differently in your life?

That is impossible to answer, as you knew when you asked it. But if you mean would I spend a good part of my life as I did working on intelligence, I would be glad to repeat the experience because I think that it was not only useful to try and get intelligence established in this country, I think it was a help to the country. I was interested in it. I enjoyed working at it, and I would like to do it over again if I had to retrace my steps.

With minor modifications?

Certainly with some minor modifications, but that is true of everyone. But in the last analysis the association with the people and the work in intelligence has been a privilege, and anybody who is fortunate enough to work there is a fortunate man indeed.

If you were drawing up a balance sheet to answer the question, "Okay, what have we got out of having the CIA since 1947? What are its triumphs? What has it achieved?" what would be your sort of condensed balance sheet?

Conducted by David Frost in Washington, DC, on May 22–23, 1978, and reprinted by the Central Intelligence Agency, *Studies in Intelligence* (September 1993), 1–29.

It would be that we had brought into being and had, up to a point, settled into American society an intelligence organization which not only was designed to prevent another Pearl Harbor, that is, an intelligence organization which could review and analyze independently and objectively all of the material coming into the United States Government, but we also made some significant contributions in the technical field. The CIA has been in the vanguard of that quantum jump in the use of intelligence derived from photographs, satellites, electronics, overflights—a whole series of technological achievements. Some were developed in concert with the Department of Defense, but the ideas for many of them originated in the Agency itself. Then last, but by no means least, we did develop a worldwide network of intelligence collection which has made a significant contribution.

What about the complaints of liberal critics of the CIA that we always end up in the name of freedom on the side of the suppressors of freedom? Where has the CIA advanced human rights?

That is simply an unfair charge. The whole history of the CIA, if you care to examine it, was to support the non-Communist left, not only in Europe but in Latin America and elsewhere, and I think the record will show that this is what was done. Obviously, we have dealt with dictatorships of the right in various places where it seemed required in the anti-Communist context which certainly governed this government's policies overseas during the '50s and the '60s. But if you examine the record, I think that a great deal was done to support the non-Communist left against takeover by the Soviets. Take the youth movement of the '50s and '60s, when the Agency was supporting the young people at international conferences. The Soviets put on about two of these meetings after we began to do so and then never put them on again, because young people from the free world were able to dominate the conferences and prevent the Soviets and their satellites from controlling youth movements the world over.

So do you think in a sense there is a double standard in the media that applies to right-wing dictators as opposed to left-wing dictators?

There is no question that there is a double standard; left-wing dictators seem to be treated very well by the media, whereas right-wing dictators are beyond the pale. We suffer, it seems to me, from a bit of provincialism in thinking that the kind of democracy that developed in the United Kingdom and in the United States is exportable everywhere. That simply isn't true.

But there are certain irreducible human values that are universal, wouldn't you say?

I would, and I believe that firmly. But I don't find that those values are adhered to any more in left-wing or Communist dictatorships than in any other.

Is it practical that the public be informed of what Intelligence is doing in its name?

I don't quite see how, particularly in the secret intelligence field. It may be possible to tell them about oil imports and wheat estimates and things of that kind, although I happen not to agree even with that. I don't think that the Agency ought to make documents public, even if theoretically they are sanitized. Anybody reading them knows that a lot of the information came from secret sources; and even if it's fuzzed up, the fact remains that there is put in the public domain more evidence, more material, for the opposition to examine and to study and to deduce how the data have been gathered.

What would happen if we were to disband the clandestine services?

We would run a real risk, particularly with a country as powerful and having as good an intelligence service as the USSR. They would simply run us off the map in the rest of the world—if they are not doing so already.

Presumably the public must accept the fact that for clandestine activities to work, some of it has to be "dirty work" by definition?

It is by definition. I believe that the American public is mature enough to understand. Except for certain very shrill voices, you don't find very much ill will when you travel around and talk to people in this country. They think it is quite sensible that we should protect ourselves. We have a right to survive, to protect our way of life. The allegation that the Agency and the FBI have eroded our civil liberties is nonsense.

This country has never been more democratic than it is today. Civil rights have never been so vigorously defended. How anyone can say that their personal liberties have been impinged upon by these various things, except in the abstract or theoretically, I don't know.

Should the American public trust CIA employees or anyone engaging in "dirty work" in their behalf?

A professional intelligence service is essential to our survival.

Who are these CIA people, after all? They are the men and women living next door, down the street, or across town—these are normal Americans who have gone through an extraordinary experience to get into the Agency in the first place.

They are interviewed, then they take a difficult intelligence test; and if they get through that, they take a probing psychological test to establish their stability and their personality and so forth. They are then the subject of a detailed security investigation during which their entire past, from the time they were born, is combed out. Last but not least, they are asked to submit voluntarily to a lie-detector test in which they are asked very intimate questions.

These are people serving this country very well and very loyally and very patriotically, in some cases under very difficult circumstances. But too often they are reviled and cast as second-class citizens. If this is the way the public wants to deal with its intelligence professionals, then we ought to disband the Agency and go back to the way we were before World War II. Otherwise, it is up to the citizens of this country, the Congress, and the President to support these people and to support them adequately, or else there is no reason to expect them to do these kinds of dirty jobs. It isn't fair, it isn't right, and it won't work.

We went from a hot war, World War II, into a Cold War, and then into something called Détente. Are we back in a Cold War situation today?

I happen to agree with George Will, who says we have never left the Cold War. The underlying antipathy between the East and the West is as real today as it was when Winston Churchill warned in 1945 about the Iron Curtain descending over Central Europe. Détente was a term used to describe limited efforts by the U.S. and USSR to get on a better footing and a better relationship, and there was nothing wrong with attempting to do so. But the basic hostility between us and the goals which the Soviet Union has espoused from Lenin through Stalin, [Nikita] Khrushchev, and [Leonid] Brezhnev have not changed.

Do you think that the weakened position of the Intelligence Community has made our ability to warn of another Pearl Harbor questionable?

I am not so concerned about that aspect. We have a first-rate indications and warning capability. The Central Intelligence Agency still has a top-notch analytical and estimative capability. There is nothing secret about that function of the CIA. Pearl Harbor might have been avoided or its impact lessened had information available been brought together and properly analyzed and presented to the leaders of the United States.

The Clandestine Service established by Executive Order can contribute only a small amount of information compared to the horde acquired by other means. Nevertheless, sometimes that tiny bit can be terribly important, particularly if it tells you what the other fellow's intentions are.

There are two memorable quotes in your speech of 1971. The first, as you may have guessed, is, "I cannot, then, give an easy answer to the

*objections raised by those who consider intelligence work incompatible
with democratic principles." And, "The Nation must, to a degree, take it
on faith that we too are honorable men devoted to our service." Do you
stand by both, and if you would want to amplify them now?*

I stand by them. I think they sound fine.

You still couldn't give an easy answer to those who are worried?

I could not. In fact, I think that it has even become more difficult,
because the problems have multiplied as a result of the charges, the allegations, and the efforts to write charter legislation in the Congress, and
so forth. In a democratic society there are endless ambiguities; it is inevitable by the very nature of the society in which we live. These things
cannot be made black and white; there have to be gray areas.

We have to do the best we can, take some chances, and hope for the
best. And this is why I advocate that authority over a Clandestine Service
should be in the Office of the President where it is now, that it should
have Congressional oversight, certainly, but that the responsibility should
not be shared. The President is the Commander-in-Chief of the Armed
Forces—he is the formulator of American foreign policy; intelligence is
a tool available to him.

*How would you compare Presidents Kennedy, Johnson, and Nixon in
their approach to the CIA? In what way were they different to deal with?*

The CIA got off to a very weak, rocky start with President Kennedy
because the Bay of Pigs came along not long after he was inaugurated,
and after that we had to pick up the pieces. One dealt with him on a personal and very straightforward basis. He held a lot of meetings, calling to
the White House experts at lower levels in the government in an effort to
find out to his satisfaction what the facts in any given case were. He
wouldn't even have the Secretary of State or the Secretary of Defense
there. Gradually, I think by the time 1963 had rolled around, we had rather
reestablished ourselves, and he could see the Agency's good points as
well as the warts, if you like.

As for President Johnson, it was not very clear to him, I believe,
what role intelligence could play until the Six Day War in 1967, when
suddenly he realized that intelligence could be premonitory and could
keep him informed in a way that was helpful to him. After that, I was
invited to the so-called Tuesday lunches which he held almost weekly. I
did not play a policy role, however. I don't want to be misunderstood on
that score. But I was at the table. If I may put it this way, having me there
kept the game honest. The other people present had to be a little careful
about the way they pushed their individual causes or policies, because

they knew very well that I probably had the facts fairly straight and wouldn't hesitate to speak up.

I think it is fairly clear that President Nixon was very distrustful of the CIA, largely because of the missile gap which was alleged to have existed at the time of his 1959 campaign against Mr. Kennedy. He felt that he lost that election because of the so-called missile gap and held the CIA at fault. He had it in for the Agency in the sense that he was very distrustful of what we advocated and felt that our estimates had been wrong at times. There was not very much opportunity to talk to him personally. He liked to deal through [Henry] Kissinger and [Alexander] Haig, and so we had an arrangement whereby written reports were sent to him and he read them. When necessary, one could talk to him, obviously, but it was a more stylized and formalized arrangement. He took it in faster through the eye and preferred to do so. So did President Johnson, for that matter. He liked to read reports; he didn't want to be talked to.

In his book, The Ends of Power *[1978], H. R. Haldeman claims Nixon also resented the fact Kennedy had been briefed by Allen Dulles on the possibility of a Bay of Pigs operation so Kennedy was able to advocate aggressive action against [Fidel] Castro while Nixon, since he knew it was really going to happen, had to seem to oppose it in order not to tip the Administration's hand.*

I have seen that, but I know nothing about the merits of the allegation.

In the same book, Haldeman refers to an unspoken feud between CIA Director Richard Helms and Nixon.

There was none on my part. He was my President. I worked for him, and I had no sense of a feud at all. I was doing the best I could to satisfy his requirements and the requirements of the office. Haldeman must have got the notion of a feud from President Nixon, not from me.

Is the story in the Haldeman book that Nixon wanted certain documents on the Bay of Pigs and that you resisted handing them over true?

It isn't only in the Haldeman book but in President Nixon's book, as well, that I was asked for certain documents by [John] Ehrlichman. I collected the documents, ones that I felt would be satisfactory for the purpose. I then insisted on seeing President Nixon because I wanted to be sure that he wanted them himself and that he, as my boss, asked me for them.

The appointment was arranged and I did go down to see him in October of '71. I turned over the documents that he had requested and, as far as I knew, they were satisfactory. He never told me later that he hadn't received what he wanted. So I don't understand the complaint in the

Haldeman book—or in Nixon's—that they asked for more material than I provided.

After all, under the law the Director of Central Intelligence reports to the National Security Council, which, in effect, is the President. He was my boss. We have one President at a time and if he wanted a document from the CIA, what right did I have to decline to give it to him?

Haldeman says in his book that when Ehrlichman read the materials you had delivered, he found that several reports, including the one on the Bay of Pigs, [were] incomplete. But they never said that to you?

They didn't. They just said it among themselves, apparently. As I recall, I took three documents with me. One was about the Bay of Pigs, the second about [the Dominican Republic's Rafael] Trujillo and his demise, and the third—written by John McCone—made it clear that the Agency had had nothing to do with President [Ngo Dinh] Diem's being killed in Vietnam.

You wanted to hear directly from the President that he wanted these documents. What were your misgivings?

The documents dealt with episodes that had occurred on other Presidents' watches, and I wanted to be very sure that Mr. Nixon himself wanted them and that they were not going to fall into the wrong hands or be used for purposes other than what I thought might be proper. It turned out that that was not the design, but I didn't know this. I just simply wanted to be sure that this wasn't an Assistant to the President asking for information which might be used politically. It seemed only proper to me that the President himself should ask for them.

Given that the motive of the President himself seems now to have been political, was that abuse of the Agency?

It might have been. He assured me at the time that he would protect the Agency, that he did not intend to use the documents for political purposes. I had no choice other than to accept his word. But I don't think in the end that actually they were used for any nefarious purposes.

Do you think there was abuse of the CIA by the Nixon Administration?

I think that the effort to involve the CIA on 23 June 1972, vis-à-vis the FBI, was an abuse. So, too, was the effort by Mr. [John] Dean to get us to put up bail money and so forth for the [Watergate] break-in men. I don't recall anything else. The materials for Howard Hunt and certain related things I didn't like, and it may just be that we should have stood up more firmly against the requests even though we didn't know what they were for. I mean, all of those second guesses by the Monday morning quarterbacks do come at issue, but the things I have mentioned were real abuses. Had we gotten involved in those, I think the consequences for the Agency would have been very serious.

The [Edward] Epstein book, Legend: The Secret World of Lee Harvey Oswald *[1978], which tries to pull together a lot of fragmented information, contains two great mystery quotes of Nixon. Presumably when he said, "We protected Helms from a lot of things," he actually probably meant the CIA; and when he said, "Bring out the whole Bay of Pigs thing," he meant the assassination plots against Castro?*

Well, Mr. Nixon makes clear in his book and also has made clear in an affidavit in a law case, that the only thing he meant when he said, "We have done a lot of things for Helms," was that he helped me get a lawyer appointed in the Department of Justice to seek to enjoin [Victor] Marchetti from publishing a book about the Agency. That is the only case mentioned in his book, and the only case mentioned in a legal affidavit, and I assume that is the only case he had in mind. I know of no favors he did me, other than the perfectly official interchange of business.

As for the Bay of Pigs, I don't know what Haldeman was talking about. All I knew was that that was a failure that the Agency had had, but I didn't see any reason to drag it into conversations that we were having at the time. The efforts to upset Castro are well known, and I didn't have a moment's thought about this. So if this is Haldeman's interpretation, it is his and his alone.

When I talked to Richard Nixon in Monarch Bay in the Spring of '77, his criticism of the CIA was that it had not done a good job on Cambodia, that it failed to warn of the [1973 Arab-Israeli] Yom Kippur War, and that it thought that [Salvador] Allende was likely to win the Chilean election, albeit not with the plurality. Do you think he was right on those three things?

We did miscalculate the flow of arms, weapons, and supplies provided to the Viet Cong or North Vietnamese forces through the port of Sihanoukville in Cambodia. The economists built a model to try to do so, and we underestimated, I think rather considerably underestimated, what was going through Sihanoukville. Later, when we had access to things in Cambodia and found the bills of lading for the ships that had called at Sihanoukville, they totaled up to a larger volume than we had estimated.

As for the Yom Kippur War, I was in Tehran as Ambassador and I don't know the merits of that case.

I don't see how he could assert that we were mistaken on Chile, because we said relatively early on there was a very real question whether

Allende could be defeated. And all of that hugger-mugger that took place in Chile was a result of that estimate. I can't imagine that President Nixon should have been surprised when Allende was the winner.

Did the Nixonian idea that there must be a sort of "bamboo Pentagon" somewhere in Cambodia, a sort of "Dr. No's Palace," to be found by the April 30 incursion, emanate from the CIA?

They were looking for but never found something called COSVN [Central Office of South Vietnam], which was the North Vietnamese command of the forces in South Vietnam. The CIA had no illusions of a "bamboo Pentagon." We knew that there was kind of a command structure which may have been no more than a general and two or three aides and maybe a table that moved from place to place, but you can't run armies without communications and without a headquarters.

If President Nixon had kept the American troops in the area longer and really had cleaned it out, as the operation was designed to do, I think we would have found a lot more. But the operation started and then stopped suddenly, and the troops withdrew because of domestic pressures in the United States. It is hard to say today that there was no headquarters in there just because we didn't find it.

There are people who told us that the idea of an incursion into Cambodia was one of Nixon's greatest passions, and that in fact there was a good deal of information that such an incursion would not be successful, that you had some of that material but you thought that it was hopeless to show it to Nixon, because he was intent on doing it come what may. Did you have evidence that the thing wouldn't be a success that you didn't give to Nixon?

I don't really know, in this context, how you define success. We did our very best to provide Mr. Nixon information on what we thought was there. There was a very real concern about what would happen if Cambodia were invaded. We had no illusions about the domestic dissent in the United States either, but that wasn't our job to assess.

It has always seemed to me, quite frankly, that President Nixon early-on paid a very high price for that invasion and therefore should have seen it through to the bitter end. It didn't help him any to pull out before it was finished. And we will never know whether it could have been more productive.

Do you have evidence that it wouldn't be successful unless he stayed there for a long time?

That is too minute a detail for me to remember.

Do you think that overall the CIA was responsible for overly optimistic assessments by both Presidents Johnson and Nixon of how we were going to do in Vietnam, or do you think that was political optimism overlapped on not overly optimistic CIA estimates?

I don't think that the CIA was in the vanguard of optimism about the Vietnamese war at any time. As a matter of fact, one of the most difficult problems for the DCI during that period with both President Johnson and President Nixon was the charge of negativism—that, after all, you are Americans, you are on the team, why is it you see these things so negatively? Why is it these things are never going to work? What is the matter with you fellows?

The OPEC [Organization of Petroleum Exporting Countries] oil embargo came about in October '73, but the Nixon people seemed to have resented the lack of any contingency plans for an embargo going back months or years. Is that a fair point?

I would not have thought so. I would have thought that the United States Government should have had a contingency plan for an embargo of that kind because it affected the entire country.

Were there ever CIA people in any other government department without the knowledge of the head of that department?

Never. But there might have been instances in which a responsible person in the department knew, whereas the head may not have been personally aware, if you want to make that qualification. However, the CIA did not go about planting agents or spies or the like in any agency of the government or, most importantly, in the White House. I would like to put this myth to rest forever.

There were as many as ninety or one hundred employees of the CIA in various parts of the White House at different times—in communications, handling telegrams in the Secretariat, in the Situation Room. There were Agency secretaries working in parts of the White House. We loaned telephone operators. It was our effort to help the White House staff itself in the way that it thought was required. There was nothing secretive about it. For a long time, the White House was staffed largely by people seconded from other agencies—the Department of State and Defense, the CIA—and from any place that they could borrow people. That was one of the ways the President kept the White House budget down.

To revert to H. R. Haldeman, was Alexander Butterfield a CIA plant?

He was not.

Let's come on to that 15 September 1972 meeting after Allende had already won the popular election on 4 September, though not with a plu-

rality. You said later that if ever you left the Oval Office with the marshal's baton in your knapsack, it was on that day.

Well, that was one of those zingy phrases which one should refrain from ever using.

But it is basically true, that Nixon was extremely exercised?

He was very interested in preventing Allende's accession to the presidency. There wasn't one of us who thought we had any chance whatever of achieving that objective, and I had tried to make that point, but it was like talking into a gale. We were to go out and do the best we could, and that was all there was to it. The possibilities of succeeding in the short time span were so remote that we had a most difficult time putting together anything that was even a semblance of an effort.

One of the things not generally realized by people who are not familiar with the process [is] that advanced planning is critical for any covert operation. You have to have assets in place—real estate, individuals, money, and sometimes automobiles, newspapers, printing plants, and even loudspeakers. You have to have everything organized and ready to use. We had nothing in place in Chile. We really had to extemporize from the very beginning, and it was an almost impossible situation.

Why do you think Nixon was so worked up about Chile?

I think that he makes the point clearly in his book that with Castro in Cuba, right off the coast of the United States, that another Communist-led country with frontiers contiguous with Argentina and Bolivia and Peru would make things in Latin America difficult for the United States.

One of the reports critical of the operation asked, "Did the threat to vital U.S. national security interests posed by the presidency of Salvador Allende justify the several major covert attempts to prevent his accession to power?" Answering that question today, would you say yes or no?

With benefit of hindsight, I think that the Chilean business would be handled differently. I can't imagine wanting to go through such a nightmare a second time. When President Kennedy launched the Agency into the 1964 Chilean election, the work was started many months ahead of time so that there was some chance it would be effective. Against Allende it was started much too late to be very effective. The thing went from bad to worse.

Any judgment as to whether Mr. Nixon was justified in trying to defeat Allende, or whether President Kennedy was right earlier in wanting to defeat him, rests within the foreign policy establishment. The President has the right, under our Constitution, to formulate foreign policy whether everybody agrees with it at the time or their perceptions change through the years.

The Agency is often criticized, "Well, you did what the President wanted." What is the Agency for? It is part of the President's bag of tools, if you like, and if he and proper authorities have decided that something has to be done, then the Agency is bound to try to do it. We would have a very strange government indeed in this country if everybody with an independent view of foreign policy decided he was free to take or not take the President's instruction according to his own likes and beliefs.

But when you left that meeting on September the 15th, you knew that the brief was impossible?

Let's say, most difficult.

Were you tempted to resign or did you think, "This is part of my job"?

No, I thought it was part of my job.

Chile was central to what I think [British Prime Minister] Harold Macmillan once described as "local difficulties" that you experienced. Looking back on those Senate hearings at which you said "No, sir," to the question about CIA activities in Chile and so on, if you had your time over again, would you handle it differently?

I don't know how I could handle it differently, because the dilemma posed at that time has never been resolved. If I was to live up to my oath and fulfill my statutory responsibility to protect intelligence sources and methods from unauthorized disclosure, I could not reveal covert operations to people unauthorized to learn about them, and that was the predicament I was in before Senator [Frank] Church's committee. If I had to do it again tomorrow, I don't see that I would have had any choice. It should be made clear what Congressional committees a Director of Central Intelligence must confide in or to which he must provide operational details. The chairmen of at least eight committees, four in the Senate and four in the House, can summon the Director of Central Intelligence and swear him [in], ask him any questions they want, and force from him any information they want.

There have been suggestions that when you were called to Camp David and then sent as Ambassador to Iran, you held a pistol of some kind to Nixon's head. Did you? And, if so, what was in it?

I certainly did not. Of all the accusations made about me and about my leadership of the Agency and about the Agency itself, I have resented none more than the charge I blackmailed President Nixon. It is nonsense. I did not blackmail him; I threatened him with nothing. When he said that he wanted me to leave, I said, fine. It never occurred to me to argue. I was never one of those presidential appointees who thought he had an entitlement to his job. You serve at the pleasure of the President of the United States. When he wants you to leave, this is time for you to leave.

And, last but not least, why should I want to blackmail my boss, the President of the United States? I worked for him; the Agency worked for him. What point would there have been to do this?

When he asked you to leave, did he also offer you your new appointment? Did you feel you were being fired and then given another appointment or promoted or what?

He told me that he wanted me to leave and that he wanted to appoint a new man. There was some conversation about timing, and then he said, "Well, would you like to be an Ambassador?" We discussed this, and I said I wanted to think it over because I didn't know. So the two were not put together, no.

Was Iran mentioned at that meeting?

Yes, it was, because by the time I said that I wanted to think about the idea, he asked, "If you would like to be an Ambassador, where would you like to go?" I thought for a minute, and I said I thought Iran would be a good post. I never regretted it.

Presumably, one of the reasons that you thought the appointment appropriate was that the CIA has enjoyed good relations with Iran ever since it helped restore the Shah to power in 1953.

That is the conventional wisdom, and while it may be true that the Shah appreciated the help that both the British and the American governments gave him in 1952, his later feeling about the Agency had a great deal more to do with the quality of its personnel who had served in Iran and whom he came to know over the years than with the earlier events. He thought them a first-class group of officers who knew their business.

You have testified that you didn't know about the Watergate break-in in advance. Given that in an organization as large as the CIA, there are things that the Director doesn't get to hear about, like the Lee Pennington affair,* until later, I could quite believe the theory that since [Eugenio] Martínez [a Cuban-American recruited by E. Howard Hunt to report on the Cuban community in Miami] was reporting to his case officer and had reported his contacts with Hunt as early as November '71 and that

---

*Editor's note: Pennington was a secret CIA contract person who, out of friendship and acting on his own, helped James McCord's wife burn McCord's files two days after the Watergate break-in. McCord, a former CIA security officer, was a member of the burglary team.

Hunt was working for the White House in March of '72, I could quite believe that although word never reached you, somebody in the CIA knew that a break-in was going to happen.

The FBI, Special Prosecutors, grand juries, Senate committees, House committees, Lord knows who all, have been trying to find who it might have been. As far as I know, he doesn't exist. Martínez did not share his information with his case officer. Nobody has ever been found in the Central Intelligence Agency who knew about the Watergate break-in beforehand, period. And let's put a period to it right now.

But everybody has such a vast respect for the intelligence-gathering capacity of the CIA that it seems almost incredible that they didn't know that something like this was going on. Do you think they ought to have known?

No, because we don't have a charter to do any investigative work in the United States. Why would we have people around the Democratic National Committee or around the White House or around the CRP, the organization [rather, Committee] to re-elect the President?
The CIA had nothing to do with any of them. We were very conscious that we ought to stay out of anything having to do with the political process in the United States, and to the best of my knowledge we did. So why would a tip-off to the break-in come to our attention?

Only under the guise of self-protection, I suppose. But once you had found out that Hunt was a potential troublemaker in August of '71, shouldn't some one of your underlings have kept track of him in self-protection?

That would have been the worst thing we could have done. Then we would have been tied into the thing and never could have extricated ourselves. I think it would have been a disaster if we had tried to keep an eye on Howard Hunt. He was working for the White House. He was their man, and he was doing their bidding, and he paid a horrendous price for it, but that was the way it was.

When you first learned that Hunt had come to the Agency for help in August of '71 and you and [Gen. Robert] Cushman switched him off because he was getting to be a bore or potential danger or whatever; and when [Howard] Osborne called to say that various people with CIA connections, including Hunt, had been detained in connection with the Watergate break-in; and, without knowing any of the details, didn't your mind go click, click, click, what the whole bloody hell, and your heart sink?

Well, I didn't like the notion of any people that formerly worked for the Agency being involved, but the interesting thing about Hunt was that when I got the call from Osborne, I believe it was a Saturday evening, but then the papers the next morning made no mention of Hunt's name at all. So on Monday when we had our staff meeting, I turned to somebody and said, "Osborne tells me that Hunt is involved in this. I haven't seen his name in any of the papers. How come he is making that allegation?" Then I called Osborne, and he said that Hunt was involved in it and in what way. So during the twenty-four hours in between, I was more concerned about the names in the paper than I was about Hunt.

To go back just a moment, I don't know why [FBI Director L. Patrick] Gray didn't believe me when I told him early-on back at the time of the Watergate break-in, that those fellows were involved with Ehrlichman. I did tell him that. I am certain he will tell you I told him. But for some reason his people seemed to feel that the Agency was involved. But I didn't hold back from the head of the FBI. As a matter of fact, I told him in a telephone call I made at the time of the break-in. I think he was in Los Angeles. I said, "You'd better watch out because these fellows may have some connection with Ehrlichman." I knew Ehrlichman was the one who had arranged for the hiring of Howard Hunt.

We were notified when the White House hired Hunt. We were never asked about it beforehand. We never asked about his background or anything. Not that it might have changed the course of history, but it interested me that the White House hired him without ever going to his employer of many years' standing for a recommendation or a reference.

There have been allegations since, whether in books by prosecutors or committee reports, that while the CIA wasn't involved and didn't know about Watergate in advance, it could have been more cooperative sooner. Do you regret that the CIA didn't blow the whistle a bit quicker and perhaps shorten the agony of Watergate?

I don't think that it would have shortened the Watergate agony. That should have ended in 1974 with President Nixon's resignation, but it seems to have been continuing. Something in our psyche likes to keep working this one over. My problem as Director was to distance the Agency from anything which looked like involvement. That problem began the minute the announcements about the break-in were made. Who were those fellows? They were Cubans that had worked for the CIA. There was [James] McCord and there was Howard Hunt.

I knew that we were not in any way culpable with respect to Watergate; and it seemed to me that the thing I had to do, and what I was paid to do, was to adhere to truth, to distance the Agency from the whole problem. I recognize that I have been accused of not having turned out my pockets and made everything available to the prosecutors, but the fact remains that their office and the FBI and so forth were leaking information to the press in a way that looked very dangerous to me. If I had said to them, "Talk to this man; here is a fellow who did such and such," the next thing you know we would never be able to unsnarl the Agency from the Watergate thing. If I was wrong, I was wrong. Monday morning quarterbacks always have a better way to play the game.

To clarify the record, Haldeman says in his book: "Interestingly, the CIA never allowed the [Sam] Ervin Committee investigators to see reports of Martínez's case officer. . . ." When they asked to interview the case officer, they were told he was on safari in Africa. There were no reports from Martínez's case officer for them to see?

I don't recall ever having gotten into it and they may not have been able to get them, but certainly the FBI could have, if they had wanted to, or a Special Prosecutor or a grand jury. You know there is nothing that you can deny to a grand jury if they want to subpoena it.

Again, Haldeman, in November of '73: "Andrew St. George said in Harper's Magazine *that he had visited CIA Headquarters and discussed the break-in with his former associates. What he discovered was that Martínez had indeed reported to the CIA hierarchy on the planning of the Watergate break-in."*

Who said this?

Andrew St. George said it in Harper's Magazine.

That fellow is a discredited individual. The Senate Armed Services Committee went into his background and so forth, and if you take Andrew St. George as a witness, you can believe anything.

When did you realize that what you had been invited to take part in was a cover-up?

"Cover-up" became a word of art much later in 1973. At this particular point the things that concerned me were Dean's requests to give money for bail and things of that kind.

Now, this is not the first time that the Agency had been asked to use its unvouchered funds for things that were not strictly our business. I don't want to go into the history of this; there is no sense in dredging it up. But this was not the first time by any means and we were used to turning these things off—or pointing out that we had an understanding with the Chairmen of the Appropriations Committees of the Senate and the House, that any monies expended this way would be reported to them.

This we religiously abided by. So when Dean's request was denied and then the pressure dropped off and so forth, we resumed our own normal business. Now this whole area of cover-up and so forth developed much later.

In fact, it was May '73 before [Vernon] Walters informed the Department of Justice of these White House efforts to have the CIA stop the FBI investigation—eleven months after they happened. It was 11 May before General Cushman provided testimony that it was Ehrlichman who had telephoned him to assist Hunt, rather than that he couldn't recall. It was the same month, May '73, before the first James McCord letter, which Osborne had shown you in August '72, came to light. It was January '73 before the casting photographs of the [Lewis] Fielding break-in [at the offices of Daniel Ellsberg's former psychiatrist] came to light. Those four things together might have held up the investigation considerably. In retrospect, perhaps it was a mistake that those things were not brought to light sooner?

Possibly, and I don't have any reason to argue with your recital of the events. I left the Agency in February of 1973 and I don't remember any more the exact dates on which these things came out. But I don't recall either any people from the Department of Justice or any place else up until the 1972 election asking for any of this material.

The real investigation began in March 1973 and that was when the thing really started to move. The Ervin Committee was organized, et cetera. There were just small pieces of it being nibbled around the edges in February of 1973 when I was being confirmed as Ambassador to Iran. The first questions were being asked about it. Prior to that, I don't recall anybody asking about these things. If they did, I have forgotten about it. I am not ducking here; I just don't recall it.

Your priority was that you felt the whole future of the Agency might be at stake here, in fact?

I did indeed.

And you told Gray right at the time of the break-in that there was a link between Hunt and Ehrlichman?

I did indeed.

It was a major lead?

I would have thought so.

Given that the CIA got quite a lot of "stick" for the fact that for eleven months General Cushman didn't name Ehrlichman as the man who called him about Hunt, as I mentioned, why didn't the CIA ever get credit for your call to L. Patrick Gray right after the break-in, when you said that it was Ehrlichman who had called Hunt?

I don't know to this day, because at the time we were attempting to deal with all of these various factors. I didn't see Gray. I had asked to see him on one occasion, but he cancelled the appointment. I learned later he cancelled on instructions from the White House.

I think that he was in a most unfortunate position. He had taken over the Bureau [the FBI] at a most difficult time. I think he had a very tough time of it. And I have no interest in picking on Pat Gray. He doesn't deserve it.

Who was [informant] "Deep Throat," do you think?

I haven't the faintest idea.

Someone I talked with yesterday is convinced it was you. Was it?

No, I never even met Bob Woodward or Carl Bernstein [of the *Washington Post*]. I think it is most unlikely that they would even have thought of me in this connection.

Wouldn't it be very good for your image if you had been?

I would prefer not to have that image. There would be no reason for a person in my position to sneak around in garages and so forth to keep a couple of reporters straight. If I had all of this information, I should have walked out and said something about it publicly, or before a properly authorized body.

Moving away to broader issues of Watergate, taking a broader philosophical view, in retrospect is there any period when you wish that you had resigned because the demands made upon you were improper?

The only time that there was a real question in my mind as to what was going on was at the 23 June 1972 meeting, because neither Walters nor I, especially, could figure out what this was all about. Everyone must realize that at that time we knew nothing about money being laundered in Mexico—we knew nothing about money at all. We couldn't figure out what the preoccupation with Mexico was. We didn't want to bring Walters into that aspect of it too much because he had only been with the Agency for six weeks, but after all he is a clever man and he obviously was wondering, too, about why they were interested in Mexico and what was going on down there that might cause a problem for the CIA. When I left that office that day, therefore, I was in a quandary trying to figure out what we could be involved with here.

But you must remember, as I had said earlier, the President was the boss, and if he had information about something that I apparently didn't have, I wanted to find out what it was and see what it portended for the Agency or for any of us. So when I got back to the Agency and we finally got to working on these things, I realized that there was nothing in Mexico that was going to affect our operations. Gray eventually was told this when we had been able to ascertain it.

Then gradually those several names came to light. They didn't mean anything to us at the time. It was only later that I understood that they had to do with something in this line of laundering the money. So, during that period, that weekend Walters and I talked frequently, and later on Dean called Walters down on Monday, Tuesday, and Wednesday.

If you had to choose an adjective to characterize your personal relationship with J. Edgar Hoover, what word would you choose?

I can't choose any adjective except "correct." I used to see Mr. Hoover at an occasional reception, and we held very pleasant conversations on those occasions. In some respects, I came to know him relatively well—in contradistinction to most [people] because he never saw very many outsiders.

When I say I came to know him relatively well, that is only by contrast; other people didn't know him at all. We always greeted each other with proper respect and cordiality. It has been said often that we didn't meet very frequently in a formal way. The reason I didn't call on him more frequently, rather than handle the business between the agencies [the CIA and FBI] through liaison officers or memoranda, was that when I went to his office, I was lectured the entire time and then left when it was time to leave. I could barely get a word in edgewise. I used to succeed a little bit when I had something important to talk about, but Mr. Hoover liked to dominate the conversation, and he was quite a figure around this town for forty years. A lot of people are throwing arrows at him and saying unkind things about him now. I didn't see very many people, including Presidents, who said unkind things about him when he was in office.

One of the reasons that is given for the feeling that you may have felt no more than correct toward him is that throughout the Nixon Administration, Hoover was adding legal attachés to embassies around the world everytime he saw Nixon and that he was encroaching on your territory. Broadly speaking, is that so?

Broadly speaking, it is accurate, but it really had nothing to do with this so-called breakdown of relations because, after all, we were grown-up people. I recognized that Hoover was encroaching on my territory, and

I did my best to keep this encroachment down to a minimum. President Nixon wanted it, and since he did, we would accommodate to it.

There is no sense in being immature about these things. I felt that the breakdown over the Colorado affair was quite unnecessary, but this was obviously in a fit of petulance on Mr. Hoover's part, and, like most things that come as a fit of pique or petulance, it was short-lived. [In February 1970, after a seemingly insignificant incident in Denver, all policy-level liaison betwen the CIA and FBI was severed by the FBI and restored only in November 1972.] It wasn't very many days before we were back to the status quo ante, but the papers had been going back and forth, and people were talking informally, and the work of the two agencies was not impeded.

A lot has been made out of it. It is one of those episodes that are easy to dramatize, but the working level in both agencies kept things on an even keel. After all, you must recognize that if these two organizations don't work together, the United States is ill served, and I think most of us had that sense.

You knew that Hoover was trying to encroach on your territory. How did you limit that encroachment?

I think the word "encroach" is too strong. There have been so-called legal attachés in embassies abroad since World War II. Those legal attachés were Hoover's men. Hoover wanted to expand those legal attaché officers in certain places. This would not "encroach" on the CIA's efforts. We have a great deal of work to do. There is a certain specialized kind of work the FBI did overseas and it did not get in our way. What was involved here, more than encroachment, was the fact that the embassies had to absorb additional people, which the State Department and the Foreign Service obviously didn't like very much. I didn't like it much either, but I was in no position to remonstrate about it, since it was quite clearly delineated that the legal attachés were not going to duplicate any of the work that our people did.

Do you think Hoover, knowing Nixon didn't like the CIA, sold the plan to him partly by intimating that he could also keep an eye on the CIA?

I never suspected that because, frankly, what was there to keep an eye on? We had a highly disciplined organization overseas with first-quality people doing the best job they knew how to do, and if somebody wanted to mind their business for them, let them mind it. But I doubt very much that the FBI fellows wanted that kind of job or would have done it anyway.

In the last resort, who do you think was responsible for exposing CIA to the public? Was it Ehrlichman? Nixon? Daniel Schorr? Was it William Colby?

I don't think there is any place to lay it except at the feet of Director Colby, who, after all, was the one who made available all of this material. To this day, I am not sure why he handled matters the way he did. He explains his reasons in his book, and obviously I am required to accept his explanation. But the thing that had bothered me, quite frankly, is Mr. Colby's belief that he had a constitutional obligation to do all this. I am no lawyer, but it has always been my understanding that any question of constitutionality has to be decided by the courts, with the Supreme Court the final arbiter.

But the legality or the requirement for the release of these hordes of documents [regarding questionable CIA activities that might be construed as outside the legislative charter of the Agency] to the House and Senate Committees never was tested before the fact in the courts. Finally, President Ford stood aside and watched it happen when, if it was going to be stopped, he had to dig in his heels and say, "Don't send down those documents. We are going to find out here whether it is required that secrecy be breached in order to conduct this investigation in public." That would have forced the issue into the courts. If the Congress then insisted on subpoenaing the documents, the courts would have had to decide.

I would have felt a lot more comfortable if they had done so, if there had been an order from the courts to Director Colby to turn over those documents, but this never happened. In the end, it was decided by Mr. Colby's interpretation of the Constitution.

Could Colby have stopped the hemorrhaging? What should he have done?

Once one starts to bleed, it becomes a question of quantity. The time to try to head this off was at the beginning. That was the time for the President of the United States to take a firm stand in favor of the security of the CIA's files. President Ford could have forced the issue into the courts and maybe to the Supreme Court. I would have felt a lot more comfortable if the Supreme Court had directed the Executive to turn over those secret documents to the Legislative Committee. But they didn't have a chance to rule. We must not forget that the Office of Strategic Services, the forerunner of the CIA, a secret service or a clandestine service, was founded just before our involvement in World War II, and the concept never has been tested in the courts.

One review of Colby's book said that he could have scarcely done more damage to the cause of U.S. intelligence or counterintelligence if he had been a KGB [Russian] agent. Would you go along with that?

I think Colby did considerable damage, but he explains in his book why he took the actions he did. He has gone to great pains to explain himself, and I think only History can judge the merits of the case. I don't believe that Colby was a KGB agent. I don't believe that we had any KGB agent in the inner circle of the Central Intelligence Agency. The nightmare of every Director is that one day he will be told that somebody inside his immediate organization has been spying for a foreign power. So I was very conscious always of the charges and countercharges that some individual might be off base or something of this kind. It was my conviction that none of the people with whom I was closely associated was in any way working for any foreign intelligence organization. I certainly do not believe it about Colby, and I don't think such allegations serve the cause of the United States at all.

So much paper and so much information were released that it is almost impossible to tell what has been compromised. Moreover, the legal requirement to satisfy inquiries under the Freedom of Information Act [FOIA] is further eroding security. The Agency is trying to be careful about what it releases, but blotting out something with black ink on a piece of paper doesn't mean it can't be re-created by somebody who knows the facts. I find that this is a very difficult ongoing kind of "leaking," and I put the "leaking" in quotations because it is done under the guise of legality and by law. I have pleaded with the Senate Select Committee to exempt the intelligence and security agencies from the Freedom of Information Act.

FOIA is good legislation if it results in someone learning from the Department of Transportation or the Department of the Interior or elsewhere information the American public has the right to know. But it is used as a device to ferret out information about intelligence and security operations, and I think that is bad and ought to be changed. I realize that I am opening myself up to criticism about the public's right to know, but the public's right to know is the Russians' right to know; it is everybody else's right to know. The Russians read our newspapers and our magazines and our technical journals very carefully indeed.

Colby says in his book that he felt that he had to go to the Attorney General's office and that it was an unpleasant thing for him to do and so on. How do you feel about it?

Obviously I have always wondered why he did it, but I haven't anything further to say. If he felt he had to do it, then he did and it has been done. I would have preferred, however, that he had gone first to the President, his boss, and said, "Mr. President, I am going to turn over this material on one of my predecessors, and I just want you to know it is being turned over to the Attorney General."

Have you seen Mr. Colby on a personal basis since he decided that he had to advise the Attorney General's office that you might have committed perjury in the Chile hearings?

We have seen each other in public since that time, but we haven't had any detailed conversation. But I don't mark it from that time. I just haven't had any detailed conversation with him since sometime in 1975, when I went to his office for lunch and talked about a particular situation. That was the last time I had any conversation with him.

In retrospect, do you agree with the findings of the Rockefeller Commission that some domestic activities, such as Operation CHAOS, exceeded the CIA's statutory authority?

Yes, I think there were two or three cases in the Operation CHAOS context where we went too far. I would like to explain, though, if I may, that the word "chaos," which has such an unhappy connotation, was not chosen because it was descriptive of the operation. You will remember that Winston Churchill always said that you should have happy optimistic cryptonyms [code names] when engaged in any big undertaking in the world. This was not all that big an undertaking. We didn't think anything about it at the time. But I have noticed since that the word "chaos," although only a cryptonym, has been seized on as an indication of some terrible thing that the Agency was involved in, whereas in point of fact the operation was an attempt to collect information on foreign involvement with American dissidents and domestic bombings and things of that kind.

What about the mail opening, HTLINGUAL or SRPOINTER, from '52 to '73? The Rockefeller Commission said that was unlawful. Do you think it shouldn't have happened?

Mail opening is a very important counterintelligence technique, particularly if it can be done as we did it, under conditions of secrecy. Whether it should have continued as long as it did is debatable, but it was useful at the outset. The Korean War was just winding down and then American soldiers were being killed in Viet Nam. We were looking for evidence of the involvement of Americans with the Soviets and so forth. After all, the Soviets were backing the North Vietnamese, just as they had backed the North Koreans.

I can't imagine that Allen Dulles embarked on the program without President Eisenhower's knowledge. President Kennedy was briefed. There is some controversy over whether I informed President Johnson, but I am relatively certain that I did on 10 May 1967 when we went over certain things that the Agency was doing. There is no record of it, however. I did not testify to this effect before the Church Committee because there was no document to support such testimony. It was solely my word; President Johnson can't speak for himself, so I didn't want to get this into any controversy. I don't feel, however, that it was the wrong thing to do in terms of our efforts to see what the Soviets were doing to us.

Let me say that this issue is important for the future. We still have a problem with counterintelligence in this country. Not only has it fallen into disrepute, but there isn't very much being done. Now is the moment for the Executive and Legislature to decide how they are going to protect this country against spies, saboteurs, and terrorists at home.

It is an important question. Our young people seem to be rather cavalier about such questions because of a lingering distaste for the Vietnamese war and other things, but they are the ones who are going to be affected. I think they ought to decide whether the right of survival of the country takes precedence over human rights in certain cases.

But the Agency did end up with files or a cross-index or whatever on over three hundred thousand Americans, files on protest organizations and seven thousand details of those figures?

These were names—most provided to us by the FBI. To hold names you need lists. Sometimes you open a file, but that doesn't mean you are targeting anyone. As a matter of fact, most of the files in the CIA aren't targeting anybody. They simply hold material, like the filing case in your office, the kind of correspondence you conduct.

For example, someone in the CIA today receives a letter from the FBI mentioning David Frost. Now, do you file the letter or throw it away? Usually you file it, because you don't destroy material in the government except under a certain process. So it would be filed and henceforth there would be a file on David Frost, who might be innocent as a lamb. Maybe it just said you went across the street and had a beer. So that this question of the files on Americans has been blown out of all proportion, and I am delighted to have the opportunity to set the record straight.

Including photographing individuals attending anti-war demonstrations?

There were two cases of this. There were two fellows for whom we were trying to build overseas cover so that when they went abroad, they would have the proper credentials to penetrate foreign dissidents working against the United States. We overstepped the line by encouraging these two to become a part of the demonstration, to get their credentials by meeting the leaders, so they could say when they went overseas that I was with Joe in that May Day demonstration and so forth.

In one of these cases all that material was put aside and never used or passed to anybody. But when the boss of the section left, a new man arrived, found this material, and distributed it all over the place. When finally it was taken down to the Senate, it looked as though we had been spying on everybody in the United States. I want to wipe out that impression. We were not spying on people in the United States. We were not spying on anybody; we were trying to get this fellow prepared to go overseas. In retrospect we overstepped the line, and I am sorry. Nobody was damaged that I know of and nobody was disadvantaged.

Do you agree with the Rockefeller Commission's view that you exercised poor judgment in January of '73 by destroying documents that might have contained evidence?

Tapes, not documents, were destroyed. No, I don't agree. One recorder was attached to my telephone and the other could be used to record conversations in my office. Neither, may I say, was activated by sound; both required the pushing of a button.

These tapes contained material having to do with foreign policy and U.S. intelligence; they would have been damaging to our foreign policy if they had gotten into the public domain. I thought that then; I think so now. I would do the same thing today. A great deal has been made of the fact that Senator [Mike] Mansfield wrote various government agencies not to destroy material having to do with Watergate. I did not destroy material having to do with Watergate. Nobody can examine those tapes, so there is no way to verify my assertion—but I promise you it is true.

In the case of Operation MUDHEN, do you think you overstepped the line there with the surveillance of [syndicated newspaper columnist] Jack Anderson?

When I was testifying before the Senate Select Committee in May 1978, I said this is a totally unclear area and needs to be looked at. I was criticized in the Rockefeller Commission Report for undertaking this surveillance of Anderson, saying I had no authority to do so under the Director's charge by statute to protect intelligence sources and methods from unauthorized disclosure. Now if you are going to give the Director this responsibility in the future, then I think you have either got to define it, give him the wherewithal to achieve his purpose, or don't give him the responsibility. This is an unclear area to this day, and I think it ought to be cleared up one way or the other.

The drug testing is a mystery to me. How did the CIA feel that LSD and such things fitted in with national security?

All of this started back in the very early fifties, when you will recall we were just coming out of the Korean War and there was deep concern over the issue of brainwashing. As a matter of fact, a man named [Edward] Hunter had written a book entitled *Brainwashing in Red China,* and "brainwashing" was a literal translation of the Chinese words, and we wondered what it was all about. Did they use sodium pentothal or drugs of one kind or another? We had learned that something called LSD had been discovered in Switzerland by a scientist named [Albert] Hoffman. It was tasteless, odorless, and colorless and, taken even in small quantities, created a kind of schizophrenia.

Coincidentally, I think it was in 1952, Ambassador [George F.] Kennan came out of Moscow and made a speech in Berlin that the Soviets regarded as so egregious that they declared him *persona non grata.* We wondered whether he'd be administered some drug that caused him to act in such an aberrant fashion. There were a number of things going on that puzzled us.*

We felt that it was our responsibility not to lag behind the Russians or the Chinese in this field, and the only way to find out what the risks were was to test things such as LSD and other drugs that could be used to control human behavior. These experiments went on for many years. There is the inevitable question of whether they should have been ended sooner.

Allen Dulles, who was the Director back in those days, authorized this thing to be undertaken, but we all felt that we would have been derelict not to investigate this area. Who else in government was going to investigate it? It was our field. Maybe our people abroad would be administered drugs. In other words, in a defensive way we felt we would have failed in our responsibilities if we hadn't investigated what was there, if anything.

*The remarks in question were delivered at a plane-side press conference at Templehof in Berlin on 19 February 1952. Ambassador Kennan, en route to a Chiefs of Mission meeting in London, had learned shortly before his departure from Moscow that his study in Spaso House had been bugged and had seen Soviet militia keeping Soviet children away from his two-year-old son at play in the Embassy garden. In his own words, he was both depressed and irate. He thought that his remarks to the press in Berlin were off the record, but later admitted that they and particularly a young reporter for the *Herald Tribune* may not have sensed his intent. In any event, when asked by the reporter for the *Tribune* whether diplomats in Moscow enjoyed social contacts with the Russian people, Kennan snappishly compared life in the Embassy in Moscow with that which he had known in an internment camp where he was imprisoned by the Germans in 1941–42. On 26 September he was attacked by *Pravda* in an editorial which said he'd "lied ecstatically" and made "slanderous attacks" on the Soviet Union. He was declared *persona non grata* on 3 October. For a full account of the incident, see George F. Kennan, *Memoirs, 1950–1963,* vol. 2 (Boston, 1972), 145–67.

The commission said it is clearly illegal to test potentially dangerous drugs on unsuspecting U.S. citizens.

There was one instance in which that was the case, and in retrospect I agree we should not have done it.

There is virtually no drug-related MK-ULTRA [CIA code name for drug and counter-drug research projects] material in the files, we gather? In terms of destruction of those files, [in] the seven boxes of progress reports that I think you had recalled from the Archives and destroyed on 31 January was a booklet called "LSD 25, Some Unpsychedelic Implications." Why did you decide to do that?

It was a conscious decision that there were a whole series of things that involved Americans who had helped us with the various aspects of this testing, with whom we had had a fiduciary relationship and whose participation we had agreed to keep secret. Since this was a time when both I and the fellow who had been in charge of the program were going to retire, there was no reason to have the stuff around anymore. We kept faith with the people who had helped us, and I see nothing wrong with that.

In principle, do you think there is ever an occasion when somebody has a right to lie in the national interest?

I don't recall specific episodes, but it seems to me that if one goes through history, there are examples of it and that it has been upheld by public opinion at the time. I don't encourage lying. I have never been confronted with this problem. I testified many years before various Congressional committees cleared to hear my testimony. This is the first time I was questioned about operational matters before a committee that I had understood the Congress did not want me to testify before on such matters. The consensus in the Congress, it always seemed to me, was quite clear. There were two attempts, one in 1955 and another in 1965, to broaden the committees that had oversight of the CIA. Both were defeated in the Senate. That should have settled the matter, it would seem to me, but apparently it didn't.

So that there can be situations in which a Director of the CIA would have a right to lie in the national interest?

I don't think there is any question about that, just as other officials of the United States Government would. I would suggest that if you unearth the transcript of the hearings of the Senate Foreign Relations Committee after the U-2 was shot down over Russia, you will find that there were very high members of the United States Government who were not telling the truth, the whole truth, and nothing but the truth. They were trying to protect the President. He later admitted that he knew about the U-2 flight and revealed it. I am sure there are other examples of testimony before the Senate and House where the whole truth was not disgorged by members of the Executive Branch.

In fact, you were not charged with lying, but rather with withholding information. I suppose that critics of the Intelligence Community would say that the sorry state that the intelligence business finds itself in now is not so much that things were made public but that the CIA and other agencies had done things which made news—that if there hadn't been assassination plots, if there hadn't been Operation CHAOS, if there hadn't been drug testing and so on, then public disclosure would not have been harmful?

If the CIA had done nothing, then there would have been nothing to expose. When Vice President [Hubert] Humphrey came out to speak at the twentieth anniversary of the founding of the Agency, he made the point to the audience very strongly that "you are criticized and you will be criticized, but if you are an activist and get out and do the work that you are supposed to be doing in the world, you ought to be able to bear the criticism, but the only people that aren't criticized are those who do nothing, and I would hate to see this Agency get in that state." I grant you that the point you make is a valid one, except that I would like to submit in evidence that the way that these matters were brought to public attention, in the most flamboyant manner possible and sometimes almost in an atmosphere of hysteria, was most unfortunate.

Have you ever had any doubts about the Warren Commission's conclusions that JFK was killed by a lone gunman acting alone?

No, I have never had any doubts about it. I didn't have any doubts when the Warren Commission made its report, and I don't have any today. I have never seen any persuasive evidence that anyone other than Lee Harvey Oswald shot President Kennedy.

How close did either of the Kennedy brothers get to ordering attempts on the life of Fidel Castro?

I can't answer the question directly. If you read the transcripts of the Church Committee, and there are many pages in the public domain, you can see what the problem is all about. All I would like to ask is, what did these so-called assassination plots against Castro amount to? The business about the suit that was supposed to have powder put on it and some big seashell and so forth are just pipe dreams. There were fellows trying to figure out if some device could do this, but the idea was never seriously considered and the gadgets never left the laboratory.

As for the Mafia, that is one of the great regrets of my life. We were under great pressure to make contacts in Cuba. I let the pressure to do something—because we didn't have very many contacts—overwhelm my judgment. We never should have gone forward the second time with that [John] Roselli thing.

When I found out about it, I should have corked it off then and there. I am genuinely sorry that I didn't. It was a case of poor judgment. I was told Roselli was attempting to find out if there were Mafia elements or organized crime elements still in Havana. That was all I authorized, but I shouldn't even have authorized that, and I am sorry.

On the other hand, let's not exaggerate what was involved. There isn't the slightest creditable evidence that any poison pellets ever reached Havana. We have only the word of a gangster that they did, and I don't believe him. I think he and his case officer grossly exaggerated what they were trying to accomplish.

What about the testimony of [Yuri] Nosenko, the Soviet defector who is referred to in the Epstein book? You told Earl Warren there were two opinions about Nosenko. Do you believe his claim that the KGB had no contact with Lee Harvey Oswald while he was in the Soviet Union?

I went to Chief Justice Warren because I didn't know what to believe then; and I don't know what to believe now. I don't know what the facts are today. But it did strike me at the time that it would be a great mistake for the Warren Commission to shape its findings on the basis of a statement made by a man whose bona fides we could not establish. I told Justice Warren that I did not know what the truth was but that we could not vouch for Nosenko, and the Commission should take this into very serious consideration in their conclusions. I think that was the right thing to do.

When Nosenko was given a new identity, after three years of hostile interrogation, had you decided on his bona fides?

By this time the issue was what to do with him. Obviously, I recognized we couldn't keep him in durance vile, as we had, against the laws of the United States. Lord knows what would happen if we had a comparable situation today, because the laws haven't been changed, and I don't know what you do with people like Nosenko. We sought guidance from the Justice Department at the time. It was clear we were holding him in violation of the law, but what were we to do with him? Were we going to release him and then a year later have it said, "Well, you fellows should have had more sense than to do that. He was the whole key to who killed President Kennedy."

The controversy has been bad enough without our having done that, but everything would have come down on our heads, I am sure, if we had released him before we did, and we would have been bitterly criticized. So we did the best we could, but eventually it became necessary to give him a chance to go on about his life. There were those who felt he was bona fide and others who felt that he was not. As far as I know, that controversy endures. May I say one of the most difficult things about counterintelligence is that it tends to be very untidy. There is no answer to the Lee Harvey Oswald and Nosenko cases, and there won't be unless the KGB in Moscow or the Soviet leadership is going to tell the United States exactly what the facts were. I think that unlikely to happen, and therefore these cases are going to remain untidy. They don't end up like novels; they end up with long Irish pendants.

What about the assertion that during his residence in the USSR, Oswald provided information on the U-2 to the Soviets?

I was totally unaware of that until I read Mr. Epstein's book, and I know nothing about the merits of the assertion. In other words, I have no way of verifying it. I don't call up the Agency about matters of this kind. After all, when I was DCI, I wasn't interested in having former Directors guide my hand.

In retrospect, do you think the Warren Commission should have known about AMLASH [code name for a Cuban agent, Maj. Rolando Cubela Secades, recruited by the CIA to eliminate Castro] and those contacts?

This is a very confused area, as far as I am concerned. Allen Dulles, who had been Director of the Agency for many years, was on the Warren Commission. I don't know what he did or did not tell the Warren Commission about what the CIA was doing. When one is running secret operations, there is a great reluctance to spread knowledge of them. In retrospect, I can't question the fact that it might have made for some clarity if these things had been laid on the table for the Warren Commission.

On the other hand, that is a hindsight judgment. I just don't know why Allen Dulles didn't make these things clear to them or John McCone go down and talk to the Warren Commission about these, or the Attorney General go down, or somebody go down. But suppose they had known it—what different conclusion would they have come to? This is a question I simply raise. I am not making a judgment; I am simply raising it as if to say, what does it signify?

One of the Senate reports makes the point that you were on the horns of a dilemma because you were in contact with the Warren Commission and you knew about AMLASH.

It wouldn't have occurred to me to go to the Warren Commission with information about ongoing covert operations without the clearance of the Director, and maybe the clearance of the executive committee that passed on those things at the time. In those days I think it was known as the Special Group.

But the thing that seems to be quite forgotten, with respect to the Kennedy Administration and Castro, was the missile crisis. Nobody talks about that anymore. The Russians came along at Castro's invitation in 1962 and were about to score one of the great strategic coups of the century by placing medium-range ballistic missiles in Cuba—missiles which could shoot right into the American heartland and hold us hostage in a way which their intercontinental ballistic missiles could not. We seem to have forgotten that Castro was a co-conspirator of Khrushchev's; he was making it possible. But that never seems to be mentioned anymore. We became snarled up in the question of whether CIA was running this or that operation against Cuba, as though that had everything to do with what later happened to President Kennedy, whereas the antipathy between Mr. Kennedy and Castro was manifest at the time of the missile crisis and for good and serious reasons.

The missile crisis happened in October 1962. In December 1962, when the Brigade that had landed at the Bay of Pigs, Brigade 2506, was repatriated as a result of the arrangements made by Attorney General Robert Kennedy in exchange for drugs and medical supplies and so forth, President Kennedy went to the Orange Bowl in Miami and greeted them with words to the effect that "I can assure you that this flag will be returned to this Brigade in a Free Havana."

President Kennedy himself was keeping the pressure on the Castro government. This wasn't anything hidden or anything of that kind. I mean, if provocations were needed, both Castro and Kennedy had provided fine provocations for each other. But what does it say in the end?

If History renders the verdict that President John F. Kennedy did not rule out the assassination of Castro, and even said in so many words that he would quite welcome it, would History be unfair?

I don't know how to answer that, and I think one is simply going to have to wait for History.

You were asked if Robert Kennedy told you to kill Castro and you said, "Not in those words, no." Can you remember what the words were?

No, I don't recall anymore. Let's leave this judgment to History. We are not going to contribute anything by trying to make a judgment today.

If the Kennedy family, for reasons of national security and so on, had endorsed or not turned off assassination plans, if the CIA didn't want the details of something like AMLASH to be made public, then there was a vested interest between the CIA and the Kennedys that these facts not be put before the Warren Commission, just as you didn't mention them to Rusk in '66 or LBJ in '67.

I know of no conspiracy about these matters. If there were oversights and things that should have happened didn't, I assure you there was no conspiracy involved.

Turning to the subject of assassinations in general, you made your point that you think assassination is unacceptable as a policy tool, both because of the public aversion to it and also for practical reasons. Is the most practical reason the danger of reciprocity?

No, that is not the most practical reason. But I think this is a good place to note that the CIA never has assassinated anyone. There were many of us who never liked any idea of assassination. Plotting such an act is one thing and committing it is another. Plotting is a buzz word—all you have to do is say somebody is plotting, and it reeks of crime and all kinds of horrible things. But the fact remains that none of this happened.

Let's leave aside the notion of theology and the morality of all good men for just a moment. Leaving that aside, one comes smack up against the fact that if you hire someone to kill somebody else, you are immediately subject to blackmail, and that includes individuals as well as governments. In short, these things inevitably come out. That is the most compelling reason for not getting involved.

But then there is an ancillary consideration. If you become involved in the business of eliminating foreign leaders, and it is considered by governments more frequently than one likes to admit, there is always the question of who comes next. If you eliminate one leader, have you really improved your position? That is a very critical point. And if you kill someone else's leaders, why shouldn't they kill yours and so forth?

On the other hand, may I say that there isn't a chief of state or chief of government in the world today who does not feel vulnerable to some terrorist or would-be assassin, and they all take great precautions. There isn't one so naive as to think he isn't a possible target by someone, some disgruntled individual.

Do you feel the world would be a safer place if those assassination attempts on Castro had succeeded?

It is an awfully hard thing to bring a case against a specific individual. But I think the world would have been a nicer place if somebody had gotten to Hitler before he had a chance to eliminate six million Jews and cause God knows how much destruction.

Discussing assassinations is a very difficult thing for an American, particularly for one of any religious persuasion, because we are against killing. But we are peculiarly ambivalent; we are glad to have certain people eliminated if we don't have to do the eliminating.

I cited the case of Hitler, but there are others. What about the thousands of people killed in Cambodia in 1977–78? There would be a revulsion in this country if it was thought anybody in our government was trying to kill Pol Pot. The same was true with [Uganda's] Idi Amin, and yet the death of a tyrant might save hundreds of innocent people. A human life is a human life. Nevertheless, assassination is not a way for the American government. It is not a way for the CIA. Nonetheless, I can only say I agreed with Clark Clifford, when he testified that it should not be barred by law. That would make us look silly.

It makes us look silly, or there might be a Hitler-type situation where it should happen?

If there were, maybe you would have to break the law, but I don't think anybody would notice particularly. We don't notice if laws are broken in the best causes. It is when somebody questions the causes that we get uptight, but the fact remains that if you say we are going to bar assassination and to bar this and to bar that, there are a lot of other things you are going to permit—by implication.

When you say that the subject of eliminating foreign leaders is discussed more than anyone would like, does that mean that you, on your initiative or that of others, actually said "No," or turned off such discussion, or had suggested to you other assassination plans?

I don't want to go into any details, but obviously I have heard such suggestions and turned them off. But the idea does come up because it looks like a quick and relatively cheap way of achieving something in the foreign policy or national security area.

Right. You said "No" for the reason that you have just given, I suppose?

Yes. I have never believed in assassination.

There are two accounts, one of them very fresh, to put it in perspective, in the case of [Patrice] Lumumba, where lethal biological substances were supposed to have been transmitted to the Congo and two Europeans with criminal backgrounds were allegedly involved. I have read that you told CIA officer Michael Moroney that you thought that the Lumumba plan was ill-founded.

Now, Leonard Mosley in his book, Dulles: A Biography of Eleanor, Allen, and John Foster Dulles and their Family Network *[1979], says that in fact you planned one operation with lethal toothpaste, but that*

Lumumba did not use toothpaste and that the joke was that he preferred halitosis to no breath at all. Which is the truth?

Leonard Mosley has a fascinating imagination. I don't know the gentleman. I have never met or talked to him. I don't believe that story. I have no recollection of any such plot. I had nothing to do with the Lumumba business. Moroney, as you call him, which is obviously not his name, asserts that he came to discuss this business with me, and I intimated that I didn't think that this was a very good idea. But I was not the boss, and it was the boss who was talking about this at the time.

But I don't think we should leave on the record any suggestion that anything came of this, even though certain things may have been transported to the Congo. The final decision was to do nothing, and that is the important thing. What happens in the end is important—this is what we are all judged on.

But given there were so many plots.

There weren't so many plots.

There were plots against five leaders.

What five?

Well, there was Castro, obviously.

We have discussed Castro.

To quote the Senate report, which you said is your Constitutional right to say was wrong, the CIA encouraged or was privy to coup plots which resulted in the deaths of Trujillo, Diem, and [Chile's Gen. René] Schneider. That was the final result. But there were also plans against Lumumba and Castro?

A "coup plot" is very different from an assassination—maybe. Let us take an example. President [Mohammad] Daoud of Afghanistan was killed in a coup. Was he intentionally assassinated, or was he simply killed in the course of the coup? I don't know—but he is dead.

The Agency had nothing whatever to do with the demise of Diem and didn't plot it. If there was any plotting, it was someone else in the United States Government. As far as Trujillo was concerned, he was killed, but there has never been any real evidence that those guns that were allegedly sent to the Dominican Republic were used to shoot him. We did not pull the trigger.

I think that it has been abundantly pointed out that Schneider was killed accidentally, that he was not killed intentionally by anybody, let alone the CIA. I think that what this line of questioning tends to lay out is that no matter which of these leaders dies, if the Agency was anywhere around, they were the ones who are assumed to have plotted. Whereas if you had an objective rendition of history, I think you would find that a lot of people at all levels of the United States Government were involved in these things.

But I suppose the point on Schneider is that if the CIA gave ammunition, albeit to other kidnap groups, as they did, the Agency must have been aware that ammunition might be used in a kidnap. Isn't that fair?

It is perhaps a fair question, but who can prove that any ammunition was given? One of the difficulties with the Senate report about this business in Chile was that it is all based on second-hand stuff—from CIA case officers' documents, allegations, and so forth. But nobody has ever demonstrated exactly what went on down there, and in 1975 it was very popular to pick on the CIA and give the worst cast to all of these things. Someday, with the aid of the Chileans who took part, maybe the proper history of this will be written, and then maybe we will have a correct rendition.

My own feeling about the Schneider affair is the irony of it, that given President Nixon's instructions, the United States was a party to removing a democrat in order to install somebody else who would support overthrowing the democratic process in Chile?

Who was the democrat in this?

Schneider was the man who believed in constitutionalism in Chile.

That is a better term, constitutionalist, rather than democrat.

Should we really not have been on the side of a constitutionalist, rather than trying to have him removed?

We could discuss for hours the backings and forthings of what went on during this period of time in Chile, but I agree that it is ironical. Let's leave it there. I have no other insights to contribute, to help unwind the tangled skein of who did what to whom in connection with Schneider's kidnapping and death. I don't know the facts to this day, and I don't believe they have ever been put down anyplace accurately.

It will only be with the aid of the Chileans that were involved?

I would think so.

How many Chileans were involved?

I don't remember anymore.

It has often been reported that Israel, with the help of persons in the United States, achieved the wherewithal for the atomic bomb. What was the reaction in the Intelligence Community to the news that the Israelis had almost certainly joined the nuclear club?

Intelligence officers are so used to the Quixotic developments of life that what they are really interested in is trying to make a correct assessment and getting something right. In the study of the proliferation of nuclear weapons, there were certain countries referred to as "threshold countries." These were countries thought to have the capability to make an atomic bomb if they chose, but most have not done so.

If you don't test such a bomb, it is not difficult to make one secretly. You can put the bomb together, and the only way that anybody is going to know that you have it is either to spy it out and take a photograph or have you explode it. Anyone who wants to assume that the Israelis have nuclear weapons is free to do so. There has been enough evidence in the newspapers and so forth to argue both ways.

For the record, during the Johnson Administration, did you hear that the Israelis probably had a nuclear capability, and did President Johnson tell you that that must remain a secret?

I have no recollection of President Johnson ever enjoining me in this fashion. I don't think it happened, but I obviously can't swear to it.

One of the most interesting incidents in your life must have been when you had the opportunity to interview Hitler.

It was unforgettable, particularly since I was only twenty-three years old and didn't expect it. It was only on Saturday afternoon (the day before) that I had been invited to have lunch with the Fuehrer. He talked with us for almost an hour, so that I had a chance, being as close to him as I am to you, to hear his views and see his gestures, the expressions on his face, how he treated various questions, and so on.

One of the problems of dealing with history is that everybody wants to run it together—run it on real time, rather than historical time. But this happened in 1936 when one couldn't help being impressed then with how astute he was in the geopolitical sense, what a good politician he was, German-style. He understood his people very well, what they wanted, what their aspirations were, how to appeal to them.

The luncheon took place in connection with the Party Congress, which was run annually in Nuremberg, and in the course of the conversation somebody asked him, "Why have this party congress?" He said, "Well, this is the way I reward the faithful party workers. . . . Besides, they come for two days and then they go back home, and it is exactly the kind of an operation that the German railways would be involved in if we had a mobilization, so it is very good practice." The statement gives you pause in the light of what happened later.

Whereas former secret agents in Britain tend to defect to the Russians, in America former secret agents tend to defect to their publishers. When you look at somebody like Philip Agee [whose books exposed CIA clandestine agents], would you describe what he does as treason or what?

I find the terminology a little bit difficult to come by. I am not a lawyer, and I realize that certain words have legal implications which other words do not have, but I don't have any difficulty agreeing that what he did and the way he did it was treasonable.

What about people like Frank Snepp that have a moral crusade about the fall of Saigon, or [John] Stockwell talking about Angola?

Well, I would think of them in a different category entirely. I am not in favor of turning off dissent or suppressing disagreement. The thing that I think somewhat unfortunate about Snepp and Stockwell is that they published without abiding by earlier agreements both made to clear their writings with the Agency. It doesn't seem to me that is such a bad agreement. I can't conceive that the points that these gentlemen wanted to make about mistakes and misfeasance and so forth would have been censored by anybody at the CIA. They certainly were not classified or anything. I don't know why they didn't go the normal course and submit their books for review. [Snepp, a CIA analyst who served in Saigon, wrote *Decent Interval* (1980), which criticized Agency failures in evacuating CIA personnel and Vietnamese co-workers from Saigon in 1975; Stockwell's *In Search of Enemies* (1978) described CIA activities in Angola.]

It is very different, it seems to me, to want to correct abuses by making points in a book rather than by going out and compromising the names of agents in a way designed to do harm literally to human beings. And that is what I criticize about Agee.

TED GITTINGER: *It seems to me that around this time [1961], and it partly is a result of the Bay of Pigs, there was a policy decision that the CIA should not be so involved in large-scale paramilitary sorts of things. Is that correct?*

RICHARD HELMS: There was no question about the fact that the Bay of Pigs taught everyone, whether they were involved directly or marginally,

Conducted by Ted Gittinger in Washington, DC, on September 16, 1981. Oral History Interviews, Lyndon Baines Johnson Library, Austin, Texas.

a lesson—and that is that when one undertakes a military operation in which actual troops, planes, logistics, training, all the rest of these things are involved, that an organization like the CIA should not undertake such a mission, because they don't have the general staff system and the support mechanisms to underpin an activity of that kind and of that size involving that much support equipment, such as boats, airplanes, training camps, and all the rest of it. But that did not affect the Kennedy Administration's view that CIA should do its best to handle the tribal dissidents in Laos, because after the Geneva Accords there was no way for the United States to be involved on a full military basis. So the CIA was selected by President Kennedy to work with the Meos and the tribes in Laos, and to do everything possible to keep a resistance against the North Vietnamese and the Pathet Lao organized there. In other words, to keep Laos from going Communist.

Even though that activity became later known as the "secret war," I have rarely come across any greater nonsense than that. The Congress, the Congressional committees to which Directors of the CIA—or of Central Intelligence, which is the proper title—reported, knew about our activities in Laos from the very first day. They had to appropriate the money for it. The appropriations subcommittees were kept briefed in detail at regular intervals. And later on, when Senator Stuart Symington got up and started talking about a "secret war," he knew far better than that. In fact, he had been out to Laos on a couple of occasions to visit the installations that the Agency had there. On one occasion he invited a man who was then the Chief of Station in Laos to come before the full Senate Armed Services Committee and tell it in great detail what the Agency was doing in Laos. This was early on; this wasn't late in the game; this was early in the game. And the senators were very approving and felt it was a much cheaper and better way to fight a war in Southeast Asia than to commit American troops. The date of that meeting of the Senate Committee is available, but I don't know that it's particularly relevant to this oral history.

But let me put it this way as a final note. The CIA activities in Laos in the sixties and seventies were well known (a) to key people in the Administration, and (b) to key members of Congress.

Let me pose a thesis to you: if the CIA had been left to run the war in Vietnam from the beginning, they would have done a much better job than the militarization that took place later.

It's awfully hard to answer a question like that. I would like to take advantage of the opportunity you've given me, but I do think that one has a problem here of making a comparison between unequal things. Let me put it this way. If the CIA work with the tribes and with the various Vietnamese units had been kept at a low level of civil war—and by civil war

I'm not talking about civil war in the sense of Vietnamese versus Vietnamese, I'm talking about it at a level where military components, regular military units, do not get involved—I think that the CIA could have done a very good job of keeping the Viet Cong at bay. The problem was, though, that with the arrival of American troops, more North Vietnamese troops became involved. You have a little bit of a chicken-and-egg situation—which came first and which came second—but that's not important. The war as later fought was on an entirely different scale from the way the CIA was attempting to fight it in the late fifties and early sixties. That's the way I'd like to answer your question. Since this is history, I don't think we ought to go overboard. There's been enough misconception about the war in Vietnam as it is.

Well, I'd propounded that thesis because it has been put forth by some highly placed people.

There is truth in it. If it had been allowed to run that course, it probably never would have escalated to the next level above.

Of course, we don't know whether the Communists would have escalated it or not.

That's the point.

Good. In 1961, General Lansdale, I think, went on special mission...

Before you get to that . . . You have a question here whether there were disputes concerning what the CIA should or should not be doing in regard to activities in Vietnam and Laos. Back in the late fifties and early sixties on up through the Johnson Administration the arguments about how the CIA should be deployed in Southeast Asia were nonexistent. Everybody was anxious for them to do everything they possibly could. So that controversy arose much later.

Okay. Were you familiar with the Lansdale report of 1961?

Yes, sure, because Lansdale, after his time in the Philippines during which, as you recall, he helped get President [Ramon] Magsaysay elected, then went on to Saigon in the middle fifties. While he was there, he obtained a fair reputation for himself as a fellow who knew how to operate and was good at teaming up with the Vietnamese and staying behind the scenes, had been advising them on political warfare and covert action and things of this kind. So when he went back again—was sent back again—and wrote this report in 1961, obviously it attracted a good deal of attention. Also, the Kennedy brothers thought Lansdale was a pretty unusual fellow in that he understood these things a lot better than most people, and that one should depend on Lansdale as the man who was a good initiator of proper work with locals and how to influence them and how to affect them and so forth. Lansdale's program, as I recall it now—his recommendation—was for what later turned out to be known variously but I guess the most familiar term is pacification. I believe that when he made that report, that was about the time that Dan Ellsberg was involved in these matters in Vietnam. But, in any event, it was widely read in government, let's put it that way.

You don't have to answer this if you don't like, and I'll understand why you wouldn't, but Lansdale was a rather legendary figure, I think, in the press and popularly, although I think Graham Greene didn't think as much of him as a good many other people and saw him as rather a sinister figure than otherwise. But within the CIA, was his reputation equally illustrious?

He was well regarded in the CIA, but one must realize that those who were working side by side with him and examining exactly what was going on did not think that he was the hot ticket that a lot of other people did. Lansdale was a very good promoter, and he was a very good promoter of Lansdale. One can't blame a person for being that. I'm not being critical; I'm just stating a fact. But those who worked side by side with him didn't believe that he was the miracle worker that other people made him out to be.

The clay feet became more visible the closer you got to him.

And later on, you know, he became very much involved in the Cuban operations of the Kennedy Administration, Operation MONGOOSE and various others that have become well known now, and obviously he did not shine up his reputation in those activities.

I believe he has since recorded that he was very much opposed to the Bay of Pigs operation. Do you have any knowledge of that?

I have no knowledge of that one way or the other.

Now later in 1961 there was another famous mission to Vietnam, the Maxwell Taylor-Walt Rostow mission. Did CIA have any input into that?

I think that CIA had an input into everything to the extent that people obviously went around and talked to the CIA officers. They did not have an official input as papers written in Headquarters and added to these reports, but obviously people were talked to; and in the Taylor-Rostow mission to which you refer here, I have no doubt that they did talk with the people that were in Vietnam for the CIA at that time. I never actually saw this report as best as I can recollect; I think I was briefed on it orally. It obviously had an influence on President Kennedy; there wasn't any doubt about that. I don't know whether that is precisely the reason, but at least it is one of the contributing reasons why the United States got more militarily involved in the whole Vietnamese affair.

I bring that up because Mr. Colby has written that he had been off to a meeting in the Philippines and only got a few minutes with . . . I don't know who he talked to on the Taylor-Rostow team, but in any case he arrived back in Saigon just in time as they were leaving, and he seems to feel that the real CIA solution or opinion in Vietnam didn't get much attention as a result of that. Do you have any recollection of that?

I have no recollection of that whatsoever. I must confess that I get a little bit tired of all this hindsight that people try to put into history these days to prove that they were right. I was fascinated to read last night an article in *Encounter* Magazine [August 1981] written by a man named Robert Elegant . . .

He's a British journalist, I believe.

In which he blames the U.S. press for giving a totally distorted version of the Vietnamese war and makes his case very eloquently.

I believe that's entitled "How to Lose a War," isn't it?

Yes. Have you read that?

Yes, sir.

Well, I think it's a fascinating article. I think that President Johnson would agree with every word of it.

There are some fascinating inserts in that article, too, as I recall, about the role of doubles in the South Vietnamese government.

Well, I'm glad you have a copy of that article, because I think it's an important one.

I think it is, too. Now, there was hot debate in the Kennedy Administration about the suitability of President Ngo Dinh Diem, I believe.

Yes.

Was the debate equally contested within the CIA about how suitable Diem was?

One of the problems that you—and I mean you as the oral historian—must keep in mind, I think, is that John McCone, who was Director of Central Intelligence at this period, was a man who believed that he had two hats: one hat was running the Agency, and the other hat was as one of the President's policymakers. But he was the only one at the Agency who felt that way. Now what his various inputs into matters of this kind may have been, orally and otherwise, is a little hard for me to assess. As for the operational people in the Agency, I don't think that you would have found any consensus that President Diem should have been let go. I think our feeling at the time was that this immolation of the Buddhist monks was a lot of window dressing, that it received far too much attention from President Kennedy and Averell Harriman and various people in Washington who were working on these matters at the time, and that the move the Administration made, in that famous telegram the date of which I've now forgotten . . .

I think that's the August 24 [1963] telegram.

I wouldn't be surprised. But this is a telegram devised by Averell Harriman, and I think there was also some input probably from . . .

Was it Roger Hilsman, perhaps?

Roger Hilsman, and I don't know the extent that Mike Forrestal played a role in this. But in any event that telegram was pushed through the various policymakers and the various people with whom it would normally have been cleared in government, pretty much as though President Kennedy had already approved it. If you wanted to object and go to him, you could object, but the thing to do was stand aside. This was a truck that was rolling down the road. It was this telegram, I haven't the slightest doubt, that ended the career of President Diem finally. Now in saying what I have said, I don't want to be guilty of a lot of hindsight, but as best as I can recall the atmosphere at the time, and we would sit at the table in the White House hearing these things debated, this immolation of the Buddhist monks received far more attention and was played up as a reason why Diem and particularly his brother, [Ngo Dinh] Nhu, should be got rid of. As so frequently happens in life, you succeed in getting rid of one, but who do you get in his place? After that we had a revolving door of prime ministers in Vietnam, which certainly did not help the American cause at all.

Now I'm not pointing a finger, a critical finger, at anyone, because I can understand the political reasons why certain of these decisions may well have been taken. But I'm simply saying that these people did focus on this, there was much discussion of it, and that I'm sure the decisions that were made were made very thoughtfully. So I'm not being critical; I'm simply responding to your notion that the operational people who were knowledgeable about Vietnam were far more reluctant to see Diem got rid of than the other people were, the political figures in the government. As one looks back on those events, the field operatives were fairly critical in the way things went in Vietnam after this time—I mean, from that time onward. I think one must come to the conclusion that whatever Diem may have represented, whatever his brother Nhu and Madame Nhu represented, Vietnam under their aegis was a stronger political entity than it was later.

Could Diem have been sustained, do you think?

Have been sustained?

Could he have been kept [in power]? A lot of people were saying that he . . .

I don't know any reason why not.

Okay.

And all of the allegations—I guess they come in subsequent questions here, but we might just as well hit them now—the allegations that the Agency was responsible for unseating Diem, that was absolutely untrue. As a matter of fact, there was no Agency desire particularly. We were following orders and we were doing what we were supposed to do, but we had no role in this. The Harriman telegram had to do with economic support and so forth. It was the Vietnamese who got together and chopped up Diem and Nhu.

But what the Agency role at that time was, if it had any role at all, was that Lucien Conein—he's known as Luigi Conein—was put on the job of keeping in touch with some of the dissident generals in Vietnam at the time. After all, we were responsible for the collection of intelligence; we weren't responsible for being the nice guys and dealing just with the government the way the Embassy does. We were trying to keep our lines out into all parts of South Vietnam. He happened to have a catbird seat at what went on in those days, because he had been tipped off that there was going to be some trouble. He reported from an intelligence standpoint what the events were, and he did a good job of it. But he was under no instructions and did nothing whatever to assist this whole process of unseating Diem.

If this oral history is useful, it's to put to rest once and for all some of the reports that have been kicking around these years which seem incendiary and exciting and all the rest of it. But it simply is not true that the Agency had anything to do with the assassination of Diem and Nhu. I believe John McCone as Director had an entire study written of that affair to demonstrate that the Agency was not responsible for this. But that study aside, I'll just tell you as one of the fellows who was not only theoretically but practically in charge of the operational people out there, I just know it isn't true.

I'm going to ask you a standard question I ask everybody. Who killed President Diem?

I don't know.

That's the usual answer I get.

I don't know who killed him.

Although I have about eight other candidates that have been put forward, the most frequent answer is that nobody knows. Had Diem's brother, Nhu, been secretly trying to make a deal with Hanoi? That's been reported in a few places.

I don't know. We were not aware of it at the time if he was. But on the other hand, no sane man wants to sit in a chair and say that one Vietnamese hasn't been dealing with another Vietnamese. I have no doubt that there were elements in South Vietnam that were working for the Communists, that were agents and sleepers and agents of influence and all kinds of people under Hanoi's control. Somehow or other I don't see Nhu trying to make a deal with Hanoi, but that's just on form. I don't know whether he did or whether he didn't. I would think that he did not.

It has been suggested to me that Nhu was capable of virtually any kind of Byzantine intrigue.

Well, that was exactly what is alleged, but that's sort of a popularized version of a fellow who had a very strong and articulate wife and who was obviously a fairly devious Oriental. Why [do] we in the West insist on categorizing various people as being capable of anything in our terms, when by Oriental standards he probably was no worse than a lot of other people? We just don't understand these cultures, and we are in many respects silly in our comments about them.

How much is there to the sinister sort of aspect that is reported of Nhu so often in the popular books and press? You see him as the bad guy, the guy who led Diem astray and so on.

Well, I don't know the merits of that case. I think it would be far better to get that story from somebody who knew him a lot better than I did. I simply am putting up the cautionary flag that American reaction to Orientals is usually rather juvenile.

I think that's very, very true. From my reading of the documents at the LBJ Library, after the coup the CIA cables seemed to focus entirely on political developments. I don't know if there was a policy decision or . . .

Oh, I think that was a passing phenomenon. In intelligence work, as it's presently constituted in the United States Government, when there's a hot affair going on, the President and other officials start shouting for information. One of the quickest ways to get it is to ask the CIA fellows to get it, because the other reporting mechanisms in most cases seem to be so slow. Obviously, when Diem and Nhu were assassinated, this was a most important event to the whole Administration as to what had happened, why it had happened, where it had happened, and so forth, so it was only natural that we would be sending queries out constantly, saying: find out this, find out that, who did this, who did that, where was Conein at such and such a time, are you sure he didn't have anything to do with this, et cetera? No, I think that was just a passing phenomenon, a reaction to the events of the time.

You know, there's a very interesting sidelight in connection with this whole affair of Diem. President Johnson, for reasons which are totally unclear to me, had some kind of belief or conviction I don't know how strong it was, that because President Kennedy had been in a sense responsible for Diem's demise, he in turn was assassinated himself. I mean, it was a strange and rather bizarre view he held. I don't know how convinced he was about it, but I've heard him say it, and it rather surprised me, because I was wondering exactly how he'd put this together in his head. Since I had great respect for President Johnson, I didn't know whether this was just like the fly fisherman flick over the water to see if it has any takers, or whether he really believed it.

Sort of a divine retribution aspect, do you think?

That's the idea. That's the idea.

Well, I have heard the remark quoting him many times, "They've done it over there and now they're doing it here," or something to that effect. Of course, President Johnson never specified who "they" were; it was always "they."

Can we talk about Laos a little bit? Realizing, of course, that you were not the operational man on the spot and were not perhaps handling the nuts and bolts of this thing, but were there policy problems involved in arming and training the tribesmen that we recruited in Laos?

My direct answer to that is that the Agency, working closely with the Ambassador on the scene and with the military attaché in the Embassy, was flat out in its effort to keep the tribes viable militarily in that Plain of Jars [Plaine des Jarres] area of Laos. You remember the Agency had a base at Long Tieng—and it is L-O-N-G and T-I-E-N-G; it isn't a lot of the other things it's been called. That was the operational base where General . . .

Was it Vang Pao?

Vang Pao had his base and where the logistics support was provided, where the airplanes could come in with additional supplies, and the whole affair was run from there. This was a major operation for the Agency, as you can imagine. It took manpower, it took specially qualified manpower, it was dangerous, it was difficult. One was living in the boonies, a long way from Broadway, and I think frankly the Agency did a superb job. I don't normally go around trying to praise this or criticize that particularly; I try to keep things on an even keel. But I do think that over the years it was a remarkable job that the Agency did, with support from Air America and the United States Army; the whole government worked together with CIA in the lead. And when you read the history of that war factually, I think you will agree with me that it was a superb job.

There has been a lot of speculation about the opium traffic that was so notorious in this area. Weren't some of the tribes involved in that trade?

There is no argument that many of the Meo tribes raised opium. After all, opium was indigenous to that area and areas in Thailand and Burma and Vietnam around and about Laos. I have no doubt that the Meos trafficked in drugs at various times, but they did *not* do it with the CIA's blessing or with the CIA's connivance. There have also been allegations that pilots for Air America flew opium in and out of places like Laos. I don't know the merits of this charge. It was certainly not condoned. If they did it, they did it behind the backs of their superiors. There *may* have been a little bit of this, but I can assure you that they were very brave and courageous fellows who flew those Air America helicopters and planes. They landed in fields that you would never regard as air fields. They were doing this constantly, and they were supporting troops under fire. They were an extremely able bunch of airmen, there is no doubt about it, and if one or two of them got off the reservation at some time or other, I don't know the merits of the case. But I do know that the Agency was not conniving or condoning any drug smuggling.

It's one of the things that I think probably irritates me more than any of the allegations against the Agency, and that is that we were involved in the drug traffic at any time. We never were! After all, the people who ran the Agency, the people who worked in various places on the operational side all over the world, were perfectly decent Americans. You have to go through a security clearance, you have to go through a psychological check, you have to go through a lie-detector test, you have to go through a physical examination, you have to do all of these things to get into the Agency in the first place. They were a perfectly decent bunch of human beings. They know very well what drugs do to people in the United States and what they have done to our society and so forth, and none of them had any desire to connive in that kind of business or to make our domestic problems worse. These allegations are just simply irresponsible.

On the other side, did CIA get requests to furnish intelligence to other agencies on the drug traffic so that it could be suppressed?

Yes. And we offered all kinds of information to them about drug smuggling in the Golden Triangle [jungle area at the borders of Burma, Thailand, and Laos], and we gave information to elements in the United States Government so that if they wanted to, they could raid these camps and so forth. I once reported to Senator [John] Stennis, who at that time was chairman of the Armed Services Committee and therefore the committee to which the Agency reported, that we were doing everything we could to help the drug-enforcement agencies and various other elements of the government in this field. He paused after I had said this and shook his head and said, "I'm not sure you people ought to be getting involved in things like that. I don't know that that's a proper activity for you." I said, "Well, Mr. Chairman, how could we possibly not help the United States Government when we've got such a hideous drug problem in this country?" In any event, we did help. . . .

I might say, if you would like an observation in hindsight, that the great sadness of the entire affair in Vietnam *was not*—this is all my opinion—that the United States went in there and tried to help the South Vietnamese maintain their freedom, and *was not* that we felt that this was an opportunity to show strength against the communism from the North which was pushing down into Southeast Asia, but it was the fact that we were dealing with a complicated cultural and ethnic problem which we never came to understand. In other words, it was our ignorance or innocence, if you like, which led us to mis-assess, not comprehend, and make a lot of wrong decisions which one way or another helped to affect the outcome.

As one looks back on the whole Vietnamese war, I think it very important to look at Southeast Asia today. I agree with Lee Kuan Yew, the Prime Minister of Singapore, that American firmness in South Vietnam permitted Indonesia, Malaysia, Singapore, and the Philippines to maintain their independence, to get themselves straightened out from the effects of World War II. And now look at the economic prosperity of that part of the world—the A-S-E-A-N or ASEAN nations are doing extremely well, Vietnam is a basket case, so is Cambodia, Laos not much better— that those nations that had a chance to get their legs under them and get themselves organized and get their industry going and their commerce going and their trade going are now in great shape. And they owe that to the United States. In other words, that was a very important by-product of this whole affair in Vietnam.

If I interpret you correctly, you're saying we gained everything we would have lost if we didn't fight?

That's just about right. . . .

I simply want to comment on one controversy that was raging about American policy in Vietnam. And in doing so I want to make it clear at the outset that I have the greatest regard and respect for Clark Clifford. I like Tim [Townsend] Hoopes very much. I regard both of them as friends; I think they regard me as a friend. So what I'm saying has no personal overtones whatever and is not intended to be critical. It simply has to do with the facts of the case. I believe that Hoopes in his book [*The Limits of Intervention* (1973)] makes the contention that it was Clark Clifford who was responsible for "turning President Johnson around" on the Vietnamese war during the short period that he, Clifford, was Secretary of Defense.

Hoopes asked me about this point before he ever wrote his book. I told him I did not believe this to be the case. I had never seen any evidence of it, I was in all the meetings, I believed that President Johnson had come to his own conclusions for his own reasons. There was no single individual who had set him on one course or the other or been the one who influenced him most in this direction. Despite my stating that, Hoopes went ahead with his book, and I believe Clifford was the one who was responsible for giving him that point of view. I know that later, after he was out of office, President Johnson, when I was at the Ranch [the Johnson home in Texas] one time, asked me whether or not I knew of any particular papers or notes I might have taken in meetings which would help clarify this matter. So I realized from what he said to me on that occasion that President Johnson didn't believe this was true either. I mention this, because I think that in an effort to nail down some of these things, it is useful for you to have my view of the situation or of what transpired.

By all means.

Another thing: on the slightly amusing side, you're aware of President Johnson's inclination when he didn't like somebody or something that somebody had done, to get his name wrong on purpose. I remember on the occasion of Marie Fehmer's bridal dinner in Washington, my wife, Cynthia, was sitting next to President Johnson. He suddenly turned to her and said, "Cynthia, who is that fellow Hoopeez?" pronouncing it H-O-O-P-E-E-Z. So it was quite clear that the line Hoopes took in his book was not congenial to President Johnson. That's all I've got to say on the subject.

10

William E. Colby

For WILLIAM COLBY, THE CENTRAL INTELLIGENCE AGENCY promised more than a career—it offered a tough and challenging profession. As he himself put it, "Joining the CIA back in 1950 was a highly esteemed, indeed a rather glamorous and fashionable and certainly a most patriotic thing to do. In those days the Agency was considered the vanguard of the fight for democracy and it attracted what nowadays we would call the best and the brightest, the politically liberal young men and women from the finest Ivy League campuses and with the most impeccable social and established backgrounds, young people with 'vigor' and adventuresome spirits who believed fervently that the Communist threat had to be met aggressively, innovatively, and courageously" (*Honorable Men: My Life in the CIA* [New York, 1978], 77).

The son of professor and World War I veteran Elbridge Colby and Margaret Mary Egan Colby, Bill was born in St. Paul, Minnesota, on January 4, 1920. Young Bill witnessed his father's return to Army officer status, and the family began regular tours of duty in Panama, China, Georgia, and Vermont. As his father had before him, Bill enrolled at Princeton University at age sixteen, but modest finances together with Army ROTC training and part-time jobs left him little time for Princeton's social circles.

Graduating in 1940, he then enrolled at Columbia Law School and completed one year's studies before entering active military service as an Army officer at Fort Bragg, North Carolina, followed by parachute training at Fort Benning, Georgia. In mid-1943 the Office of Strategic Services (OSS) recruiting officer, promising highly hazardous missions, won Colby's enlistment. Trained in special guerrilla warfare in the south of England, Colby adapted quickly to this instruction. Dropped behind German lines in France and Norway, this tough officer practiced the arts and skills of covert warfare until Germany surrendered. Peacetime and marriage to Barbara Heinzen preceded Colby's resumption of his studies at Columbia and his graduation with a law degree in 1947. William Donovan, his former OSS commanding general, welcomed him to his influential New York law firm. After two and one-half years there, Colby, dissatisfied with New York legal challenges, joined the National Labor Relations Board in Washington, DC.

In June 1948, President Harry Truman approved a special National Security Council recommendation and established a clandestine political and paramilitary unit, the Office of Policy Coordination (OPC). Soon after the Korean War began in 1950, Colby joined the ranks of this Central Intelligence Agency unit. Secret assignments in Scandinavia for two years and then Italy for five years with the Directorate for Plans were followed by a tour in Saigon as Deputy Chief of Station beginning in 1959 and as Chief of Station in 1960. In these early years of the Vietnam War, the CIA worked in coordination with the Agency for International Development (AID) on the Strategic Hamlets Program. These hectic years in South Vietnam continued Colby's guerrilla warfare education.

Late in 1962, Colby returned to Washington, where in 1963 he became chief of the Far East Division, Directorate of Plans. He witnessed ill-coordinated planning as the Kennedy Administration turned against the Diem regime in South Vietnam. In late 1967 an increasingly frustrated President Lyndon Johnson asked CIA Director Richard Helms to have Colby go on leave from the Agency and join Civil Operations and Rural Development Support (CORDS) in Saigon where, as Ambassador, he would head the Phoenix Program. This joint AID-military group, heavily staffed with tough South Vietnamese agents, targeted Viet Cong agents who were running huge espionage operations in South Vietnam. Phoenix tactics of torture, assassination, and kidnapping reflected the bitter brutality of this vicious war as Colby and other American leaders struggled against the Viet Cong infrastructure, one of the largest in twentieth-century warfare.

Called back again to the United States in 1972, Colby became Executive Director-Comptroller under Helms at the CIA and later Deputy Director for Operations under James Schlesinger. Following Schlesinger's brief five-month tour as Director, President Richard Nixon in May 1973 appointed Colby to lead the Agency, with his appointment becoming effective in September. For the next two and one-half grueling years, this careful, scrupulous, and tough administrator faced an increasingly hostile media, Congress, and public fed up with the defeat in Vietnam, the Watergate hearings, and an imperial Presidency. Colby, fighting for the Agency's survival, revealed many of the intelligence organization's secrets in 1975, first to the Rockefeller Commission appointed by President Gerald Ford and later to two Congressional committees headed by Frank Church and Otis Pike.

Fueled by intensive media coverage, these investigations into CIA activities reflected the frustrations and sometime naiveté regarding the question: How does a secret espionage agency operate in an open society, especially in peacetime? Colby tried with only modest success to answer this question and address the central issue. And during that year-long set of hearings, President Ford and his advisors decided to replace Colby with George Bush in January 1976, a presidential election year. Colby returned to the practice of law and wrote two books on his intelligence career and the war in Vietnam. He died in May 1996.

TED GITTINGER: *[Regarding South Vietnam], if what [Ngo Dinh] Nhu and [Ngo Dinh] Diem were trying to do was create a new elite, is it fair to say that the elite they were trying to create then turned on them in the form of the army?*

WILLIAM COLBY: Well, the army eventually turned on them, but that's another feature. I mean, we caused that, let's face it. No, I think the weakness was that Diem first started thinking in terms of creating a new trained elite out of the National Institute of Administration and so forth. Nhu later turned to this new idea of a new popular elite coming out of the villages. There's a contradiction between the two, obviously. The beneficiaries of Diem's effort were the elites in the cities who were able to still be there and not be eliminated as they were in the North. They certainly turned on Diem, and they turned on him because of an idealistic feeling that he hadn't made things good enough, and that certainly he had changed

Conducted by Ted Gittinger in Washington, DC, on June 2, 1981, and March 1, 1982. Oral History Interviews, Lyndon Baines Johnson Library, Austin, Texas.

the old systems to their detriment and yet had not solved the problems by his changes. Then they got intoxicated, some of them, by the idea that if we just have more democracy, everything will be all right. I just don't think that would have been the case any more than it was in Chang Myon's Korea in 1960 when the country started to come apart after [the presidency of] Syngman Rhee. It was only rescued by Park Chung Hee putting it together. I think the same come-apart phenomenon would have occurred if Diem had been assassinated in 1960. In fact, he had that revolt against him, parachute attack, and he put it down. He had enough loyal troops to put it down. It wasn't the army that turned on him; those were a few excited paratroopers and a few local politicians. I think that he could control that problem.

What he couldn't control later were two things: one, the forerunner of the Ayatollah Khomeini [later in Iran in the 1970s], the Buddhist *bonzes* [monks] that burned themselves. Because I think that's an exact forerunner—total rejection of the changes going on, modernization, an idealistic return to some religious base which, if you ever talk to any of these people, you really see that it's all words and no content. I mean, very, very strange. Then the effect, however, of the Buddhist thing—again, I'm a little contentious about this because I believe that the Buddhist revolt, which blew up in June of 1963, had its major impact not in Vietnam but in the United States. When that picture of the burning *bonze* appeared in *Life* Magazine, the party was almost over in terms of the imagery that was affecting the American opinion. That put enormous pressure on President Kennedy. "How can you possibly support a government that has people doing this against it?" [It] led to his vacillation, which is what I have to say it was in terms of what we should do about this problem, and then led to Diem's forceful suppression of the Buddhist revolt in the August raids. Frankly, I think he suppressed them in the same way that he suppressed the sects in 1955.

Now, the problem he couldn't control was the United States reaction. But the Buddhists were not a factor in September and October—the factor was the difference between the Americans and the government. It wasn't a matter of the Buddhists being a major problem in the countryside. They were not a major problem, and he had not lost the authority of his state. Sure, there were unhappy people, but he hadn't lost authority and he had been through tough challenges like that before.

The thing that really led to the revolt, of course, was the American signal, given by President Kennedy, that new personalities would be necessary. Our fight with them [was whether] to send Nhu and Madame Nhu—who didn't help at all over here, that's for sure, she had a terrible impact on American opinion—out of the country and Diem's refusal to knuckle under, as he would have said it, to American domination on that issue, and to demonstrate in part his independence and his belief that the Americans were wrong. [Diem had] the genuine feeling that the Americans were making a mistake and it was up to him to struggle hard enough against them to prevent them from doing so. Then that led to the big fight in Washington that occurred all that summer as to whether we'd go with President Diem or think of replacing him—you know as much about that as I do—and eventually ended up with a few signals by the Administration, a statement by President Kennedy, suspension of our commercial import program, the assurances to the generals that we would be prepared to resume it if they moved against the government.

What was the generals' original complaint against Diem?

That he was creating such confusion in his programs and in his policies that he was risking American support of Vietnam against the Communists. That was their fundamental feeling, that he was going to lose the war because the Americans were going to back away.

I see. It's been contended that they were saying he was botching the effort against the Communists, rather than alienating the Americans.

Right, those are the two arguments. I mean, you can pay your money and take your choice. But the one argument was that his policies, particularly vis-à-vis the Buddhists and the authoritarian nature of the regime, were antagonizing the people, therefore giving encouragement to the Communists to develop more support among the people and therefore threatening the future of Vietnam, and that we could never hope to win the war against the Communist attack with Diem. A lot of very sincere people believed that.

The other argument was that the countryside was essentially unaffected by the whole Buddhist struggle and that in fact the programs of the countryside were going along. I happen to think that that is a little exaggerated, because I think the really critical thing that happened was the outburst of the Buddhist revolt, which turned the attention of the palace away from the Strategic Hamlet Program, which until that time had been quite successful but required an enormous amount of palace attention and stimulus and drive. When the Buddhist thing blew up and then the fight with the Americans developed, all of that stimulus and drive had to be diverted onto the other problems. The program was let lag at exactly the time when the Communists had identified it as a major threat, in the spring of 1963, and had instructed their people that they were to destroy this program at all costs because it really did threaten them strategically. So they began to attack it in about June or July, and you can see the terrorist incidents grow at that time against it. One interpretation is that this was a reflection of the disenchantment with Diem; the other is that it was an expression of Communist strategic focus on a dangerous program. I take the Communist direction as the key element. I know these are arguable, and I don't mind. But the fact was that they wouldn't have had a revolt if the United States had not encouraged it. There was no doubt about that whatsoever. I think it's the greatest mistake we made. I know Mr. [Lyndon] Johnson also thought it was a terrible mistake, but Vice Presidents don't have much power.

This is speculative, of course, but do you think in the face of the opposition Diem was experiencing from the Buddhists and the unrest in the army and so forth, could he have been sustained through that crisis?

Oh, yes. Yes. If the Americans had maintained their commitment, their support, no doubt about it. But when the Americans indicated a change, then bing, it was gone, it went.

Where does this put Roger Hilsman?

Well, I think Roger and some of the others, and [Averell] Harriman, I disagreed with on various [things] at times—I just think their assessment of the problem, of the nature of the problem, and the policies that we followed were mistaken. Now I must admit that they weren't entirely free in that because they had a lot of pressure behind them from the American people and the American press. That's why I say, when that picture appeared in *Life* Magazine, the game was almost over. Because we do have a government which has to reflect strong attitudes by the American people. That certainly had a strong element, a strong impact on the situation. Now I'm not one of those who believe that you can ignore the American people. You cannot. You've got to listen to them. You've got hopefully to educate them as to what the reality of the problem is, but they are the ultimate repositories of power; and when they decide something, it's done. And it was done with Diem on that image, and it was done with Vietnam on the Tet image. . . .

In the raid on the pagodas [in August], Diem, I think, came to the conclusion that he had to suppress the Buddhists. As I said earlier, I think he succeeded. But he came to the conclusion that they were not just a religious force, but a political force that was attacking the authority of his state, and he had no choice but to suppress them. He used the Special Forces because he happened to have them, they were handy and easy and he didn't have to explain them to a whole general staff or anything, just reach out and tell them to do it.

Didn't he make an effort, or someone make an effort, to pin this on the ARVN [Army of the Republic of Viet Nam] rather than on the Special Forces?

Well, that was the fuss that we got into afterwards. I think, as I remember it, the question was whether the army had participated in it. They had army uniforms on. And then the army had always been unhappy about the Special Forces having a separate line of command to Nhu's structure. That's why they eventually shot Colonel [Le Quang] Tung in the most outrageous murder of all, frankly. A very mild, straightforward, decent guy.

But the army then, with the reaction, you see, of the Americans to this, insisted this wasn't army. [Henry Cabot] Lodge took this point up and made something of it; and at a time when we were building our contacts with the army and wanted to maintain that option of the army, then that became important. You see, quite obviously, Diem and Nhu took the interregnum between [Lodge and Frederick] Nolting that they did respect and realized that he was losing the battle of supporting them and had been kicked out obviously and replaced by Lodge, who was a very unknown quantity at that point. They didn't know which way he'd go. They thought they'd take the interregnum between those two Ambassadors and just eliminate the Buddhist thing and present Lodge with a *fait accompli*, that it had been eliminated, wasn't there anymore. Well, Lodge is not one that takes that kind of a gesture lightly, and this affected his entire attitude towards them.

Did Lodge interpret that as a challenge, an insult perhaps?

No, . . . they deliberately had acted before he got there in order to just do away with the Buddhist problem before they had the problem of dealing with him. [Interruption.]

There is an interesting series of blank spots and conjectures concerning their relationship right before the coup, between Lodge and General [Paul] Harkins, the MAAG [Military Assistance Advisory Group] chief, and Mr. [John] Richardson, the station chief of CIA. Can you sort that out?

Well, Lodge came out to Vietnam having been chosen, as the former vice presidential candidate for the Republicans in 1960, by President Kennedy, in order to de-politicize our problems in Vietnam and get the Republicans on the hook as well as the Democrats. As I said, this challenge to his authority by Diem and Nhu affected Lodge's entire approach.

Harkins, in the MAAG position, was convinced that the war was going relatively well—not perfectly, but moving along. The programs actually working of improving the armed forces and the Strategic Hamlet Program seemed to be in the right direction and so forth, and that the Buddhist problems were some political thing that were off in a corner and shouldn't affect our main interest in the support of the South Vietnamese and the war effort.

Richardson, by direction and by tradition, was in direct touch with Nhu, had talked to Nhu over the year and a half since I'd left, and had a frank relationship with him, understood what he was talking about and trying to do, and basically sympathized with the concept of a political, hamlet-based solution to the insurgency problem—that we also shouldn't be diverted by the urban, religious problems from our main interest in the major challenge to our interests there, which was from the North.

Lodge came in with much more of a sense of the American reaction to the Buddhist problems and the intensity of feeling in the United States, much more aware of the sharp difference of opinion within the Administration as to what ought to be done, and probably a little better informed about President Kennedy's basic thinking, that something had to be done about Diem and Nhu. So he came in after the raid on the pagodas, determined to distance himself from, and distance the United States from, total identification with Diem and Nhu. This, of course, conflicted with Richardson and Harkins's view of what was important and what was the significant element of the problem, which was the countryside problem. This led eventually to his dismissing Richardson in order symbolically to indicate the end of the relationship with Nhu, because Diem was not yielding to Lodge's demands, and they were demands. Diem was not yielding to those demands. The chemistry between the two didn't work at all.

One of the more wry aspects was one of Lodge's first cables when he got there, and he went to some ceremony at the palace. Diem had appeared in a traditional Vietnamese mandarin's coat, and I guess the other people there, too. Diem for a long time had adopted the sort of French white sharkskin suits that all the bureaucrats did, and then increasingly he turned to putting on a traditional Vietnamese costume. Lodge's cable is rather amusing because it talks about the medieval court with all its connotations. Of course, the really fascinating thing was that when Lodge finally left Vietnam about a year and a half later, *he* put on a Vietnamese costume for the final ceremony. . . .

All right, sir, I hate to make you repeat yourself, but in Honorable Men *[1978] you wrote a good deal about the coup of 1960, and you have just said, although we didn't get it on tape, that there was a good deal of dissatisfaction in the military and so on.*

Frustration, I would call it, more than dissatisfaction—frustration that the enemy seemed to be getting away with acting the way he wanted. Let's remember we're dealing in the time frame of another military coup; 1961 was the coup in Korea, but there was one prior to that in Pakistan, where a group of colonels took over—some place like that, I've forgotten where it was, and I think that was a little contagious. So that when you had a combination of the soldiers feeling a little frustrated that we weren't winning the war immediately, and some of the opposition politicians stressing their distaste for the Diem government, you had an atmosphere which did produce the attempt by the Colonel [Nguyen Chanh Thi] and a battalion or two that he had in an attack on the palace. Now, he had not thought through the thing; he didn't know where he was going. I think his basic motivation, as it came out later, was that he wanted to capture the palace and then secure the President's approval of a more vigorous program against the enemy. In other words, not to overthrow the President, but to get him to go along with a stronger effort.

Why do you think this was true?

Well, that was his feeling. He certainly had no idea of a substitute government. He didn't have any views on that at all. And the civilian politicians essentially joined him rather than being a part of his plot. They assembled after the coup had started to try to give it some general direction and political direction. But by that time the President had reacted, had called upon the forces from outside the area, and particularly from the South and a couple from the North. They moved in the next day and the coup was over without any fighting particularly, other than the little shooting at the first part of the coup.

Now, you said that your first indication of the coup, or at least you knew the coup was in progress, [was] because the troops went by your house. Did we have no warning, no advance notice of this?

I don't think any particular warning, no. I remember I went out to dinner the night before with the Ambassador and we certainly had no thoughts of that. We knew there was some dissatisfaction, but to isolate, to prognosticate a coup from some individual colonel is really quite an effort. After it happened, our people got onto it and gave very full and complete reporting. We had a network of voice radios around town that we used. We put people with the different elements of the coup, both with the government and with the coup leaders, so that we had a very full reporting of everything that was happening after that happened.

So there was somebody from the CIA with the coup leaders when the confrontation was taking place at the palace?

There was a CIA officer with the civilians, who sat with them and reported to me what was happening by the phone, radio, or whatever we had at the time. There was another officer who just walked in on the Colonel and sat with him pretty much. They did not appear when they were going to meet the government side, they weren't part of that, but in the councils they were there reporting on what was happening so we'd know about it.

Now, [Gen.] Tran Van Don says there was a CIA man with the coup leaders, and he even goes as far as to say his name was Miller. Does that ring any bells in your mind?

Well, I am probably under some constraints as to whether I can say the names. I do know the names of the two men that I mentioned and they are the main ones, as I recall, the one with the civilians and the one with the others. There may have been some others, but I'd rather not give the names without knowing whether I'm authorized to or not.

That's understandable. I'm not trying to drag that sort of thing in.

No, it's fair enough. No problem.

I have heard stories that a CIA man—and I'm going to quote some-body—got caught on the wrong side of a coup about 1960 and they had to take him out, and I was wondering if that was this one?

Oh, yes. I've described that in the book [*Lost Victory: A Firsthand Account of America's Sixteen-Year Involvement in Vietnam* (1989)] a little bit, the subtle way in which Nhu arranged for him to be taken out.

They threatened him out?

Yes. It was kind of transparent in the way it was done, but it was very subtle, and I thought quite amusing.

Why was Nhu so upset if all that was going on was reporting?

Well, he, I think, had an idea that more was going on. After all, from his point of view, even the presence of an American in those councils would be a form of participation. I mean, I tried to draw the distinction between reporting and encouraging as two different things, but to the outsider sometimes the mere presence is an encouragement. So I appreci-ated Nhu's problem on it; that's why I wasn't morally indignant or any-thing about it. I knew exactly what his problem was, and that the problem we needed was some face-saving way of getting around the impasse, which I still think he provided.

Did this have a lingering effect in Nhu or Diem's mind, do you think, about what the CIA might or might not do in future coups?

Oh, I think both of them were aware that CIA had its independent links in various places and would try to get independent reporting. And, of course, in the summer of 1963 when our government and the Vietnam-ese came to issue, the mouthpiece there, the English-language paper, ran a great story about how the CIA had tried to run a coup in 1960. Well, they're right, we did, it's not exactly news. But to find them turning on CIA at that point, at a point when CIA was probably one of their strongest advocates within the American government. . . . But they were using it because they were dealing with the American government, and if the

American government had turned hostile to them. they had to assume that CIA would.

You're referring to John Richardson, now, I think.

Yes. Well, and I've forgotten—it was about August, as I remember, of 1963 [that] the whole series of headlines [appeared] about the CIA coup uncovered and so forth. And it's true; we had to go on out to try to find one at that point under instructions and had not found it but certainly had looked hard.

Were the Diems floating this, or did they know something?

Oh, I suspect they knew about it. I suspect they ran into enough evidence of it. We had talked to a bunch of officers there and I think scared a number of them. I think some of them reinsured and told the government about the conversations. I don't have any doubt about that whatsoever.

So when the coup plotters finally did begin their plotting, this . . .

Well, you remember the end of that effort. The generals told us to go away, but if something happened, they would be back: "Just rest quietly; this is not the time. If something happens, we'll be back." Sure enough, they called one of our officers in the afternoon they decided to move in November.

At least some people had sort of despaired that the generals were ever going to move, didn't they?

Well, that I couldn't say for sure. I was spending a good part of my time trying to argue against encouraging them. But always in a situation like that, yes, there were people who wanted it to happen. It wasn't happening for a month, and a month, and a month, and they would probably get impatient.

Right.

I don't recall any such conversation, although it may be in the records for all I know.

I'm intrigued by the use of CIA communications by people who don't normally use CIA communications. Was it not common but did it happen that foreign officials would use CIA communications in the belief that they were more secure, more direct, or whatever?

Foreign officials?

Yes.

Yes, sometimes, in various parts of the world. In various places a foreign leader might think that he could be dealing with CIA and have kind of a direct shot into the policy levels in Washington rather than going into the kind of more bureaucratic concept of the Department of State and the Foreign Service and all that. And [they thought] they would receive more of an understanding transmission of their ideas than might occur through the diplomatic channel. Now this can become a problem. It can either become a problem or it can be very useful, depending upon the attitude of the Ambassador and the local Chief of Station and the head of CIA and whoever's the Secretary of State. Because in some situations, if those four people have enough confidence in each other that they're going to play the same game, then the foreigner can be given the impression that he's getting this direct shot so that he's going to be perhaps more revealing of his ideas. And nobody will be out of sympathy, because everybody will be consulted and there'll be no feeling that something's going on behind his back. On the other hand, if the Ambassador gets persnickety about his privileges, or if the Chief of Station begins to think he's the Ambassador, then you've got trouble and it doesn't work.

Does this happen?

It has happened in various places that the Ambassador has been upset and said, "No, if the chief of government wants to deal with the Americans, he's got to deal with me."

Did this happen in Saigon?

Well, Lodge, of course, cut off the Richardson contact in order to make the point that there wasn't an indirect way around him. When I went out there on a trip, he told me I couldn't go see the people in the palace, which I think was also making his point that they had to deal with him. Other than that, no. [Elbridge] Dubow used the technique very well. We very easily keep each other totally informed—no question about who was the Ambassador, and it worked very well. With Nolting the same, no problems whatsoever, total confidence. With [Maxwell] Taylor, I would have had a hard time. That was such a confused period after the overthrow.

Now, you said that Lodge broke that contact primarily as a signal to Diem?

Yes.

He was not upset or had the feeling that anybody was [undermining him]?

I don't think so, no. I think he was giving it as a signal to the regime. I don't believe, he never gave any indication, that he thought the CIA was cheating on him and running a separate policy. Even though we'd disagree from time to time, there'd be no question of CIA people there, under my instructions, that they would respond to the Ambassador, and he was the boss there. And I don't recall any problem about that. The move of Richardson was a policy decision just to indicate the end of a close relationship with Nhu.

Now, this is a subject that's been hashed over endlessly and has raised an awful lot of smoke and that concerns the effectiveness of a number of methods used in pacification. There were Provincial Reconnaissance Units, or PRUs, People's Action Teams. The Marine Corps had its own concept, Combined Action Program, County Fairs, and of course the Phoenix Program, which you supervised. Is there any easy comparison to make between all of these things, their effectiveness, and so on?

Well, the easiest comparison is that Strategic Hamlets started in 1961, early 1961. Wilfred Burchett says that they had become so effective that in 1962 the year belonged to the government, and that was a Communist appraisal of the fact. There was still a lot of criticism about how good they are. That's what gets confusing. When you look at a program, you can see all the faults and you complain about them, but if you're on the enemy's side, it may be having quite an effect despite its faults. Of course, Strategic Hamlets stopped with the overthrow of Diem. They stopped before, when the attention of the palace drifted off after May of 1960 to the problems with the Buddhists and with the Americans. The Strategic Hamlets essentially stopped. After the overthrow, the Communists mounted an attack on them because they thought they would—well, they began substantially to attack them in about July and were beginning to have an effect because of the lack of priority and the preoccupation of the government with other things. Then with the overthrow, they mounted a final one that pretty well destroyed it. I mean, there just wasn't any program after November. So you're starting at ground zero at that point. . . .

Then the thing [internal security forces] began to get organized when [Robert] Komer organized CORDS [Civil Operations and Rural Development Support] to try to put our programs together; and we, using our influence with the Vietnamese, tried to put together a program that would be an integration. After the Tet attack, this became the government's primary program, the priority program. It was an integrated program of political, economic, and security elements. The political element was the revival of village government, and a variety of other things: a little propaganda activity, the receipt of the defectors from the other side, the amnesty program for them, and various things like that. But the politics of it was to try to get the village to assume its own responsibilities for its own destiny and for decision-making on the civilian side, you might call it. Even though there were a few soldiers in the line, it was essentially the civilian government attempting to get the participation of the people at the village level.

At the economic level, again, [it was designed] to try to get activity at the village level. Not great national plans for a school in every hamlet, but what does this hamlet need? What kind of activity does it need—a ditch, a wall, or a road or a bridge or whatever? And [there was] self-help and some contribution by the government to the program to, again, [encourage] this sense of participation.

Then on the security side, [there was] a very substantial increase in the strength and the effectiveness of the weaponry of the popular forces and the regional forces, the territorials, in other words, as distinct from the main army. [We were] supplementing them by the self-defense force, which were unpaid people just doing a night or two [of] guard [duty] a week but giving them arms. We gave five hundred thousand weapons to the villagers for use in that kind of a program, not to the police or the military but to those villagers, again, [so] that they would be able to participate, the key thinking being that if you have a village of three hundred people and five men walk in with pistols, they dominate it. But if you've got ten people on guard, and they're kind of scared and they may shoot once and run away, but the five men don't dominate it. They can't come in and totally dominate it and run it anymore. So, in that sense, the motive again was political.

Now, Phoenix was an element of that security side, which is to try to identify the political order of battle of the enemy. We had lots of order of battle about the regular forces and the local forces and all that sort of thing and battalions and all the rest of it. But the question was, Who are the internal, subversive, secret apparatus in the country? Who are they? What are they doing? Until you know about them, you can't do anything much about them. So this was an attempt to regularize the intelligence coverage: decent interrogations, decent record-keeping, evidence, all that sort of thing, the whole structure of the struggle against the secret apparatus. That was Phoenix.

Well, I'm fairly simple about this, because I say that the combination of the three, and the number-one priority that President [Nguyen Van] Thieu and Ambassador [Ellsworth] Bunker and General [Creighton] Abrams gave to this triple approach—and it was the principal government program after 1968, there's no question about it—in my opinion won the guerrilla part of the war. And it's very easy to show it. I won't give you any numbers or percentages or any of that jazz, but the fact was that in 1968 the Tet attack was a massive, countrywide guerrilla attack supported by some military forces. It happened to have failed in its objectives, but it certainly had an enormous psychological victory. Nonetheless, it showed that the enemy had a countrywide guerrilla apparatus.

The pacification program was then started. Four years later, in the spring of 1972, there was another major attack which took place at three points on the border of South Vietnam: Quang Tri and Kontum and An Loc. It consisted of purely military actions with artillery, tanks, all the rest of it, bombing, all the rest. The South Vietnamese were totally unbothered in all the rest of South Vietnam, to the extent that they took the 21st Division out of the Delta and put it up in An Loc to fend off that attack. In other words, the guerrillas weren't there, and in the final attack of 1975 the North Vietnamese commander in his report clearly says that he was just dealing with military movements and had no role for the guerrillas at all. Fascinating.

So the answer is, that's a pretty objective test. You have a countrywide guerrilla attack, and four years later they have to attack you from the outside by regular forces. It means they've lost anything inside. Now, there's all sorts of allegations about how they overexposed themselves at Tet and then shot their wad and all the rest of it. I'm sure there's some truth to that, but the conscious nature of the program to develop the degree of cohesion in the countryside, the participation, I think, really did it. As you know, I did a lot of travel there; and by 1971, when I left, I could go to places that I'd have had my head shot off three years before— no question about that. I rode through the countryside in the night and rode up the canals in the Delta, all sorts of places that I never could have gone a very few years before. And it wasn't because we had forces with us, because you'd see a nondescript-looking bunch of fellows up the canal and they'd wave to you with their guns. They were a local self-defense group.

Have you ever heard the story that Barry Zorthian had a plan to drive from Ca Mau to Quang Tri by himself in a Jeep just to prove to people how much better it was?

Yes. Well, John Vann and I drove across the Delta from Can Tho to Chau Doc on Tet 1971, and we had nobody with us, just the two of us on a couple of motorcycles.

How was Vann feeling about things by that time?

Oh, he felt that it was doing well; and he, of course, was so satisfied with what had happened in the Delta, because it had been totally cleaned out of any enemy problems, except for minor little things, that he was interested in moving up to II Corps to take over the effort there. That's where he was killed in the 1972 attack. But I think he felt very satisfied about it, even to the extent of keeping his mouth shut once in awhile, which was an extreme sacrifice for John. He told me that one time. He said, "You know, I feel so strongly about the way this thing is working and the way we're running it that I'm even not going to criticize."

I'm sure you've heard the famous story of his confrontation with Walt Rostow, right at Tet, in fact. He came in and Rostow said, "Now, before you start, Vann, I know where you're coming from, but don't you think the war is going to be over by July?" And Vann said, "Oh, hell, no, I think we can hold out longer than that."

Yes, I do remember that. [Laughter.]

I've become a little interested in some of the developments within the CIA itself by way of my Vietnam adventures. Can you give me any commentary on the effect on the Agency of the changes of leadership which took place in the decade of the sixties?

Do you mean [John] McCone to [William] Raborn to [Richard] Helms?

Yes.

Well, McCone came in, of course, following Allen Dulles. McCone was, I thought, a splendid Director. He used the Agency for what it could do very effectively. I think he rebuilt a great deal of the morale following the Bay of Pigs, which people felt was a disaster, which it was. He changed a few people, but generally he really put it back to work. He used particularly the analytical side of it very effectively and brought them into advising on decision making and that sort of thing.

Can I interrupt you there? I know that McCone felt in early 1965 that a gradual escalation of bombing was not going to work. I've seen memos in which he said either you've got to hurt them badly or not venture this at all. Was this a reflection of the analyst's view?

No, I don't think it was the analyst; it was John McCone largely. I mean, McCone had the courage of his convictions. He'd say things that were pretty far out, but he would say them as recommendations. His estimates would be well founded. He would use the analysts very well for their estimates, but he'd make his judgments about what we ought to do. That was his business, not theirs.

A related criticism is a criticism which has been made that the Agency, in some rather important cases, has a tendency to make very good analyses and then not do what the analysts said would work.

Well, what I think you can find . . . and replete through the *Pentagon Papers* are a series of estimates that, you know, bombing won't get the

North Vietnamese to change their minds. [There were] the estimates that the various kinds of military actions were not going to solve the problem of the infrastructure and the guerrilla force problem in South Vietnam, that the military approach wasn't the answer, that more military would not solve the problem, such as cutting the Ho Chi Minh Trail. Sometimes they were wrong. They were spectacularly wrong on Cambodia because the analysts said that the supplies coming down the Ho Chi Minh Trail were enough to satisfy the needs of the Communists, and there was no evidence that they were coming through Cambodia Of course, after the overthrow of [Norodom] Sihanouk in 1970, we found the bills of lading in Cambodia where they'd been shipping it through by the bushel. The military had always thought that it was there, but it was so obvious. It was easy and not very hard but we had never gotten good evidence of it, and the analysts, in the absence of good evidence, had said it can't be happening. I disagreed with that at the time. I wasn't working for CIA at that point, but that sounded pretty silly to me. But they had a big fight about it.

But the answer was that the analysts, I think particularly in the sort of mid-sixties, did a very good job of trying to say this is a much more complicated fight than you're thinking it is. It's not a military fight—it's much more of a political fight—and your military actions are not going to solve it. The enemy is very hardheaded; they're very tough and they're very effective in running their operations. On the government side, God knows the governments were weak, but unless something is developed here, you're not going to get anywhere. Now, that was their approach, and they were basically right. I sympathized with them.

Where I think they began to go wrong—the analysts—is after 1968, when I think they were somewhat infected with the general academic view of Vietnam as a lost cause. I don't think they paid enough direct attention to what was actually happening but instead were hung on their earlier projections. Because what was actually happening was, I think, that change in the country atmosphere that I was demonstrating. That doesn't mean that the North Vietnamese were going to quit; the question was whether the North Vietnamese could be pushed back to the borders and then held there. And if they came across again, bop them on the head. [There would be] what I used to call the residual level of violence you were going to have there all along, because the North Vietnamese were not going to quit, and the peace treaty in 1973 was just a pause as far as they were concerned. It was pretty obvious. We signed the peace treaty in order to get our POWs out more than anything; we already had most of our forces out. We yielded on a couple of the key things, which is whether the North Vietnamese would be allowed to be in Cambodia and the areas which they then proceeded to build up with a great logistics accomplishment on the borders there and then launched their attack in 1975, and it won.

But I think the contrast is between 1972 and 1975. In 1972, with large-scale logistic support, with a minute number of Americans—I don't think there were any combat forces to speak of there—and some B-52 bombing, they stopped the North Vietnamese, and it was South Vietnamese forces that stood up and did it. In 1975, when their munitions had been cut back very substantially by the Congress—when Congress said no, it wasn't going to get them another appropriation for even the weapons of war—and there's certainly no possibility of B-52 help, they failed.

Now, one allegation in that respect has been that there were, in fact, enough munitions in the country at current rates of expenditure to have held out until August, that the big blow of the Congressional move was a blow against morale more than material.

Both. Both. The fact was that the estimate as to what the enemy was going to do, which turns out to be exactly what the report by the North Vietnamese said was their intention—it's fascinating, the coincidence—was that they were going to launch an attack in early 1975. But it was going to be the beginning of a long series, and they hoped to bring it to culmination in 1976, which was our election year. Of course, if they got a target of opportunity, they were going to go ahead and exploit it, which is exactly what they did.

Now, that was our estimate, and it was the South Vietnamese government's estimate. The government looked at the American attitude toward additional logistical aid[?], thinking ahead to that 1976 major attack, and realized the stocks were going to have to be stretched if they were going to have anything at all. This brought about a totally different tactical [approach] toward the problem by the Thieu government. For instance, when there was a move into—what the hell's the name of the province just up north of Saigon? [Phuoc Long.] Never mind. Anyway, in the previous times, a move like that would have resulted in a very extensive South Vietnamese air mobile operation up to drive them out. They took the province capital. The province capital's about fifty or a hundred houses, so it's not all that important, quite frankly. But they did not move, because they wanted to conserve their fuel, their weaponry, their helicopters, the wear and tear and all the rest of it, because there weren't any more. So instead of the forward defense that they had been fighting with their military, they were not fighting a forward defense. They were fighting a conservative defensive approach, and that began in the fall of 1974. . . . You had guns that were held to one round a day, two rounds a day. I mean, that was their allocation and that's all there were; that's all they were allowed to supply. Sure, back in the depot there were probably more, but if they shot them up then, they wouldn't have them in 1976. And that's what happened to Vietnam, in my mind.

Do you think that the move out of the highlands was a great mistake?

Oh, it was a disaster, yes. Well, it was a disaster the way it was done. The general who went up there gave the orders and then walked away and it was really astonishing. But you had similar failings in 1972, you remember. There was a division that broke and ran up at Quang Tri in 1972, but they picked up and patched it together and held before they got to Hue. I remember my estimate in 1972 was that they might lose Hue, but they would be held before they got to Da Nang. Well, they didn't even lose Hue that time. They did lose Quang Tri, but then they drove them back out. So you had those tactical errors in both 1972 and 1975, but in 1972 they were then picked up, compensated for; in 1975 it just began the whole process of unraveling.

Do you think it would have been a viable policy to try to hold the Delta, you know, a defense line north of Saigon?

No, not that. No, by that time the rout phenomena had gone too far, and the enemy had too many forces. They had about, what, twelve or fourteen divisions or something? I've forgotten, something like that.

Something on that order, yes.

They had more forces than could be met on that basis. Now, the place to have held them was right at the three places where they came over the frontier, and they didn't have the forces to do it with and the logistics.

To return to the original question about the CIA, we got . . .

Let me say another . . . McCone left after President Johnson took over. McCone was so oriented towards serving President Kennedy that I think President Johnson had a few doubts about him and vice versa. There just wasn't that much warmth between the two, as I remember. Then, of course, when he left, they put in Admiral . . .

Admiral Raborn?

Admiral Raborn. But he only lasted for about a year. He had been sent in because he'd done such a good job with the Polaris [nuclear submarine missile program]. He was not a subtle fellow in terms of political estimates and so forth, and there was, I think, kind of a hatchet job done on him too by some of the more intellectual types around town.

I'd heard that the word around the Georgetown cocktail circuit, whatever that is, was that Raborn was committing faux pas after faux pas.

Well, he might have had a little trouble. You know, he's a smart-enough guy in his field, but he just wasn't in the right field when he was getting into the subtleties of the Dominican Republic or something. So anyway, he left, and then Helms became head. You ask, did that have an impact? It did in a way, because Helms came up through the intelligence professional channel, and a general feeling in the intelligence professional channel is that the more vigorous political operations and paramilitary operations usually backfire because they become known and they become criticized. The Agency really ought to focus on the really hard intelligence targets and get out of these forward position activities and programs. That was not a new thought. I mean, the process had begun in the early sixties, really. The fifties were a time when the Agency was doing everything, and then the Bay of Pigs made that somewhat dubious, and then it was costing more money and the money crunch was on a little bit.

So over the sixties, from about 1962 or so to about 1970, the Agency was very substantially reducing its role in various parts of the world. Now, they did a few things—the Chile thing and some others—but very minor compared to what they were doing in the fifties.

I was going to say, is it too much to say that this was an anti-covert action feeling in general?

It wasn't an anti, it was just a feeling, well, that they were of somewhat dubious value, some of these things. And they certainly exposed the Agency. And the *Ramparts* thing in 1967 [a February article on CIA support for the National Student Association] was another example of getting an awful lot of heat for what didn't seem to be that important. I think it was very important in the fifties; it probably kept on going too long, that particular program. You know, it's hard to close a program once you get it going.

Covert action was your specialty, wasn't it?

Yes. Oh, yes.

Well, how did you feel?

Oh, I felt there was still something to do. I was all for doing things. But by then I was out at Vietnam at that other job doing what I would have done in the Agency but in an open area, which I must say is a better way to do it if you can do it.

Well, some people would say that that was the CIA.

Well, it wasn't. But the fact is that you were able to work informally because of the wartime funding problems or techniques. That you didn't have to, you know, have every little jot and tittle approved by Washington and a different agency in Washington. I got money from AID, from USIA, from the military, got people from there and CIA and every place,

State Department people, everything, and just put them into one team. The GAO [General Accounting Office] came over to investigate how much money we were spending at one time, and I quite frankly, in some cases, had to tell them that I didn't know, because the material was passed into the stream back in Washington, and I didn't know how much money was involved. I had nothing to do with the money; I wasn't handling the money. I was just handling the strategy and ensuring that the weapons went to the right places and things like that.

From what I know of GAO, that must have shocked them right out of their shoes.

It really did shock them, but they did understand it. They wrote a very good report. They said, "Well, there ought to be some better controls on this, but we understand the point." I said, you know, you can't have guys out there with a machine gun counting the damn bullets. They were pretty good about it, but it was initially quite a shock to them. But that function, then, you see, was what had previously been a CIA function, the various teams and some of the local security stuff.

Well, a lot of CIA personnel were used, were they not?

Not very many. A few, yes, but surprisingly few. I'd say ten, twenty, something like that.

Is that all?

Not many more than that in the CORDS program. The CIA had their own station. They had some of the people in the countryside, and I worked out a coordination so that we didn't trip over each other's feet. But they pretty much stayed to themselves. And we borrowed a few CIA people to use them in the CORDS program, like myself.

That's an interesting story about how you were sort of picked off the tree here in Washington.

Yes. Well, it made sense. If I'd spent so much time on Vietnam, I really should go out and contribute what I could.

But let me just give you one more figure. I looked up the figures one time. In the mid- to late fifties, I think that about half of CIA's budget went into covert action, paramilitary and political and things like the Bay of Pigs and some other things. By the early seventies—and this was before the investigations—that figure had sunk to something like 4 or 5 percent.

That's astonishing.

And that was a real comparison. I mean, the total was different, but it was a real diminution of the amount of effort being put on there. Well, we had turned over to Defense Department funding the Laos operation, Vietnamese operations, all the RDF teams—the rural development [force] teams—and all the rest of it that we had started, the Vung Tau Training Center which CIA had started. The old Phoenix Program became funded and became a CORDS program. So all of that stuff dropped out of the CIA budget, and the war in Laos dropped out of it, so you really had very little left. I think it went down too far, and then you had the investigations and the uproar. I suspect it's a little bit on its way up. I don't think it'll get back to 1950, but I hope it gets up a ways, because I think there are things you can do subtly with CIA covert action. . . .

The best testimony, I think, to the effectiveness of one element of the program, the Phoenix Program—and believe me, if you read the documents, the monthly reports from our people about Phoenix, they're a continual stream of criticism about "this program isn't doing what it should be," and "damn it, it isn't working right," and all the rest of it, "the Vietnamese don't seem to be able to get the idea of how to do this," and "oh, records are just awful," you know.

That's pretty discouraging.

Yes, I knew it was going on, but I still said, "Just keep at it. Let it grow; let them improve. Just like the Strategic Hamlets in 1960 and 1961, let them improve. It'll take time. It'll get going." But there were still [comments], "Oh, gee, it's not working right." Well, by 1971 the effect not just of Phoenix but of the whole effort came to a situation where the Communists were losing contact with the people. The provincial committee of Long An province, for instance, would be over in the Parrot's Beak in Cambodia.

That was a very tough province in the sixties.

Yes, because it couldn't stay in Long An. They had lost contact, and they weren't able to maintain their links there, and a variety of others [were] similarly going pretty well. The biggest testimony, of course, has happened since the war when several people, including Stan Karnow, were out there a few months ago; and the Communists that he talked to said that the period of Phoenix was the worst time they ever had during the war, *the* worst time; it had almost put them down. Now, I'm not sure that they just mean Phoenix, and I asked Stan whether that's really what they meant or whether they didn't mean the overall pacification program, the whole integrated effort, which is what I think put them down rather than just the targeting of who these fellows were. He said, no, they said Phoenix, but I don't know whether they really know what they mean or not. . . .

But you see the theory that this was some great Southern rebellion then is just absolute nonsense. The Southerners for awhile were subject

to fear and some lingering degree of nationalist feeling about the flawed
credentials of the government as a nationalist government. That certainly
existed for awhile. I think it was pretty well overcome in the late fifties
by Diem's vigorous social and economic programs. It was revived in the
early sixties with the rather intense subversive program that the Communists launched in 1960, stressing the American Diemists as the continuing puppet colonialist masters. And they did some recruiting then, and I
think the Strategic Hamlets threw that back.

Then, of course, the government collapsed and everything was a mess,
and then they were just holding on. In that time I think the Communists
did some real recruiting, you know, had a very substantial number of recruits, some ideologically, some out of fear, fear that they had to go along.
As I say, those five men with the pistols, they dominate the village when
they're there, so you go along with them. Then after the Tet attack and it
began to look as though the government was going to survive—and actually even earlier, which is the whole light-at-the-end-of-the-tunnel controversy. You had a constitution, you had a government, you're beginning
to put the order together, the Tet attack was thrown back, and then the
pacification program went into high gear. The Americans began to leave,
and the combination of all of that, I think, then brought the Southern
people to a feeling that they were on to a pretty good thing, the land
reform, the various other programs. Then, of course, we got sick and tired
of it, and when they did throw off the 1972 attack, that was a great success. When Thieu made the treaty, I think he had his reservations and his
fears about it, but he really didn't have much choice, because we put such
pressure on him to make it. He thought if he could just keep the arms
coming and the airplanes, he'd be able to hold the next attack off, if necessary. He didn't, because the weapons weren't there, and by that time
we'd thrown our President Nixon out and there wasn't any chance of using the Air Force in support of him.

*Let me broach a subject which has gained a lot of currency recently,
and this is the order-of-battle controversy. I don't know if you saw the
Mike Wallace show . . .*

I saw about two-thirds of it, I guess.

*Okay. In light of this, would you comment on that controversy as you
saw it from your point of view?*

I wasn't really very much involved in it. I was head of the Far East
Division at that time, but this was an analyst problem, and so it wasn't the
operations side of the Agency that was involved in it. It was really the
analytical side that was debating this. I knew generally what was going
on. As I understand the argument, there were two arguments, and they got

confused. The one argument is whether there was or was not a surge in infiltration in late 1967. I frankly don't know the answer to that question. I mean, I'm sure the records are full of it and that it'll get itself solved one way or the other. I think there is a technical explanation for some differences in numbers in that we had certain information which was delayed in getting to us at one point, and then we broke through and had it on a contemporary basis rather than three or four months later.

Was three or four months a common lag?

It was in infiltration figures for that period, because we were getting this at a certain point and it would take them three or four months to get down to where they'd be near us. But I don't know; I'm not sure on that. I didn't really have anything to do with those figures.

The other point was an argument about what the strength of the enemy was, and I testified on this a couple of years ago, or five years ago, whenever it was, in some detail. Sam Adams was making his charges, and I answered them with what I thought was the story. The Sam Adams argument is that the military were just counting soldiers—even irregulars, but soldiers—and that there were a lot of other people that ought to be counted if you were going to get a comprehensive look at the kind of war you were facing. The Agency agreed with that. Adams then took a couple of villages, as I understand, as samples and then projected a nationwide force out of those samples. The Agency at that point said, "Oops, no, you can't do that. Your evidence is not good enough to make that kind of hard projection into absolute figures at that stage, although you're right that there is something other than the pure military forces." I don't recall that there was much argument about whether there were that many—three hundred thousand—military. I think that was understood and accepted. The argument was about whether you could quantify the other group.

And we finally stuck, and the estimate that went to the President said there are about three hundred thousand military forces of various kinds. And then there was a note that said there's an unquantifiable additional element to the war in terms of the people who have just casual connections with it that must be considered when you're thinking of the total force you're facing, but no numbers. Now, Adams was upset that his number wasn't used. He got mad and resigned and all the rest of it, and he's been carrying on this campaign ever since. Then I guess Westy [General William Westmoreland] quite obviously got a little confused about the details of some of the questions which were handled way down below him. You ask me how many VC [Viet Cong] there were in Quang Tin province in 1971, and I tell you I don't know. You know, I'd have to go look at the records for that.

Now, Wallace seems to have been particularly upset with the possibility that there was within the military intelligence order-of-battle people, their own debate, and he makes it appear at least that Westmoreland simply said, "Well, we're going to put a lid on this and this is what the number's going to be."

I know that allegation, but I think it relates to this, not whether the three hundred is three hundred. It's my understanding that that was pretty well accepted. The only question is this additional category as to whether you should give numbers to them, and I know the Agency said, no, you couldn't. I don't think the military thought you could either. But Adams did, and that's where it comes from. But that's separate from the infiltration argument. I don't know how they all patch together.

Of course, the main conclusion that Wallace seems to draw is that we had fundamentally miscalculated the whole thing.

And that's nonsense. The fact is that Fred Weyand moved a division down near Saigon just before Tet because he knew something was happening in that area that was very important in the battle, Rostow's own remarks about the various indicators of troubles, and, of course, the basic fact that the attacks failed. I mean, let's go back to that. That's fairly important.

No, this is not in the area of expertise of CIA, but I think you probably have an opinion on it. It's been said that one of the reasons for the great psychological impact of Tet was the recent progress that had been emphasized so heavily; and if we knew that there was something coming, why, for God's sake, didn't we prepare the public a little better for it?

I don't know. I think that the people were fairly content that 1967 had been a positive year in terms of what had been developed, mainly in structure, which gave a basis for now going out into the country and beginning to really do something well. The light at the end of the tunnel wasn't actually a bad phrase, when you think about what developed. But the short attention span of the American people had begun to be effective. The casualty rates were up and bothering, and the opposition in the schools and in the various intellectual communities to the war in Vietnam, which now was touching ten years—or eight, anyway—began to have its effect. At that point, you know, there were enough mistakes that had been made: the Diem thing, the huge commitment of forces into a non-military kind of a problem, the frustration of our forces as they're looking around for the war to fight and couldn't even find the enemy. It looked like things weren't really that well off and then suddenly they get the TV screens all full of fellows in the Embassy, and people kind of panicked. That's what happened; they panicked.

Did the media panic?

Oh, clearly. You've seen this Peter Braestrup piece [*Big Story: How the American Press and Television Reported and Interpreted the Crisis of Tet 1968 in Vietnam and Washington* (1977)]. Clearly the media panicked.

There's a current fashion among some journalists and ex-journalists who I hesitate to say beat their breasts, but it's hard to call it anything else: "Mea culpa, mea culpa, we blew it." How do you feel about that?

Well, I think they have a responsibility to call things right. The problem with the competitive nature of the American media is that there's a high premium on the dramatic event, and the perspective is very difficult to present. I remember taking a journalist out on one of my twice-a-week ventures to spend the night in the countryside. We went out and we talked to the various people and had a briefing about what the situation was there and all the rest of it, and on the way back I said, "What do you think?" And he said, "Well, nothing very dramatic." And I said, "What do you mean?" And he said, "No action, nothing very special." I said, "For Lord's sake, go over there and ask that lady over there where she was a year ago. I'll bet that she will tell you that she was in a refugee camp about thirty miles away [from] here which the Communists rocketed or mortared, that her three sons were missing, she didn't know where they were, and she just didn't know anything about it. Here she is back in her hometown, two of the sons are back—one's still missing—they're standing guard, they're back at their own farm, they've gotten some help to get the thing going again, the town's getting started again. This area that used to be a battlefield is now starting to come back into a village. You ask her if she doesn't think her life's dramatically different from what it was a year ago." "Yes, I suppose so, but . . ."

But not news.

But not news, yes. It's the biggest news of all. The most important news, and yet nothing. I mean, that's the dangerous part of it. And I know some of the more serious media are concerned about this problem. Well, that *bonze* burning, I think, made it absolutely impossible for President Kennedy to do anything but move more or less the way he did. The thing was almost over when that happened. And it had nothing to do with reality, but it was just so strong a picture. . . .

Just to finish off this order-of-battle thing so that there aren't any loose ends as far as this is concerned, it's also alleged that the White House was ignorant that there was a debate on this question.

I really don't know. It wouldn't necessarily be informed. I mean, you have arguments all over the bottom ends of the Intelligence Community every day that you don't tell the White House every detail of.

Well, some people say that Rostow, for instance, was passing not only summaries but raw intelligence to [President] Johnson in late September.

I'm sure he was. I'm sure he was.

Wouldn't that have made it a little difficult for Johnson to have been in the dark?

No. The problem is, you see, the way intelligence works. The theory of it is that all the raw stuff goes to the center, and then the analysts put it into final form for their great President. Well, that was fine until electric transmission came to work, and then it became absolutely essential that the White House be in on the original transmission of the electrical message. So the White House gets all the raw stuff by wire; then it gets the summary. Now, depending on the predilection of the individual President, the National Security Assistant, whoever, he'll pull raw things out. I've seen President Kennedy read it right off the teletape machine. Well, you say that's a violation of the way it ought to work, that's right, but he's not going to wait that extra two hours for that thing to get to him. If he thinks it's important, he's going to read it right there. . . .

What haven't we talked about that you think needs to go on record? [Interruption.]

A rather, in my mind, poignant remark that must have been about 1970 or 1971 when I was going around the country with President Thieu. I had a conversation with one general who was working on the pacification, and he was happy. I guess it was about 1969 or 1970 when we really started getting in stride. He said, "This is the first time I've seen anything with this degree of cohesion and drive and initiative since the Strategic Hamlets Program." The other interesting remark was a remark by President Thieu one time in which he mentioned President Diem, and he said, "He actually ran the country pretty well."

Thieu said that?

So I said—I don't know that Thieu said this, but I remember thinking it myself—"And you, Mr. Thieu, are running it approximately the way he did."

It was Colonel Thieu that furnished some key troops in 1963, wasn't it?

In 1963, yes. Oh, yes, sure. That's my point, that the overthrow of Diem was the worst mistake we made.

This is a terrible question, but I'm going to ask it anyway. How far back did it set us?

Well, clearly, if President Johnson had not sent in the troops in 1965, the enemy would have won the war in early 1966, probably. If President Diem had not been killed, it was my feeling that we never would have gotten a large number of forces in there, that we might have lost the war— it was about a fifty-fifty chance of it—that Diem would have suppressed the Buddhists, which I think he had successfully done in about September or October. [He] would have cranked up the Strategic Hamlets Program again and would have gotten some initiative going and had a fifty-fifty chance of reducing the enemy threat by about 1965 or 1966. On the other hand, they might have put in enough additional force to have made it beyond him to do alone, in which case I don't think we would have had the compulsion that I think President Johnson felt that he had, because of our involvement with the Diem overthrow, to send our troops in to do it. I think in that case he, President Johnson, could have let the thing go down and said it wasn't his, he didn't cause it, and that we'd done a fair, decent deal. And we would have saved about ten years of war with all the effects of it, especially the effects in the United States.

If Diem had been sustained. Could he have been sustained?

Yes, I think so. I think so. You would have had some troubles. President Kennedy or President Johnson—President Johnson would have had a fairly clear shot, I think, at, "Well, let's work out a very clear relationship here. We're not going to be totally responsible for everything he does, and I'm not going to be told by our press that I'm a monster just because I'm supporting these guys. But on the other hand, we'll support them to the extent that they'll fight for themselves, but we're not going to fight for them." And I think he could have avoided most of the rest of the war, which is a hell of a note.

Index